'This book does a great service. It takes really important contemporary issues – issues that affect all of us, from our sexual relationships to the quality of the air we breathe – and roots them in the analysis of one of the masters of political science, Robert Dahl. At times it made me more optimistic about democracy – and at times very concerned.'

– *Chris Hanretty, University of East Anglia, UK*

'*Democratic Transformations in Europe* is an outstanding contribution to the description and analysis of European democracy. It is broad, covering a large number of topics. It is structured by a theoretical perspective, which leads to important generalizations in the concluding chapter. It is comparative, analysing 31 European nations, and finally, it is balanced. It not only looks at deficits of current European democracies, but it also emphasizes achievements and developments furthering a future democratic Europe.'

– *Klaus Armingeon, University of Bern, Switzerland*

'Following Stein Rokkan the University of Bergen has established an excellent tradition of studying democracy and political parties. *Democratic Transformations in Europe: Challenges and opportunities* has been assembled by two very talented scholars that bring together research strengths of scholars from that Bergen tradition. In the aftermath of the recent UK referendum to exit the European Union ("Brexit"), this book addresses a number of particularly current and relevant questions for Europe moving forward on nationalism, migration, the welfare state, party decline, democratic satisfaction, terrorism, and a range of other important issues. As billed in the title, this volume is crucial for understanding challenges that face Europe, and it brings together a cohesive set of chapters to do so.'

– *Lawrence Ezrow, University of Essex, UK*

DEMOCRATIC TRANSFORMATIONS IN EUROPE

Democracies evolve. Their evolution is not only key to their survival; it is also a reflection of the changing environment in which they operate. This book contributes to the analysis and understanding of how democratic states have transformed over time by examining a number of challenges and opportunities that they face.

With a focus on 'Europe 31', understood as the EU28 plus Switzerland, Norway, and Iceland, the book brings together separate strands of literature which often remain disconnected in political science narratives. Looking at citizen–state relations, the restructuring of politics and institutions of the state, and developments which reach 'beyond and below' the state, it interrogates a variety of issues ranging from the decline of parties or the re-emergence of nationalism as a political force, to liberal challenges to social democracy, terrorist threats, and climate change. The book combines these different dimensions into a comprehensive overview of the state of contemporary democracy, its challenges and opportunities, and its dynamic capacity to adapt. In other words, it deals with the perpetual threats to and transformations of democracy, and the state's ability to protect and strengthen its democratic attributes.

This text will be of key interest to scholars of European Politics, Comparative Politics, and Democracy Studies.

Yvette Peters is a Postdoctoral Researcher in the Department of Comparative Politics, at the University of Bergen, Norway. Her research focuses on institutions, political participation, and political representation, as well as the functioning, development, and interactions between representative and direct democracy. Her work can be found in the *European Journal of Political Research*, *West European Politics*, and *Political Studies*.

Michaël Tatham is a Professor in the Department of Comparative Politics, at the University of Bergen, Norway. He is Chairman of the Council for European Studies research network on Territorial Politics and Federalism, Editor of the international journal *Regional and Federal Studies*, Editor of the *Comparative Territorial Politics* book series, and Director of the interdisciplinary BA programme in European Studies in Bergen.

Routledge Advances in European Politics

DEMOCRATIC TRANSFORMATIONS IN EUROPE

Challenges and opportunities

Edited by Yvette Peters and Michaël Tatham

Routledge
Taylor & Francis Group

LONDON AND NEW YORK

First published 2016
by Routledge
2 Park Square, Milton Park, Abingdon, Oxon OX14 4RN

and by Routledge
711 Third Avenue, New York, NY 10017

Routledge is an imprint of the Taylor & Francis Group, an informa business

British Library Cataloguing in Publication Data
A catalogue record for this book is available from the British Library

Library of Congress Cataloging in Publication Data
Names: Peters, Yvette, editor. | Tatham, Michaèl, 1981– editor.
Title: Democratic transformations in Europe : challenges and opportunities / edited by Yvette Peters and Michaèel Tatham.
Other titles: Democratic transformation in Europe thirty one
Description: New York, NY : Routledge, 2016. | Includes bibliographical references and index.
Identifiers: LCCN 2016027945 | ISBN 9781138100473 (hardback : alk. paper) | ISBN 9781138100480 (pbk. : alk. paper) | ISBN 9781315657646 (ebook : alk. paper)
Subjects: LCSH: Democracy—European Union countries. | Political participation—European Union countries. | Welfare state—European Union countries. | European Union countries—Politics and government—21st century.
Classification: LCC JN40 .D4435 2016 | DDC 320.94—dc23
LC record available at https://lccn.loc.gov/2016027945

ISBN: 978-1-138-10047-3 (hbk)
ISBN: 978-1-138-10048-0 (pbk)
ISBN: 978-1-315-65764-6 (ebk)

Typeset in Bembo
by Apex CoVantage, LLC

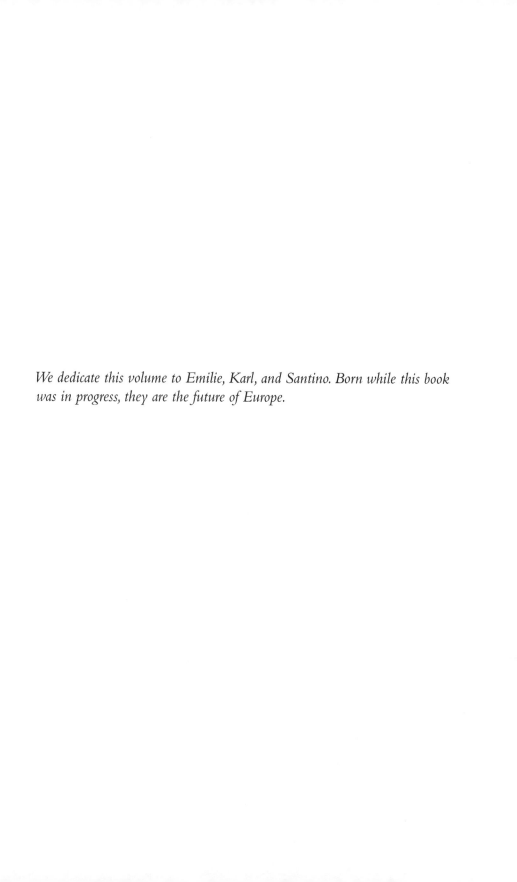

We dedicate this volume to Emilie, Karl, and Santino. Born while this book was in progress, they are the future of Europe.

CONTENTS

PART 4
Conclusions 295

FIGURES AND TABLES

Figures

Tables

FOREWORD

The idea behind the book came to us in December 2013 while on a walk around Zegerplas in The Netherlands. Once back in Norway, the Bergen research group on *Challenges in Advanced Democracies* provided it with a home for the following two years. We are very grateful to its then Coordinators, Michael E. Alvarez and Cornelius Cappelen, for their support of this project in its infant days. Similarly, a number of colleagues provided further support and much-valued input throughout the maturing process. Special thanks have to go to Elisabeth Ivarsflaten, Jonas Linde, Stein Kuhnle, Jan Oskar Engene, Hakan G. Sicakkan, and Terje Knutsen.

The project immensely benefited from a workshop held at Solstrand in Norway in December 2014. At this occasion, first drafts of all chapters were presented and discussed over two days. It was a privileged experience to be able to take this time to collectively analyse and question the transformation of democracy in Europe 31. This workshop played a key role in improving individual chapters and in reassessing what they taught us about democracy and its evolution. We are very thankful to Gunnar Grendstad and the Department of Comparative Politics of the University of Bergen for the partial funding of the workshop.

At that occasion, we were also extremely fortunate to benefit from the comments and wisdom of three distinguished reviewers. Lawrence Ezrow, Klaus Armingeon, and Chris Hanretty provided invaluable feedback on the book as a whole and on its individual chapters. The insights they shared helped tremendously to shape the better aspects of this collective endeavour. Martin Lodge also provided feedback on Part 2 of the book. Clearly, any remaining mistakes and shortcomings are ours.

We hope this book can contribute in its own way to a better understanding of the current state of democracy in Europe 31 and trigger further discussions as to the direction of change and its empirical, theoretical, and normative implications.

Yvette Peters and Michaël Tatham
Bergen, Norway
28 March 2016

CONTRIBUTORS

Michael E. Alvarez is Associate Professor in the Department of Comparative Politics, at the University of Bergen, Norway. He is co-author (with Przeworski, Limongi, and Cheibub) of *Democracy and Development: Political Institutions and Well-Being in the World, 1950–1990* (Cambridge University Press, 2000). This work won the 2001 American Political Science Association (APSA) Woodrow Wilson Foundation Award for the best book published on government, politics, or international affairs, as well as the 2002 Lipset/Przeworski/Verba Data Set award from the Comparative Politics Section of the APSA. He has also published in the *Journal of Democracy* and in *Studies in International Comparative Development.*

Lise Lund Bjånesøy is a PhD candidate in the Department of Comparative Politics, at the University of Bergen, Norway. Her general fields of interest concern voting preferences and right-wing populism, public opinion, and attitudinal change. She is assisting with the coordination of the Norwegian Citizen Panel.

Cornelius Cappelen is a Researcher in the Department of Comparative Politics, at the University of Bergen, Norway. Together with Stein Kuhnle, he is the Principal Investigator of a cross-national research project funded by the Norwegian Research Council (NRC) on intra-EU labour migration and the moral sustainability of the welfare state. He is also co-Investigator of a cross-national research project funded by the NRC, exploring issues related to the redesign of the Chinese welfare state.

Stefan Dahlberg is Associate Professor in the Department of Political Science and database manager at the Quality of Government Institute at the University of Gothenburg, Sweden. His research focuses on representative democracy, democratic legitimacy, and survey methodology. His work can be found in the *European Journal* *of Political Research*, the *European Sociological Review*, *West European Politics*, *Electoral Studies*, *Public Opinion Quarterly*, *Political Studies*, the *Journal of Elections, Public Opinion and Parties*, the *International Political Science Review*, *Scandinavian Political Studies*, the *Review of Public Administration and Management*, the *International Journal of Public Administration*, the *Journal of Prejudices*, and a number of book chapters.

Jan Oskar Engene is Associate Professor in the Department of Comparative Politics, at the University of Bergen, Norway. He is the founder of the Terrorism in Western Europe: Events Data (TWEED) dataset. It covers eighteen West European countries for more than half a century and is the first cross-national dataset to focus on internal terrorism. He has published his research in monograph format (Edward Elgar) and in journals such as the *Journal of Peace Research*, *Metaphor and Symbol*, or the *Tidsskrift for samfunnsforskning*.

Elisabeth Ivarsflaten is Professor in the Department of Comparative Politics, at the University of Bergen and Adjunct Professor in the Centre for Research on Right-wing Extremism (C-REX), at the University of Oslo, Norway. She is an expert on right-wing populism and public opinion. Her work appears in the *American Journal of Political Science*, *Comparative Political Studies*, the *British Journal of Political Science*, and the *European Journal of Political Research*. She is the principal investigator of the Norwegian Citizen Panel.

Terje Knutsen is Associate Professor in the Department of Comparative Politics, at the University of Bergen, Norway, where he is leading a Master's Degree in Democracy Building. His research interest is in the fields of European nationalism and processes of democratization. He also holds a Professor II position at the Norwegian University Centre in St. Petersburg. The author of several monographs and edited books, his latest publication is *The Handbook of Political Change in Eastern Europe* (Edward Elgar, third edition, 2013).

Stein Kuhnle is Professor of Comparative Politics at the University of Bergen, Norway, and Professor Emeritus of the Hertie School of Governance, Berlin, where he was Professor of Comparative Social Policy from 2006 to 2013. He is Honorary Professor in the Centre for Welfare State Research at the University of Southern Denmark, Odense, as well as at Sun Yat-Sen University, Guangzhou, China; Fudan University, Shanghai, China; and Northwest Normal University, Lanzhou, Gansu, China. He is a leading expert on welfare state studies.

Jonas Linde is Professor in the Department of Comparative Politics, at the University of Bergen, Norway. His research interests are within the fields of political support, public opinion, comparative corruption, democratization, and post-communist politics. His research has been published in journals such as the *European Journal of Political Research*, *Governance*, *Political Studies*, the *Government Information Quarterly*, the *International Political Science Review*, the *International Journal of Public Administration*,

Government and Opposition, the *Journal of Communist Studies and Transition Politics*, *Politics in Central Europe*, *Problems of Post-Communism*, and a number of book chapters.

Hilmar L. Mjelde is a Senior Researcher at the Uni Research Rokkan Center, Bergen, Norway. He has published research on political parties, party membership, elections, and the U.S. presidency in *Representation, Regional and Federal Studies, German Politics*, and *The Norwegian Journal of Political Science*. Together with Robert Harmel and Lars Svåsand, he is the co-author of the book *Institutionalization (and De-Institutionalization) of Rightwing Protest Parties*, which is to be published by the ECPR Press. He has appeared regularly in Norwegian media since 2012 as an expert commentator on U.S. politics.

Johannes Andresen Oldervoll is a Research Assistant in the Department of Comparative Politics, at the University of Bergen, Norway. His work focusses on welfare state and labour market change.

Yvette Peters is a Postdoctoral Researcher at the Department of Comparative Politics, at the University of Bergen, Norway. Her research focuses on institutions, institutional change, political participation, and political representation, as well as the functioning, development, and interactions between representative and direct democracy. Her research has appeared in the *European Journal of Political Research, West European Politics, Political Studies*, a forthcoming research monograph at Routledge, and a number of book chapters.

Hakan G. Sicakkan is Associate Professor in the Department of Comparative Politics, at the University of Bergen, Norway. His research themes include politics, democracy, citizenship, and the public sphere in transnational contexts of diversity. He initiated and directed the international projects GLOCALMIG (FP5, 2002–2004) and EUROSPHERE (FP6, 2007–2012). In addition to a series of journal articles, book chapters and journal special issues, he has authored and edited five different books. He is the founding editor, and was the editor-in-chief from 2011 to 2014, of the *Nordic Journal of Migration Research*.

Lars Svåsand is Professor of Comparative Politics at the University of Bergen, Norway. He has published research on political parties in established and new democracies in several international journals, including *Comparative Political Studies, West European Politics, Democratization, Party Politics, Representation, Democratization, Government and Opposition*, the *International Political Science Review, Commonwealth and Comparative Politics*, and the *Forum for Development Studies*.

Friederike Talbot is a Scientific Assistant in the Department of Social Sciences at the The Humboldt University of Berlin, Germany. She had previously worked as the Chair of Comparative Politics at the same institution. In her work, she specialises on questions related to climate change and environmental policies.

Michaël Tatham is Professor at the Department of Comparative Politics, at the University of Bergen, Norway. He is the Chairman of the Council for European Studies research network on Territorial Politics and Federalism (Columbia University, U.S.), Editor of the international journal *Regional and Federal Studies* (Taylor & Francis, Routledge), and Editor of the *Comparative Territorial Politics* book series (Palgrave Macmillan). He is a territorial politics, public policy/administration, and EU scholar. His research can be found in *Comparative Political Studies*, the *Journal of Public Administration Research and Theory*, the *International Studies Quarterly*, *European Union Politics*, the *Journal of European Public Policy*, the *Journal of Public Policy*, the *European Political Science Review*, and *Regional and Federal Studies*. He has a research monograph forthcoming at Oxford University Press.

Vegard Vibe is a PhD candidate in the Department of Comparative Politics, at the University of Bergen, Norway. His work focuses on LGBT rights in developed and developing democracies. Together with colleagues at the Christian Michelsen Institute (CMI) and the University of Oslo, Norway, he has built the Sexual and Reproductive Rights Lawfare database, which involves numerous scholars across the world. He is also an affiliate with the Center on Law and Social Transformation in Bergen.

1

THE TRANSFORMATION
OF DEMOCRACY

Yvette Peters and Michaël Tatham

In a nutshell

This book is about the challenges democratic states are facing. Although our primary focus is on Europe, many of the arguments presented here extend farther. We identify two types of challenges. Both types affect how democratic states evolve and transform. The first type represents *threats* to our democratic systems, ranging from radical right populism and nationalism to terrorism or global warming. These are challenges our democracies have to rise up to and deal with for fear of otherwise perishing altogether or compromising their democratic nature. These challenges have different normative and policy implications. The second type represents *transformations* that our democratic systems have undergone, ranging from the decline of parties and the evolution of the welfare state to the emergence of transnational public spheres. These challenges are both causes and consequences of wider developments such as the changing nature of political participation, demographic evolutions, or the breakdown of national borders. These challenges, too, pose important normative and policy questions. However, they also come along with opportunities for democratic renewal and systemic reform, which may enhance our political systems.

For both types of challenges, we explore the existing empirical trends, the various issues these generate for our democracies, what solutions may exist, what opportunities may arise as a result, and finally what the main normative and policy implications are. To this end we have selected thirteen challenges which seem to have the greatest implications for Europe's democracies. Terrorism has been high on the political agenda for a long time, though for changing reasons: from separatist or nationalist expressions, as found in the Basque country, Corsica, or Northern Ireland, all the way to its more international expressions, as crystallised by the 9/11 al-Qaeda attacks. Sometimes related to terrorism, nationalism has decisively re-emerged as a political force in Europe, driven by a plurality of European crises such as those related to the economy, immigration, or identity. This nationalistic resurrection is sometimes – though certainly not always – intertwined with radical right populism. Indeed, both share a number of determinants such as increasing cross-border migration and community/identity crises, which have become salient in the face of economic hardship and the reform of welfare state policies. Together with the evolution (and in some cases decline) of political parties, citizens have expressed discontent with how their democratic systems have performed. They have grown distrustful of both their politicians and institutions of government, and they have come across as blasé, in the best of cases, or, in the worst of cases, as outright disillusioned about the democratic process.

This 'threat from within' may be related to the evolving structure of the state and, namely, the diffusion of power away from central government. Such 'displacement' of politics has meant that political equality – and hence the community dimension of politics – has suffered, with negative consequences for the health of democracy. Inequality and the definition of a system's political community, linked to migration flows, economic hardship, and a number of demographic trends (e.g. aging population, declining fertility rates), have generated a debate about the redefinition of the welfare state and its policies, thereby giving rise to new political conflicts and divisions, as symbolised by discussions on 'welfare tourism' in the United Kingdom, the Netherlands, or Germany. The steps from labour market dualisation, to welfare dualisation, to de facto 'second-class citizenship' or the dualisation of rights and duties within the political system, all appear less and less remote and directly question the principle of equality – a core building block of any democratic political system. These debates, about the welfare state, inequalities, and the displacement of politics, all feed into the tension between two centripetal concepts of democracy: a social and a liberal one. Both clash on political, ideological, and economic fronts and synthesise a number of key elements of the above discussion.

This discussion, however, has spread beyond that of the state. As politics has been displaced from central government, mobilisation has also occurred outside of the purely national sphere. In this sense, transnational public spheres come with a number of challenges and opportunities, but their emergence is as irreversible as it has been slow and fragmented. Within a European context of deeper integration, characterised by growing interdependence and magnified negative externalities, such spheres provide a new dimension to the political debate. Among these debates, that of climate change has perhaps represented the most pressing but also the most disjointed and contested issue. However, such common pool problems, which cut across political boundaries, both beyond and below the state, only further accentuate the rise of multi-jurisdictional politics. The consequence of states both decentralising and supranationalising political authority, multi-jurisdictional politics represents an answer to a series of policy problems and citizen demands, but in turn also generates its own set of challenges. In this context, the politically loaded issue of LGB rights illustrates how social movements have mobilised at both the national and supranational levels, whilst exploiting opportunities for judicial policy-making at regional, national, and supranational venues. Their twofold strategy of both pressurising and bypassing state institutions is characteristic of the questions raised by the evolution of citizen–state relations, the changing nature of the state's own institutions and politics, and the tensions generated by pressures for change from both below and beyond the state.

Democratic states in Europe 31 face numerous other challenges in addition to those outlined above. A number of these are indirectly assessed by different chapters. Migration trends (Fassmann et al., 2009; Geddes, 2000; Zincone et al., 2011), for example, have to some extent fed into (and have been instrumentalised) by radical right populist parties, nationalist movements, or advocates of welfare chauvinism. The regulation of financial markets and the sovereign debt crisis (Helleiner, 2014; Helleiner et al., 2010) have also, to some extent, nourished debates related to populism, nationalism, or welfare state reform, and have been captured by the broader tension between the liberal and social visions of democracy. A number of such topics (i.e. migration, the financial crisis) run through the various contributions and are therefore not dedicated as a stand-alone chapter. Other – to our minds less central – themes are only touched upon briefly in individual chapters. For example, technological progress in the form of new means of communication or the social media (Bray, 2002; Edwards et al., 2012) may contribute to the development of transnational public spheres, the displacement of politics, the decline of parties, or democratic discontent, but nonetheless remain in the background. The same extends to three other important topics to which we have not allotted a unique chapter. The rise of New Public Management logics (Pollitt & Bouckaert, 2011) and the framing of citizens as customers of their political system (Denhardt & Denhardt, 2011) play a relevant role in the displacement of politics and are in part reflected in the divide between liberal and social democratic models. The advent of judicial politics in Europe, otherwise known as *Eurolegalism* (Kelemen, 2011), emerging to some extent as a consequence of the spread of regulatory politics (Majone, 1994), means that regulation through litigation has dramatically increased. This development contributes to both the displacement and the multi-jurisdictionality of politics and is further illustrated by the cases of LGB-rights mobilisation and of the governance preferences of dissatisfied democrats and radical right populists. Finally, democratic innovations, such as deliberative polls, participatory budgeting, e-voting, or 'minipublics' (Geissel & Newton, 2012; Saward, 2004; Smith, 2009) concern mostly local politics and new forms of citizen expressions, which are only marginally touched upon when discussing democratic discontent, the displacement, and the multi-jurisdictionality of politics.

Overall, we present a broad but concise analysis of the main challenges facing our democracies. These are articulated around the three central themes of (1) citizen–state relations, (2) the restructuring of the politics and institutions of the state, and (3) governance beyond and below the state. The book combines these into an overview of the state of contemporary democracy, its challenges, opportunities, and especially its dynamic capability to adapt. In other words, this book deals with the perpetual *threats to* and *transformations of* democracy and the state's ability to protect and strengthen its democratic component. In essence, it deals with democracies that are in flux.

Why this book?

Democracies evolve. Their evolution is not only key to their survival, but it is also a reflection of the changing environment in which they operate. This book contributes to the analysis and understanding of how democratic states have transformed over time by examining a number of challenges and opportunities that they face. The book stands out from other contributions by bringing together separate strands of literature which often remain disconnected in political science narratives. For all themes covered, the book outlines how these developments constitute a challenge to democracy but also what solutions are possible and what opportunities may arise from those challenges. The chapters also reflect on the normative and policy implications generated by each challenge, hence highlighting their societal relevance. Indeed, each author discusses what trends, challenges, and opportunities are observable, but also how democracies could respond to such challenges.

We believe that the book's coverage – both topical and geographical – can appeal to a diverse readership ranging from undergraduate[1] and post-graduate students to advanced researchers and policy-makers. The thirteen topics covered are discussed for a wide sample of countries defined as 'Europe 31', which includes the European Union's 28 member states plus Switzerland, Iceland, and Norway. Few books cover such a broad spectrum of relevant topics related to the transformation of democracies for such a wide sample of European countries. The challenges these democracies face are near universal to all democracies worldwide and will continue to generate much debate within both academic and practitioner circles. In this sense, the book contributes to the wider discussion on the evolution of democracies, their adaptations, and the challenges and opportunities that are arising as their environment evolves.

Main aims and themes

We map out challenges that European democracies are facing. These challenges – ranging from radical right populism to climate change – generate pressures for democratic states to evolve and transform, but they also provide some opportunities for democracies to re-define their relations to their citizenry and to adapt their policies and structures to an increasingly *glocalised* environment.

The book is structured around three core themes. The first – Part 1 – is that of *citizen–state relations*. Such relations have been put under strain by the emergence and consolidation of radical right populist parties but also by the re-emergence of nationalism as a political force. In parallel, most European democracies have been characterised by a decline of their political parties (in terms of membership, identification, trust, or vote volatility) while democratic discontent – as expressed by citizens towards the performance of their political system – has received increasing attention.

The second theme – Part 2 – is that of *the restructuring of the politics and institutions of the state.* These concern three highly salient dimensions, which consist of the liberal challenge to social democracy, the evolution of the welfare state and its changing demography, boundaries, and normative underpinnings, and, finally, the diffusion of state power and its impact on the citizenry.

The third theme – Part 3 – deals with processes which have simultaneously reached *below and beyond the state.* These processes regard terrorism and counter-terrorism (of the domestic and international kinds), the quest for climate change mitigation and greater LGB rights, the emergence of transnational public spheres, and, finally, the advent of multi-jurisdictional politics through the decentralisation and supranationalisation of state competences.

The originality of this contribution resides in the wide range of challenges identified and how their discussion can help us reflect on the evolution of democracy. All individual chapters reach out to other chapters and hence encourage us to further think about possible intersections between the themes. For example, between the displacement of politics, the rise of multi-jurisdictional politics, and transnational public spheres, between radical right populism, nationalism, and minority rights, between liberal challenges to social democracy, the evolution of the welfare state, and climate mitigation, or between democratic discontent, the decline of parties, and the displacement of politics.

More generally, the book aims to complement the existing literature on the challenges democracies face. This literature is fragmented, and it tends to either focus on themes such as those that we cover in Part 1 (e.g. Dalton, 2004; Hay, 2013; Norris, 2011) or deals with issues that we cover in Parts 2 and 3 (e.g. Leibfried et al., 2015). We seek to bring together both sets of literatures into a single, yet succinct contribution.

This contribution can indeed be studied in parallel to that of Dalton (2004), which focuses on the question of political support using survey data. Twelve years on, Dalton's critical work dialogues well with our Chapters 4 and 5 (on the decline of parties and democratic discontent in times of crisis, respectively) as well as, to some extent, Chapters 2, 3, and 9 (on nationalism, radical right populism, and the displacing of politics). The same holds for Hay's more recent contribution (2013), which centres on the themes of political disenchantment, participation, and de-politicization, or Norris's crucial book on the democratic deficit (2011), which explores the determinants and consequences of citizens' political disaffection. This essential literature can be fruitfully combined with our part on citizen–state relations, while our second and third parts (on the restructuring of politics and institutions of the state, and on governance beyond and below the state) tend to be treated by separate strands of research which have failed to dialogue with the literature embodied by Norris's, Dalton's, or Hay's seminal works. It is one of the added values of this book to discuss these themes within a unified study of Europe's democratic transformations.

To the best of our knowledge, the only current contribution which adopts a similarly broad and structured approach is Leibfried et al.'s *Oxford Handbook of Transformations of the State* (2015). As above, we therefore recommend a parallel use of their momentous Handbook and our more succinct study. Their contribution complements a certain number of themes that we also cover. For example, our chapter on multi-jurisdictional politics is nicely complemented by Leibfried et al.'s chapters on "Multi-level Governance and the State" (Chapter 14), on "Internationalisation and the State: Sovereignty as the External Side of Modern Statehood" (10), and on "Beyond the State: Are Transnational Regulatory Institutions Replacing the State?" (15). Similarly, our two chapters on the welfare state dialogue well with Leibfried et al.'s chapters 24 and 27, as does our chapter on the struggle between liberalism and social democracy with Leibfried et al.'s chapters 12, 20, 21, and 22. There are further synergies, beyond these more obvious ones. While Leibfried et al.'s groundbreaking Handbook explores a number of themes that we also cover in Parts 2 and 3, and numerous other themes which provide critical and complementary insights to the work we present here, it generally does not address the themes covered in Part 1.

In sum, much of the existing literature dealing with the broad topic of the democratic transformations of the state either tends to focus on our first part (i.e. citizen–state relations), as Dalton, Hay, or Norris do (2004; 2013; 2011), or on elements of our second and third parts (on the restructuring of the state, and challenges below and beyond it), as Leibfried et al. do (2015). We hope that the present book can help foster further dialogue between these two strands of research and encourage the scholarly community to bring together interrelated but often segregated issues relevant to the better understanding of the evolution of our democratic political systems. We bring together the empirical insights from Parts 1, 2, and 3 in our concluding chapter. There we discuss what they collectively teach us about the transformation of democracy in Europe 31 using the conceptual framework provided by the work of Robert Dahl.

The concept of democracy: a Dahlian perspective

When discussing democracy across such a broad range of challenges, common tools and concepts help to collect the insights provided by each contribution. The different chapters often relate – implicitly or explicitly – to a Dahlian conception of democracy. The democratic framework of Robert Dahl refers to a series of requirements of what a democratic process entails, which in effect are (a) the congruence between popular preferences and policy, (b) political equality, and (c) citizenship rights for most permanent adult residents. This framework emphasizes people's involvement much more than some other, more minimalist, concepts of democracy which, for example, focus on 'competition' to the detriment of 'inclusion' (Schumpeter, 1942: 273). Dahl's requirements do not necessarily prescribe in what way a political system should be organised institutionally, nor does Dahl argue that this conceptualization is necessarily realistic. In fact, he made a distinction between democracy and *polyarchy*, where the latter describes the contemporary political systems that we call democracies and that come closest to the ideal of democracy.[2]

A common thread to emerge across chapters is a comparison between the observed changes to democracy and an ideal notion of democracy. This provides a standard for comparison. With this benchmark, it is possible to evaluate the state of democracy based on the changes that occurred. It can be used as an ideal type against which real cases can be compared, and this can be done for all trends that are dealt with here. It does not mean that Dahl's democratic ideal is fully desirable, or even possible. We emphasise instead his concept of democracy and the path that countries can travel to come closer to that ideal. Similarly, not all challenges relate equally to the different elements of Dahl's framework. Whilst for some the link is clearer and more explicit (such as in the case of the displacement of politics, climate change mitigation, or the liberal vs. social models of democracy), for others the link is more indirect or partial.

Dahl (1989, 1998) formulated five necessary conditions for a democratic process – four to assure *political equality* and one referring to *who* should be politically equal. The first opportunity that people within the system (or association) should have, *necessary condition nr. 1*, is that of effective participation. This principle implies that people must have equal and effective possibilities to make their preferences, ideas, and considerations concerning a policy known to one another. Members should be able to discuss and deliberate on the different aspects and possible outcomes/alternatives of the policy, and they should have equal opportunities to do so. The second requirement for a democratic process is voting equality (*necessary condition nr. 2*), where every member must have the equal and effective opportunity to cast a vote concerning the decision on a policy. Every member should have one vote, and all votes should weigh equally. *Necessary condition nr. 3* is members' enlightened understanding – the notion that everyone should have equal and effective possibilities to learn about the relevant aspects and alternatives of policies, within a reasonable limit of time. This implies that people should have the opportunity to obtain information relevant to the policy at stake or possible alternatives to that policy. The next requirement for the democratic process is the control of the agenda (*necessary condition nr. 4*), where the members of the association or system must have the exclusive right to decide on what matters and should hence be placed on the political agenda. This also means that the decisions that have been taken in the past, for example, can be challenged again if members of the system wish to do so. Last, *necessary condition nr. 5* entails that all or most permanent adult residents should have full citizen rights, defined by *necessary conditions nr. 1 to 4*, which together also form the conditions for political equality.

Related to Dahl's 4+1 necessary conditions is his discussion of conceptions and interpretations of democracy in his *A Preface to Democratic Theory* (Dahl, 2006). Some of the chapters explicitly deal with a trend or phenomenon that relates to one or more of these discussions, such as the tension between a Madisonian model of democracy (as reflected by the growth of non-majoritarian institutions such as regulatory agencies or the spread of judicial policy-making) and a more Populistic model of democracy (emphasising unchecked majority rule). Along with Dahl's *necessary conditions*, the model of democracy towards which Europe 31 seems to be heading equally influences our assessment of the health and prospects of the democratic experience in these countries. Consequently, we come back to these questions in the book's concluding chapter, where we discuss the contemporary state of democracy in a 'transformed' Europe. In light of the insights provided throughout the book, we also make some recommendations regarding the evolution of our democratic systems.

Notes

1 To this end we also provide a Teaching Companion at the close of each individual chapter. There we outline three further readings (usually in the form of journal articles or book chapters) for students to deepen their understanding of the chapter's theme, and three questions for discussion which may prove fruitful to trigger exchanges within the classroom.
2 Dahl has drawn up a list of principles and institutions that relate to the requirements of a democracy but which are also observable among all or most *polyarchies* (Dahl, 1971).

References

Bray J (2002) *Innovation and the Communications Revolution: From the Victorian Pioneers to Broadband Internet*. Stevenage: Institution of Engineering and Technology.

Dahl R A (1971) *Polyarchy: Participation and Opposition*. New Haven: Yale University Press.

Dahl R A (1989) *Democracy and Its Critics*. New Haven: Yale University Press.

Dahl R A (1998) *On Democracy*. New Haven: Yale University Press.

Dahl R A (2006) *A Preface to Democratic Theory: Expanded Edition*. Chicago: University of Chicago Press.

Dalton R J (2004) *Democratic Challenges, Democratic Choices: The Erosion of Political Support in Advanced Industrial Democracies*. Oxford: Oxford University Press.

Denhardt J V and Denhardt R B (2011) *The New Public Service: Serving, Not Steering*. New York: M.E. Sharpe.

Edwards A, Edwards C, Wahl S T and Myers S A (2012) *The Communication Age: Connecting and Engaging*. London: SAGE Publications.

Fassmann H, Haller M and Lane D S (2009) *Migration and Mobility in Europe: Trends, Patterns and Control*. Cheltenham: Edward Elgar Publishing.

Geddes A (2000) *Immigration and European Integration: Towards Fortress Europe?* Manchester: Manchester University Press.

Geissel B and Newton K (eds.) (2012) *Evaluating Democratic Innovations: Curing the Democratic Malaise?* London: Routledge.

Hay C (2013) *Why We Hate Politics*. New York: Wiley.

Helleiner E (2014) *The Status Quo Crisis: Global Financial Governance After the 2007–08 Financial Meltdown*. New York: Oxford University Press.

Helleiner E, Pagliari S and Zimmermann H (2010) *Global Finance in Crisis: The Politics of International Regulatory Change*. London: Routledge.

Kelemen R D (2011) *Eurolegalism: The Transformation of Law and Regulation in the European Union*. Cambridge: Harvard University Press.

Leibfried S, Huber E, Lange M, Levy J D, Nullmeier F and Stephens J D (eds.) (2015) *The Oxford Handbook of Transformations of the State*. Oxford: Oxford University Press.

Majone G (1994) The rise of the regulatory state in Europe. *West European Politics* 17(3): 77–101.

Norris P (2011) *Democratic Deficit: Critical Citizens Revisited.* Cambridge: Cambridge University Press.

Pollitt C and Bouckaert G (2011) *Public Management Reform: A Comparative Analysis – New Public Management, Governance, and the Neo-Weberian State.* Oxford: Oxford University Press.

Saward M (ed.) (2004) *Democratic Innovation: Deliberation, Representation and Association.* London: Routledge.

Schumpeter J A (1942) *Capitalism, Socialism, and Democracy.* New York: Harper & Brothers.

Smith G (2009) *Democratic Innovations: Designing Institutions for Citizen Participation.* Cambridge: Cambridge University Press.

Zincone G, Penninx R and Borkert M (2011) *Migration Policymaking in Europe: The Dynamics of Actors and Contexts in Past and Present.* Amsterdam: Amsterdam University Press.

PART 1
Citizen–state relations

2

A RE-EMERGENCE OF NATIONALISM AS A POLITICAL FORCE IN EUROPE?

Terje Knutsen

Europe today is a continent beset by multiple crises. Europe is ageing; at the same time, immigration to the continent is booming. The great European project of integration and moving towards an ever-closer union is faltering in the midst of an economic crisis, polarising the debate between integrationists and integration sceptics. Europe's identity is unclear and under attack from many sides.

Into this volatile mix of uncertainty about the future, we see nationalism once more emerging as an ideological guiding force for many of those who feel let down, excluded or alienated by current politics. Parties both on the extreme left and the extreme right are advocating national solutions, protectionism and harsher demands for integrating external immigrants. Xenophobia and uncertainty about the future is being used to whip up nationalist fervour. This chapter will look at this possible re-emergence of nationalism as a political force in Europe, exacerbated by the continuing financial crisis that has undermined belief in the European project. The 2014 European elections showed a marked growth in support for parties being sceptical towards the European project, advocating national solutions instead. In both France and Britain, parties whose agenda may clearly be called nationalistic gained over 25 per cent of the vote. Using survey data, this chapter takes a closer look at the attitudes and perceptions of European voters in this area.

The foundations of nationalism

What is nationalism? There are no universally accepted definitions of the concept, which means that the concept will have to be explored. That it has to do with the idea of a nation – or nationhood – is obvious. In its weakest form, it may be likened to some form of civic patriotism, what Jürgen Habermas called "verfassungspatriotismus" (Habermas 1990). In practice, however, it is difficult to speak about nationalism in this context without taking into consideration the dimension of ethnicity. Nationalism expresses itself through manifestations of national identity. One of the most commonly used definitions of the term "nation" is coined by Anthony D. Smith. According to him, a nation is "a named community possessing a historic territory, shared myths and memories, a common public culture and common laws and customs" (Smith 2002:15). This definition is, however, not without its own problems, as it closely mirrors the definition of what Smith calls an *ethnie*. An ethnie is defined by Smith as "a named community of shared origin myths, memories and one or more element(s) of common culture, including an association with a specific territory" (Smith 2002:15). The nation is conceived as growing out of the ethnie, as the title of Smith's 1986 book *The Ethnic Origin of Nations* shows. But this makes it very difficult to distinguish a nation from an ethnie, and moreover it still seems that Smith is linking nation to territory. Thus, the problem of defining an ethnic group versus that of defining a nation lies at the core of the debate on nationalism that Smith's contributions have created. This is problematic in today's Europe, where, according to Smith, many states consist of more than one nation within their borders.

But far from all who have written on nationalism agree with the focus on history and the ethnic origins of nations. For Ernest Gellner, the industrial revolution and the state's response to it triggers the development of nationalism. In order to promote growth by making the state stronger, the state attempts to force cultural homogeneity onto its citizens (Gellner 1983:73). Gellner sees this as a rational response to the demands of the emerging industrial society. The state becomes an agent for cultural homogenisation and standardisation among its citizens, creating a drive towards greater mobility and egalitarianism. Nationalism in this sense is a protection against alienation and anonymity and assures individuals that they all have equal status within the nation (Tamir 1995:433f). According to Gellner and others, the emergence of nationalism in the industrial age was an impulse towards democratisation; not being satisfied with being equal within the context of a nation, citizens also wanted political participation through mass politics to achieve true equality. In this early stage, nationalism could be perceived as both liberal and democratising, driving forward political, social and electoral reforms. It was in this context that the democratic political foundations of modern Europe were created.

When Gellner originally came to this conclusion in the late 1970s, European history seemed to prove him right. It was an era when the great conflicts regarding nations had been solved and the continued integration of Europe had become the common goal. Nations like Portugal and Spain were being welcomed into the European Community as they threw off their former nationalistic, authoritarian regimes and embraced democracy. But nationalism did not fade quietly into the past. In the 1980s, nationalism became an important part of the ideology of regionalist or separatist movements across Europe. And after the fall of communism, nationalism became an integral part of the identity that many of the East European countries felt a need to strengthen. Some countries in Central and Eastern Europe, like Latvia and Slovakia, had to go through simultaneous processes of both state- and nation-building. For others, it was more a question of reaffirming their identity and history after 40 years or more of communism. Nationalism was likewise a crucial factor in the disintegration of the multinational empire states of Yugoslavia and the Soviet Union. Recent history has shown that nationalism as an ideology is alive and well, in both Eastern and Western Europe. The 2014 Scottish referendum on independence is a potent example of this.

Nationalism and modernity

Industrialisation may have led to the creation of nationalism, although nationalism as an ideology is built upon pre-existing communities and structures (Schnee 2001:6; Smith 1998:36). The idea and concept of national identity predates nationalism as an ideology by several hundred years. The formation of national identities began in England in the sixteenth century and in France somewhat later (Greenfeld 1992:6). In Germany, national identity emerged as a consequence of resistance against the Napoleonic occupation, half a century before industrialisation took its hold of the country (Kedourie 1993:143). But seen in view of the re-emergence of nationalism in Europe, the perhaps greatest puzzle unexplained by Gellner is the passions that nationalism generates. This is not just a matter of feeling patriotic when the national team gains a victory. Why are people willing to put their lives on the line to defend or protect their respective nations, when they are generally not willing to do so for other societal constructions?

It may be that nations are actually some form of imagined communities – imagined as both inherently limited and sovereign (Anderson 1991:6). It is imagined because it is an abstract symbol; we sense a common bond among its members, although we will never meet more than a tiny fraction of them. It is limited in the sense that it has borders, and outside of those borders are other nations and states. It is sovereign and the final arbiter of affairs within its borders. Anderson ascribes this to the time when nations and nationalities became a cultural construction. He dates this to the end of the eighteenth century, a time when one worldview replaced another, and the effect of the Enlightenment finally came into force. The nation is a community, a horizontal comradeship transcending all other worldly realities like class or religion. If we accept Anderson's argument, the nations of Europe today are under attack from several angles. Forces of globalisation, regionalism and multiculturalism are eroding its foundations. Different and competing imagined communities are emerging. But if the concept and legitimacy of the nation-state is becoming weakened, then what is the alternative for its inhabitants?

A full review of the different theories of nationalism is outside the focus of this chapter. I have tried to present some views concerning what a nation is and what nationalism constitutes, showing different directions within the literature.

This will have relevance when I examine data showing the current state regarding nationalism and xenophobia, later in this chapter. Some decades ago, it was usual to classify nationalism according to how rooted it was in the ethnic perception of itself. France was seen as an example of a nation that expressed a very "civic" and open-ended nationalism. Living in France, speaking the language and immersing oneself in French culture was seen as enough to gain citizenship and become French. Germany represented the opposite attitude; citizenship here was based on ethnic bonds, being of ethnic German origins, of German blood and territory. Nationalism along these lines was perceived to be of a more closed and inward-looking type. Scholars today realise that such ideal types do not exist. Nationalism in all countries is a blend of these two impulses, although some countries may at times show more of one impulse than the other. Furthermore, nations show a tendency to close up and withdraw from the global discourse when they perceive threats to the nation and its history, culture and way of life. In the last decades, growing forces of globalisation, "Americanisation", immigration from different cultures and an ageing population have influenced the "blend" of nationalism across Europe. In the literature, we can ascertain three broad "schools" as to the different forms of nationalism, but most of the recent debate concerning nationalism today is between those who claim that nationalism was an invention of the nineteenth century and those who seek continuation with the ethnic and cultural roots of nationalism.

Nationalism: an East–West divide?

A hundred years ago, most countries of Central and Eastern Europe did not exist. Many of them were created after the First World War, while some disappeared after the Second World War and reappeared again after the fall of communism in 1989. Thus, a lot of both state- and nation-building has been going on since they were freed from communism. In Western Europe, the grand project since the end of the Second World War has been European integration, binding the nation-states together in an ever-closer union. Until recently that has left little room for nationalism except on a purely symbolic level. That has not been the case in Eastern Europe after the fall of the Berlin Wall. Here, mainstream political parties often express nationalistic attitudes, although more moderate than extremist. Moreover, this is not a phenomenon restricted to right-wing politics. Such attitudes are expressed by parties as varied as the left-wing HZDS in Slovakia and the right-wing Fidesz-MPS in Hungary (Mudde 2005:184). In Western Europe, nationalistic rhetoric has been more the domain of right-wing or populist parties like the UK Independence Party (UKIP) or the French Front National Party.

We do not see such expressions as dangerous to democracy in itself. History has shown that nationalism can be a powerful force for good in supporting and maintaining democracy. More worrying in Eastern Europe is that racist and anti-Semitic attitudes are far more widespread among both elites and ordinary people than in the West. No less than 50 per cent of respondents in a Polish survey indicated negative feelings towards Jews or Israelis, while 23 per cent asked in Lithuania and Slovakia would not like to live in a neighbourhood with Jews (Mudde 2005:181). Despite this response, some describe the level of nationalism as remarkably low (Kopecky and Mudde 2000:529). Indeed, purely racist extremist parties in Central and Eastern Europe tend to be both more extreme and to have less support than their western counterparts (Mudde 2005:165).

This does not mean that there are not significant differences between East and West in Europe. Research indicates that there is an East–West divide concerning nationalism. Citizenship policy is more restrictive in the East, and people are less likely to support the civic elements of nationality, focusing more on ethnic elements (Ariely 2013). In general, nationalism in Western Europe is more based on civic values, while nationalism in Eastern Europe is tuned towards more primordial values. People who feel a strong attachment to their country are not a threat to its democracy, but if national identity is accompanied by inward-looking ethnocentrism, then it can be a hindrance to democratic stability in countries with sizeable minorities.

In today's Europe, there is an extra dimension to this issue, and it is closely connected to the increasing storm of globalisation that is sweeping over Europe. Globalisation is not a new concept; during the last five centuries, with Europe in the driving seat, globalisation has swept over the world, bringing profound changes all around the globe. The growth and promotion of capitalism and democracy have been a part of this process, and it has been astoundingly successful. Democratic nation-states have in many ways been presented as the ideal end state in this process, but in a Europe that was formed by the traumatic experiences of the Second World War, leaders dreamed of an even greater ideal – a United States of Europe. And since the establishment of the Coal and Steel Community in 1951, the elites of Europe have had a relentlessly driven agenda towards an ever-closer union, towards ever-closer integration in Europe. This project has in many ways been a huge success; 28 European countries are today bound together in the European Union (EU), most with a common currency and all of them subject to extensive common regulations made to create a common market bringing benefits to all its inhabitants.

This process of European integration has, however, met an increasing amount of resistance, which has become stronger in the past few decades. The reason for this is simple; it is eroding the concept of the nation-state, without offering a clear alternative. According to the DHL Global Connectedness Index for 2014, Europe is the world's most globally connected region, with nine of the ten most connected countries, averaging the highest scores with regard to trade and people flows (Ghemawat and Altman 2014). In addition, a new element has been introduced: immigration across borders, both within Europe and from outside Europe, has not been addressed well enough by European elites. This immigration is in many cases both wanted and needed, but Europe has also been facing an influx of unwanted immigration. Handling these challenges well politically in the eyes of voters has often proved difficult, finding a balance between legal, ethical, work and social issues (Carling 2011; Jurado and Brochmann 2013). Not just immigration, but also integrating those who are becoming new citizens, is of importance in this context. Unsuccessful integration means social unrest, disproportionate unemployment among immigrants and critique of welfare benefits being wrongly allocated, weakening the legitimacy of existing welfare policies. Some of the problems and challenges connected to this situation are explored in greater detail in this book's chapters on right-wing populism by Bjånesøy and Ivarsflaten (Bjånesøy and Ivarsflaten 2016), within-EU immigration and welfare by Cappelen (Cappelen 2016), and the challenges that the European welfare states are facing by Oldervoll and Kuhnle (Oldervoll and Kuhnle 2016).

Globalisation also brings with it a pressure for economic liberalisation, both domestically and internationally. The EU's inner market is a good example of these mechanisms. While a free flow of work, capital and services across borders may enhance efficiency and lower costs, it also creates losers in the process. Neoliberal impulses vie for supremacy, clashing with the idea of a more social Europe (Hutter et al. 2012:229ff). All of these issues have different saliency in national politics across Europe, changing the manifestations of nationalism. The EU is not a state – yet. This means huge challenges in managing these flows and forces when politics and policies need to be multi-jurisdictional. Thus, a separate chapter in this book is devoted to these challenges and their possible solutions (Tatham 2016).

Classifying nationalism

Classifying the different ways nationalism is being expressed is a difficult exercise where there is often little overlap between authors (Gat and Yakobson 2013; Lawrence 2005; Özkirimli 2005). But in taking a more empirical look at Europe, it is possible to arrive at some tentative conclusions. In analysing data from the International Social Survey Programme (ISSP), Bart Bonikowski has used cluster and factor analysis in analysing respondents' answers to twenty-six questions that can be used as indicators of nationalism (Bonikowski 2011:119ff). See also Hjerm (2003) for a similar study done earlier. Bonikowski finds that respondents' attitudes towards nationalism can be divided into four different categories, which he calls liberal nationalism, critical nationalism, populist nationalism and ultra-nationalism. Those named *critical nationalists* in general score low on all questions connected with nationalism, leaning clearly towards civic nationalism. Concerning national pride, respondents in this classification exhibit either ambivalence or simply a lack of pride. Those labelled *liberal nationalists* also lean towards a civic dimension concerning the idea of the nation but show a high degree of pride in all aspects of the nation-state. The form of nationalism shown by these respondents is more liberal than uncompromising; on "supremacist" questions such as if one's country is better or more superior than others, they show little support. *Populist nationalists*, on the other hand, show little regard for the more civic aspects of nationalism, tapping deeper into the ethnic dimension of nationalism. Respondents belonging to this group score high on questions such as if ancestry and birth are important in order to be seen as a citizen. They positively value the nation's achievement while rejecting many of the state institutions. Nativist sentiments are strong. *Ultranationalists* also have strong ethnic identification, but they also strongly support the institutions of the nation-state. In short, they score high on almost all indicators of nationalism. Based upon this classification, we will later compare the mix of different manifestations of nationalism across Europe. But before that, I examine evidence of some of the changes that are currently transforming Europe.

A changing Europe

Europe is changing, due both to the internal processes of integration and assimilation and to processes of globalisation and internal pressure from below. The survey data presented as follows clearly show that confidence in the European project is dwindling. Some of this undoubtedly has to do with the financial crisis that shook Europe in 2008–2009, the repercussions of which are still being felt today. After the introduction of the euro and the successful admission of many East European countries, confidence in the EU soared, reaching almost 60 per cent in 2007, as Figure 2.1 shows.

This was unfortunately about the same time the financial economic crisis hit Europe, and confidence started deteriorating rapidly. A bungling approach to the crisis by both the EU and national governments did not help create confidence. From a peak in 2007, where almost 60 per cent of respondents said they tended to trust the EU, numbers have declined to around 30 per cent in 2014. The numbers of those who tend to trust their own government have shown the same development

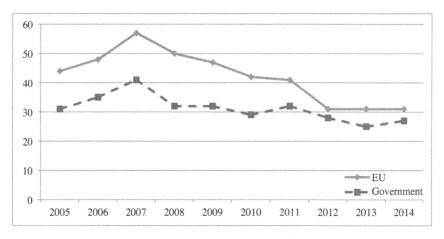

FIGURE 2.1   Per cent who tend to trust national and EU institutions

Source: Eurobarometers 64–81

over time, although even fewer respondents tend to trust their own government in the EU as a whole. These numbers shown in Figure 2.1 are a clear indication of a crisis of confidence between respondents and the elites they elect to represent them. Figure 2.2 illustrates the problem.

In this figure we clearly see that a change has taken place in the European electorate, as the financial crisis took hold. A positive view of the EU has been replaced by a more pessimistic one of lack of confidence in the EU. While lack of confidence in national governments is often connected to a rise in unemployment, this lack of confidence in the EU and its institutions seems more connected to the perceived financial and economic crisis that took hold from 2008 onwards (Roth and Nowak-Lehmann 2011). This can be perceived as a crisis of legitimacy, an uncertainty among respondents if the EU really is the way forward when it comes to Europe's future. In Figure 2.2, we also see that respondents over time have developed a more pessimistic view about this project of European integration. In 2012 and 2013 close to 50 per cent voiced a pessimistic outlook when thinking about the future of the EU.

This development is paradoxical, since the EU in many ways can be seen as a great success story. The introduction of a common currency, the abolition of internal border controls and a freer flow of goods and services is felt by its citizens every day. But in questions like those reported above, respondents are asked to evaluate what we might call the systemic performance of both national and supra-national institutions, including governments. And they are clearly not satisfied with recent performance. Respondents do, however, seem to be more pleased attitudinally with European integration. In Figure 2.3, respondents have been asked about their national and European identity.[1] The figure shows the percentage of respondents that indicated having either or both identities.

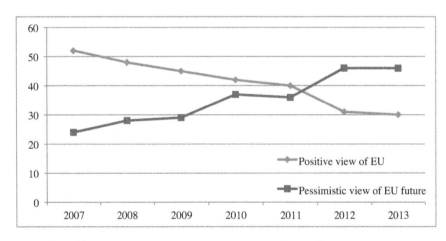

FIGURE 2.2 Percentages who hold a favourable view of the EU and those who are pessimistic about the future of the EU

Source: Eurobarometers 67–79

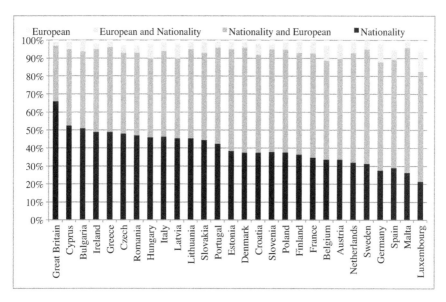

FIGURE 2.3   Per cent answering question on identity

Source: Eurobarometer 81 (2014)

Not surprisingly, as many as 64 per cent of British respondents have said they feel British only. Within the EU, Britain is the odd man out, having opted out from many of the different measures of integration that the rest of the union has implemented, like the Schengen border agreement and the introduction of the euro. In addition, the British Isles have very strong regional identities. These numbers are another argument for the idea of a core EU versus a more peripheral EU. Figure 2.3 illustrates that most countries that have mostly respondents with a single, national identity either lie in the peripheries of Europe or are new East European members, such as Great Britain or Bulgaria. The respondents of the original six member states show lower single national identity values as a general rule. Only about 20 per cent of respondents from Luxembourg have this identity as the only one, but most of those who feel they have two identities put the national one before the European one.

Does membership in the EU over time make respondents feel more European? A possible answer to that question can be read out of Table 2.1, which compares the development of a single, national identity over time.

The numbers in the table strongly indicate that time is an important part of the development towards a more nuanced identity – that of feeling both a national and a European identity. In some countries the development has been remarkable over time. In two of those countries that became members of the EU in 1994, Sweden and Austria, the high numbers of respondents with a single national identity remain basically unchanged from 1995 to 2004. In the third country, Finland, we even see a surge of single identity among respondents, from 47 to 60 per cent, making a

TABLE 2.1 Per cent answering "Nationality only" on question of identity

Country	1995	2004	Change 1995–2004	2014	Change 2004–2014
France	28	31	3	34	3
Belgium	33	40	7	33	−7
The Netherlands	34	49	15	32	−17
Germany*	34	38	4	27	−11
Italy	22	29	7	45	16
Luxembourg	17	28	11	21	−7
Denmark	48	43	−5	37	−6
Ireland	40	50	10	49	−1
Great Britain	53	65	12	64	−1
Greece	52	55	3	49	−6
Spain	42	33	−9	27	−6
Portugal	44	47	3	42	−5
Finland	47	60	13	36	−24
Sweden	56	58	2	31	−27
Austria	52	53	1	33	−20

*Average: 32% in West Germany in 1995, 43% in East Germany. In 2004 the numbers were 35% and 51%, respectively.

Source: Eurobarometer 43, 61 and 81.

single exclusive national identity almost as common as in Britain. But from 2004 to 2014, we see a marked decrease in single exclusive identity of over 20 per cent. In the period as a whole, we basically see a weakening of a single identity and a growth of a dual identity, although with some notable exceptions. The increase of respondents adhering to a single identity increased in the Netherlands by over 15 per cent between 1995 and 2004, which can probably be explained by two political assassinations that shook the country in 2002 and 2004, starting a polarising debate about multiculturalism and immigration (Vasta 2007). Likewise, the increase of Britons feeling only British in the same period is probably linked to the gradual self-exclusion of Britain from important core parts of European integration. Fuelled by a back-bench rebellion in 2011, the Conservative party has turned deeply Euros-ceptic, at the same time as the anti-EU, populist UKIP has gained ground (Gamble 2012). In light of this, and the fact that 52 per cent of British voters decided to leave the EU in June 2016, it is no wonder the number of respondents who still hold on to a single British identity remains stable around 65 per cent.

Unfortunately, comparable data is not available for all EU countries in order to examine the new East European member countries that joined in 2004 and 2007 for the period up to 2014, as questions in the time period have been asked using different wording. But for most countries examined, the development concerning exclusive national identity from 2004 to 2014 has been one of decline. Feelings of territorial identity have become dualistic and inclusive over time, although the national identity is still of most importance to respondents. Even in Luxembourg in 2014, only 17 per cent put a European identity first.

Another country also needs mentioning here. Although single national identity respondents have increased somewhat in France, numbers increased from 29 per cent in 2004 to 45 per cent in 2014 in Italy. This is a surprising development, as Italy for decades has been the one, big EU country where national identity has been deemed weakest. In 1995, as many as over 60 per cent of respondents felt Italian and European, 11 per cent European and Italian and 6 per cent European only. Recent changes in Italian politics are probably the main cause for this upsurge of a single national identity, in addition to a growing disillusionment with the decision of joining the euro-zone as a cure-all for Italy's economic ailments (Giurlando 2012). Politically, Italy was thrown into flux by the earthquake elections of 2013. During the Berlusconi era of Italian politics (1994–2013), Italy experienced a polarisation on moral issues and immigration, while a convergence of the socio-economic platforms of parties took place. Market issues, environmental issues and issues concerning the welfare state became de-politicised (Conti 2014:218). This pattern was overturned in the 2013 elections, when environmental issues and social protection became the main concern of voters. The upstart left-populist Five Star movement managed to capture this voter segment, leaving traditional parties scrambling for the hills. The reaction of right-wing parties like Forza Italia and the Northern League has been an appeal towards cultural nationalism, opposition to the EU and a harder stance on immigration issues.

The anatomy of European nationalism

In the previous section, I discussed a possible typology for classifying the different manifestations of nationalism in Europe. Based upon Bonokowski's classification, Table 2.2 displays the distribution of the different forms of nationalism in many European countries in 2003. The countries in the table are ranked in descending order based on the number of respondents who show the highest amount of critical nationalism (i.e. respondents leaning towards civic nationalism), displaying either a lack of pride in their country's achievements or ambivalence thereof.

It is not surprising that Germany, with its chequered nationalist past, is high on this list. More surprising perhaps is the fact that as many as 35 per cent of Russian respondents are found in the same category. On the other side, nowhere else, with the possible exception of Poland, do we find so many respondents who can be classified as populist nationalists. Populist nationalism seems more common in those countries in Eastern Europe that are part of this sample, while liberal nationalism (i.e. the civic type) seems more common among West European countries.

Ultranationalism, on the other hand, is not that usual a manifestation as liberal or populist nationalism, but especially one country makes an exception: Austria. The

TABLE 2.2 Types of nationalism in per cent by country in 2003

	Critical	Liberal	Populist	Ultra	N of cases
Slovakia	55	14	28	4	866
Germany	39	43	12	7	779
Czech Rep.	38	21	36	5	885
Russia	35	10	49	6	1389
Poland	32	17	44	7	880
Slovenia	30	35	29	7	843
Sweden	29	51	14	6	747
Netherlands	27	57	10	6	1216
Hungary	20	32	33	11	661
Norway	20	52	14	15	1025
Spain	19	50	10	21	874
Great Britain	18	51	12	18	526
Ireland	13	50	7	30	770
Austria	9	37	13	41	666

Source: ISSP 2003, adapted from (Bonikowski 2011:198).

number of people who were critical to nationalism is exceptionally low, with only 9 per cent. The high number of respondents being identified as ultranationalists may have several explanations. First, Euroscepticism is quite strong in Austria and has been quite high for a long time (Fallend 2008). Second, the survey was done at a time when the right-wing FPÖ (Freedom Party of Austria) had been record-high, gaining 27 per cent in the 1999 elections. But a third factor may be a result of the country's authoritarian past. Research has shown that some form of "underclass authoritarianism" exists in Austria and is closely connected with ethnic intolerance (Weiss 2003:396). A legacy of authoritarian attitudes may also explain the relatively high numbers of ultranationalists observed in countries like Ireland and Spain.

Xenophobia and attitudes towards migrants

Xenophobia, or the fear of other people who do not belong to your own perceived group identity, has been quite usual among people from time immemorial. To a certain extent, it may also be a useful reaction when confronted by something new or unexpected. But in modern societies, it is also a major impediment to creating functioning and harmonious societies, including all segments of society. Xenophobia, in its ugly manifestation of racism, normally becomes a more acute problem when countries are going through societal transformations (Wimmer 1997). Right-wing parties often use fear and distrust of foreigners to mobilise support for their policies in times of crisis. The logic of nationalism is a simple one in such situations; the nation looks after its own first.

Xenophobia and negative attitudes towards immigrants and others who seek a safe harbour in Europe are a potential threat towards European integration and cooperation. What we have seen since the late 1990s is that far-right parties have used their increasing electoral power to press governments into adopting more strict citizenship policies (Howard 2010). This has happened, for instance, in countries like the Netherlands, Belgium and Austria, where these parties have highlighted the challenges immigration can bring when it comes to integration. Challenges, however, are not necessarily the same as threats towards society. Ariely finds that national identification does not necessarily lead to increased xenophobia towards immigrants (Ariely 2012). He finds that the more inclusive the citizenship regime is, the weaker the relations between national identification and xenophobia. But a number of studies also show that the sheer size of immigrant communities and their competitiveness in the local job market can bring out resentment towards foreigners (Alonso and da Fonseca 2012; Mudde 2013). In a multi-level study, Rustenbach (2010) tries to puncture this implicit hypothesis and partially succeeds in doing so. According to her results, the size of immigrant communities is not important in itself, but other factors are more important:

> Anti-immigrant attitudes were influenced by regional and national interpersonal trust, education level, political interest, individual and national left/right political leaning, and foreign direct investment, among others. However, sheer numbers of immigrants, having been discriminated against or economic variables as a whole were not consistently associated with anti-immigrant attitudes.
>
> (Rustenbach 2010:70)

This is a complex matter, but an interesting question in the context of this chapter is to what degree attitudes towards immigrants change over time. In Table 2.3, respondents have been asked to tell whether they agree or disagree with a statement that immigrants contribute a lot to one's own country. The overall results do not point to more sceptic attitudes towards immigrants over time. Given that these questions were polled just before and at the current end of the European financial crisis, the numbers may be a bit surprising. In Greece and Cyprus, two countries that were hit hard by this crisis, numbers are down significantly, but in all other countries, numbers are stable, or in many cases show a significant increase. Within the EU there is a large variation when it comes to this question. Few respondents in Eastern Europe feel immigrants contribute to their country. In all probability this may be linked to the fact that these countries have relatively few immigrants. Indeed, most of these countries export immigrants to other EU countries farther west and north, where both salaries and the standard of living are higher. Even in countries that receive a lot of immigrants, like Germany, Great Britain and Sweden, respondents have become significantly more positive. In Sweden, as many as 89 per cent in 2014 feel immigrants contribute positively. Taken at face value, this may be a sign that the free flow of work across borders is working as intended in many parts of Europe.

TABLE 2.3 Per cent agreeing that immigrants contribute a lot to one's country

Country	2006	2012	Difference 2006 and 2012
France	44	48	4
Belgium	40	39	−1
Netherlands	53	61	8
Germany	30	53	23
Italy	41	44	3
Luxembourg	56	77	21
Denmark	45	58	13
Ireland	56	54	−2
Great Britain	47	57	10
Greece	43	32	−11
Spain	40	48	8
Portugal	66	66	0
Finland	54	64	10
Sweden	77	89	12
Austria	37	47	10
Poland	33	44	11
Cyprus	30	21	−9
Slovenia	28	43	15
Malta	21	25	4
Lithuania	20	38	18
Hungary	19	22	3
Czech Republic	17	18	1
Estonia	16	17	1
Latvia	16	21	5
Slovakia	12	21	9
Romania	43	48	5
Bulgaria	23	26	3

The percentages are those who either totally agree or tend to agree with the statement.
Source: Eurobarometer 66 and 77.

These results are in line with a study that uses data from the European Social Survey going from 2002 to 2012. This study finds that anti-immigrant attitudes remain basically unchanged over time, the average value differing between 4.5 and 5.0 on a scale from 0–10, turning slightly downwards over time, with high numbers marking strong anti-immigrant values (Hjerm and Bohman 2014:51). It also shows that East European respondents tend to have stronger anti-immigrant attitudes, while Swedes clearly have the most positive attitudes when it comes to immigration. This is being confirmed by our own data from the Eurobarometers.

Of course, the term *immigrant* is a relatively loose term that can mean different things for different respondents. The term may also have different connotations in different countries. The Spanish will probably think more of immigrants from Northern Africa, while Swedes and Britons may associate the term with job seekers from Eastern Europe. But the data available allows us to take a closer look at some groups that people may have some ambivalent attitudes towards. Table 2.4

TABLE 2.4 Per cent saying they do not want a named group as neighbours

	Immigrants		Jews		Muslims	
	2008	Change from 1990	2008	Change from 1990	2008	Change from 1990
Malta	34,1	25,2	20,8	12,7	31,6	19,6
Estonia	32,2	15,1	22,3	9,4	33,9	13,3
Czech Republic	30,2	7,5	11,9	−0,8	30,7	8,3
Lithuania	28,6	13,8	28,3	10,6	47	13
Slovenia	28,5	−12,1	28,2	−9,9	29,3	−9
Austria	23,2	3	17,3	5,9	30,9	16,7
Latvia	20,9	−9,9	9,8	1,3	28,6	2,7
Romania	20,8	−9,4	18,6	−9,5	22,9	−11,6
Bulgaria	18,1	−16,3	14,9	−15,3	19,5	−21,3
Poland	17,5	7,5	17,9	0,2	25,1	5,5
Slovak Rep.	16,6	−6,8	12,5	−13,6	23,1	−3
Italy	16,1	2,7	12,1	−0,2	22,7	8,4
Finland	16	11,4	4,9	0,1	23,4	13,5
Netherlands	15,4	6,5	8	4,7	18,9	4,8
Hungary	15,2	−7	6,4	−3,9	11	−7,3
Great Britain	14,9	4,1	3,2	−3,5	12,9	−3,5
Ireland	14,1	9	10,9	4,5	22,7	9,3
Germany	11,6	−5,5	6,1	−1,4	26,2	6,2
Portugal	7,9	−2,2	12,6	−9,4	14,8	−4,4
Denmark	6,8	−4,8	2,1	−1	13,1	−2,3
Sweden	6,4	−2,5	3,1	−2,5	15,8	−1,2
Belgium	6,2	−14,1	3,9	−9,1	14,5	−12,1
Norway	6	−9,8	2,9	−6	13,3	−7,9
France	4,3	−8,5	2,4	−4,3	7,6	−9,9
Spain	4,2	−3,3	2,5	−5,7	12,9	2,4
Iceland	3,4	−4,3	2,6	−4,7	8,1	−3,6

Source: European Value Survey 1990 and 2008.

shows how many of the respondents do not want people from specific groups as neighbours. This is a very concrete question that measures very concrete attitudes. One might generally be in favour of immigration, or of different subgroups, but the final test is in many ways if you are willing to accept people from different groups in your own neighbourhood.

First of all, the results are somewhat counterintuitive from what might have been expected. People in general have become more tolerant of potentially vulnerable groups in the last twenty years, but there are some very clear exceptions to this rule. In many East European countries, the number of people who say they do not want immigrants, Jews and Muslims as neighbours has increased in the period from 1990 to 2008. This may be connected with the fact that the political discourse regarding nationalism, racism and immigration is taking place more on the right wing of the political spectrum. On these issues, mainstream politics is more to the right than is the case in most West European countries (Mudde 2005). It is also in Eastern Europe that people are most reserved when it comes to having Jews as neighbours, although the numbers tend to be much higher when it comes to Muslims. In Lithuania, as many as 47 per cent do not want Muslims as neighbours, while 28 per cent are sceptical towards Jews, an increase of 10 per cent since 1990. It may be difficult to explain these high numbers; before the Second World War, countries like Poland and Lithuania were seen as safe havens for many Jews, and in both countries they made up around 7 per cent of the inter-war population. Hardly any were left in 1990. The fact that both racist and right-wing nationalist attitudes are more widespread may be part of the explanation. The type of nationalism, according to the classification by Bonikowski presented earlier, also tends to be of a more populist kind in many East European countries.

Among West European countries, Malta stands out, having roughly one-third of the population that do not want immigrants or Muslims as neighbours. These sentiments may be easier to explain. Since around 2000, the number of illegal, mainly Muslim immigrants to the island has increased dramatically, making irregular immigration perhaps the most important policy issue among voters (Lutterbeck 2009). The relatively high Austrian numbers may be partly explained by the "underclass authoritarianism" previously discussed, but elsewhere in Western Europe, the number of respondents who do not want immigrants, Muslims or Jews as neighbours tends to be relatively small. And it is worth noting that, in general, respondents in most countries have become less sceptical over time. This trend is the same as seen in Table 2.3, where the number of respondents who think that immigrants contribute a lot to one's country showed a general increase between 2006 and 2012, even in the midst of the euro crisis.

Conclusions

In a famous definition of when democracy is truly consolidated, Juan Linz and Alfred Stephan once stated that this would happen when democracy had become "the only game in town" (Linz and Stepan 1996). Democracy would have had to become consolidated behaviourally, attitudinally and constitutionally in the minds of the people. In comparison, the process of European integration is still far from being consolidated. State and nation – and the identities emanating from them – are still far stronger than any European identity, but the data we have examined also tell us another story. It is the story of dual, complementing identities, where more and more respondents are feeling both national and European identities. In generating this change, the EU may well be regarded as a success story.

The numbers also tell another story, however. They tell of a Europe that respondents think is in systemic crisis, where both the EU and national governments are losing legitimacy. This development may have long-term implications for the project of European integration. In the article referred to previously, Linz and Stephan pointed to another issue that had to be solved before a state could come so far along the road towards democracy that democratic consolidation even became a topic: the problem of "stateness". The territorial stability and indivisibility of the state must not be in doubt. This is an issue in many countries in Europe, like Spain, Italy, Belgium, Great Britain – in which Scotland in a 2014 referendum decided still to be a part of Britain – Latvia and Estonia, as well as a destabilised Ukraine. This is also an issue for the EU itself, whose legitimacy has been weakened.

At the same time we see populist, radical and extremist parties gaining support on the fringes of the political system, sometimes turning themselves into mainstream parties by their sheer size, as is the case with the Flemish Bloc in Belgium and the National Front in France (Bjånesøy and Ivarsflaten 2016). The increased electoral appeal of parties like this can be taken as a sign that something is not working in the interaction between the national and supranational level. Europe is in many ways at a crossroads – and has been for some time. A decrease in legitimacy at both the national and supranational levels is creating a vacuum that can easily be filled by more extreme or populist voices. The emergence of populist movements like Syriza in Greece or Podemos in Spain is a symptom that politics as usual is not working anymore. This is paradoxical, in the sense that the Europeanisation of feelings of identity and belonging seems to be working. An increasing number of people across Europe share not only a national identity but a European one as well. The real danger in this development is that people who have not taken part in this process of Europeanisation may become alienated and disenfranchised. If so, Europe may stand before a development not towards an ever-closer union but a Europe more divided. Such a development would lead towards an ever-looser union and the end of the project of European integration as we know it. Nationalism in such a context is far from a spent force, but something that needs to be taken very seriously.

Further reading

Ariely, Gal. 2013. "Nationhood across Europe: The Civic-Ethnic Framework and the Distinction between Western and Eastern Europe." *Perspectives on European politics and Society* 14 (1):123–43.

Howard, Marc Morje. 2010. "The Impact of the Far Right on Citizenship Policy in Europe: Explaining Continuity and Change." *Journal of Ethnic and Migration Studies* 36 (5):735–51.

Mudde, Cas. 2013. "Three Decades of Populist Radical Right Parties in Western Europe: So What?" *European Journal of Political Research* 52 (1):1–19.

Key questions for discussion

1   What impact has the financial crisis had on trust in national and European institutions?
2   Are Europeans becoming more nationalistic?
3   Is there evidence of growing xenophobia in Europe?

Note

1   On questions of identity, respondents have been asked: Do you feel like "Nationality only", "Nationality and European", "European and nationality" or "European only"?

References

Alonso, S., and S. C. da Fonseca. 2012. "Immigration, Left and Right." *Party Politics* 18 (6):865–84.

Anderson, Benedict. 1991. *Imagined Communities: Reflections on the Origin and Spread of Nationalism.* Rev. ed. London: Verso.

Ariely, Gal. 2012. "Do Those Who Identify with Their Nation Always Dislike Immigrants?: An Examination of Citizenship Policy Effects." *Nationalism and Ethnic Politics* 18 (2):242–61.

———. 2013. "Nationhood across Europe: The Civic-Ethnic Framework and the Distinction between Western and Eastern Europe." *Perspectives on European Politics and Society* 14 (1):123–43.

Bjånesøy, Lise Lund, and Elisabeth Ivarsflaten. 2016. "Right-Wing Populism." In *Democratic Transformations in Europe: Challenges and Opportunities*, ed. Y. Peters and M. Tatham. Abingdon: Routledge, pp. 33–50.

Bonikowski, Bart. 2011. *Toward a Theory of Popular Nationalism: Shared Representations of the Nation-State in Modern Democracies.* Princeton, NJ: Princeton University Press.

Cappelen, Cornelius. 2016. "Intra-EU Migration and the Moral Sustainability of the Welfare State." In *Democratic Transformations in Europe: Challenges and Opportunities*, ed. Y. Peters and M. Tatham. Abingdon: Routledge, pp. 143–162.

Carling, Jørgen. 2011. "The European Paradox of Unwanted Immigration." In *A Threat Against Europe? Security, Migration and Integration*, ed. J. P. Burgess and S. Gutwirth. Brussels: Brussels University Press.

Conti, Nicolò. 2014. "New Parties and the Transformation of the Italian Political Space." *Contemporary Italian Politics* 6 (3):205–21.

Fallend, Franz. 2008. "Euroscepticism in Austrian Political Parties: Ideologically Rooted or Strategically Motivated?" In *Opposing Europe? The Comparative Party Politics of Euroscepticism*, ed. A. Szczerbiak and P. Taggart. Oxford: Oxford University Press, pp. 33–46.

Gamble, Andrew. 2012. "Better Off Out? Britain and Europe." *The Political Quarterly* 83 (3):468–77.

Gat, Azar, and Alexander Yakobson. 2013. *Nations: The Long History and Deep Roots of Political Ethnicity and Nationalism.* Cambridge: Cambridge University Press.

Gellner, Ernest. 1983. *Nations and Nationalism*. Oxford: Blackwell.

Ghemawat, Pankaj, and Steven A. Altman. 2014. *DHL Global Connectedness Index 2014*. Bonn: Deutsche Post DHL.

Giurlando, Philip. 2012. "Vicarious Evaluation: How European Integration Changes National Identities." *Review of European and Russian Affairs* 7 (2):1–14.

Greenfeld, Liah. 1992. *Nationalism: Five Roads to Modernity*. Cambridge, MA: Harvard University Press.

Habermas, Jürgen. 1990. *Die Nachholende Revolution*. Frankfurt am Main: Suhrkamp.

Hjerm, Mikael. 2003. "National Sentiments in Eastern and Western Europe." *Nationalities Papers* 31 (4):413–29.

Hjerm, Mikael, and Andrea Bohman. 2014. "Is It Getting Worse? Anti-Immigrant Attitudes in Europe during the 21 Century." In *European Populism and Winning the Immigration Debate*, ed. C. Sandelin. Falun: European Liberal Forum, pp. 41–64.

Howard, Marc Morje. 2010. "The Impact of the Far Right on Citizenship Policy in Europe: Explaining Continuity and Change." *Journal of Ethnic and Migration Studies* 36 (5):735–51.

Hutter, Swen, Bruno Wüest, Edgar Grande, Marc Helbling, Martin Dolezal, Hanspeter Kriesi, and Dominic Höglinger. 2012. *Political Conflict in Western Europe*. Cambridge: Cambridge University Press.

Jurado, Elena, and Grete Brochmann. 2013. *Europe's Immigration Challenge: Reconciling Work, Welfare and Mobility*. London: I.B.Tauris & Co. Ltd.

Kedourie, Elie. 1993. *Nationalism*. 4th, Exp. edn. Oxford: Blackwell.

Kopecky, P., and C. Mudde. 2000. "What Has Eastern Europe Taught Us about the Democratisation Literature (and Vice Versa)?" *European Journal of Political Research* 37 (4):517–23.

Lawrence, Paul. 2005. *Nationalism: History and Theory*. Harlow: Pearson Longman.

Linz, Juan J., and Alfred Stepan. 1996. "Toward Consolidated Democracies." *Journal of Democracy* 7 (2):14–33.

Lutterbeck, David 2009. "Small Frontier Island: Malta and the Challenge of Irregular Immigration." *Mediterranean Quarterly* 20 (1):119–44.

Mudde, Cas. 2005. "Racist Extremism in Central and Eastern Europe." *East European Politics and Societies* 19 (2):161–84.

———. 2013. "Three Decades of Populist Radical Right Parties in Western Europe: So What?" *European Journal of Political Research* 52 (1):1–19.

Oldervoll, Johannes Andresen, and Stein Kuhnle. 2016. "The Sustainability of European Welfare States: The Significance of Changing Labour Markets." In *Democratic Transformations in Europe: Challenges and Opportunities*, ed. Y. Peters and M. Tatham. Abingdon: Routledge, pp. 120–142.

Özkirimli, Umut. 2005. *Contemporary Debates on Nationalism: A Critical Engagement*. Basingstoke: Palgrave Macmillan.

Roth, Felix, and Felicitas D. Nowak-Lehmann. 2011. "Has the financial crisis shattered citizens' trust in national and European governmental institutions? Evidence from the EU member states, 1999–2010." *Centre for European Policy Studies Working Document* (343).

Rustenbach, Elisa. 2010. "Sources of Negative Attitudes toward Immigrants in Europe: A Multi-Level Analysis." *International Migration Review* 44 (1):53–77.

Schnee, Walter. 2001. "Nationalism: A Review of the Literature." *Journal of Political and Military Sociology* 29 (Summer):1–18.

Smith, Anthony D. 1998. *Nationalism and Modernism: A Critical Survey of Recent Theories of Nations and Nationalism*. London: Routledge.

———. 2002. "When Is a Nation?" *Geopolitics* 7 (2):5–32.

Tamir, Yael. 1995. "The Enigma of Nationalism." *World Politics* 47 (3):418–40.

Tatham, Michaël. 2016. "Multi-Jurisdictional Politics: State Adaptation and Mixed Visions of Democracy." In *Democratic Transformations in Europe: Challenges and Opportunities*, ed. Y. Peters and M. Tatham. Abingdon: Routledge, pp. 269–294.

Vasta, Ellie. 2007. "From Ethnic Minorities to Ethnic Majority Policy: Multiculturalism and the Shift to Assimilationism in the Netherlands." *Journal of Ethnic and Racial Studies* 30 (5):713–40.

Weiss, H. 2003. "A Cross-National Comparison of Nationalism in Austria, the Czech and Slovac Republics, Hungary, and Poland." *Political Psychology* 24 (2):377–401.

Wimmer, Andreas. 1997. "Explaining Xenophobia and Racism: A Critical Review of Current Research Approaches." *Ethnic and Racial Studies* 20 (1):17–41.

3

WHAT KIND OF CHALLENGE?

Right-wing populism in contemporary Western Europe

Lise Lund Bjånesøy and Elisabeth Ivarsflaten

Introduction

During the past three decades, populist radical right parties have become influential political actors in a number of Western European countries. In the elections to the European Parliament in June 2014, populist radical right parties won the largest share of the vote in France, the UK, and Denmark. They received a substantial number of votes in Finland, Sweden, the Netherlands, Flanders, and Austria. In addition to the remarkable EU parliamentary election results, populist radical right parties entered government in Norway and Finland and have been established as one of the largest political parties in Switzerland. What kind of challenge does the rise of the populist radical right raise in advanced contemporary democracies?

In this chapter, we argue that the challenge of the populist radical right to advanced contemporary democracies can be interpreted in two substantially different ways. On the one hand, these parties can be seen as representing an alternative democratic vision to that of mainstream parties. On this view, populist radical right parties do not represent a fundamental threat to the democratic system, but they want to change – and in their view improve – the way democracy operates. The essence of the alternative democratic model associated with the populist radical right is the emphasis they put on the will of the majority and unmediated decision-making. On the other hand, populist radical right parties can be seen as representing a more fundamental alienation from, and even rejection of, core democratic principles. In this logic, the populist radical right is, for the time being, playing by democratic rules, but the values and voters they represent are not committed to the democratic order.

These questions strike at the core of the normative political conflicts that surround the populist radical right parties in Western Europe. These conflicts have resulted in non-cooperation pacts in various parliaments, street demonstrations, international sanctions, and legal bans. The fundamental question raised implicitly or explicitly in these conflicts is, to what extent are populist radical right parties and their voters a threat to democracy? This question relates to the politically contentious line drawn between right-wing extremism, on the one hand, and right-wing populism, on the other. While extremism refers to a lack of support for core democratic principles, populism need not do so. Populism may be conceived as a particular majoritarian vision of democracy, which many politicians and citizens disagree with and even dislike, but it is not on its own a rejection of core democratic values.

Democracy and new nationalism

Existing studies of the radical right have tended to focus most on nativism and strict integration and immigration policies when examining the ideology and voter appeal of the populist radical right (Bornschier 2010; Ivarsflaten 2007; Mudde 2007). Central to these studies has been the contention that the electorally successful radical right parties in contemporary Western Europe were "new" in the sense that they distanced themselves from the extreme nationalists, the Nazis and the fascist parties of the 1930s. The French radical right party, Front National (FN), is in this account seen as a paradigmatic case (Rydgren 2004). The ethno-nationalist or nativist ideology – towards which the other radical right parties later converged (Ignazi 2005; Mudde 2007; Rydgren 2005) – was initially formulated in the French New Right circles that inspired the formation of the French FN (in 1972). The New Right's – and by extension the FN's – claim to ideological innovation lay in their attempt to separate a cultural basis for national unity and first-preference from a biological basis for such political goals.

Taking a stance against old nationalism and racism, narrowly understood, is today nearly universally perceived as a necessary part of a viable electoral strategy on the radical right side of politics in contemporary Western European democracies (Blinder et al. 2013; Ivarsflaten et al. 2010).[1] Still, establishing some ideological distance between themselves and Nazism or fascism is far from sufficient to be considered a democratic party. Therefore, in this chapter we address the "extremism vs. populism" debate, not by examining whether or not the radical right represents an old or a new version of nationalist ideology. Instead, we address analytically and empirically to what extent and how the voters of those parties that pose as "new," "right-wing populist," and "non-extremist" are committed to core democratic principles.

The populist vision of democracy

Populism has proved to be a difficult concept in the literature on radical right parties. Most scholars use the concept of "populism" to describe or define the party family, but Mudde, for example, argues that populism is a thin ideology that comes on top of the core ideology, which in principle can be either right- or left-wing (Mudde 2007).

Jagers and Walgrave take the concept of a thin ideology even further and refer to a "populist style" of communication (Jagers and Walgrave 2007).

Unlike in studies of anti-immigration sentiment, not much evidence has been found for populist mobilization from the side of voters. Van der Brug et al. firmly rejected in a comprehensive study that support for the populist radical right was driven by an identifiable pattern of protest voting. They conclude that, "voting for anti-immigrant parties is largely motivated by ideological and pragmatic considerations, just like voting for other parties" (Van der Brug et al. 2000: 77).

What has been mostly missing from these previous analyses is a discussion and analysis of populism as thick ideology – as an alternative, majoritarian vision of democracy. In a more recent discussion of the populist challenge, Kriesi identifies exactly this missing piece when stating that "the populist theory of democracy is rarely made explicit, but it provides the key to understanding of the populist ideology" (Kriesi 2014: 363). In line with conventional thinking in political science (e.g. Dahl 1956), Kriesi defines the populist vision of democracy in contrast to liberal or Madisonian democracy. In the Federalist papers, James Madison worried that democracy would turn out to be "the tyranny of the majority" if left unchecked by division of power and the rule of law that could protect the rights of minorities.

By contrast, the majoritarian or populist vision of democracy draws no distinction between the will of the people and what is normatively right. In this logic, it is important to devise democratic institutions that most effectively, and without cumbersome institutional procedures, translate the will of the majority into policy. Dahl similarly singles out the accordance with "the preferences of the greater number of citizens (voters, or legislators)" as the "necessary and sufficient condition for government policy" in the populist argument for democracy (Dahl 1956: 44–45). With the Madisonian argument, Dahl argues, "accordance with the preferences of the greater number of citizens ought to be a necessary condition but not a sufficient condition for government policy" (Dahl 1956: 45).

Manin describes how a worry about democracy as "mob rule" in Ancient Greece helped establish representative democracy as the standard vision of democracy. Today, Manin argues, representative democracy is seen as the natural form of democracy, but he emphasizes that it is not the only conceivable manifestation of democratic principles. In fact, representative democracy in Manin's account is more correctly understood as a combination of a democratic and a more aristocratic, or elitist, impulse (Manin 1997).

When viewed in opposition to the idea of representative democracy, the populist vision emphasizes direct and unmediated decision-making. According to the populist vision, the essence of democracy is rule by the people in a spontaneous way. This view of democracy makes populism as thick ideology deeply critical of representative democracy. This suspicion of representative democracy takes many forms, one of which is a negative view of political parties or any representatives as being part of a corrupted elite, whose clear and honest thinking is destroyed by, for example, too much education, privilege, special economic interests, or artificial urban life. These elites are then in populist thinking distinguished from the common people, who are viewed as honest, simple, wise, and the natural heartland of democracy (Abts and Rummens 2007; Canovan 1999; Mény and Surel 2002). It follows from this way of reasoning that elites and representatives are an obstacle to true democracy and that direct decision-making, for example in the form of referenda, is favored.

Critiques and lines of questioning of the populist vision of democracy are many. What precisely is an unmediated link between the people and policies supposed to look like? How tenable is the assumption of a monolithic people with a general will?[2] Why do populist visions so often also include support for charismatic leaders? Nevertheless, it cannot be denied that the populist vision of democracy, the unchecked translation of popular will into political actions, is one of many possible democratic models. Interestingly, it shares with some very progressive contemporary ideals of participatory democracy a deep critique of the established institutions of liberal representative democracy as unable to deliver on the democratic promise of citizen power (Held 1987).

Lack of commitment to democratic principles?

The designation of radical right parties as "populist" or "new" has in the scholarly literature been used primarily to distinguish these parties from "old" and "extreme" right-wing parties. Ignazi's 1992 article viewed the rise of the radical right as a counter-movement to the postmaterialist mobilization of green voters. It established the now-entrenched argument that only radical right parties that offered something "new" in ideological terms had any chance of mobilizing voters in contemporary Western European politics (see also Art 2005; Carter 2005; Golder 2003; Ignazi 2005). In particular, any blatant and direct connections with Nazi or fascist organizations or ideologies have proved a losing electoral formula. By contrast, credible distancing, or "reputational shields" against accusations of racism and fascism, has proved important for successful electoral outcomes (Blinder et al. 2013; Ford and Goodwin 2014; Ivarsflaten 2007; Sniderman et al. 2014).

The quite persuasive evidence suggesting that old-style extremism is a losing strategy in contemporary Western Europe has had one blind spot, which we will address in our analysis in this chapter. In the extensive literature on the radical right voter, we have failed to examine empirically their degree of commitment to core democratic values. The radical right parties argue that they are not extreme, and they do so in particular by distancing themselves from extremist organizations of the past. But what if they in fact represent and mobilize a new form of democratic alienation or resentment? Could it be that the contemporary radical right, despite their assurances of compliance with democratic norms and distancing efforts from previous extremist ideologies and organizations, still mobilize voters who are less committed to democratic principles than are other voters?

Logically it is certainly possible that a new form of anti-democratic sentiment can be mobilized by the contemporary radical right even if a particular form of extremism is rejected – in this case Nazism and fascism. After all, political movements and parties are in the end defined by the political projects that they favor, not only the ones they oppose. It also does not follow logically that because radical right voters are ideological (i.e. not merely protest voters), they are necessarily committed to democratic principles. A voter may very well favor certain ideological political ends without recognizing the importance of democratic principles in achieving those ends. In the final instance, the question of the democratic commitment of populist radical right voters is empirical in nature.

The populist radical right parties in Europe

The political parties whose voters are examined in this chapter have been classified and labeled in many different ways. They have been labeled Extreme Right parties (Ignazi 1992; Lubbers et al. 2002), Populist Radical Right parties (Mudde 2007), Radical Right-Wing Populists (Betz 1994), Anti-Immigrant parties (van der Brug et al. 2000), and many more. In this chapter we follow Mudde and use the label populist radical right (PRR). When selecting parties for empirical analysis, we rely on previous studies, because we want to examine the democratic commitment of the voters of those parties that previous research agrees to be PRR. Furthermore, since we are interested in empirically examining voters, we can only examine parties that have experienced some electoral success. Following convention, we chose parties that received more than 5 per cent of the national vote. Furthermore, since we are interested in examining variations in democratic commitment in stable democracies, we chose to focus our analysis on Europe's oldest democracies. Eastern European parties are therefore not included in our analysis. Our final analysis then includes the voters of the eight PRR parties listed in Table 3.1 and further described in the section that follows.[3]

Fremskrittspartiet (the Progress Party)

Fremskrittspartiet was founded in 1973 (originally named Anders Langes Parti). It started out as a protest against increased taxation and not as an anti-immigrant party. In the local election of 1987, Fremskrittspartiet had made

TABLE 3.1 Populist radical right parties in Western Europe

Country	PRR party	Previous general election result
Belgium	Vlaams Belang (VB)	3.6% (2014)
Denmark	Dansk Folkeparti (DF)	21.1% (2015)
Finland	Perussuomalaiset (PS)	17.6% (2015)
France	Front National (FN)	13.6% (2012)
Netherlands	Partij voor de Vrijheid (PVV)	10.1% (2012)
Norway	Fremskrittspartiet (FrP)	16.3% (2013)
Sweden	Sverigedemokraterna (SD)	12.9% (2014)
Switzerland	Schweizerische Volkspartei (SVP)	26.6% (2011)

restrictive immigration policies part of their political platform and made substantial gains. In the general election of 2009, Fremskrittspartiet gained 22.9 per cent of the vote, which constitutes their best election result so far. In 2013 Fremskrittspartiet entered government for the first time. They joined a minority coalition, together with Norway's conservative party Høyre. Fremskrittspartiet's leader, Siv Jensen, is the Government's Minister of Finance.

Sverigedemokraterna (the Sweden Democrats)

Sverigedemokraterna made their first electoral breakthrough in the general election of 2010 when they won 5.7 per cent of the vote and passed the electoral threshold. Unlike the other PRR parties in the Nordic countries, Sverigedemokraterna primarily started as a nationalist and anti-immigrant party. Unlike other successful PRR parties in Western Europe, Sverigedemokraterna has an extreme right-wing past. The party has gone through moderations since 2005, when Jimmie Åkesson became the party leader. However, established parties still refuse to cooperate with them even after the general election of 2014 when Sverigedemokraterna gained 12.9 per cent of the vote.

Dansk Folkeparti (the Danish People's Party)

Dansk Folkeparti was established in 1995. Previous members of the party Fremskridtspartiet split from the party after a long period of conflicts and formed the new party Dansk Folkeparti. The founding leader, Pia Kjærsgaard, led the party until 2012, when she stepped down and Kristian Thulesen Dahl took her place. Dansk Folkeparti is a nationalist, Euroscept, and anti-immigrant party. In the general election of 2015, Dansk Folkeparti won 20.5 per cent of the vote.

Perussuomalaiset (the Finns Party)

Perussuomalaiset was established in 1995 and grew out from the Finnish Rural Party. The party is led by Timo Soini, a charismatic and popular figure. In the general election of 2011 the party gained 19.1 per cent of the vote, which was a significant gain. Perussuomalaiset is a nationalist party with critical views on immigration similar to the other PRR parties in Western Europe, but it also places a number of issues as equally important. They are, for example, skeptical towards the EU and want to abolish Swedish as an official language in Finland.

Vlaams Belang (Flemish Interest)

Vlaams Belang started out as Vlaams Blok but had to change its name due to a racism judgement. One of the core issues of Vlaams Belang has been Flemish nationalism and separatism. In recent years immigration and ethnic diversity have become concerns of increasing importance for the party. Vlaams Belang gained 12 per cent of the vote in the general election of 2007 but gained only 3.7 per cent of the vote in the 2014 election. The party is now in internal conflicts, and the future of the party is currently unclear.

Schweizerische Volkspartei (the Swiss People's Party)

The Schweizerische Volkspartei started out as an agrarian party but transformed itself into a populist party in the 1990s. In 2007, Schweizerische Volkspartei won 28.9 per cent of the vote, and in 2011, 26.6 per cent. It is the party with the largest electoral support in Switzerland. The party has, like the other PRR parties in Western Europe, anti-immigration and Euroscepticism at its core, together with traditional family values and law-and-order issues.

Partij voor de Vrijheid (the Party for Freedom)

The PRR in the Netherlands gained its breakthrough in the general election of 2002, when the party Lijst Pim Fortuyn won 17 per cent of the vote. The party's charismatic leader, Pim Fortuyn, was assassinated only a week before the election, ending the future of the party. In 2004 the party was succeeded by Group Wilders led by Geert Wilders. The Group Wilders was renamed Partij voor de Vrijheid in 2006. Core issues of the party are anti-immigration and multiculturalism (and especially Islam). The party gained its largest share of votes in the general election of 2009, when it won 17 per cent of the votes. In the general election of 2012 the party gained 10.1 per cent of the vote, which was a significant decline.

Front National (the National Front)

The Front National is often considered a paradigmatic case of PRR parties. The Front National was founded in 1972 and led by Jean-Marie Le Pen until 2011, when his daughter, Marine Le Pen, took over as the head of the party. Marine Le Pen came third in the presidential election of 2012, with 17.9 per cent of the vote. The core issues of the party are anti-immigration issues and nationalism. Marine Le Pen is considered a less authoritarian figure than her father Jean-Marie Le Pen, something that has broadened the appeal of the party to new groups of voters.

Data

We use the democracy module from the European Social Survey 2012 (ESS). This module contains questions about voters' principled beliefs about democracy, how they evaluate democracy, and what factors they believe to be important in a democracy. The module also contains questions about voters' perceptions of democracy; about their satisfaction with the different institutions of democracy, asking them to

TABLE 3.2 Descriptive statistics of the dependent variable

Dependent variable	(N) PRR	(N) Non-PRR	PRR voters %
Vote	915	8765	9
Norway	132	1043	11
Denmark	117	1210	9
Sweden	64	1377	4
Finland	202	1296	13
The Netherlands	96	1316	7
France	126	1130	10
Switzerland	131	612	17
Flanders	47	781	6

evaluate how they believe it works in their own country. In this study we focus on the principled beliefs about democracy.[4]

Our dependent variable, shown in Table 3.2, is respondents' self-reported vote choice. All of the respondents were asked the following question: "What party did you vote for in the last national election of [country]." This variable was then recoded into a dichotomous variable for each country, where 1 represents a vote for the country's PRR party and 0 represents a vote for one of the country's other parties. Non-voters are not the focus of this chapter and therefore not included in the analysis.

Table 3.2 shows that in the selected countries, an average of 9.5 per cent of voters chose the PRR. In this sample of voters, Switzerland is the country where the radical right makes up the largest share of voters, while Sweden is where the radical right makes up the smallest share of voters of the selected countries. As seen in the columns reporting the sample sizes, both the Flemish and Swedish samples have a limited number of PRR party voters included in the sample (47 individuals in Flanders and 64 individuals in Sweden).

Analysis

We now turn to the empirical analysis. First, we examine the extent to which PRR voters support a populist, majoritarian vision of democracy as opposed to a liberal, representative democratic vision. Second, we examine whether or not PRR voters are less committed than voters of other parties to general democratic principles.

Populist voters' vision of democracy

The ESS module contains four questions that can be said to measure various aspects of support for a populist vision of democracy. As discussed in the previous section, the populist vision idealizes the majority will and emphasizes the importance of a system that translates the majority will directly into political decisions with as few institutional barriers and intermediaries as possible. The survey asks about voters' beliefs in the importance for democracy of referenda, minority rights protection, of taking into account the views of other European countries, and of independent courts.

If PRR voters support a more populist vision of democracy than do other voters, we would expect them to consider referenda more important to democracy, because these facilitate direct decisions by the majority without elite representation. Furthermore, we would expect PRR voters to consider minority rights protection less important for democracy than other voters would. We would also expect PRR voters to be less concerned than other voters about taking the views of other European countries into account, because this adds checks onto the exercise of majority power. Finally, because constitutions and courts place restrictions on the ability of governments to freely pursue the majority will, we expect PRR voters to consider courts to be less important for democracy than other voters would.

As shown in Figure 3.1, we find exactly the result we expect on the question of referenda. Respondents were asked, "How important do you think it is for democracy in general that citizens have the final say on political issues by voting directly in referendums." The figure shows that PRR voters place themselves substantively and

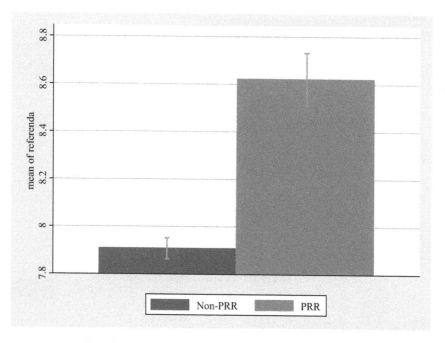

FIGURE 3.1 Referenda

significantly higher on the 11-point "important for democracy" scale than do other voters.[5] Among radical right parties there is almost full agreement on the importance of referenda for democracy. Fully 89 per cent of the radical right voters place themselves on the "important for democracy" side of the scale – between 7 and 10 on an 11-point scale, where 10 is the maximal score. The results on the referendum question thus support the contention that PRR voters favor an alternative and more direct democratic model.

Figure 3.2 shows that the PRR voters also differ from voters of other parties as expected on the question of minority rights. Respondents were asked, "How important do you think it is for democracy in general that the rights of minority groups are protected?" On this question, we find as expected, based on the majoritarian bias in the populist vision of democracy, that PRR voters find minority rights protection to be substantively and significantly less important to democracy than do voters of other parties. In the case of minority rights we find that fully 89 per cent of all non-PRR voters consider this to be important to democracy. Substantially fewer, but still a majority, of 79 per cent of PRR voters consider minority rights protection to be important for democracy. The pattern displayed in Figure 3.2 thus further supports the contention that PRR voters support a more populist and majoritarian vision of democracy than do voters of other parties.

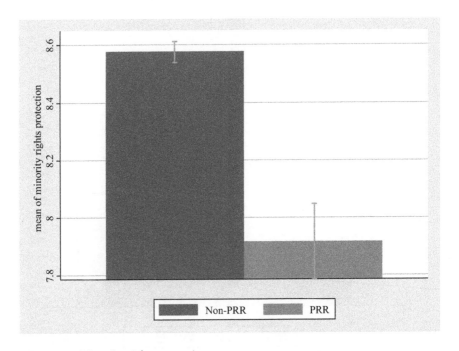

FIGURE 3.2 Minority rights protection

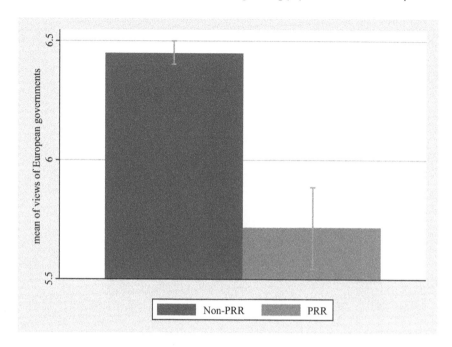

FIGURE 3.3   Take into account views of other European governments

Figure 3.3 shows that on the question of taking the views of other European governments into account, PRR voters differ substantively and significantly from voters of other parties. Respondents were asked, "How important do you think it is for democracy in general that politicians take into account the views of other European governments before making decisions?" As expected, voters of PRR parties consider any kind of barriers to the process of turning majority decisions into policy not so important. In this case, a minority of 44 per cent of PRR voters consider it important for democracy that other countries' views should be taken into consideration. This judgment contrasts with non-PRR voters, where a majority of 56 per cent believes this to be important.

The final question, where a populist vision of democracy will lead to different judgments, concerns the importance of courts. The question asked of respondents was, "How important do you think it is for democracy in general that the courts are able to stop the government acting beyond its authority?" As Figure 3.4 shows, we do not find the expected pattern in this case. On this question PRR voters answer exactly the same as voters of other parties. Support for the importance of courts is overwhelming in both cases; around 90 per cent of both PRR and non-PRR voters think that it is important for democracy that courts can constrain government authority. In fact, among PRR voters this principle receives the highest level of support of all the questions asked about principled beliefs about democracy. This

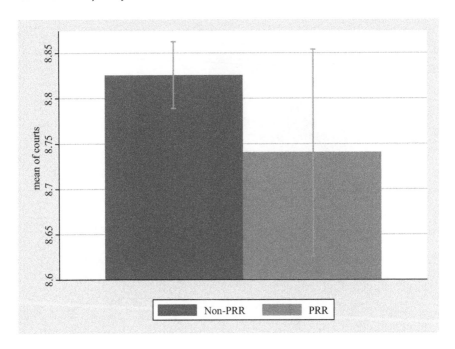

FIGURE 3.4   Courts

result contradicts the idea that PRR voters support an unconstrained majoritarian democratic vision. The result is also at odds with the relatively low importance placed on minority rights protection by the PRR voters. Future studies should try to formulate the question about the importance of courts differently to learn more about the reasons for this somewhat surprising result.

Populist voters' principled beliefs about democracy

In this section we examine voters' principled beliefs about democracy in general. We focus the analysis on three such core principles: (1) the overall belief that it is important to live in a democracy, (2) the belief that free and fair elections are important, and (3) the importance of a free press. The purpose of the analysis is to examine the extent to which PRR voters are less attached to core democratic values and institutions than are voters of other parties. An account that emphasizes the role of democratic alienation or lack of general democratic commitment among PRR voters would lead us to expect PRR voters to place less importance on living in a democracy, be less concerned about free and fair elections, and put less emphasis on a free press.

As shown in Figure 3.5, we find a pattern of weaker attachment to democracy in general among PRR voters. Respondents were asked, "How important is it for you to live in a country that is governed democratically?" The figure shows that

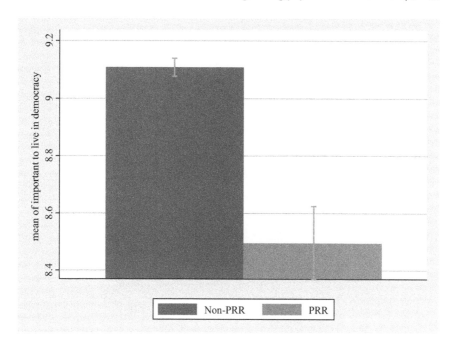

FIGURE 3.5 Important to live in a democratically governed country

PRR voters place themselves substantially and significantly lower on this scale than do other voters.

The figure demonstrates that it is less important for PRR voters to live in a democracy than it is for voters of other parties. Note that both PRR voters and non-PRR voters believe that it is important to live in a democratically governed country. Nevertheless, PRR voters believe that it is significantly *less* important than do other voters. Fully 94 per cent of non-PRR voters consider this to be important. Substantially fewer, but still a majority at 85 per cent, PRR voters consider living in a democracy to be important.

Figure 3.6 shows that also on the question of free and fair elections, PRR voters differ significantly from voters of other parties in Western Europe. Respondents were asked, "How important do you think it is for democracy in general that national elections are free and fair?" Also on this question, we find that PRR voters are significantly different from voters of other parties.

Still, Figure 3.6 shows that support for free and fair elections is high in both groups of voters. Approximately 95 per cent of all non-PRR voters consider free and fair elections to be important for democracy, while 89 per cent of PRR voters believe that this is important for democracy.

Figure 3.7 shows that PRR voters also differ from voters of other parties with respect to the importance of a free media. Respondents were asked, "How important

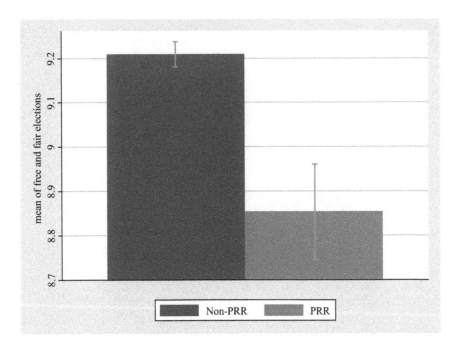

FIGURE 3.6 Free and fair elections

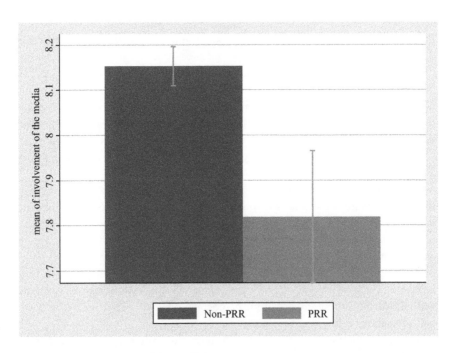

FIGURE 3.7 Involvement of the media

do you think it is for democracy in general that the media are free to criticize the government?" Also on this question, we find that PRR voters are significantly different from voters of other parties. We find that 81 per cent of all non-PRR voters consider this to be important for democracy. Fewer, but still a majority at 74 per cent, PRR voters consider a free media to be important for democracy.

Discussion and conclusion

In this chapter we have shown that there are significant differences between PRR voters' support for democracy and that of other voters. When asked questions tapping support for a populist or majoritarian conception of democracy, PRR voters score higher than do other voters. When asked about their principled beliefs about democracy, PRR voters are significantly less attached to core democratic principles than are other voters. To be sure, the majority of PRR voters support these core democratic principles, but PRR voters score significantly lower on these items than do other voters. Together, the PRR voters' combination of support for majoritarian, unchecked, political power and weaker attachment to core democratic principles suggest that the PRR is a difficult challenge to contemporary European democracies.

PRR voters are on the whole supportive of democracy but not as much as other voters are, and a substantial subset of PRR voters in Europe's oldest democracies are, we find in this study, not democratic. This chapter thus adds fuel to the ongoing academic and societal debates about the nature of contemporary PRR parties in Europe. The analysis we have presented suggests that even in some of the world's oldest and most established democracies, the battle for democracy still goes on, and support for core democratic principles cannot be taken for granted.

Further reading

Ford, Robert and Goodwin, Matthew (2014) *Revolt on the Right: Explaining Support for the Radical Right in Britain* (2014). London: Routledge.

Mudde, Cas (2007) *Populist Radical Right Parties in Europe.* Cambridge: Cambridge University Press, Chapters 1, 2 and 7.

Sniderman, Paul M., Petersen, Michael Bang, Slothuus, Rune and Stubager, Rune (2014) *Paradoxes of Liberal Democracy: Islam, Western Europe, and the Danish Cartoon Crisis.* Princeton: Princeton University Press.

Key questions for discussion

1   Which political parties belong to the populist radical right party family? Why?
2   Why do voters vote for populist radical right parties?
3   Are you worried about the political influence of populist radical right parties in Europe today? Why or why not?

Notes

1 For an in-depth discussion of nationalism in contemporary Europe, see Knutsen, Terje (this volume), "A Re-Emergence of Nationalism as a Political Force in Europe?" In Peters, Y. and Tatham, M. (eds.), *Democratic Transformations in Europe: Challenges and Opportunities.* Abingdon: Routledge.
2 For an extended discussion of minority rights in contemporary democracies, see Vibe, Vegard (this volume), "Minority Rights under Majority Rule: LGB-Rights in Europe." In Peters, Y. and Tatham, M. (eds.), *Democratic Transformations in Europe: Challenges and Opportunities.* Abingdon: Routledge.
3 Lega Nord is excluded from the analysis because of the 5-per cent threshold. Vlaams Belang is still included in the analysis because they reached the threshold of 5 per cent in the election of 2010, before the collection of the European Social Survey (ESS, 2012). For the Belgian case, only the Flemish voters are included in the further analysis. Austria is excluded from the analysis because the country is not part of the ESS 2012.
4 The ESS is an academically driven cross-national and large-scale survey that has been conducted every two years since 2001. The respondents are selected by strict random probability sampling, and the data collection is conducted by face-to-face interviews (ESS 2014).
5 The graph shows means scores with confidence intervals.

Bibliography

Abts, Koen and Rummens, Stefan (2007) "Populism versus Democracy". *Political Studies 55*, 405–424.

Art, David (2005) *The Politics of the Nazi Past in Germany and Austria.* Cambridge: Cambridge University Press.

Betz, Hans-Georg (1994) *Radical Right-Wing Populism in Western Europe.* London: MacMillan.

Blinder, Scott, Ford, Robert and Ivarsflaten, Elisabeth (2013) "The Better Angels of Our Nature: How the Antiprejudice Norm Affects Policy and Party Preferences in Great Britain and Germany". *American Journal of Political Science 57*(4), 841–857.

Bornschier, Simon (2010) *The New Cultural Conflict in Western Europe.* Philadelphia: Temple University Press.

Canovan, Margaret (1999) "Trust the People! Populism and the Two Faces of Democracy". *Political Studies 47*, 2–16.

Carter, Elisabeth (2005) *The Extreme Right in Western Europe: Success or Failure?* Manchester: Manchester University Press.

Dahl, Robert A. (1956) *A Preface to Democratic Theory.* Chicago: University of Chicago Press.

ESS (2014) The European Social Survey: ESS Round 6 (2012/2013). *Technical Report.* London: Centre for Comparative Social Surveys, City University London.

ESS Round 6: European Social Survey Round 6 Data (2012) Data file edition 2.1. Norwegian Social Science Data Services, Norway – Data Archive and distributor of ESS data for ESS ERIC.

Ford, Robert and Goodwin, Martin (2014) *Revolt for the Right: Explaining Support for the Radical Right in Britain.* New York: Routledge.

Golder, Matt (2003) "Explaining Variation in the Success of Extreme Right Parties in Western Europe". *Comparative Political Studies 36*, 432–466.

Held, David (1987) *Models of Democracy.* Stanford: Stanford University Press.

Ignazi, Piero (1992) "The Silent Counter-Revolution: Hypotheses on the Emergence of the Extreme Right-Wing Parties in Europe". *European Journal of Political Research 22*, 3–34.

Ignazi, Piero (2005) *Extreme Right Parties in Western Europe.* Oxford: Oxford University Press.

Ivarsflaten, Elisabeth (2007) "What Unites Right-Wing Populists in Western Europe?: Re-Examining Grievance Mobilization Models in Seven Successful Cases". *Comparative Political Studies 41*, 3–23.

Ivarsflaten, Elisabeth, Ford, Robert and Blinder, Scott (2010) "The Anti-Racism Norm in Western European Immigration Politics: Why We Need to Consider It and How to Measure It". *Journal of Elections, Public Opinion and Parties 20*(4), 421–445.

Jagers, Jan and Walgrave, Stefan (2007) "Populism as Political Communication Style: An Empirical Study if Political Parties' Discourse in Belgium". *European Journal of Political Research 46*(3), 319–45.

Knutsen, Terje (2016) A Re-Emergence of Nationalism as a Political Force in Europe? In Peters, Y. and Tatham, M. (eds.), *Democratic Transformations in Europe: Challenges and Opportunities.* Abingdon: Routledge, pp. 13–32.

Kriesi, Hanspeter (2014) "The Populist Challenge". *West European Politics 37*(2), 361–378.

Lubbers, Marcel, Gijsberts, Mérove and Scheepers, Peer (2002) "Extreme Right-Wing Voting in Western Europe". *European Journal of Political Research 41*, 345–378.

Manin, Bernard (1997) *The Principles of Representative Government.* Cambridge: Cambridge University Press.

Mény, Yves and Surel, Yves (2002) The Constitutive Ambiguity of Populism. In Mény, Yves and Surel, Yves (eds.), *Democracies and the Populist Challenge.* New York: Palgrave, pp. 1–24.

Mudde, Cas (2007) *Populist Radical Right Parties in Europe.* Cambridge: Cambridge University Press.

Rydgren, Jens (2004) *The Populist Challenge: Political Protest and Ethno-Nationalist Mobilization in France.* New York: Berghahn Books.

Rydgren, Jens (2005) "Is Extreme Right-Wing Populism Contagious? Explaining the Emergence of a New Party Family". *European Journal of Political Research 44*(3), 413–437.

Sniderman, Paul M., Petersen, Michael Bang, Slothuus, Rune and Stubager, Rune (2014) *Paradoxes of Liberal Democracy: Islam, Western Europe, and the Danish Cartoon Crisis.* Princeton: Princeton University Press.

Van der Brug, Wouter, Fennema, Meindert and Tillie, Jean (2000) "Anti-Immigrant Parties in Europe: Ideological or Protest Vote?". *European Journal of Political Research 37*, 77–102.

Vibe, Vegard (2016) Minority Rights under Majority Rule: LGB-Rights in Europe. In Peters, Y. and Tatham, M. (eds.), *Democratic Transformations in Europe: Challenges and Opportunities.* Abingdon: Routledge, pp. 231–251.

Appendix

TABLE A1 Exact question wording of the variables in the analyses

Referendum	How important do you think it is for democracy in general that citizens have the final say on political issues by voting directly in referendums?
Democracy	How important is it for you to live in a country that is governed democratically?
Elections	How important do you think it is for democracy in general that national elections are free and fair?
Media	How important do you think it is for democracy in general that the media are free to criticize the government?
Courts	How important do you think it is for democracy in general that the courts are able to stop the government acting beyond its authority?
Minority rights	How important do you think it is for democracy in general that the rights of minority groups are protected?
European gov.	How important do you think it is for democracy in general that politicians take into account the views of other European governments before making decisions?

TABLE A2 Voters' principle beliefs about democracy in per cent

Variable name	PRR	Non-PRR	Difference*
Voting by referendum	89	80	−9
Minorities	79	89	10
European governments	44	57	13
Courts' involvement	90	91	1
Important to live in democracy	85	94	9
Free and fair elections	89	95	6
Involvement of the media	74	81	7
Mean percentage	78	83	

* The percentages were calculated by dividing the values of each variable (eleven-point scale) into three categories. The first category "not important for democracy in general" is represented by those who answered from 0 to 3 on each of the questions. The mid-category "Neither important nor unimportant" is represented by those who answered between 4 and 6. The last category "important for democracy" is represented by those who answered between 7 and 10 on each of the questions. This table compares the final category "important for democracy" for those who voted for a populist radical right party with those who voted for a party other than the populist radical right.

4

PARTY DECLINE?

Hilmar L. Mjelde and Lars Svåsand

Introduction

One of the most popular conceptions of the state of political parties in contemporary democracies is their 'decline'. Since David Broder's (1972) "The Party's Over", there has been an 'avalanche' of publications lamenting the sorry state of parties in many established democracies (van Biezen et al. 2012; Bille 1994; Clarke and Stewart 1998; Coleman 1996a; Crotty and Jacobson 1980; Daalder 1992; Scarrow 2002; Togeby 1992; Wattenberg 1984, 2002; Webb 1995; Widtfeldt 1999). The 2005 introduction to a special issue of *Parliamentary Affairs* on British parties had as its subtitle: "Do parties have a future?" (Needham 2005). The widespread perception of decline is partly understandable, as parties are among the least trusted institutions across democracies. However, 'decline' is a term for a change of something in a direction perceived as negative, and for some indicators of party strength, decline is discernible, but there are also aspects of political parties in which they have *not* been declining. Moreover, we must distinguish between decline of *particular* parties vs. decline of the party as a collective actor. Another problem with the notion of party decline is that it is sometimes conflated with change. When existing parties decline and are being replaced by new parties, we have a case of party system *change*, not of *decline* of the party as an institution (Ignazi 1996).

Party decline has been perceived as a challenge for democracies because of the perception that parties are *necessary* institutions (Dalton and Wattenberg 2002; Lipset 2000; Stokes 1999). This view is based on the functions that parties perform, such as nomination of candidates to office, articulating and aggregating policy preferences, and forming the basis for governments and opposition (Aldrich 1995). Thus, the decline of parties may have consequences for the way democracies work. In the following sections, we outline how decline may be measured and apply these measures to ascertain the extent of party decline in primarily Western European democracies, although some findings may apply to parties in other regions to the degree that parties there operate in a similar environment. We identify how parties have declined in their relation to the electorate, but not necessarily as organizations, and least of all in government (Key 1964). After discussing the three faces of parties, we outline how parties have been able to adapt to some challenges: the rise of alternative forms of linkages between citizens and government, and the potential impact of new technologies. We summarize findings and discuss implications in the conclusion.

The party in the electorate

The party in the electorate refers to the linkages between parties and voters who consider themselves allied or associated with a party, and are indicated by party identification, electoral turnout and volatility, and trust in parties as institutions.

Party identification

Party identification refers to ties between voters and parties, and denotes a psychological-affective attachment of citizens to a political party (Bengtsson et al. 2014; Campbell et al. 1960; Dalton and Weldon 2007; Holmberg 2007). Various measures have been developed to gauge it (Dalton and Weldon 2007), the most common of which are how strongly attached to parties voters feel, the percentage of non-partisans (i.e. independents), and at which point in time during an electoral cycle the voter makes the decision on which party to vote for. Although there is some variation in magnitude and exceptions to the trends, the literature on party identification concludes that it has clearly gone down in Western European democracies: both the voters who do not report a strong attachment to a party and the percentage of independents increased decidedly from the 1960s to the late 1990s irrespective of electoral systems, the number of parties, and cleavage structure. Rohrschneider and Whitefield (2012) find that more than half of Central and Eastern European voters are independents. Moreover, the proportion of voters who decide what party to vote for close to Election Day has increased (Dalton 2002 [2000], 2004; Mair 2013). For example, in Sweden, a country with a stable party system until the late 1980s, the percentage of party identifiers declined consistently from 65 per cent in 1968 to 47 per cent in 1994 (Holmberg 1999). In the UK, party identification dropped from above 90 per cent in 1964 to below 80 per cent in 2005, and similar patterns are found in the U.S., France, and Germany (Dalton 2010). More recent European Social Survey (ESS) data reveals that the percentage of party identifiers in European democracies fell from 48,7 per cent in 2002 to 45,9 per cent in 2012,[1] and the percentage of those strongly identifying with a party declined from 74,3 per cent to 71 percent in the same period (ESS 2002, 2012).[2] As a proxy to when voters decide what party to vote for, we measure the difficulty of respondents in making up their mind about political issues: the percentage of respondents finding this difficult increased modestly, from 36,1 per cent in 2002 to 37 per cent in 2008 (ESS 2002, 2008).[3] In Sweden, the share of voters deciding during the last week of the electoral campaign increased from 29 per cent in 1991 to 34 percent in 2014 (Holmberg 2014). Similarly, while only 5 per cent of Norwegian voters in 1965 decided which party to vote for just before the election, 27 per cent did so in 2009 (Aardal 2011: 21). The decline trend in party identification is consistent with the contraction of party memberships in the same countries over the same time period, but the decline is not necessarily an expression of distrust in parties as institutions, which we examine next.

Trust in parties

Trust in parties is critical for the quality of democratic government (Putnam and Goss 2004 [2002]; Schuller et al. 2000). If they lack trust in parties, more voters may opt for 'exit' from the electoral arena, which in turn undermines parties' linkage function (Hirschman 1982; Lawson 1988). Available data covering advanced democracies from the 1990s to 2013 shows that trust in political parties is low but fluctuating: in Dalton and Weldon's (2005) 1997–2004 survey of fifteen EU member states, an average of 17 per cent of voters trust parties throughout the period; Norris (2011) reports trendless fluctuations in trust between 20 and 30 per cent in most European countries from 1997 to 2009, but overall a positive net change in trust in parties in this period; and finally, a 2013 Organisation for Economic Co-operation and Development (OECD) survey of 23 European member states shows that trust in parties on average fluctuated between 18,6 and 24 per cent between 2005 and 2013 (OECD 2013b). This is consistent with ESS data, which shows that the percentage of respondents with no trust in parties increased from 15,7 per cent in 2004 to 21 per cent in 2012 (ESS 2004, 2012). But across time there are also recent examples of increased trust. In Sweden, trust in parties rose from 29,6 per cent to 38,2 per cent from 2004 to 2012 (ESS 2004, 2012), and in Norway it increased from 24,7 per cent to 42,6 per cent in the same period.[4] These deviations from the trend should be seen in the context of the generally high trust levels in these nations (Bergman and Strøm 2010). On balance, the majority of voters consider parties to be rather untrustworthy.

Voting: turnout and volatility

Low trust in parties should translate into declining, if not low, voter turnout. Mair (2013) reports that electoral participation in Western European countries decreased from 84,3 per cent in the 1950s to 75,8 per cent percent in the first decade of the twenty-first century, a trend that accelerated from the 1990s and onwards, and is consistent with the marked decline in turnout in OECD countries from the 1950s to 2011 (OECD 2013a; Wattenberg 2002 [2000]). Recent ESS data supports this evidence: turnout fell from 74,8 per cent to 69,8 per cent from 2002 to 2012 (ESS 2002, 2012).[5] There is country-level variation, however: while turnout dropped more than 10 per cent from the 1950s to the 1990s in a number of countries, including the U.S. and Norway, no decline was seen in Denmark and Sweden (Hague and Harrop 2004). In the latter, turnout increased over the three most recent elections, with 85,8 per cent of the electorate voting in 2014, a percentage that is on par with the average post-war turnout up until 2006 of 86,4 per cent (09.09.14 SVT 2014; 20.09.14 DN 2014). Nonetheless, as Mair (2013) notes, the fact that a large majority of citizens in advanced democracies still exercise their voting rights should not divert attention from the general long-term decline trend in advanced democracies.

The development in electoral stability is similar to voter turnout: as measured by the Pedersen volatility index,[6] electoral volatility remained relatively low and stable from the 1950s to the 1980s in Western European democracies, with a net increase of 1,4 points from 8 to 9,4. A rather sudden and marked increase began in the 1990s, when volatility jumped to 11,3 and averaged 10,5 from 2000 to 2009 (Gallagher et al. 2011; Mair 2013). Thus, late-twentieth-century lows in electoral participation correlated with simultaneous highs in electoral volatility. In sum, modern parties operate on shaky electoral grounds, with declining party identification, low trust, declining turnout, and rising volatility.

Party organization

As organizations, parties consist of activists and staffers carrying out the day-to-day business of the party. In this section we track changes in party membership, both with respect to numbers and member activity level, intra-party democracy, party finance, and party staff.

Party membership: numbers and participants

Party membership in advanced democracies has generally declined markedly in the post-war era, although its magnitude, acceleration, and starting point have varied across countries.[7] Measured in absolute numbers, there was no uniform trend of falling membership in Western European democracies between 1960 and 1990, but from 1980 to 2009 drops were discernible in all long-established democracies. Raw figures indicate the membership status for individual parties, but both steady and growing memberships could conceal relative declines when the post-war expansion of Western electorates is considered. Membership as a proportion of the electorate (M/E) tackles this, however, and by this measure a clearer trend of membership losses is evident throughout the region and for the entire time period. The average M/E ratio across Europe was just 4,7 per cent in 2009, and in thirteen long-established democracies[8] together the average membership ratio decreased by nearly 5 percentage points since 1980 (Katz and Mair 1992b; Mair and van Biezen 2001; van Biezen et al. 2012; van Biezen and Poguntke 2014). Scarrow's (2002 [2000]) overview of membership changes in sixteen OECD countries from 1950 to the mid-1990s, including Japan, New Zealand, and Australia, is consistent with these findings, as is Delwit's (2011) 1946–2006 overview of thirteen Western European countries, Krouwel's (2012) 1945–2010 overview of fifteen Western European countries, and survey data (Scarrow and Gezgor 2010; Whiteley 2011). The percentage of self-reported party members decreased from 3,9 per cent to 3,3 per cent from 2002 to 2010 (ESS 2002, 2010). Although an overall trend of party membership declension in recent decades is evident, there are numerous individual exceptions to it (Delwit 2011; Kölln 2014). For example, Delwit considers membership figures in the context of parties' organizational characteristics and finds a significant difference between mass-based and cadre parties: the former lost two-thirds of their members between 1975 and 2005, while the cadre parties' 2005 memberships were 88 per cent of their 1975 memberships.

Less evident is the decline of participation inside parties (e.g. branch meetings, holding an elective position, campaigning, donating money) (Heidar and Saglie 2003). Granted, the activists' involvement varies substantially according to the nature of the party, their own motivation and capacity, and the opportunities available to them (Duverger 1959 [1954]; Heidar 2006). Overall, evidence shows that only a minority of members partake in party activities regularly (Bruter and Harrison 2009; Scarrow 2002 [2000]),[9] but whether or not the amount of active members has gone down over time is unclear. According to Putnam (2004 [2002]), participation in election campaign activities has been in nearly universal decline in recent decades, and case studies show declining member activism in some British and Irish parties in the 1990s (Gallagher and Marsh 2004; Seyd and Whiteley 2004). Furthermore, ESS data shows that the percentage of respondents who did work for either a political party or an action group in the last year dropped slightly from 4,3 per cent to 3,9 per cent from 2002 to 2012 (ESS 2002, 2012). While it is not possible to distinguish between party and action group participants, we surmise that the decline partially reflects lower participation in parties. Others, however, report that the share of activists has not changed much or has even increased when it comes to online participation in Danish and Norwegian parties in the 2000s, which could arguably be expected given the relative ubiquity of the Internet in advanced democracies (Heidar et al. 2012; Scarrow 2007). However, as Heidar et al. (2012: 162) note with reference to old parties, '[a] stable proportion of activists combined with declining membership figures means that both passive and active members seem to disappear at the same rate'.

Internal party democracy

One aspect of party activism is internal party democracy. An ambiguous concept (Cross and Katz 2013), internal party democracy typically refers to rank-and-file participation in the selection of candidates for public office, the election of party leadership, and the development of programmatic policy. Historically, the first parties in Western democracies existed only in public office, but with the emergence of mass parties at the turn of the twentieth century, internal decision-making became representative, with leaders being at least nominally accountable to the members (Katz and Mair 1995; Michels 1962). But in post-war advanced democracies, both parties in (national) public office and ordinary members have been empowered, with the former dominating the party in central office while the latter have been granted more direct-democratic rights at the expense of mid-level activists (Katz and Mair 2002, 1994). Accordingly, there is a discernible trend of ordinary members being given more say (Enyedi 2014; Krouwel 2012; Scarrow 2007) and the 'selectorate' becoming more inclusive through the blurring of the member/non-member distinction (Cross and Blais 2012; Katz 2014; Mjelde 2014a; Pennings and Hazan 2001). Numerous parties have also changed their procedures for selecting the party leader by including the membership in the selection process, such as in the British Conservatives, where the parliamentary group selects two candidates for the party leadership position, but where the final vote is by party members. Direct membership ballot for selecting the leadership has also been introduced in Israeli and French parties, for example. Also the nomination of parliamentary candidates has been opened up from taking place in delegates' meetings to membership voting (Hazan 2002; Narud et al. 2002). Moreover, there is evidence of 'stratarchy', whereby the public office tends to national affairs and the local party organization deals with local party matters, in what may be characterized as a division of labor (Katz and Mair 2002; Mair 1997). While Loxbo's (2011) case study of the Swedish Social Democrats finds activists to be more influential in the 1990s than in the 1950s, Katz and Mair argue (1994: 16) that members in general are 'at once more docile and more likely to endorse the policies (and candidates) proposed by the party leadership and by the party in public office'. Thus, Michels (1962) may be correct that internal decision-making in parties in advanced democracies is still a top-down process. However, changes that have been made are in the direction of widening the selectorate for leadership and candidate nominations.

Party finance

Originally, parties were funded primarily by their members or sympathetic sponsors. The decline of party membership could therefore have put financial strain on the party as an organization, were it not for state subsidies that are now commonplace in advanced democracies. State subsidies were introduced in the 1950s to sustain extra-parliamentary party activities,[10] first in Latin American countries (Costa Rica 1954, Argentina 1955, and Puerto Rico 1957), while West Germany pioneered it in Western Europe in 1959 (Nassmacher 1989; Pierre et al.

2000; Scarrow 2006). Public subventions have since been instituted worldwide (Casas-Zamora 2005; Fogg et al. 2003; Koß 2010; Nassmacher 2010), and evidence suggests that over the last fifty years, parties in advanced democracies have at an increasing rate been co-funded by the state, which lessens the relative importance of other sources (Mair 1997; van Biezen and Kopecký 2014). For example, Belgian, Italian, and Spanish parties get 80 to 90 per cent of their funds from the state, while subsidies make up less than 50 per cent of total income only in German and Dutch parties (van Biezen and Kopecký 2014: 172–3). Public subsidies nevertheless have introduced an element of uncertainty for the party as an institution. As the public subsidy part of the total finance increases, electoral volatility leads to short-term fluctuations in party finance. Also, the costs of electoral campaigns have increased (Farrell and Webb 2002 [2000]). On the whole, though, parties in advanced democracies are doing well financially, being in the unique position where they can change the 'rules of the game', including party finance.

Party staff

The primacy of the party in public office has been propelled by the expansion in party staff, which comprises amateurs and professionals (Webb and Kolodny 2006). Furthermore, external agents (state and private-sector employees) may contribute knowledge/expertise and time (Krouwel 2012). Although comparative data on party staff developments are scarce, Mair's (1997) 1960 to 1990 survey of growth in number of staff employed by Western European parties documents an increase in all countries, ranging from a 330 per cent increase in Ireland, and nearly as much in Germany, to relatively modest growth in the UK and the Netherlands.[11] Notably, a significant cause of staff expansion is the professionalization of party operations accompanying 'catch-all' politics and the integration of new media and campaign technology (Farrell and Webb 2002 [2000]; Krouwel 2006; Semetko 2006). Krouwel's (2012) overview of eleven Western European countries confirms previous accounts: the number of professional staffers in both the extra-parliamentary organization and in the party in public office has risen markedly. He reports a particularly high ratio of professional staffers to party members in Ireland and Italy at party headquarters, and most professionalization in the German and Dutch parliaments over the last three decades (Krouwel 2012: 245, 247). While modern parties still need members to perform many functions (Mjelde 2014b; Scarrow 1996), they have become increasingly reliant on professionals.

Thus, the decline of voluntary participants that is evident in many parties should not be conflated with general organizational decay, as public subventions have enabled parties in advanced democracies to professionalize their organizations. Its precondition has been parties' deep entrenchment within the government apparatus, dimensions of which we discuss next.

The party in office

Independents vs. party candidates

To some extent, the dominance of parties in elections for public offices is a consequence of institutional rules tilting the electoral playing field in favour of them, as opposed to independent candidates. Examples of such rules are proportional electoral systems that for the most part make it impossible to vote for individual candidates, candidate registration in which registered parties do not have to fulfil signature requirements to be placed on the ballot but individual candidates and minor parties must (Massicotte et al. 2004), and rules on national TV-debates participation, which tend to exclude independents and minor parties (Katz and Mair 1992a). With the exception of the UK, France, the U.S., Australia, and Canada, all established democracies apply a variant of proportional electoral districts. By implication, candidates cannot run alone, but have to appear on a slate of candidates. Technically, a slate may be constructed prior to each election and/or for individual constituencies, but in practice parties with established organizations have an advantage over individuals. Moreover, the introduction of public subsidies for parties provides them with financial resources that are denied to independent candidates. Brancati (2008), in her analysis of the frequency of independent candidates in thirty-four old and new democracies for elections held between 1945 and 2003, found that for each electoral district, on average 6,94a per cent of all candidates were independents, but they win on average only 1,73 per cent of the vote. Independent candidates appear more often and succeed more in new democracies, before the emerging party system consolidates. Although Bolleyer and Weeks (2009) refer to several examples of successful independent candidates in the U.S. and Japan, in most political systems it is still rare that non-partisans succeed in winning parliamentary seats, even in countries with single-member constituencies.[12] Recruitment to presidential offices is also dominated by partisan candidates. In no established democracy have candidates running as independents succeeded.

There are many cases of political recruitment through *new parties*, outside of the *established* parties. Most of these are parties seeking to occupy a political space on the left-right dimensions, or they are advocates of specific issues. There are also some examples of 'anti-party parties', most notably in Central and Eastern Europe (Meseznikov et al. 2013), but it is too early to tell if these are viable. In local elections, where the issue of government formation is not at stake, and where many policy issues do not reflect the national cleavage patterns, parties nevertheless have a dominant position in the recruitment of councillors in most established democracies (Reiser 2008). In Norway, for example, there have always been a number of non-partisan or local slates of candidates. In the municipal elections in 2007, voters in 40 per cent of the municipalities could choose slates of candidates who did not run for one of the national parties. Yet, only 2,9 per cent of voters supported such lists (Berg and Bjørklund 2009: 147). Only the Netherlands deviates from this pattern. In 2002 and 2006, local parties won 26,3 per cent and 23,7 per cent of the votes (Boogers 2008), respectively. Poland, on the other hand, is an extreme example of how little parties are able to penetrate local politics in a new democracy. Less than half of the mayors and councillors have been elected as party representatives, even if Poland now has experienced more than two decades of multiparty democracy (Gendzwill and Zoltak 2014). Thus, parties remain the main channel for recruitment to elected offices and retain their grip on elected representatives.

Party loyalty among MPs

If the party-in-office is declining, we should see a decline in the cohesiveness among members of party caucuses. Yet, party discipline remains high among members of parliament (MPs). Second, we should expect that more MPs leave the parties they were elected to represent and become independent (party defection) or join other parties (party switching). However, both party defection (Sieberer 2006) and party switching (Heller and Mershon 2009b) remain rare events in established democracies, for two reasons. The first is that MPs are nominated by their parties precisely because they are seen as the individuals most likely to pursue the policy goals of their respective parties. Candidates nominated to run often have a track record from party organizational work and/or representation locally and are therefore trusted to promote party objectives. Second, many MPs harbor ambitions of a political career or at least wish to be re-nominated. Studies show that the prime factor explaining nomination is incumbency. Only in the U.S., where the nomination process has been decoupled from the party organization as such, are incumbents in danger of losing to challengers. Hence, as the party organization 'controls' their career, representatives have every incentive to be loyal to their party (see e.g. Tavits 2013). Party switching is quite frequent in a number of new democracies, such as Russia and Brazil, but it is relatively rare in established democracies (Heller and Mershon 2009a: 11). Italy is a deviant case among West European democracies: more than one-quarter of MPs changed caucus affiliation between 1988 and 1992, when the party system as a whole collapsed (Heller and Mershon 2005). When a party splits over issues, multiple defections may occur, but *individual* defections are rare in established democracies.

In short, parties remain government's gatekeepers. Because parliamentarism is the dominant form of democratic governance, the executive power, the cabinet is accountable to the parliament. As parties dominate parliament, forming a government outside of parties is almost impossible. There are very few cabinet members who are not party members, except when care-taker governments are appointed. Next, we address democratic decentralization and its implications for political parties.

Decentralization

Across time there have been several institutional reforms in Western democracies that represent both challenges and opportunities to parties. In countries with long traditions of elected local government, the trend has been towards fewer units, as smaller municipalities have merged to create larger ones. For example, the number of municipalities in Norway declined from 744 in 1950 to 465 at the end of the 1960s, and in Denmark the number of municipalities was reduced from 274 in 1970 to 98 in 2007. On the one hand, then, with fewer units, there is declining need for parties to find candidates to fill the council seats (Sundberg 1989), but on the other hand, territorially and numerically larger units increase the coordination cost of elections for which parties are better placed to compete than other collective actors. Strong regional branches and regionalist/autonomist parties may resist national parties, however (see e.g. Aarebrot and Saglie 2013; Palermo and Wilson 2014; Toubeau 2010). Second, there has been a change in several countries towards decentralization, devolution, and various forms of federalism (Spain, Belgium, the UK; see Tatham, 2016, this volume) with the creation of more elected bodies. Thus, parties are provided more opportunities to compete for office and for implementing policies. Hence, key functions that parties are seen to perform in democracies – leadership recruitment and the formation of government and opposition – are still dominated by parties.

Parties have shown a remarkable ability to adapt to changing circumstances. The main parties in many established democracies have existed for more than a century. Just as Mark Twain dismissed reports of his death as 'exaggerated', the alleged decline of parties was followed by a revisionist line of publications arguing that parties should not be seen as heading for extinction but as able to adapt to changing circumstances (Coleman 1996b; Daalder 2002; Gunther et al. 2002; Lawson and Merkl 2007; Lawson and Poguntke 2004; Reiter 1989; Sabato 1988). Furthermore, we must distinguish between *party change* and *party decline*. While existing parties and party systems may have declined in some ways since the 1970s (Webb et al. 2002), there is no shortage of new parties being formed and achieving electoral success. Hug (2001) counted 361 new parties appearing in 261 national elections in twenty-two countries from 1945 until 1990. On average, in each national election there were 1.38 new parties. In a recent study, Bolleyer identifies 140 new parties in seventeen established democracies that successfully won seats in at least two elections in the period 1968–2011 (Bolleyer 2014: 39).[13] The Netherlands, Switzerland, and the UK had seventeen, fourteen, and thirteen new parties, respectively. If the party as an institution is in decline, there should be less interest in forming new ones. Despite many institutional changes in communication patterns and alternative forms of mobilization, political parties remain the backbone of modern democratic government. Table 4.1 summarizes the trends.

TABLE 4.1 Party trends – empirical indicators

Empirical indicators of party strength	Status
The party in the electorate	
Party identification	Decline
Trust	Contingent
Turnout	Decline
Volatility	Increase
The party organization	
Party membership	Decline*
Internal party democracy	Contingent
Party finance	No decline
Party staff	Increase
The party in office	
Party candidates	No decline
MP loyalty	No decline

*A clear member activity trend is not discernible.

Challenges and opportunities for political parties: alternative linkages and new technologies

Notwithstanding the decline of membership and the low public trust in parties, the party as an institution continues to be regarded as necessary in democracies. Dalton and Weldon (2005) show that in all democracies, new as well as old, a majority of the electorate sees political parties as necessary. Even in countries that have experienced a significant decline on several of the indicators of decline, such as the Scandinavian countries and the Netherlands, a substantial majority of the voters agree with the statement that parties are necessary in a democracy. Nevertheless, democracies are also political systems with an enormous ability to adjust their institutional arrangements. Most notably is the expansion in the number of referenda at all levels in the political system (LeDuc 2002), but it is not clear that direct democracy is associated with weak parties (Peters 2016). It has been argued that many voters will take cues from their party's position when making up their mind on how to vote in a referendum (Budge 2006: 5–6), and empirical studies in Switzerland, which has more referenda and initiatives than any other country, do not find a clear link with weaker parties (Ladner and Brandle 1999). In addition to referenda, there are several supplements to the standard representative democracy model where voters' participation in decision-making is limited to choosing a group of representatives. Smith (2009) analyses fifty-seven additional mechanisms, including various forms of direct democracy, citizen assemblies, and consultative forums, which do not necessarily involve parties. While possibly bypassing parties, it is worth noting that these alternatives are *supplementary* to representative democracy, not replacements for it (see the chapter by Peters 2016, this volume). To the degree that parties reduce information costs for voters also in these arenas, the supplements can reinforce parties' bonds with the citizenry.

A second type of change that could potentially alter the role of political parties is the spread of information technologies and social media. Such technologies have been described as challenges to the traditional way parties operate, with their formal hierarchical structures, regular meetings, and campaign activities. These innovations have enabled activists to mobilize support for issues outside of regular interest groups and parties and thereby drained these institutions of resources. But parties have also proved adept at incorporating new technology and social media into their organizational routines and in election campaigns (Gibson and Ward 1998; Giebert 2014; Pedersen and Saglie 2005; Römmele 2003; Tumasjan et al. 2010). The new technology has supplemented rather than replaced the way parties traditionally have worked. Perhaps the main consequence has been to alter internal communication patterns within the parties. The party leadership can communicate directly with the members and supporters, which earlier had to go via the intermediate organizational units at the local and regional levels. Moreover, as Karlsen (2011) shows, it may change the relative significance of individual candidates vs. the parties by encouraging candidates to run campaigns emphasizing themselves rather than their parties.[14] Thus, it is not a given that new technologies will undermine parties. They may also provide opportunities for parties to improve communications within as well as with the electorate.

Conclusion

The so-called decline of parties is debatable when considering each of the three faces of parties. For the party in the electorate, the decline is fairly consistent across different indicators and also across parties and countries. For the party organization, there is undoubtedly a decline in membership, but not necessarily in the ability of parties to function as organizations, due to public subsidies. While the 'supply' of new parties indicates a persistence of party as an attractive instrument to gain office, at least some of the new parties represent fundamentally new ideas for why they have an organization in the first place. For 'entrepreneurial parties' totally dependent on their leader, such as Berlusconi's Forza Italia, the idea of a party organization seems fundamentally different from that found in movement-based parties. For the party in office, however, it is not possible to talk of decline. The parties remain the main channel for recruitment to public office and for organizing the relationship between parliament and the executive. As long as representative democracy is the main institutional solution to decision-making in a democracy, particularly regarding the need for interest aggregation and government formation, the political party has an advantage over other types of political actors (Aldrich 1995).

Taken together, the main challenge these trends imply for representative democracy is declining popular engagement. Parties can be said to organize and structure representative democracy by performing their many functions, but particularly declining voter turnout and intra-party participation may render elected government less representative and less legitimate by loosening linkage between rulers and the ruled. Democratic government relies on the ruled perceiving it as legitimate, and while elected governments in advanced democracies do not yet face any legitimacy *crisis* given the still considerable electoral turnout in these countries, declining popular engagement may make advanced democracies more vulnerable to political actors who are less committed to representative democracy and its institutions (see the chapter by Bjånesøy and Ivarsflaten 2016, this volume). The more the declining involvement reflects citizen dissatisfaction rather than lack of political interest, the more grave these challenges could become, as many citizens can then be expected to become more receptive to alternative modes of government. On the other hand, Mjelde (2014a) argues that parties have shown a willingness to lower barriers for participation by welcoming non-members to partake in their activities. This appears to be a response to declining party memberships, and declining popular involvement may thus have moved parties to innovate. However, this opportunity to reinforce bonds with citizens depends on the latter's response to the invitation. Moreover, cooperation with collateral organizations such as trade unions, the use of opinion polls, and the consultation of policy experts can support representative democracy. However, parties' ability to maintain control of the levers of government is insufficient for a viable representative democracy; parties must find ways to respond effectively to the challenge of declining popular engagement.

Further reading

Dalton, Russel J., and Steven A. Weldon. 2005. "Public images of political parties: A necessary evil?" *West European Politics* 28 (5): 931–51.

Sieberer, Ulrich. 2006. "Party unity in parliamentary democracies." *Journal of Legislative Studies* 12 (2): 150–78.

van Biezen, Ingrid and Thomas Poguntke. 2014. "The decline of membership-based parties." *Party Politics* 20 (2): 205–16.

Key questions for discussion

1 Most political parties in established democracies have experienced declining membership figures. What factors can explain this development and what are the consequences for political parties?
2 Party cohesion is generally strong in established democracies. Why is this so even when the party system as such is in flux and the parties are experiencing declining membership figures?
3 Voters are highly skeptical of political parties, compared to other public institutions. Why is this the case and how does it matter for the parties?

Notes

1 Variable: 'Feel closer to a particular party than all other parties'. Design and population size weights were applied to all ESS data used in this chapter.
2 Cumulative percentages of respondents reporting that they feel either 'Very Close' or 'Quite Close' to a party.
3 Cumulative percentages of respondents reporting that they find it either 'Very Difficult' or 'Difficult' to make up their mind about political issues. The variable was not included in the 2010 and 2012 ESS rounds.
4 This variable is measured on a 0–10 point scale (0: No trust at all; 10: Complete trust). Values 6 and above were added to one score/percentage.
5 Voters who voted in the last national election.
6 Pedersen calculates the level of volatility by summing the aggregate gains/losses of all winning/losing parties in a given election (Pedersen 1979).
7 There are two sources of membership data: figures provided by the parties and mass survey research data based on individual self-reporting of party membership. The most comprehensive data have been provided by parties.
8 UK, France, Norway, Sweden, Ireland, Switzerland, Finland, Italy, Denmark, Belgium, Netherlands, Austria, Germany.
9 As Heidar (2006: 306) notes, what is considered regular participation varies across parties and studies.
10 As Scarrow (2006: 620) notes, indirect subsidies were introduced earlier in many countries in the form of state-paid voter registering and ballot printing, free campaign mailings, and free access to radio and TV. Moreover, financial support to parliamentary groups also preceded support for the party organization outside of the legislature (Pierre et al. 2000: 6).
11 The time period varies from country to country.
12 Ireland may be exceptional in this regard. Bolleyer and Weeks (2009: 308) find that the number of independent candidates running in parliamentary elections in Ireland has increased from less than 10 per cent of all candidates to 20 per cent between 1969 and 2002, while the share of the vote increased from approximately 3 per cent to approximately 10 per cent. This may be due to the Irish electoral system in which *all* candidates in a constituency are listed on the same ballot paper and where voters *have to* indicate preference for one of the individual candidates, but *may* indicate a number of preferences equal to the total number of seats available for the constituency. See also Weeks (2014) for a discussion of how the ballot design can work against independent candidates in Australia.
13 Additional parties won seats during the last years of her study, but because they were newer, they did not meet the requirement of 'persistence'.
14 During the 2009 parliamentary election in Norway, 43 per cent of the candidates used Facebook in their campaign communication (Karlsen 2011).

References

09.09.14 SVT. *Statsvetaren om det höga valdeltagandet* 2014 [cited 23.10.2014]. Available from http://www.svt.se/nyheter/val2014/statsvetaren-om-det-hoga-valdeltagandet.

20.09.14 DN. *Valdeltagandet nästan 86 procent* 2014 [cited 23.10.2014]. Available from http://www.dn.se/valet-2014/valdeltagandet-nastan-86-procent/.

Aardal, Bernt, ed. 2011. *Det politiske landskap. En studie av stortingsvalget 2009*. Oslo: Cappelen Damm.

Aarebrot, Erik, and Jo Saglie. 2013. "Linkage in multi-level party organizations: The role(s) of Norwegian regional party branches." *Regional and Federal Studies* 23 (5): 613–29.

Aldrich, John H. 1995. *Why Parties: The Origin and Transformation of Party Politics in America*. London: University of Chicago Press.

Bengtsson, Åsa, Kasper Hansen, Ólafur Þ Harðarson, Hanne Marthe Narud, and Henrik Oscarsson. 2014. *The Nordic Voter: Myths of Exceptionalism*. Colchester: ECPR Press.

Berg, Johannes, and Tor Bjørklund. 2009. "Lokalvalg og riksvalg: forskjeller og likheter." In *Det nære demokratiet − lokalvalg og lokal deltakelse*, ed. J. Saglie. Oslo: Abstrakt Forlag, pp. 69–88.

Bergman, Torbjörn, and Kaare Strøm. 2010. "Nordics: Demanding Citizens, Complex Polities." In *The Madisonian Turn: Political Parties and Parliamentary Democracy in Nordic Europe*, ed. T. Bergman and K. Strøm. Ann Arbor: University of Michigan Press, pp. 356–387.

Bille, Lars. 1994. "Denmark: The Decline of the Membership Party?" In *How Parties Organize*, ed. R. Katz. and P. Mair. London: SAGE, pp. 134–157.

Bjånesøy, Lise Lund, and Elisabeth Ivarsflaten. 2016. "Right-Wing Populism." In *Democratic Transformations in Europe: Challenges and Opportunities*, ed. Yvette Peters and Michaël Tatham. Abingdon: Routledge, pp. 33–50.

Bolleyer, Nicole. 2014. *New Parties in Old Party Systems: Persistence and Decline in Seventeen Democracies*. Oxford: Oxford University Press.

Bolleyer, Nicole, and Liam Weeks. 2009. "The puzzle of non-party actors in party democracy: Independents in Ireland." *Comparative European Politics* 7 (3): 299–324.

Boogers, Marcel. 2008. "Local Political Parties in the Netherlands: Anomaly or Prototype?" In *Farewell to the Party Model? Independent Local Lists in East and West European Countries*, ed. M. Reiser and E. Holtmann. Dordrecht: Springer Link, pp. 149–157.

Brancati, Dawn. 2008. "Winning alone: The electoral fate of independent candidates worldwide." *Journal of Politics* 70 (3): 648–62.

Broder, David S. 1972. *The Party's Over: The Failure of Politics in America*. New York: Harper.

Bruter, Michael, and Sarah Harrison. 2009. *The Future of Our Democracies: Young Party Members in Europe*. Basingstoke and New York: Palgrave Macmillan.

Budge, Ian. 2006. "Direct and representative democracy: Are they necessarily opposed?" *Representation* 42 (1): 1–12.

Campbell, Angus, Philip E. Converse, Warren E. Miller, and Donald E. Stokes. 1960. *The American Voter*. New York: Wiley.

Casas-Zamora, Kevin. 2005. *Paying for Democracy: Political Finance and State Funding for Parties*. Colchester: ECPR Press.

Clarke, Harold D., and Marianne C. Stewart. 1998. "The decline of parties in the minds of citizens." *American Review of Political Science* 1: 357–78.

Coleman, John J. 1996a. *Party Decline in America*. Princeton: Princeton University Press.

———. 1996b. "Resurgent or Just Busy? Party Organizations in Contemporary America." In *The State of the Parties: The Changing Role of Contemporary American Parties*. Second Edition, ed. J. C. Green and D. M. Shea. London: Rowman & Littlefield, pp. 367–384.

Cross, William, and Andre Blais. 2012. "Who selects the party leader?" *Party Politics* 18 (2): 127–50.

Cross, William P., and Richard S. Katz. 2013. *The Challenges of Intra-Party Democracy*. Oxford: Oxford University Press.

Crotty, William J., and Gary C. Jacobson. 1980. *American Parties in Decline*. Boston, MA: Little, Brown and Co.

Daalder, Hans. 1992. "A crisis of party?" *Scandinavian Political Studies* 15 (4): 269–88.

———. 2002. "Parties: Denied, Dismissed, or Redundant? A Critique." In *Political Parties. Old Concepts and New Challenges*, ed. R. Gunther, J. R. Montero and J. J. Linz. Oxford: Oxford University Press, pp. 39–57.

Dalton, Russel J. 2002 [2000]. "The Decline of Party Identifications." In *Parties without Partisans*, ed. R. J. Dalton and M. P. Wattenberg. Oxford: Oxford University Press, pp. 19–36.

————. 2004. *Democratic Challenges, Democratic Choices: The Erosion of Political Support in Advanced Industrial Democracies.* Oxford: Oxford University Press.

Dalton, Russel J., and Martin P. Wattenberg. 2002. "Unthinkable Democracy: Political Change in Advanced Industrial Democracies." In *Parties without Partisans: Political Change in Advanced Industrial Democracies,* ed. R. Dalton and M. Wattenberg. Oxford: Oxford University Press, pp. 3–16.

Dalton, Russel J., and Steven A. Weldon. 2005. "Public images of political parties: A necessary evil?" *West European Politics* 28 (5): 931–51.

————. 2007. "Partisanship and party system institutionalization." *Party Politics* 13 (2): 179–96.

Dalton, Russell J. 2010. "Ideology, Partisanship, and Democratic Development." In *Comparing Democracies 3: Elections and Voting in the 21st Century,* ed. L. LeDuc, R. G. Niemi and P. Norris. Los Angeles: SAGE, pp. 143–163.

Delwit, Pascal. 2011. "Still in Decline? Party Membership in Europe." In *Party Membership in Europe: Exploration into the Anthills of Party Politics,* ed. E. van Haute. Brussels: ULB, pp. 25–42.

Duverger, Maurice. 1959 [1954]. *Political Parties: Their Organization and Activity in the Modern State.* London: Methuen.

Enyedi, Zsolt. 2014. "The discreet charm of political parties." *Party Politics* 20 (2): 194–204.

ESS. 2002. *European Social Survey Round 1 Data (2002): Data File Edition 6.3.* Bergen: Norwegian Social Science Data Services, Norway – Data Archive and distributor of ESS data.

————. 2004. *European Social Survey Round 2 Data (2004): Data File Edition 3.3.* Bergen: Norwegian Social Science Data Services, Norway – Data Archive and distributor of ESS data.

————. 2008. *European Social Survey Round 4 Data (2004): Data File Edition 4.2.* Bergen: Norwegian Social Science Data Services, Norway – Data Archive and distributor of ESS data.

————. 2010. *European Social Survey Round 5 Data (2010): Data File Edition 3.1.* Bergen: Norwegian Social Science Data Services, Norway – Data Archive and distributor of ESS data.

————. 2012. *European Social Survey Round 6 Data (2012): Data File Edition 2.0.* Bergen: Norwegian Social Science Data Services, Norway – Data Archive and distributor of ESS data.

Farrell, David M., and Paul Webb. 2002 [2000]. "Political Parties as Campaign Organizations." In *Parties Without Partisans: Political Change in Advanced Industrial Democracies,* ed. R. J. Dalton and M. P. Wattenberg. Oxford: Oxford University Press, pp. 102–128.

Fogg, Karen, Patrick Molutsi, and Maja Tjernström. 2003. "Conclusion." In *Funding of Political Parties and Election Campaigns,* ed. R. Austin and M. Tjernström. Stockholm: IDEA, pp. 344–366.

Gallagher, Michael, Michael Laver, and Peter Mair. 2011. *Representative Government in Modern Europe.* Berkshire: McGraw-Hill Higher Education.

Gallagher, Michael, and Michael Marsh. 2004. "Party membership in Ireland: The members of Fine Gael." *Party Politics* 10 (4): 407–25.

Gendzwill, Adam, and Tomasz Zoltak. 2014. "Why do non-partisans challenge parties in local politics? The (extreme) case of Poland." *Europe-Asia Studies* 66 (7): 1122–45.

Gibson, Rachel K., and Stephen J. Ward. 1998. "U.K. Political parties and the internet: 'Politics as usual' in the new media?" *Harvard International Journal of Press/Politics* 3 (3): 14–38.

Giebert, Matthew. 2014. "Party Talk Online: The Impact of Social Media on Political Party Communication." Paper prepared for presentation at MPSA Annual Meeting, Chicago, Illinois, April 3, 2014.

Gunther, Richard, Jose Ramon Montero, and Juan J. Linz, eds. 2002. *Political Parties: Old Concepts and New Challenges.* Oxford: Oxford University Press.

Hague, Rod, and Martin Harrop. 2004. *Comparative Government and Politics: An Introduction.* Basingstoke: Palgrave Macmillan.

Hazan, Reuven Y. 2002. "Candidate Selection." In *Comparing Democracies 2: New Challenges in the Study of Elections and Voting,* ed. L. LeDuc, R. G. Niemi and P. Norris. London: SAGE, pp. 108–126.

Heidar, Knut. 2006. "Party Membership and Participation." In *Handbook of Party Politics,* ed. R. S. Katz and W. Crotty. London: SAGE, pp. 301–315.

Heidar, Knut, Karina Kosiara-Pedersen, and Jo Saglie. 2012. "Party Change and Party Member Participation in Denmark and Norway." In *Democracy, Elections and Political Parties: Essays in Honor of Jørgen Elklit,* ed. J. Blom-Hansen, C. Green-Pedersen and S.-E. Skaaning. Aarhus: Politica, pp. 155–163.

Heidar, Knut, and Jo Saglie. 2003. "A decline of linkage? Intra-party participation in Norway, 1991–2000." *European Journal of Political Research* 42: 761–86.

Heller, William B., and Carol Mershon. 2005. "Party switching in the Italian chamber of deputies, 1996–2001." *Journal of Politics* 67 (2): 536–59.

———. 2009a. "Introduction: Legislative Party Switching, Parties and Party Systems." In *Political Parties and Legislative Party Switching,* ed. W. B. Heller and C. Mershon. London: Palgrave, pp. 3–28.

Heller, William B., and Carol Mershon, eds. 2009b. *Political Parties and Legislative Party Switching.* Palgrave: London.

Hirschman, Albert O. 1982. *Shifting Involvements: Private Interest and Public Action.* Oxford: Martin Robertson.

Holmberg, Søren. 1999. "Down and Down We Go: Political Trust in Sweden." In *Critical Citizens: Global Support for Democratic Governance,* ed. P. Norris. Oxford: Oxford University Press, pp. 103–122.

———. 2007. "Partisanship Reconsidered." In *The Oxford Handbook of Political Behavior,* ed. R. J. Dalton and H.-D. Klingemann. Oxford: Oxford University Press, pp. 557–570.

———. 2014. *Väljarbeteende. SVT:s vallokalsundersökning Riksdagsvalet 2014.* Stockholm: Sveriges Television.

Hug, Simon. 2001. *Altering Party Systems: Strategic Behavior and the Emergence of New Political Parties in Western Democracies.* Ann Arbor: University of Michigan Press.

Ignazi, Piero. 1996. "The crisis of parties and the rise of new political parties." *Party Politics* 3 (2): 549–66.

Karlsen, Rune. 2011. "A platform for individualized campaigning? Social media and parliamentary candidates in the party-centered Norwegian campaign." *Policy and Internet* 3 (4): 1–25.

Katz, Richard S. 2014. "No man can serve two masters: Party politicians, party members, citizens and principal-agent models of democracy." *Party Politics* 20 (2): 183–93.

Katz, Richard S., and Peter Mair, eds. 1992a. *Party Organizations: A Data Handbook.* London: SAGE.

Katz, Richard S., and Peter Mair. 1992b. "The membership of political parties in European democracies, 1960–1990." *European Journal of Political Research* 22: 329–45.

———. 1994. *How Parties Organize: Change and Adaption in Party Organizations in Western Democracies.* London: SAGE.

———. 1995. "Changing models of party organization and party democracy: The emergence of the Cartel party." *Party Politics* 1 (1): 5–28.

———. 2002. "The Ascendancy of the Party in Public Office: Party Organizational Change in Twentieth-Century Democracies." In *Political Parties: Old Concepts and New*

Challenges, ed. R. Gunther, J. Ramon-Montero and J. J. Linz. Oxford: Oxford University Press, pp. 113–135.

Key, V. O. 1964. *Politics, Parties and Pressure Groups*. New York: Crowell.

Kölln, Ann-Kristin. 2016. "Party membership in Europe: Testing party-level explanations of decline." *Party Politics* 22 (4): 465–477.

Koß, Michael. 2010. *The Politics of Party Funding: State Funding to Political Parties and Party Competition in Western Europe*. Oxford: Oxford University Press.

Krouwel, Andre. 2006. "Party Models." In *Handbook of Party Politics*, ed. W. J. Crotty and R. S. Katz. London: SAGE, pp. 249–269.

———. 2012. *Party Transformations in European Democracies*. New York: State University of New York Press.

Ladner, Andreas, and Michael Brandle. 1999. "Does direct democracy matter for political parties? An empirical test in the Swiss cantons." *Party Politics* 5 (3): 283–302.

Lawson, Kay. 1988. "When Linkage Fails." In *When Parties Fail: Emerging Alternative Organizations*, ed. K. Lawson and P. H. Merkl. Princeton: Princeton University Press, pp. 13–40.

Lawson, Kay, and Peter H. Merkl, eds. 2007. *When Parties Prosper: The Uses of Electoral Success*. London: Lynne Rienner.

Lawson, Kay, and Thomas Poguntke, eds. 2004. *How Political Parties Respond: Interest Aggregation Revisited*. London: Routledge.

LeDuc, Lawrence. 2002. "Referendums and Initiatives: The Politics of Direct Democracy." In *Comparing Democracies 2*, ed. L. LeDuc, R. G. Niemi and P. Norris. London: SAGE, pp. 70–87.

Lipset, S. M. 2000. "The indispensability of political parties." *Journal of Democracy* 11 (1): 48–55.

Loxbo, Karl. 2011. "The fate of intra-party democracy: Leadership autonomy and activist influence in the mass party and the cartel party." *Party Politics* 19 (4): 537–54.

Mair, Peter. 1997. *Party System Change: Approaches and Interpretations*. Oxford: Oxford University Press.

———. 2013. *Ruling the Void: The Hollowing of Western Democracy*. London: Verso.

Mair, Peter, and Ingrid van Biezen. 2001. "Party membership figures in twenty European democracies, 1980–2000." *Party Politics* 7 (1): 5–21.

Massicotte, Louis, Andre Blais, and Antoine Yoshinaka. 2004. *Establishing the Rules of the Game: Election Laws in Democracies*. Toronto: University of Toronto Press.

Meseznikov, Grigorij, Olga Gyarfasova, and Zora Buturova, eds. 2013. *Alternative Politics? The Rise of Political Parties in Central Europe*. Bratislava: Institute for Public Affairs.

Michels, Robert. 1962. *Political Parties: A Sociological Study of the Oligarchical Tendencies of Modern Democracies*. New York: Collier.

Mjelde, Hilmar L. 2014a. *A New Source of Linkage: Non-Member Participation in Western European Parties*. Bergen: University of Bergen.

———. 2014b. *Still Indispensable: How Modern Parties Need Grass Roots Activists for Campaigning and Sustaining Democracy*. Bergen: University of Bergen.

Narud, Hanne Marthe, Mogens N. Pedersen, and Henry Valen, eds. 2002. *Party Sovereignty and Citizen Control: Selecting Candidates for Parliamentary Elections in Denmark, Finland, Iceland and Norway*. Odense: University of Southern Denmark Press.

Nassmacher, Karl-Heinz. 1989. "Structure and Impact of Public Subsidies to Political Parties in Europe: The Examples of Austria, Italy, Sweden and West Germany." In *Comparative Political Finance in the 1980s*, ed. H. E. Alexander. Cambridge: Cambridge University Press, pp. 236–267.

———. 2010. *The Funding of Party Competition: Political Finance in 25 Democracies*. Baden-Baden: Nomos.

Needham, Catherine. 2005. "Introduction: Do parties have a future?" *Parliamentary Affairs* 58 (3 [Special issue on British political parties]), 489–502.

Norris, Pippa. 2011. *Democratic Deficit: Critical Citizens Revisited.* Cambridge: Cambridge University Press.

Organisation for Economic Co-operation and Development (OECD). 2013a. "How's Life? 2013: Measuring Well-Being." OECD Publishing. http://dx.doi.org/10.1787/9789264201392-en.

———. 2013b. *Trust in government and in political parties in European OECD member countries (2013)* 2013b [cited 06.10.2014]. Available from http://www.oecd-ilibrary.org/governance/government-at-a-glance-2013/trust-in-government-and-in-political-parties-in-european-oecd-member-countries-2013_gov_glance-2013-graph6-en.

Palermo, Francesco, and Alex Wilson. 2014. "The multi-level dynamics of state decentralization in Italy." *Comparative European Politics* 12: 510–30.

Pedersen, Karina, and Jo Saglie. 2005. "New technology in ageing parties: Internet use in Danish and Norwegian parties." *Party Politics* 11 (3): 359–78.

Pedersen, Mogens N. 1979. "The dynamics of European party systems: Changing patterns of electoral volatility." *European Journal of Political Research* 7 (1): 1–26.

Pennings, Paul, and Reuven Y. Hazan. 2001. "Democratizing candidate selection: Causes and consequences." *Party Politics* 7 (3): 267–75.

Peters, Yvette. 2016. "(Re-)join the party! The effects of direct democracy on party membership in Europe." *European Journal of Political Research* 55: 138–59.

———. 2016. "Displacing Politics: The State of Democracy in an Age of Diffused Responsibility." In *Democratic Transformations in Europe: Challenges and Prospects*, ed. Yvette Peters and Michaël Tatham. Abingdon: Routledge, pp. 163–186.

Pierre, Jon, Lars G. Svåsand, and Anders Widfeldt. 2000. "State subsidies to political parties: Confronting rhetoric with reality." *West European Politics* 23 (3): 1–24.

Putnam, Robert D. 2004 [2002]. *Democracies in Flux.* Oxford: Oxford University Press.

Putnam, Robert D., and Kristin A. Goss. 2004 [2002]. "Introduction." In *Democracies in Flux*, ed. R. D. Putnam. Oxford: Oxford University Press, pp. 3–19.

Reiser, Marion. 2008. "Conclusion: Independent Local Lists in East and West European Countries." In *Farewell to the Party Model? Independent Local Lists in East and West European Countries*, ed. M. Reiser and E. Holtmann. Dordrecht: Springer, pp. 277–294.

Reiter, Howard L. 1989. "Party decline in the West: A skeptic's view." *Journal of Theoretical Politics* 1 (3): 325–48.

Rohrschneider, Robert, and Stephen Whitefield. 2012. *The Strain of Representation: How Parties Represent Diverse Voters in Western and Eastern Europe.* Oxford: Oxford University Press.

Römmele, Andrea. 2003. "Political parties, party communication and new information and communication technologies." *Party Politics* 9 (1): 7–20.

Sabato, Larry J. 1988. *The Party's Just Begun: Shaping Political Parties for America's Future.* New York, NY: Scotts, Foreman and Co.

Scarrow, Susan E. 1996. *Parties and Their Members: Organizing for Victory in Britain and Germany.* New York: Oxford University Press.

———. 2002 [2000]. "Parties without Members? Party Organization in a Changing Electoral Environment." In *Parties without Partisans*, ed. R. J. Dalton and M. P. Wattenberg. Oxford: Oxford University Press, pp. 79–101.

———. 2002. "Party Decline in the Parties State? The Changing Environment of German Politics." In *Political Parties in Advanced Industrial Democracies*, ed. P. Webb, D. Farrell and I. Holiday. Oxford: Oxford University Press, pp. 77–106.

———. 2006. "Party subsidies and the freezing of party competition: Do Cartel mechanisms work?" *West European Politics* 29 (4): 619–39.

————. 2007. "Political Activism and Party Members." In *The Oxford Handbook of Political Behavior*, ed. R. J. Dalton and H.-D. Klingemann. Oxford: Oxford University Press, pp. 636–654.

Scarrow, Susan E., and Burcu Gezgor. 2010. "Declining memberships, changing members? European political party members in a new era." *Party Politics* 16 (6): 823–43.

Schuller, Tom, Stephen Baron, and John Field. 2000. "Social Capital: A Review and Critique." In *Social Capital: Critical Perspectives*, ed. S. Baron, J. Field and T. Schuller. Oxford: Oxford University Press, pp. 1–38.

Semetko, Holli A. 2006. "Parties in the Media Age." In *Handbook of Party Politics*, ed. R. S. Katz and W. Crotty. London: SAGE, pp. 515–527.

Seyd, Patrick, and Paul F. Whiteley. 2004. "British party members: An overview." *Party Politics* 10 (4): 355–66.

Sieberer, Ulrich. 2006. "Party unity in parliamentary democracies: A comparative analysis." *Journal of Legislative Studies* 12 (2): 150–78.

Smith, Graham. 2009. *Democratic Innovations: Designing Institutions for Citizen Participation*. Cambridge: Cambridge University Press.

Stokes, Susan C. 1999. "Political parties and democracy." *Annual Review of Political Science* 2: 243–67.

Sundberg, Jan. 1989. "Premisser for politiskt massmedlemskap: partierna i Danmark i en nordisk jamførelse." *Politica* 21 (3): 288–311.

Tatham, Michaël. 2016. "Multi-Jurisdictional Politics: State Adaptation and Mixed Visions of Democracy." In *Democratic Transformations in Europe: Challenges and Opportunities*, ed. Yvette Peters and Michaël Tatham. Abingdon: Routledge, pp. 269–294.

Tavits, Margit. 2013. *Post-Communist Democracies and Party Organization*. Cambridge: Cambridge University Press.

Togeby, Lise. 1992. "The nature of declining party membership in Denmark: Causes and consequences." *Scandinavian Political Studies* 15 (1): 1–20.

Toubeau, Simon. 2010 *The Accommodation of Nationalism: Regional Nationalist Parties and Territorial Restructuring in Great Britain, Spain and Belgium*. PhD Thesis, European University Institute, San Domenico di Fiesole.

Tumasjan, Andranik, Timm O. Sprenger, Philipp G. Sandner, and Isabell M. Welpe. 2010. "Predicting Elections with Twitter: What 140 Characters Reveal about Political Sentiment." In *Proceedings of the Fourth International AAAI Conference on Weblogs and Social Media*. Association for the Advancement of Artificial Intelligence, pp. 178–185.

van Biezen, Ingrid, and Petr Kopecký. 2014. "The cartel party and the state: Party – state linkages in European democracies." *Party Politics* 20 (2): 170–82.

van Biezen, Ingrid, Peter Mair, and Thomas Poguntke. 2012. "Going, going, . . . gone? The decline of party membership in contemporary Europe." *European Journal of Political Research* 51 (1): 24–56.

van Biezen, Ingrid, and Thomas Poguntke. 2014. "The decline of membership-based parties." *Party Politics* 20 (2): 205–16.

Wattenberg, Martin P. 1984. *The Decline of American Political Parties, 1952–1988*. Cambridge: Harvard University Press.

————. 2002. "The Decline of Party Mobilization." In *Parties Without Partisans: Political Change in Advanced Industrial Democracies*, ed. R. J. Dalton and M. P. Wattenberg. Oxford: Oxford University Press, pp. 64–76.

Webb, Paul. 1995. "Are British political parties in decline?" *Party Politics* 1 (3): 299–322.

Webb, Paul, David Farrell, and Ian Holliday, eds. 2002. *Political Parties in Advanced Industrial Democracies*. Oxford: Oxford University Press.

Webb, Paul, and Robin Kolodny. 2006. "Professional Staff in Political Parties." In *Handbook of Party Politics*, ed. R. S. Katz and W. Crotty. London: SAGE, pp. 337–347.

Weeks, Liam. 2014. "Crashing the party: Does STV help independents." *Party Politics* 20 (4): 604–16.

Whiteley, Paul F. 2011. "Is the party over? The decline of party activism and membership across the democratic world." *Party Politics* 17 (1): 21–44.

Widtfeldt, Anders. 1999. "Losing touch? The political representativeness of Swedish parties, 1985–1994." *Scandinavian Political Studies* 22 (4): 307–26.

5

DEMOCRATIC DISCONTENT IN TIMES OF CRISIS?

Jonas Linde and Stefan Dahlberg

Although representative democracy enjoys overwhelming support from citizens all over the world – and is today seen as the only legitimate means to gain political power – we are often approached by reports recalling the debate about 'the crisis of democracy' in the 1970s (see Crozier et al. 1975; Hay 2007; Runciman 2013). The spread of democracy since the beginning of the 'third wave of democracy', which has made democracy a truly global phenomenon, seems to have lost momentum. Many countries that experienced breakdowns of dictatorships have not entered the family of liberal democracies but have rather transformed into corrupt 'hybrid regimes' where incumbents take advantage of a political playing field that is skewed in favour of the ruling party and where political rights and civil liberties are restricted.

At the same time, voices within the academic community express strong concern about dropping levels of public satisfaction with the performance of democracy in Western democracies, often interpreted as something like a 'confidence crisis' (Torcal and Montero 2006a). Claims of democratic crisis have increasingly intensified in the wake of the recession that started in 2007–08, which has been shown to have resulted in substantial drops in different dimensions of political support and trust in most European countries (Armingeon and Guthmann 2014). Decreasing levels of trust in fundamental democratic institutions such as political parties and governments have for quite some time been observed all over the world. Consequently, repeating the main claim from earlier generations of political culture research that solid public support for democracy and its institutions is a prerequisite for system stability, some have concluded that the most pressing challenge to contemporary democracies comes from its own citizens. Thus, democracy is said to be under pressure from large shares of citizens who have grown distrustful of politicians and institutions, expressing discontent with the performance of democratic government and, more generally, the democratic process in itself (Dalton 2004). Thus, anxiety about growing public discontent, and subsequently a crisis of legitimacy, seems to have become the dominant view in discussions about the state of contemporary European democracy.

However, scholars disagree about the potential danger of political discontent among citizens. Recent evidence from large-scale cross-national surveys points toward a somewhat contradictory situation. Although large shares of people around the world are discontented with the performance of democracy in their country, allegiance to the principles of democracy seems to be as strong as ever. Thus, the prevailing trend in many democracies seems to be one of increasing 'democratic deficits' in terms of high democratic aspirations mixed with high levels of discontent with the ability of democratic regimes to deliver the 'goods' to its citizens (Norris 2011). This issue of democratic discontent is also tapping into other challenges to representative democracy covered in this volume, such as the decline in party membership (see Mjelde and Svåsand 2016, this volume), the resurgence of nationalism and right-wing populist parties (see Bjånesøy and Ivarsflaten 2016, this volume; Knutsen 2016), new pressures on the welfare state (see Cappelen, 2016; Oldervoll and Kuhnle 2016), the globalization and supranationalization of politics (see Peters 2016, this volume) and terrorism (see Engene 2016, this volume), to name a few.

Drawing mainly on recent data from the sixth round of the European Social Survey (ESS) conducted in 2012, this chapter sets out to examine empirically the phenomenon of democratic discontent in contemporary Europe. Although the general focus in this volume is on Europe 31, the availability of comparable data limits the scope in the empirical analysis of this chapter. However, our empirical base is wide and covers democracies from both Western and Eastern Europe.

In the first part we review the scholarly debate regarding the nature of 'dissatisfied democrats', or 'critical citizens'. In this part we also present our definition and operationalization of dissatisfied democrats and democratic discontent. The second section presents an empirical investigation of European citizens' views of the importance of democracy and their evaluation of its performance. We present recent data on the distribution of dissatisfied democrats in European democracies and discuss trend changes over the last decades. In the following section we examine European citizens' views of the importance of democracy and their evaluation of its performance, focusing on a number of important elements of modern democracy. The section ends with an analysis of the relative importance of three broad elements of democracy for democratic discontent on the individual level. The chapter closes with a discussion of democratic discontent and state of democracy in the light of the empirical data presented.

The scholarly debate on democratic discontent and dissatisfied democrats

The concepts of 'dissatisfied democrats' and 'democratic discontent' draw on a multidimensional understanding of the concept of political support, which has become the dominant analytical perspective in the literature (cf. Dalton 2004; Easton 1975;

Klingemann 1999; Linde and Ekman 2003; Norris 1999, 2011). Many studies of contemporary politics in different contexts have demonstrated a gap between strong public support for democracy as a system of government and more negative evaluations of the actual performance of democracy and its institutions (see Booth & Seligson 2009; Klingemann 1999; Norris 2011, 1999; Schmitter 2015). Hence, when studying political support, it is important to acknowledge the theoretical and empirical distinction between popular support for the *principles* of the regime and support for the *performance* of the regime.

Support for the principles of the democratic regime concerns citizens' beliefs in fundamental democratic values and principles, such as the importance of having a democratic political system with free and fair elections. The regime performance dimension concerns citizens' perceptions of the workings of the democratic regime, such as satisfaction with the actual performance of the political system. The multidimensional nature of support thus makes it possible – and probably perfectly logical – for an individual to be convinced that democracy constitutes the best – or least worst – system of government for his or her country, but at the same time to feel discontent with the way the democratic system works in practice. This is the basic political orientation of the type of citizens who in the literature have been labelled 'dissatisfied democrats' and 'critical citizens' and makes up the phenomenon we set out to empirically investigate.

In *Critical Citizens*, Pippa Norris and collaborators directed attention towards the discrepancy between citizens' strong support for democracy in principle and their extensive discontent with the performance of democratic regimes (Norris 1999). The relatively large shares of dissatisfied democrats found in different parts of the world were generally interpreted in positive terms. Dissatisfied democrats have been perceived as being 'critical' because they have been assumed to be highly educated, well informed, politically interested and active, and thus could constitute a potential driving force in strengthening and deepening democracy. For example, in the context of authoritarian and post-authoritarian countries, it has been argued that a general commitment to democracy as a system of government is not a sufficient condition when it comes to the importance of mass attitudes for democratization, but rather that it is pressure for change from critical democrats on authoritarian leaders that may lead to improvements in terms of democratization (Qi and Shin 2011). In a recent analysis of dissatisfied democrats in old and new democracies drawing on data from the European Values Survey, Klingemann finds some support for the democratizing potential of dissatisfied democrats. The dissatisfied democrats are more likely to harbour post-materialist values than are satisfied democrats, which in turn could mean that dissatisfaction very well could be a driver of alternative political activism and thus in the end 'strengthen the participatory elements of a democratic political culture as it shifts into an assertive direction' (Klingemann 2014, 141).

Not everyone subscribes to this positive notion of democratic discontent, however. In his acclaimed book *Why Politics Matters*, Gerry Stoker argues that the growing scepticism towards political institutions and discontent with the functioning of democracy are more than just a reflection of healthy scepticism and could constitute a threat to the legitimacy of representative democracy (Stoker 2006; see Doorenspleet 2012). It has also been shown that this is the case particularly in new democracies (Torcal and Lago 2006).

In one of the few empirical analyses of the political orientations of dissatisfied democrats, Doorenspleet found that in African democracies 'satisfied democrats are generally more likely to vote and have a higher level of political interest than dissatisfied democrats, who are less involved and less active' (2012, 290). Thus, Doorenspleet found no evidence for the often-made claim that dissatisfied democrats are more inclined to be politically active, struggling to improve the quality of the democratic political system. Moreover, in an analysis of different types of content and discontent and their relationship to 'democracy promoting' attitudes, Geissel (2008) shows that neither content nor discontent with the performance of the political system are the decisive orientations that promote democracy, but rather the political attentiveness in terms of perceiving monitoring of politicians and government institutions as important. Moreover, from a somewhat different angle, Hay (2007) argues that the 'critical citizen thesis' is problematic, since it assumes that discontent and dropping levels of political participation are the result of a change towards a more post-materialist political culture on the demand-side of politics (citizens/voters) and thus does not take the supply-side of politics sufficiently into account. However, much of the debate about the consequences of democratic discontent and the emergence of dissatisfied democrats has been on a theoretical level and often quite speculative. The following empirical analyses are intended to shed some new light on the issue of democratic discontent in contemporary Europe. We approach this issue from a macro- as well as an individual-level perspective. On the macro-level we focus on levels and trends in democratic discontent in European democracies. On the individual level we investigate the importance that European citizens ascribe to a wide variety of elements of democracy and also their evaluation of these elements in practice. We also assess the importance of evaluations of different aspects of democracy for democratic discontent.

Old and new democracies

Many studies on political support have demonstrated systematic differences in levels of political support across different types of democracies. The most apparent difference regards the one between established democracies and more recently democratized countries. As we will see later, this is true also in the European context, where the most obvious demarcation line is to be found between the established democracies in Northwestern Europe on the one hand and the post-authoritarian countries in Southern and Eastern Europe on the other (see Dahlberg et al. 2015; Marien 2011; Torcal and Montero 2006a). Earlier research has also shown that different types of democracies face different challenges, and that this has consequences for explanations of democratic discontent (Dahlberg et al. 2015). One important factor regards the consolidation of political institutions. For example, old and new democracies differ in terms of the institutionalization of cleavage structures, party system stability, electoral volatility, political participation, and the extent of programmatic appeal of political parties (Karp and Banducci 2007; Mainwaring and Zoco 2007), and they also differ substantially when it comes to different aspects of political performance and corruption (Keefer 2007; Treisman 2000).

Dahlberg et al. (2015) argue that citizens in established democracies have greater expectations in terms of general performance, both on the input as well as on the output side of the political system, since they have longer experience of political stability and economic growth. Moreover, in many new democracies, corruption and clientelism are more or less integrated aspects of politics, while citizens in established democracies expect politicians and public officials to behave in a non-corrupt and impartial manner. While not having much trust in the cleanness and representation of the political system in the first place, citizens in new democracies seem to first and foremost look to the government's ability to deliver the goods in terms of economic development and basic welfare. Thus, it could be expected that the factors that are driving the democratic discontent among citizens differ as a consequence of institutional consolidation at the aggregate level. Hence, in most of the analyses we distinguish between the established democracies in Western Europe and new democracies in Central and Eastern Europe. Also, in line with earlier research, we regard Portugal and Spain as 'old' democracies, since they have been democracies for almost forty years and members of the European Union since 1986 (see e.g. Aarts and Thomassen 2008; Anderson et al. 2005; Karp and Banducci 2007).

Dissatisfied democrats: operationalization and measurement

We construct our measure of democratic discontent by combining two individual-level variables; the first one tapping the extent of importance citizens attach to living in a democratic political system and the other measuring satisfaction with the way democracy works in practice. The first asks respondents to answer the question 'How important is it for you to live in a country that is governed democratically?' Respondents are then asked to choose an answer on a scale from 0 (not at all important) to 10 (extremely important). We then classify those who score the importance of democracy from 6 to 10 as 'democrats'. The other item is the ESS version of the frequently used question on satisfaction with democracy: 'on the whole, how satisfied are you with the way democracy works in [in country]?' Also here, respondents choose an answer between 0 (extremely dissatisfied) and 10 (extremely satisfied). Respondents who state that democracy is important (choosing a value ranging from 6 to 10) and at the same time express dissatisfaction with democracy (0–4) are then classified as dissatisfied democrats. On the macro-level, the country aggregates constitute our measure of democratic discontent in each country.

We are thus choosing a simple dichotomous operationalization of the concept of democratic discontent but nonetheless used in the few earlier empirical analyses concerned with dissatisfied democrats (Dahlberg et al. 2015; Doorenspleet 2012; Hofferbert and Klingemann 2001; Klingemann 2014). Thus, consisting of only two dimensions of political support, each measured with only one variable, the concept applied here should not be confused with more encompassing definitions that can be found in the literature, for example, the concept of 'political disaffection', which is the topic in Torcal and Montero's volume on *Political Disaffection in Contemporary Democracies* (Torcal and Montero 2006a). They view political disaffection as a broader syndrome of disaffection from politics and define it as 'the subjective feeling of powerlessness, cynicism, and lack of confidence in the political process, politicians, and democratic institutions, but with no questioning of the political regime' (Torcal and Montero 2006b, 6). Our straightforward operationalization does of course provide a cruder measure of democratic discontent – which is admittedly a complex concept – but nevertheless one that is possible to apply to a broad range of European countries in one comparative study.

European citizens' views of the importance of democracy and their evaluation of its performance

We start our empirical examination by assessing the relationship between European citizens' support for democratic regime principles and their evaluation of the performance of the democratic political system they live in. With reference to the general literature on system support, we expect to find a systematic difference between aggregate levels of support for democracy as a system of government and corresponding levels of satisfaction with the performance of democracy. This pattern is clearly manifest when looking at the data presented in Figure 5.1, which plots the

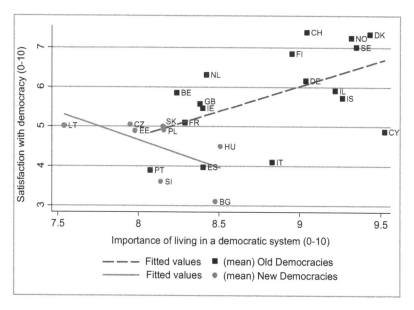

FIGURE 5.1 Satisfaction with democracy and importance of living in a democracy

Source: European Social Survey round 6 (2012)

aggregate levels of support for democracy and satisfaction with the way democracy works. In all countries, levels of citizens' aspirations of democracy exceed the corresponding evaluations of its performance. Looking at the importance of democracy, all countries have mean values above 7.5 on the scale ranging from 0 to 10, testifying to strong support for the principles of democracy in general.

The data show a strong relationship between democratic experience and the importance citizens ascribe to democratic government. When it comes to evaluations of the performance of democracy, levels are significantly lower – between 3 and 7.5 – and the newer democracies in Eastern Europe – together with the Southern European countries – tend to display substantially lower levels of satisfaction than the older democracies do.

The data provide solid evidence of the 'democratic deficit' found in many studies of different types of democracies in different parts of the world (Dahlberg et al. 2015; Linde 2012; Norris 1999, 2011). Focusing on the distinction between old and new democracies, the data reveal an interesting pattern when it comes to the relationship between the two variables.

Interestingly, the relationship between support for regime principles (importance) and evaluations of performance (satisfaction) is different in the two groups of countries. Among old democracies the relationship is quite strongly positive (the dotted line), indicating that in countries where citizens are more satisfied with the way democracy works, they also tend to believe that living in a democracy is important in itself. Among the new post-communist democracies we find a reverse, negative, relationship. Although we cannot make any claims about the causal order of these two variables, a feasible interpretation could be that in countries where the quality of democracy is lower, public dissatisfaction yields a demand for a stronger and better-functioning democracy.

Mapping democratic discontent in contemporary Europe

Applying our definition of dissatisfied democrats, we start out by investigating the variation among the countries by presenting the shares of dissatisfied democrats in each country in Figure 5.2. A quick inspection of the data presented leads to two main conclusions. First, there is substantial cross-country variation when it comes to democratic discontent: from a low 5 per cent dissatisfied democrats in Switzerland to a massive 71 per cent in Bulgaria. Second, we can observe an almost perfect division between old and new democracies. The thirteen countries displaying the smallest shares of dissatisfied democrats are all established democracies. On the left-hand side of the figure, we find the post-communist democracies, together with Portugal, Spain and Italy. Portugal and Spain are here classified as old democracies, but they are the most recent newcomers in that group. That Italy shows a high level of democratic discontent is hardly surprising considering that the Italians have experienced economic problems in the wake of the financial crisis and that several earlier studies have demonstrated high levels of dissatisfaction among the Italian public (Armingeon and Guthmann 2014; Dahlberg et al. 2015; Klingemann

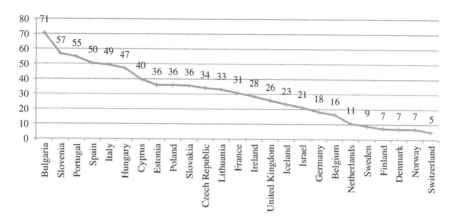

FIGURE 5.2 Cross-country variation in shares of dissatisfied democrats

Source: European Social Survey Round 6 (2012)

1999; Norris 2011; Segatti 2006). Furthest to the right we find, as expected, the wealthy countries in Northern Europe and in particular the Nordic countries, which are well known for their high levels of political and social trust (Delhey and Newton 2005).

The data presented in Figure 5.2 are interesting and suggest that the economic recession has had strong negative effects on public evaluations of political performance in the countries that were hardest hit by the crisis, as recently shown by Armingeon and Guthmann (2014) in a study of the effects of the financial crisis on support for national democracy in European countries, using aggregated survey data from the Eurobarometer covering the period from 2007 to 2011 (see also Teixeira et al. 2014). Thus, an interesting question is whether levels of democratic discontent in European democracies have increased during the crisis.

Trends in democratic discontent

Unfortunately, since the question about the importance of democracy has not been included in earlier rounds of the ESS, we are not in a position to conduct such an analysis of the development of democratic discontent measured in this way. However, the question about satisfaction with democracy has been asked in all modules of the ESS, which makes it possible to track changes in satisfaction with democracy over time in an effort to investigate if evaluations of democratic performance have decreased during the economic recession. From earlier comparative studies, we know that political trust and satisfaction with government in Europe were stable during the early years of the 2000s (i.e. before the financial crisis), although more so in old than in new democracies (Marien 2011). In the Eastern democracies, levels of political trust have shown to be lower and also much more fluctuating (Rose and Mishler 2011). We start out by looking at changes in average country levels of satisfaction with the way democracy works, as measured by the EES in 2006 and 2012.

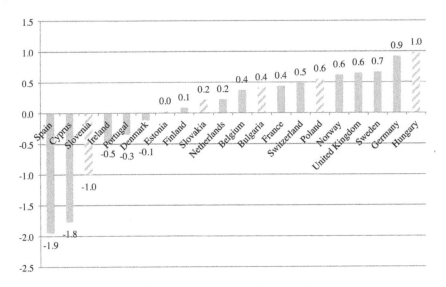

FIGURE 5.3 Changes in aggregate levels of satisfaction with democracy, 2006–2012

Source: European Social Survey round 6 (2012). Bars with the pattern fill represent new democracies

Then we will investigate the development of democratic dissatisfaction over a substantially longer period of time using a similar question from the Eurobarometer.

Figure 5.3 presents changes in aggregate levels of satisfaction with democracy from the third round of the ESS (2006) to the latest survey conducted in 2012. Unfortunately, the country coverage is not exactly the same in the two surveys, which means that we are not able to track the change in interesting countries such as Italy and Lithuania. However, we have data for twenty of our twenty-five countries. Some of the figures might come as a surprise. Levels of satisfaction with the way democracy works have actually increased in thirteen out of twenty countries when measured just before the crisis in 2006 and again in 2012. During this period satisfaction with democracy has dropped in only five countries and has been unchanged in Estonia, which was – together with its Baltic neighbours – quite severely affected by the recession.

On average, satisfaction with the way democracy works actually increased marginally from 5.40 to 5.45 in these twenty countries. If we start by looking at the negative changes, two countries stand out. Both Spain and Cyprus have seen quite dramatic drops in satisfaction between 2006 and 2012. In fact, average drops by 1.9 and 1.8 on the 11-point scale indicate sharp declines in evaluations of regime performance in a relatively short time. In Spain the average level of satisfaction with democracy dropped from 5.9 to 4.0 and in Cyprus from 6.6 to 4.9. Also Slovenia experienced quite a sharp drop from 4.6 to 3.6, placing the country in the top of the dissatisfaction list, only distanced by Bulgaria (Figure 5.2).

As expected, the data also show decreasing levels of support in Ireland and Portugal, which both experienced severe economic downturn during the period. We also find a slight decline in satisfaction among Danes, but this is a very marginal drop from the highest recorded level of satisfaction in this group of countries in 2006 (7.5). Movements in the other direction are more frequent but smaller in magnitude. The most surprising finding is probably the relatively large increase in satisfaction with the way democracy works in Hungary, although it is an increase from an already low level. The data presented in Figure 5.3 indicate that the effects of the financial crisis on political support have been quite limited in general, at least not as dramatic as could be expected. This in turn points to the fact that democratic discontent is not contingent on economic factors alone.

It is, however, difficult to draw any conclusions about the development of democratic discontent over time from only two points in time. In order to get a more nuanced picture, we turn to other data sources. The Eurobarometer (EB) has surveyed citizens in the EU member states and EU candidate countries about political issues since the early 1970s. Many of the surveys contain a version of the question on satisfaction with the way democracy works. However, as in earlier versions of the ESS, the EB surveys do not include any questions about democracy as a system of government. This means that we cannot distinguish between 'democrats' and 'non-democrats'. Thus, in the following we present levels of dissatisfaction with the way democracy works and use this as a proxy for democratic discontent. Since the EB focuses on the EU member states, some countries have significantly longer series of data on satisfaction with democracy than others do. However, taking advantage of the Central and East Eurobarometers and the subsequent Candidate Countries Eurobarometer, it is possible to construct reasonably long time series also for the post-communist countries that became members of the EU in 2004 and 2007. Figures 5.4 and 5.5 present country levels of dissatisfaction with the way democracy works for seventeen old democracies and eleven new democracies over time. The lines depict the share of citizens stating that they are 'not very' and 'not at all' satisfied with the way democracy works for each year the question has been asked.

Starting with the established Western democracies, it is quite hard to observe any systematic pattern. Levels of dissatisfaction fluctuate substantially over time, and there is a great deal of variation among countries. However, it seems clear that the South European countries have experienced quite a dramatic increase in dissatisfaction rates since the start of the financial crisis. In Cyprus, Greece, Portugal and Spain, the share of dissatisfied citizens has more or less skyrocketed and reached around 80 per cent in 2013. A similar pattern can be observed in other countries that have been hit hard by the crisis, such as Ireland and Italy. However, in Ireland the dramatic increase has been from a much lower level of discontent, and in Italy recent levels are actually lower than they were in the 1970s, '80s and '90s. When it comes to the West and North European countries, the general trend is one of steadily decreasing levels of discontent with the way democracy works, although with some quite substantial fluctuations, as in Belgium, France and Germany. In Germany, the dramatic increase in dissatisfaction that started in 1990 is to a large extent the consequence of the re-unification of West and East Germany, where citizens in the post-communist eastern part have consistently come to demonstrate higher levels of discontent with the working of democracy.

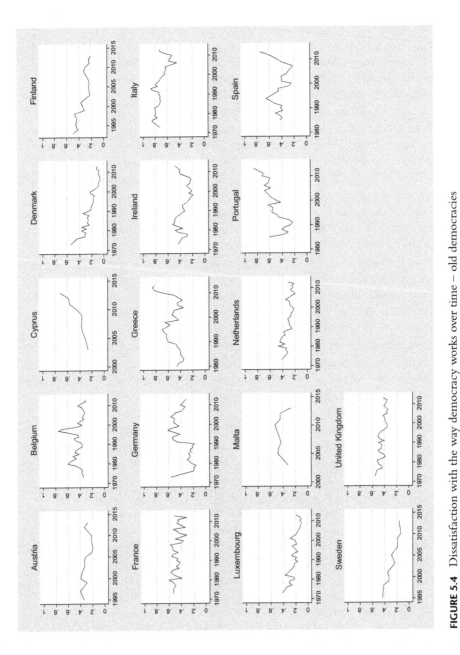

FIGURE 5.4 Dissatisfaction with the way democracy works over time – old democracies

Source: Eurobarometer 1973–2013

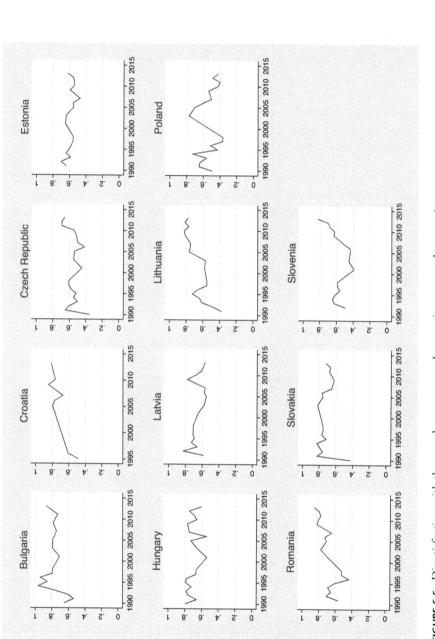

FIGURE 5.5 Dissatisfaction with the way democracy works over time – new democracies

Sources: Eurobarometer; Candidate Countries Eurobarometer; Central and East Eurobarometer; New Europe Barometer (2001)

The Nordic countries stand out as a group, demonstrating low and steadily decreasing levels of discontent, thus mirroring the ESS data on democratic discontent presented in Figure 5.2. All in all, when looking at dissatisfaction from a longer time frame, there is no clear evidence of a general increase in dissatisfaction with the way democracy works in the established European democracies. Rather, in several countries satisfaction with the performance of democracy – here illustrated as decline in discontent – has increased in the last 40 years. However, the longer trend perspective also demonstrates that in the countries that were most affected by the economic crisis, the governments have to deal with quite extreme levels of public discontent with the performance of the political system.[1]

Taking the literature on system support into account (e.g. Easton 1965, 1975; Linde and Ekman 2003; Norris 1999), it is not unlikely that in the longer run, the low levels of support for the performance of the regime may generate more general discontent with democracy as such. In the worst case, this might lead to a situation where democracy is no longer embraced as 'the only game in town' by a strong majority of the citizens, in the end generating a legitimacy problem for the democratic regime.

This is definitely something we need to keep in mind, when moving on to the most recent European democracies in Central and Eastern Europe (Figure 5.5). Here, dissatisfaction seems to be the prevailing public mood and has been so during most of the post-communist era. As has been shown in many empirical studies of political support in post-communist countries, the optimism that characterized the first few years after the fall of communism in 1989–90 was soon replaced by a more pessimistic, and perhaps also more realistic, outlook already in the early 1990s (e.g. Linde 2004; Rose et al. 1998).

In eight out of eleven countries, dissatisfaction has increased since the outbreak of the financial crisis. In most countries around eight out of ten citizens state that they are dissatisfied with the way democracy works. In the mid-1990s, levels of dissatisfaction reached above 95 per cent in Bulgaria. These are clearly the highest levels of discontent recorded by the Eurobarometers, which has tapped democratic satisfaction since the early 1970s.

In this regard, Poland stands out as an exception with a continuous decline in dissatisfaction from 2003 to 2013, in recent years displaying levels of dissatisfaction on par with many West European democracies, between 40 per cent and 50 per cent. In general, however, the state of political support in post-communist countries might be regarded as somewhat troublesome.[2] However, it is important to remember that most of these countries have struggled hard during the crisis, and several of them have a post-communist history characterized by corruption and political instability. Also, it is important to note the fact that although citizens in post-communist democracies seem to be very sceptical of the performance of their political leaders and the political system in general, there is a strong demand for stronger and improved democracy, as will be demonstrated in the next part of this chapter. In the following section, we set out to investigate how dissatisfied democrats perceive the political system in their countries in terms of the importance they ascribe to salient aspects of democracy and how they evaluate the functioning of these aspects in practice.

Democratic aspirations and evaluations of dissatisfied democrats

Free and fair elections make up necessary conditions for democracy. However, there is a wide consensus among theorists that elections need to be accompanied by several other institutions. For example, the literature on 'quality of democracy' highlights the rule of law, horizontal accountability and equality as essential components of democracy. A high-quality democracy thus needs to provide citizens with democratic equality and representation on the input-side of the political system as well as effective and fair decision-making and implementation of public policy on the output-side (Dahlberg et al. 2015; Diamond and Morlino 2004, 2005; O'Donnell 2004; Rothstein 2009; Rothstein and Teorell 2008).

Figure 5.6 presents views of importance and actual evaluations of a number of crucial aspects of democracy related to the institutions of elections and political parties (i.e. indicators of democratic representation) and thus arguably connected to the input-side of the political system (Dahlberg and Holmberg 2014). The figure presents mean values for five such elements, with the bars representing satisfied and dissatisfied democrats. The elements are fair elections, political parties offering clear alternatives to one another, freedom for opposition parties to criticize the government, the possibility for citizens to have the final say on political issues in referendums, and that government parties are punished in elections when they have done a bad job.

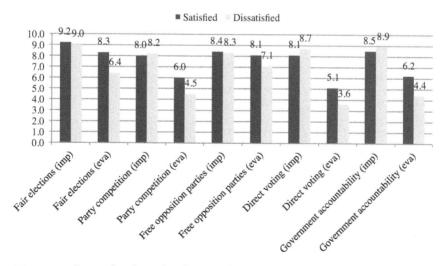

FIGURE 5.6 Demand and supply of input-related elements of democracy among satisfied and dissatisfied democrats

Source: European Social Survey round 6 (2012)

For each aspect of democracy, we present both the importance citizens attach to each element and also their evaluation of the working of each element. In general, there is a gap between the desire for and subjective evaluation of the supply with regard to all five aspects. Overall, the data demonstrate a relatively wide discrepancy between what citizens believe are important aspects of democracy and their perceptions of how the current political regime fulfills these demands. However, there is a systematic difference between dissatisfied and satisfied democrats, where the dissatisfied democrats express less favourable evaluations of the actual working of all five core democratic elements. Dissatisfied democrats are most discontent with the possibility to vote directly in referendums on the most important political issues, that poor performance of governmental parties is not punished in elections and the supply of different alternatives by the political parties. There is also a quite substantial difference between satisfied and dissatisfied democrats with regard to their view on elections as free and fair.

Next we turn to a number of elements of democracy that might be argued to be more strongly related to the output-side of the political system, or factors that sometimes are described as indicators of political performance. Recently, the ability of the political system to assure rule of law and and impartial implementation of public policy, or *quality of government*, has been shown to be of great importance for political support and democratic legitimacy (Magalhães 2014; Rothstein 2011; Wagner et al. 2009).

Figure 5.7 presents average levels of demand and the corresponding levels of perceived regime supply for three output-related elements of democracy. The first element regards the protection of minority groups' rights, which is arguably an important aspect of 'quality of government' (Rothstein 2009). In all democracies

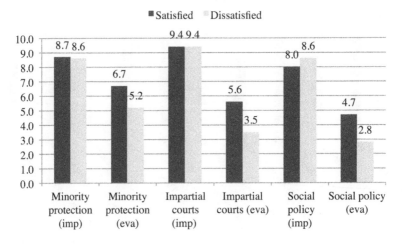

FIGURE 5.7 Demand and supply of output-related elements of democracy among satisfied and dissatisfied democrats

Source: European Social Survey round 6 (2012)

there are minority groups who know that they probably never will constitute the majority, no matter how many democratic elections are held. Thus, among minorities legitimacy is probably not created through the means of free elections but rather through the rule of law and universalistic and impartial government institutions (Rothstein 2009).

As can be seen in Figure 5.7, the protection of minority rights scores relatively high on the importance scale in both groups. When it comes to the implementation of minority rights, dissatisfied democrats are more sceptical. The rule of law is a fundamental aspect of democracy and quality of government. It is here measured by asking respondents about how important it is that the courts treat everyone the same, and then to what extent this is the case in the country where they live. The data demonstrate a quite dramatic rule-of-law deficit. Impartial treatment by the courts is regarded as the single most important element of democracy. At the same time, there is widespread discontent with the performance of the rule of law, and mostly so among the dissatisfied democrats.

Thus, at this point the argument of Rothstein and others within the 'quality of government school' – that impartial implementation of public policy is utterly important for legitimacy – seems to have substantial empirical merit. The last item presented in Figure 5.7 concerns redistribution in terms of whether or not the government should take measures to reduce income differences. Also here the gap between ascribed importance and evaluation is quite substantial, and particularly so in the dissatisfied camp. The ability of the political system to deliver on these aspects is, however, evaluated in negative terms in both groups. Thus, active policies in order to even out income differences are seen as an important aspect of democracy among most Europeans, but for a majority of citizens the measures taken by the governments are not seen as good enough.

The ESS includes two items about the role of the media when it comes to criticizing the government and as a provider of reliable information that can be used by the public in order to judge the actions of government. The questions are thus posed taking into account the important role of the media as a watchdog of the powerful and thus an important aspect of democracy and horizontal accountability (O'Donnell 1998; Schedler et al. 1999).

The data presented in Figure 5.8 suggest that the media's role both as a supplier of information and as a watchdog and critic of the rulers is judged as highly important by both satisfied and dissatisfied democrats. In general, citizens are quite positive to the media's performance in criticizing government but less so regarding the function as a provider of important information. Dissatisfied democrats are particularly critical in this regard.

All three types of democratic elements investigated here are thus coming forward as important to dissatisfied democrats. However, when it comes to the political system's performance on these important aspects, we find relatively high levels of discontent among those who are dissatisfied with the general performance of democracy. Judging from the elements investigated in the descriptive analyses above, the largest gaps between aspirations and evaluations are found with regard to

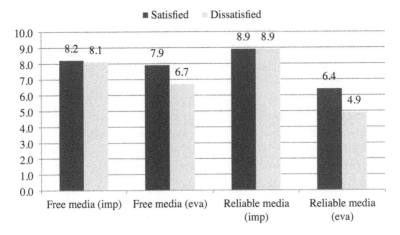

FIGURE 5.8 Ascribed importance and performance evaluation of the media as a watch-dog and provider of important information among satisfied and dissatisfied democrats

Source: European Social Survey round 6 (2012)

equal treatment by the courts, redistributive measures in order to decrease income differences, and the possibility to directly influence public policy by referendums.

Evaluations of democracy and democratic discontent

In order to assess the importance of these factors for democratic discontent, we move on to test the explanatory potential of the three broad factors (democratic input, governmental output and the media) on the individual level. Figure 5.9 presents the main results from two logistic regressions, one for old democracies and one for new democracies. The dependent variable 'democratic discontent' is the dichotomous measure presented above, with value 1 if the respondent is a dissatisfied democrat and 0 if satisfied. The main independent variables – for which coefficients are depicted in Figure 5.9 – are three indices constructed from the 'evaluation items' of the democratic elements presented in Figures 5.6–5.8. We also apply controls for gender, age, education, employment status, income, party identification, voted in last election, political interest and institutional trust.

Looking first at the democratic input elements, we find positive evaluations of input-related democracy items to have a relatively strong and statistically significant negative effect on discontent, which means that discontent is decreasing with more positive evaluations of the working of democracy. This is the case in both old and new democracies, although the effect is stronger in old democracies. The importance of 'governmental output' for democratic discontent is also substantial and statistically significant. Interestingly, evaluations of output-related aspects of democracy are much more important for discontent in the new democracies. When it comes to the media situation, it is more important for democratic discontent in new democracies.

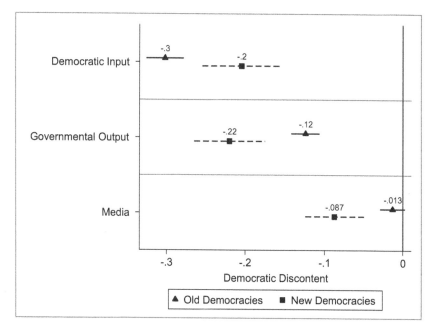

FIGURE 5.9 Determinants of democratic discontent in old and new democracies

Comment: Logistic regression with random intercepts (data is weighted using the provided ESS design weights). Control for gender, age (7 categories), education (4 categories), employment status, income (3 categories based on percentile values), party identification (yes/no), voted in last election (yes/no), political interest (4 categories), and institutional trust based on trust in the legal system, the police, politicians, political parties, European Parliament and the United Nations (Cronbach's alpha = .87). **Democratic input** is an index based on five different survey items: *fairelc:* "In country national elections are free and fair"; *dfprtalc:* "In country different political parties offer clear alternatives to one another"; *oppcrgvc:* "In country opposition parties are free to criticise the government"; *votedirc:* "In country citizens have the final say on political issues by voting directly in referendums"; *gptpelcc:* "In country governing parties are punished in elections when they have done a bad job" (Cronbach's alpha = .73). **Media** is an index based on two survey items: *medcrgvc:* "In country the media are free to criticise the government"; *meprinfc:* "In country the media provide citizens with reliable information to judge the government" (Cronbach's alpha = .65). **Governmental output** is an index based on three survey items: *rghmgprc:* "In country the rights of minority groups are protected"; *cttresac:* "In country the courts treat everyone the same"; *grdfincc:* "In country the government takes measures to reduce differences in income levels (Cronbach's alpha = .71).

Source: European Social Survey round 6 (2012)

In old democracies it does not reach statistical significance. Thus, the regression analyses suggest that both democratic input and governmental output are important determinants of democratic discontent in both old and new democracies. However, democratic input is more important in old democracies than in new democracies, where governmental output comes out as the clearly most important factor.

These results mirror findings from earlier research on dissatisfied democrats. Using data from the Comparative Study of Electoral Systems on a broader range of democracies, Dahlberg et al. (2015) have shown that both input- and output-related factors are important for democratic discontent in new and old democracies alike but that democratic input in terms of subjective feelings of representation and perceptions of corruption matter most for democratic discontent in established democracies, while perceived government performance constitutes the most important factor in new democracies. The results clearly suggest that democratic discontent is not only driven by negative evaluations of the actual policy performance of the government, but evaluations of core democratic elements, such as vertical accountability and opportunities for direct involvement in political decision-making, are also important when people make up their minds about the general performance of the democratic system.

Conclusions

The number of European democracies is higher than ever before, and for an overwhelming part of the Europeans, democracy is definitely 'the only game in town'. However, when democracy is up for public discussion, it is most often characterized in terms of crisis and erosion. In academia, books with titles such as *Democratic Deficit, Disaffected Democracies, Why We Hate Politics, The Confidence Trap* and *Vanishing Voters* depict something like a state of emergency in contemporary democracy. This is also the impression one often gets when reading about politics and democracy in the media. Is the state of democracy in contemporary Europe really that bad? In this chapter we argue and show that the situation is much more complicated and that issues of democratic legitimacy and discontent need to be viewed from different perspectives.

There is indeed a substantial discrepancy between the democratic aspirations of citizens and their evaluations of democracy in practice. The recent data from the European Social Survey investigated here thus confirm a pattern that has been demonstrated in many earlier studies drawing on a wide range of survey data from around the world. This discrepancy may be regarded as a democratic deficit and a clear indication of the fact that people want more from democracy than they think they are getting. Some view it as a problem of eroding trust in and support for the democratic political system caused by the political system's inability to deliver the 'goods', in the end affecting the legitimacy of democracy in general. The obvious solution would thus be to improve the functioning and efficiency of representative democracy. An alternative interpretation is that what we are witnessing is a widening 'expectations gap' between what is promised and/or expected and what can realistically be achieved by the political system. What would be needed then are a more realistic outlook and a reduction of the strong demands of citizens (Flinders 2013). If there is a remedy to the problem, it probably lies somewhere between these two views or in a combination of them. And, it seems like the potential for democratic regimes to meet citizens' demands can be found on both the input- and the output-side of the political system. The data investigated here indicate that a strong majority of dissatisfied democrats put great emphasis on democracy and democratic processes but also that many request improvements of the democratic processes beyond the ballot box. This is demonstrated by the large discrepancy between the importance people attach to direct voting and the perceived opportunity for direct involvement in decision making. The same room for improvement is found with regard to how Europeans evaluate the state of the rule of law. On average, impartial courts is viewed as the single most important aspect of democracy both by satisfied and dissatisfied democrats. The actual implementation of the rule of law is, however, ranked in the bottom, together with the possibility to participate directly in important political decisions and the efforts made to decrease economic inequality.

On the other hand, when looking at democratic discontent from a trend perspective, the picture looks quite different. In many West European countries, democratic discontent has actually been declining for decades. Of course, in the countries most affected by the financial crisis, dissatisfaction has grown in the wake of austerity measures and economic hardship. In the more recent Eastern democracies, the situation seems a bit more troublesome. Here, most people claim to be dissatisfied with the way democracy works. However, when investigating discontent since the 1990s, we find strong fluctuations but no dramatic increase in general. However, recent research has shown that in the countries that have been forced to introduce unpopular measures as a result of the crisis, citizens have tended to blame external agents (such as the *troika* and the European Commission) more than their national governments. This has actually resulted in a combination of eroded satisfaction with the way democracy *works* and increased attachment to the *importance* of national democracy (Cordero and Simón 2015).

Thus, the signs of democratic crisis often referred to in the public debate – dramatically dropping levels of participation, trust and confidence in politicians and the institutions of representative democracy among European citizens – need to be viewed from a broader perspective. Democracy is still perceived as the only legitimate system of government, and while discontent is widespread, most Europeans still perceive the functioning of democracy in a positive way. However, contemporary European democracies should not underestimate the importance of responding to the strong popular demands for democracy and improvements in the quality of both democracy and governance. A strong democracy requires both citizens demanding democracy and democratic governments that supply the goods perceived to be important to ordinary people, and that is not only economic prosperity but also core democratic values such as the rule of law and possibilities to participate in the decision-making process. However, the intensity of the debate about the state of democracy and declining levels of trust and confidence in democratic institutions will certainly not erode since, as pointed out by Dahrendorf (2000, 311), 'it appears that democracy is always in crisis'.

Further reading

Dahlberg, Stefan, Jonas Linde and Sören Holmberg (2015), 'Democratic Discontent in Old and New Democracies: Assessing the Importance of Democratic Input and Governmental Output', *Political Studies*, 63(Supplement S1): 18–37.

Klingemann, Hans-Dieter (2014), 'Dissatisfied Democrats: Democratic Maturation in Old and New Democracies', in Russell J. Dalton and Christian Welzel (eds), *The Civic Culture Transformed: From Allegiant to Assertive Citizens*. Cambridge: Cambridge University Press, pp. 116–157.

Norris, Pippa (2011), 'The Conceptual Framework', in Pippa Norris (ed), *Democratic Deficit: Critical Citizens Revisited*, Chapter 2. Cambridge: Cambridge University Press.

Key questions for discussion

1 What are the consequences of democratic *discontent* for democratic *legitimacy*?
2 Are dissatisfied democrats a driving force or a hurdle for democracy?
3 In what ways do new and old democracies diverge with regards to democratic discontent and why is that the case?

Notes

1 In fact, when regressing dissatisfaction on year for each country in order to grasp the direction of linear trends, the year coefficient is negative (showing an average decrease in dissatisfaction over time) in twelve out of seventeen countries (and statistically significant in ten countries). The countries that have seen an increase in dissatisfaction are Cyprus, Germany (including the post-communist GDR), Greece, Portugal and Spain.
2 However, when looking at the linear trends (OLS regression), there has been a decrease in dissatisfaction in five out of eleven countries (Estonia, Hungary, Latvia, Poland and Slovakia). Due to the low number of observations for the post-communist countries, most countries display non-significant coefficients.

References

Aarts, Kees and Jacques Thomassen (2008), 'Satisfaction with Democracy: Do Institutions Matter?', *Electoral Studies* 27(1), 5–18.

Anderson, Christopher J., André Blais, Shaun Bowler, Todd Donovan and Ola Listhaug (2005), *Losers' Consent: Elections and Democratic Legitimacy*. Oxford: Oxford University Press.

Armingeon, Klaus and Kai Guthmann (2014), 'Democracy in Crisis? The Declining Support for National Democracy in European Countries, 2007–2011', *European Journal of Political Research* 53(3), 423–442.

Bjånesøy, Lise Lund and Elisabeth Ivarsflaten (2016), 'Right-Wing Populism', in Yvette Peters and Michaël Tatham (eds), *Democratic Transformations in Europe Challenges: and Opportunities*. Abingdon: Routledge, pp. 143–162.

Booth, John A. and Mitchell A. Seligson (2009), *The Legitimacy Puzzle in Latin America: Political Support and Democracy in Eight Nations*. Cambridge: Cambridge University Press.

Cappelen, Cornelius (2016), 'Intra-EU Migration and the Moral Sustainability of the Welfare State', in Yvette Peters and Michaël Tatham (eds), *Democratic Transformations in Europe: Challenges and Opportunities*. Abingdon: Routledge, pp. 33–50.

Cordero, Guillermo and Pablo Simón (2015), 'Economic Crisis and Support for Democracy in Europe', *West European Politics* 39(2), 305–325. DOI: 10.1080/01402382.2015.1075767

Crozier, Michael, Samuel P. Huntington and Joji Watanuki (1975), *The Crisis of Democracy: Report on the Governmentability of Democracies to the Trilateral Commission*. New York: New York University Press.

Dahlberg, Stefan and Sören Holmberg (2015), 'Democracy and Bureaucracy: How Their Quality Matters for Popular Satisfaction', *West European Politics* 37(3), 515–537.

Dahlberg, Stefan, Jonas Linde and Sören Holmberg (2015), 'Democratic Discontent in Old and New Democracies: Assessing the Importance of Democratic Input and Governmental Output', *Political Studies* 63(S1), 18–37.

Dahlberg, Stefan and Sören Holmberg (2014), 'Democracy and Bureaucracy: How Their Quality Matters for Popular Satisfaction', *West European Politics* 37(3), 515–537.

Dahrendorf, Ralf (2000), 'Afterword', in Susan J. Pharr and Robert D. Putnam (eds), *Disaffected Democracies: What's Troubling the Trilateral Democracies?* Princeton: Princeton University Press, pp. 315–318.

Dalton, Russell J. (2004), *Democratic Challenges, Democratic Choices: The Erosion of Political Support in Advanced Industrial Democracies.* Oxford: Oxford University Press.

Delhey, Jan and Kenneth Newton (2005), 'Predicting Cross-National Levels of Social Trust: Global Pattern or Nordic Exceptionalism?' *European Sociological Review* 21(4), 311–327.

Diamond, Larry and Leonardo Morlino (2004), 'Quality of Democracy: An Overview', *Journal of Democracy* 15(4), 20–31.

Diamond, Larry and Leonardo Morlino (eds) (2005), *Assessing the Quality of Democracy.* Baltimore: The Johns Hopkins University Press.

Doorenspleet, Renske (2012), 'Critical Citizens, Democratic Support and Satisfaction in African Democracies', *International Political Science Review* 33(3), 279–300.

Easton, David (1975), 'A Re-Assessment of the Concept of Political Support', *British Journal of Political Science* 5(4), 435–457.

Easton, David (1965), *A Framework for Political Analysis.* Englewood Cliffs: Prentice-Hall.

Engene, Jan Oskar (2016), 'Terrorism, Counterterrorism and Democracy', in Yvette Peters and Michaël Tatham (eds), *Democratic Transformations in Europe: Challenges and Opportunities.* Abingdon: Routledge, pp. 189–208.

Flinders, Matthew (2013), 'Commentary: Explaining Democratic Disaffection: Closing the Expectations Gap', *Governance* 27(1), 1–8.

Geissel, Brigitte (2008), 'Democratic Resource or Democratic Threat? Profiles of Critical and Uncritical Citizens in Comparative Perspective', *Comparative Sociology* 7(1), 4–27.

Hay, Colin (2007), *Why We Hate Politics.* Cambridge: Polity Press.

Hofferbert, Richard I. and Hans-Dieter Klingemann (2001), 'Democracy and Its Discontents in Post-Wall Germany', *International Political Science Review* 22(4), 363–378.

Karp, Jeffrey A. and Susan A. Banducci (2007) 'Party Mobilization and Political Participation in New and Old Democracies', *Party Politics* 13(2), 217–234.

Keefer, Philip (2007), 'Clientelism, Credibility, and the Policy Choices of Young Democracies', *American Journal of Political Science* 51(4), 804–821.

Klingemann, Hans-Dieter (1999), 'Mapping Political Support in the 1990s: A Global Analysis', in Pippa Norris (ed), *Critical Citizens: Global Support for Democratic Governance.* Oxford: Oxford University Press, pp. 31–56.

Klingemann, Hans-Dieter (2014), 'Dissatisfied Democrats: Democratic Maturation in Old and New Democracies', in Russell J. Dalton and Christian Welzel (eds), *The Civic Culture Transformed: From Allegiant to Assertive Citizens.* Cambridge: Cambridge University Press, pp. 116–157.

Knutsen, Terje (2016), 'A Re-Emergence of Nationalism as a Political Force in Europe?' in Yvette Peters and Michaël Tatham (eds), *Democratic Transformations in Europe: Challenges and Opportunities.* Abingdon: Routledge, pp. 13–32.

Linde, Jonas (2004), *Doubting Democrats? A Comparative Analysis of Support for Democracy in Central and Eastern Europe.* Örebro: Örebro Studies in Political Science 10.

Linde, Jonas (2012), 'Why Feed the Hand That Bites You? Perceptions of Procedural Fairness and System Support in Post-Communist Democracies', *European Journal of Political Research* 51(3), 410–434.

Linde, Jonas and Joakim Ekman (2003), 'Satisfaction with Democracy: A Note on a Frequently Used Indicator in Comparative Politics', *European Journal of Political Research* 42(3), 391–408.

Magalhães, Pedro C. (2014), 'Government Effectiveness and Support for Democracy', *European Journal of Political Research* 53(1), 77–97.

Mainwaring, Scott and Edurne Zoco (2007), 'Political Sequences and the Stabilization of Interparty Competition Electoral Volatility in Old and New Democracies', *Party Politics* 13(2), 155–178.

Marien, Sofie (2011), 'Measuring Political Trust across Time and Space', in Sonja Zmerli and Marc Hooghe (eds), *Political Trust: Why Context Matters*. Colchester: ECPR Press, pp. 13–46.

Mjelde, Hilmar L. and Lars Svåsand (2016), 'Party Decline?' in Yvette Peters and Michaël Tatham (eds), *Democratic Transformations in Europe: Challenges and Opportunities*. Abingdon: Routledge, pp. 51–71.

Norris, Pippa (2011), *Democratic Deficit: Critical Citizens Revisited*. Cambridge: Cambridge University Press.

Norris, Pippa (ed) (1999), *Critical Citizens: Global Support for Democratic Governance*. Oxford: Oxford University Press.

O'Donnell, Guillermo (1998), 'Horizontal Accountability in New Democracies', *Journal of Democracy* 9(3), 112–126.

O'Donnell, Guillermo (2004), 'Why the Rule of Law Matters', *Journal of Democracy* 15(4), 32–46.

Oldervoll, Johannes Andresen and Stein Kuhnle (2016), 'The Sustainability of European Welfare States: The Significance of Changing Labour Markets', in Yvette Peters and Michaël Tatham (eds), *Democratic Transformations in Europe: Challenges and Opportunities*. Abingdon: Routledge, pp. 120–142.

Peters, Yvette (2016), 'Displacing Politics: The State of Democracy in an Age of Diffused Responsibility', in Yvette Peters and Michaël Tatham (eds), *Democratic Transformations in Europe: Challenges and Opportunities*. Abingdon: Routledge, pp. 163–186.

Qi, Lingling and Doh Chull Shin (2011), 'How mass political attitudes affect democratization: Exploring the facilitating role critical democrats play in the process', *International Political Science Review* 32(3), 245–262.

Rose, Richard and William Mishler (2011), 'Political Trust and Distrust in Post-Authoritarian Contexts', in Sonja Zmerli and Marc Hooghe (eds), *Political Trust: Why Context Matters*. Colchester: ECPR Press, pp. 117–140.

Rose, Richard, William Mishler and Christian Haerpfer (1998), *Democracy and Its Alternatives: Understanding Post-Communist Societies*. Baltimore and London: The Johns Hopkins University Press.

Rothstein, Bo (2009), 'Creating Political Legitimacy Electoral Democracy Versus Quality of Government', *American Behavioral Scientist* 53(3), 311–330.

Rothstein, Bo (2011), *The Quality of Government: Corruption, Social Trust, and Inequality in International Perspective*. Chicago: University of Chicago Press.

Rothstein, Bo and Jan Teorell (2008), 'What Is Quality of Government? A Theory of Impartial Government Institutions', *Governance* 21(2), 165–190.

Runciman, David (2013), *The Confidence Trap: A History of Democracy in Crisis from World War I to the Present*. Princeton and Oxford: Princeton University Press.

Schedler, Andreas, Larry Diamond and Marc F. Plattner (eds) (1999), *The Self-Restraining State: Power and Accountability in New Democracies*. Boulder: Lynne Rienner.

Schmitter, Philippe C. (2015), 'Crisis and Transition, but Not Decline', *Journal of Democracy* 26(1), 32–44.

Segatti, Paolo (2006), 'Italy, Forty Years of Political Disaffection', in Mariano Torcal and José Ramón Montero (eds), *Political Disaffection in Contemporary Democracies: Social Capital, Institutions, and Politics*. London and New York: Routledge, pp. 244–275.

Stoker, Gerry (2006), *Why Politics Matters: Making Democracy Work*. Houndsmills: Palgrave Macmillan.

Teixeira, Conceição, Emmanouil Tsatsanis and Ana Maria Belchior (2014), 'Support for Democracy in Times of Crisis: Diffuse and Specific Regime Support in Portugal and Greece', *South European Society and Politics* 19(4), 501–518. DOI: 10.1080/13608746.2014.975770

Torcal, Mariano and Ignacio Lago (2006), 'Political Participation, Information, and Accountability: Some Consequences of Political Disaffection in New Democracies', in Mariano Torcal and José Ramón Montero (eds), *Political Disaffection in Contemporary Democracies: Social Capital, Institutions, and Politics*. London and New York: Routledge, pp. 308–331.

Torcal, Mariano and José Ramón Montero (eds) (2006a), *Political Disaffection in Contemporary Democracies: Social Capital, Institutions, and Politics*. London and New York: Routledge.

Torcal, Mariano and José Ramón Montero (2006b), 'Political Disaffection in Comparative Perspective', in Mariano Torcal and José Ramón Montero (eds), *Political Disaffection in Contemporary Democracies: Social Capital, Institutions, and Politics*. London and New York: Routledge, pp. 3–19.

Treisman, Daniel (2000), 'The Causes of Corruption: A Cross-National Study', *Journal of Public Economics* 76(3), 399–457.

Wagner, Alexander F., Friedrich Schneider and Martin Halla (2009), 'The Quality of Institutions and Satisfaction with Democracy in Western Europe – A Panel Analysis', *European Journal of Political Economy* 25(1), 30–41.

PART 2

Restructuring the politics and institutions of the state

6

THE STRUGGLE BETWEEN LIBERALISM AND SOCIAL DEMOCRACY

Michael E. Alvarez

Introduction

Disagreement concerning the status of private property in productive resources has been *the* point of contention for distinguishing the ideological, theoretical, and policy dimensions of the three great philosophical-political movements of modern history: liberalism, socialism, and social democracy. More than any other policy dimensions associated with left politics and social democracy – progressive taxation, the welfare state, state provision of education, housing, etc., all of which have over time generated cross-party support, becoming in effect "valence" issues –the political struggle concerning the institution of private property in productive resources has differentiated the far left from the moderate social democratic left from the liberal and libertarian right. The implications of this struggle for democracy are decisive, and this chapter will highlight that aspect. Wolfgang Streeck (2014, 40–41) calls attention to the contemporary relevance of this problem with respect to the 2008 global economic crisis and its ongoing consequences:

> Capitalism and democracy had long been considered adversaries, until the postwar settlement seemed to have accomplished their reconciliation. . . . Today, however, doubts about the compatibility of a capitalist economy with a democratic polity have powerfully returned. . . . The legitimacy of postwar democracy was based on the premise that states had a capacity to intervene in markets and correct their outcomes in the interest of citizens. Decades of rising inequality have cast doubt on this. . . . Egalitarian democracy, regarded under Keynesianism as economically productive, is considered a drag on efficiency under contemporary Hayekianism, where growth is to derive from insulation of markets – and of the cumulative advantage they entail – against redistributive political distortions.

This tension between capitalism and democracy is the concern of this chapter. I will approach this via a contrast of liberal/neoliberal perspectives versus socialism/ social democracy, concentrating my attention on two key dimensions of their respective visions: (1) the role of the state in altering the allocation of productive resources and the distribution of incomes under capitalism and (2) the opportunities for citizens' influence over such state policies. This chapter explores debates concerning the proper role of the state with respect to productive resources and the consequences for democracy. My argument is that the contrasting liberal and social democratic positions on dimension 1 have significant implications for dimension 2. Hence the key question: *can* the conditions necessary for realizing democracy be satisfied under *capitalism*? I show in this chapter that notwithstanding the meaningful distinctions between liberalism and social democracy, both perspectives share an endorsement of some fundamental neoliberal stances regarding the private control over decisions concerning investment, production, and distribution, and hence accept some meaningful constraints upon citizen influence over this realm of decision-making.

The three sections of this chapter will trace the evolution of the struggle of these rival packages of visions, ideas, and policies, considering in turn classical liberalism, the socialist and social democratic challenge, and the neoliberal counterattack. Rival "packages" of liberal and social democratic ideologies and theories are reflected in state policies, and my objective is to highlight the importance of visions and theories for eventual state policy, and hence for advancing the interests of rival social classes. As Blyth (2002) writes, "ideas are weapons," used by conflicting interests to make sense of economic reality, mobilize collective action, and propose institutional solutions. The fundamental problem which constitutes the red thread throughout this chapter concerns the degree to which the structural context of capitalism presents structural limits to the full realization of democracy's potential.

Liberal democracy and classical economics

The key to understanding liberal social theory is summed up in what Norberto Bobbio (1989) calls the "great dichotomy," represented by distinct private (civil society) and public (state) spheres. Within the private sphere, individuals within society exercise their liberties and freedoms, understood first and foremost as the productive employment of privately owned land, labor, and capital resources (Wolin 2004). This private realm is not to be penetrated from the public sphere by the state; the latter, rather, should pursue policies oriented towards the "common good," again understood first and foremost with respect to the economic sphere: guaranteeing the reproduction of the free market capitalist system and preserving the private rights of individuals to acquire and hold productive property. Such anti-political tones, in which politics is conceptualized as physical coercion, reflected the political struggle against traditional authority and its ideological justifications. The limits thus drawn to legitimate forms of state activity, combined with the primacy of freedoms associated with market activity and private property, naturally ruled out state activities that would alter market-generated distributions of income and opposed other types of monopolistic organizations arising from within civil society:

> . The root of all evil, the liberal insists, was precisely this interference with the freedom of employment, trade and currencies practices by the various schools of social, national, and monopolistic protectionism since the third quarter of the nineteenth century; but for the unholy alliance of trade unions and labor parties with monopolistic manufacturers and agrarian interests, which in their shortsighted greed joined forces to frustrate economic liberty, the world would be enjoying today the fruits of an almost automatic system of creating material welfare.
>
> *(Polanyi 1944, 144)*

The classical recommendation for a minimal state is the natural product of a model which recognizes the regular occurrence of business cycles and unemployment, but believes that a free, competitive market with flexible prices will in and of itself restore a tendency towards full employment and the optimal allocation of productive resources. "General equilibrium models," based upon the same classical assumptions, presume that all market actors enter into transactions for goods, services, and financial assets that are available now and infinitely into the future, and show that a unique set of prices generates a state of affairs under which all markets clear. More contemporary Chicago school–based models assume that market participants form "rational expectations" of the likelihood of future events. These calculations are in turn based upon market data from the past and present wherein "individuals form their expectations by making an optimal forecast of the future using all currently available information" (Knoop 2008, 91).

> In a classical efficient market, it is presumed that there are large numbers of rational decision makers who, before making a purchase or sales decision, collect and analyze *reliable information* both on the probability of events that have already occurred and on the *probability of events that will occur in the future.* In an efficient market, it is assumed that this important information about the past and the future is readily available to decision makers and that, on the basis of this information, decision makers make optimal choices.
>
> *(Davidson 2009, 33, emphasis in original)*

All of the above variants of the classical model are rooted in Say's Law, which denies the possibility of an excess in the supply of goods and services and hence denies the possibility of free market–generated extended periods of unused productive capacity – unspent cash will eventually be reinjected into demand as excess supply generates a fall in prices and interest rates (Blaug 1996, 151).

The critical reader might wonder what justifies the assumption in these models that actors make optimal forecasts of the future, when it naturally is impossible to draw a sample from a future population and analyze it in order to calculate probabilities. The classical solution is the following:

> Since drawing a sample from the future is not possible, efficient market theorists presume that probabilities calculated from already existing past and current market data are equivalent to drawing a sample from markets that will exist in the future. In other words, calculations of probabilistic risks from the past statistics are assumed to be equivalent to calculations that would be obtained if a sample from the future could be obtained.
>
> *(Davidson 2009, 37)*

Clearly, such models, leading to the conclusion that all markets in the present and future clear and that all productive resources are efficiently allocated and fully utilized *leave no room for state activities which would alter such Pareto-optimal market allocations*. This is perfectly consistent with the ideological foundations of liberalism in that it is fundamentally anti-political: it is not the *personal* political relations, but rather the *impersonal, objective* market which most effectively distributes incomes in a manner which most accurately reflects relative marginal productivities. Therefore, even if citizens through democratic channels express the preference to alter market outcomes, state violation of property-owners' autonomy is considered to be illegitimate. The liberal (and, in its purest variant, libertarian) prescription implies the exclusion of popular influence (via democratic influence over the state) over critical domains of decisions which have enormous collective consequences: the allocation of productive resources and the distribution of incomes. To show this, I begin by explaining Robert Dahl's conceptualization of democracy.

Across the variety of subdisciplines in political science, it is difficult to find a degree of scholarly consensus on any contested concept which matches that which exists for Dahl's (1971) conceptualization of democracy. As all students of comparative politics know well, Dahl measured variation across regimes along dimensions of participation (suffrage) and contestation (party competition). Such process-oriented conceptualizations of political regimes have become the standard in the discipline: the concept of political regime is fundamentally concerned with the "choice of *procedures* that *regulate access to state power*" (Munck 2001, 123, emphasis added), or, to put it differently, "the system of rules and practices that determine who has political rights, how they can be exercised, and with what effects for the control over the state" (Przeworski et al. 2000, 18). Following this logic, then, a democratic regime is one in which universal suffrage exists under true party competition, "in which individuals *acquire the power to decide* by means of a competitive struggle for the *people's vote*" (Schumpeter 1942, 269, emphasis added). Given the near-universality of universal suffrage in today's world, the Przeworski et al. definition of democracy focuses on the contestation dimension: democracy is "a regime in which governmental offices are filled as a consequence of *contested* elections. Only if the opposition is allowed to compete, win, and assume office is a regime democratic" (Przeworski et al. 2000, 18).

For the argument presented in this chapter, a much less frequently cited element of Dahl's conceptualization of democracy is critical. According to Dahl, there exist in today's world only *polyarchies*, not democracies, because democracy is defined as "a political system, one of the characteristics of which is the quality of being completely or almost completely responsive to [the preferences of] all of its citizens, [considered equals]," wherein all citizens have the opportunity to formulate, signify, and have their preferences equally weighed (Dahl 1971, 1–2). But *why* and *how* do we not see these conditions satisfied? The key question which constitutes the red thread throughout this chapter concerns *whether* the condition that all preferences are to be given equal weight *can* be satisfied under *capitalist* democracy.

Rosa Luxemburg responded in the negative to this question: "what parliamentarism expresses here is capitalist society, that is to say, a society in which capitalist interests predominate" (Luxemburg 1970 [1900], 56). One of the most eminent contemporary scholars on the origins of the modern state concurs:

> Essentially, the liberal state was constructed to favor and sustain through its acts of rule the class domination of the bourgeoisie over the society as a whole. This was the end to which the institutional principles of the state were ultimately directed.
>
> *(Poggi 1978, 119)*

But what do "predominate" and "domination" mean in practice, in life? My argument does *not* focus on political behavior but rather, following the classic statement by Block (1977) and the subsequent elaboration by Cohen and Rogers (1983), is that under capitalist liberal democracy there exist structurally defined *constraints to political rights*. Consider the issue of inequality in income and wealth, which at the time of this writing is *the* burning issue of the day. Under capitalist liberal democracy, voters face a "demand constraint" (Cohen and Rogers 1983, 51): rights tend to be exercised in pursuit of goals that are *limited and narrow*, viz. conflicts over the distribution of income but *not* over the underlying *cause* of inequality (viz. the institutions of private property and the market). But why is this so? Well, consider the following causal chain: Consumption = f(Income) = f(Employment) = f(Production) = f(Investment), where the essential decisions concerning investment and production lie within the domain of *private* owners of productive resources. The key point is that *collective* material well-being under capitalism depends fundamentally upon *private* capitalists' propensity to invest. Under such conditions, it is *rational* for the non-propertied to avoid challenging the propertied because "the well-being of workers depends directly on the decisions of capitalists. The interests of capitalists appear as the *general* interests of the society *as a whole*, the interests of everyone else appear as merely *particular, or 'special'* (Cohen and Rogers 1983, 53, emphasis added).

Robert Dahl's contemporary, Charles Lindblom, emphasized this point in his discussion of the "privileged position of business":

> Because public functions in the market system rest in the hands of business-men, it follows that jobs, prices, productions, growth, the standard of living, and the economic security of everyone all rest in their hands. . . . In the eyes of government officials, therefore, businessmen do not appear simply as repre-sentatives of specific interest[s]. . . . They appear as functionaries performing functions that government officials regard as indispensable.
>
> *(Lindblom 1977, 172, 175)*

What we see here is a two-pronged liberal argument which restricts the range of legitimate state intervention into the economy and thus constrains the pursuit of certain categories of citizens' preferences expressed via democratic channels. On the one hand, the "demand constraint" effectively constrains state intrusion into the realm of property and significant alterations of market allocations of produc-tive resources and distributions of income. But on the other hand, the "structural dependence of the state and society on capital" (Przeworski and Wallerstein 1988) deprioritizes the priority given to any citizen preferences, which could result in a less hospitable "business environment."

The Dahlian condition of equal weighing of preferences is thus violated. Inter-estingly, liberal and neomarxist perspectives reveal very little if any fundamental disagreement on the arguments presented above: they both emphasize that the domain of private property in productive resources is first and foremost to be shielded from state intrusion under capitalist *democracy*. Furthermore, they both recognize that this privileged status of property has consequences for the Dahl-ian democracy condition concerning the weighing of citizens' preferences and relative social class power. As Claus Offe (quoted in Przeworski 1990, 92) puts it, "the political power of the capitalist class does not reside in what its members *do* politically (exert 'power' and 'influence' in the decision making process, etc.) but it resides rather in what its members can *refuse to do economically* . . . i.e. *invest*" (92, emphasis added). The difference between liberals and the political left, then, concerns whether or not this prioritization of interests associated with property is *problematic* or not.

> Liberals proved to be unconcerned about the compulsions arising from a system of property because the pressures seemed to be impersonal and lack-ing in physical duress. On the other hand, liberals could become agitated over political power because it combined both a personal and a physical element. . . . [T]he same suspicions of power exercised by a determinate, identifiable authority were coupled with an explicit preference for "the impersonal and anonymous mechanism of the market." Since the market

represented merely the registered response of the consumers, i.e. "society," the resulting compulsion and inequalities had the advantage of being not only an impersonal, collective judgment by also a "democratic" one.

(Wolin 2004, 280)

Socialists and social democrats hold a starkly different normative perspective on this "privileged position of business" and its consequences for democracy. I turn next to an elaboration of this challenge to liberalism.

The socialist and social democratic challenge to liberal democracy

The political left has always rejected the "great dichotomy" drawn in liberal theory between the "private" and "public" spheres on the following grounds: *both* state and capital produce outcomes which have *collective consequences*. The classic principle of democracy goes as follows: because "they" – state actors – *compel us* to comply with collective decisions (laws) created, implemented, and enforced by "them," then "we" the citizens should be the ultimate *source* of these laws. This is the most essential meaning of democracy: rule of the people, *self-government*. Liberty is realized only if the people are the *creators* of the laws that they live under and are treated *equally* under these laws (Przeworski 2010). So why does the same principle not apply to all types of collective decisions, including those which determine the allocation of productive resources (with their consequences for employment and for what and how much is produced), as well as those which determine the distribution of incomes? The political left has always insisted that the *economy* as well as the state constitutes a realm of the *public* sphere. As Bowles and Gintis (1986, 67) explain, the capitalist economy has three varieties of collective consequences. First, owners (and managers) of capital determine investment decisions; second, they determine production decisions; third, they have privileged influence over governmental public policy. Lindblom (1977, 172) recognizes this as well:

> [I]n any private enterprise system, a large category of major decisions is turned over to businessmen, both small and larger. They are taken off the agenda of government. Businessmen thus become a kind of public official and exercise what, on a broad view of their role, are public functions. The significant logical consequence of this for polyarchy is that a broad area of public decision making is removed from polyarchal control.

The institution of private property thus constitutes a structural barrier to the realization of democracy in the Dahlian sense. Under capitalist democracy, there exists a sphere of decision making (the allocation of productive resources and distribution of incomes) which has enormous collective consequences but which is granted the status of lying outside the realm of legitimate state intervention and thus democratic control. Although the state has the coercive capacity to cross the barrier which defines this private realm, as explained above, the enormous potential negative consequences for society as a whole – in the form of less income and employment – present tight constraints upon elected politicians, whatever their political stripe may be. We thus arrive at the classic Marxist socialist prescription, intended to remove this constraint: socialization of the means of production. Democracy was viewed by many to be a useful path for realizing this goal: the unpropertied could form parties, win elections, and use the state to transform society.

> Socialists were deeply persuaded that they would win elections, that they would obtain for socialism the support of an overwhelming numerical majority. . . . Their strength was in numbers, and elections are an expression of numerical strength. Hence, universal suffrage seemed to guarantee socialist victory.
>
> *(Przeworski 1985, 17)*

Socialists were proven to be wrong: their strategy mistakenly assumed that the working-class base of socialism would constitute a numerical majority and unify in their support for the radical transformation of capitalism. In fact, social democracy in western Europe never possessed anything close to a numerical majority of supporters which would provide a mandate for socialization of the means of production, and furthermore, as Bernstein (1993 [1899], 104) put it: "this 'proletariat' is a mixture of extraordinarily varied elements, of social groups which are even more differentiated than was 'the people' of 1789." This differentiation meant that the proletariat, defined in classical Marxian terms, constituted far from a numerical majority of voters, a situation which "imposes upon socialist parties a choice: socialists must choose between a party homogeneous in its class appeal but sentenced to perpetual electoral defeats and a party that struggles for electoral success at the cost of diluting its class character" (Przeworski 1985, 24). Hence, social democratic parties quickly identified themselves less as "workers'" parties and more as "people's" parties, which in turn influenced the self-identification of workers (Przeworski 1985, 27, 28).

The abandonment of class "purity" decisively moved social democracy away from advocating a radically interventionist stance vis-à-vis private property. The commitment to *advancing values* rather than to *controlling capital* soon came to dominate the social democratic agenda. This is well illustrated via the Swedish social democrat Ernst Wigforss. As Timothy Tilton (1979, 510–515) explains, Wigforss's values included *equality* ("make it possible for everyone to live a valuable human life") and fundamentally reformist liberal forms of *freedom*, *democracy*, and *security* (via employment, pensions, insurance, housing) alongside clear de-emphasis upon socialization, adopting a strategy that "would quietly but steadily erode capitalist domination of the economy." Social democrats came to reply upon *incentives* "that would lead private businesses to allocate their capital in socially desirable ways" (Moene and Wallerstein 1993, 185). In this vein, Kitschelt (1999) describes how late-twentieth-century contemporary social democratic parties present themselves not as *challengers* to the capitalist economy but as effective *managers* of it, more willing to employ state intervention in a manner which does not displace but rather enhances market performance.

Many socialists, for their part, had always distrusted the parliamentary road wherein the masses *delegate* the defense of their interests to elected representatives. And according to Robert Michels, in his *Political Parties*, such a strategy would likely run into the obstacle posed by the "Iron Law of Oligarchy," wherein "the socialist party will contradict its own historical mission of democratic socialism. As it grows into a powerful political movement it will professionalize, bureaucratize, and lose sight of its real purpose as it becomes preoccupied with the demands of day-to-day administration" (Esping-Andersen 1985, 16). Socialists also argued against the reformist path by emphasizing how structural constraints to radical policy posed by private property are simply insurmountable and that not only *substantive equality* but also *political democracy* cannot be fully realized under capitalism: even a "red" government would find itself by necessity prioritizing the preferences of capital over that of workers, thus violating the Dahlian condition. Kalecki (1998 [1943], 350) highlighted this necessity long ago:

> Under a *laissez-faire* system the level of employment depends to a great extent on the so-called state of confidence. If this deteriorates, private investment declines, which results in a fall of output and employment (both directly and through the secondary effect of the fall in incomes upon consumption and investment). This gives the capitalists a powerful indirect control over government policy: everything which may shake the state of confidence must be carefully avoided because it would cause an economic crisis.

Despite the critique presented by socialists, it cannot be denied that social democratic *policies*, even in their decisively non-socialist form, pursued goals which differed meaningfully from the classic liberal prescription. Progressive taxation, regulation of labor markets, cooperation with encompassing unions in order to pursue wage leveling and employment security, regulation of the private sector, a generous welfare state, state ownership of selected firms and industries – all of these forms of state intervention altered market allocations of resources and distributions of incomes in historically meaningful manners which significantly increased security for the propertyless and advanced socio-economic equality. Social democrats did not *challenge* private ownership of productive resources, but they *did* create incentives for and occasionally compelled private owners to alter market-driven choices and outcomes. But what *justifies, explains, defends* such intervention on the level of theory? Socialists had at their disposal Marx's theory, which purported to explain the "laws of motion" of capitalism and provided a theory of revolution, but given the rejection of Marxist socialism, social democrats needed a *theory*, a framework for explaining how capitalism works and justifying leftist policy interventions. John Maynard Keyes provided that theory.

The economics of Keynes was truly radical: it destroyed the foundation upon which the entire Classical edifice was built. This radicalism of Keynes provided the necessary theoretic ammunition which social democracy had lacked following its abandonment of the Marxian socialist paradigm. Keynes provided the answer to the following question: given that we social democrats have accepted capitalism, what can we *do*, given the structural constraints to policy directed towards property, to improve and correct market allocations of productive resources and reduce inequality in the distribution of income?

Keynes's fundamental argument in his critique of the Classical school was that Say's Law does not hold in reality: earned incomes will not necessarily translate into effective demand. By contrast, *excess* supply and *insufficient* effective demand constitute the "general" state of affairs under capitalism. Hence, *both* key sources of effective demand, investment and consumption, will often prove to be inadequate for generating full employment, *even in the presence of full price flexibility*. With respect to investment, even under conditions of zero interest rates, there could be excess saving, and investment will not be forthcoming if investors' "animal spirits" (expected future returns) would not incline them to sink funds into employment-generating capital. The latter state of affairs will persist whenever and as long as negative expectations concerning the uncertain future incline investors to hold back on investment, which in turn reduces production, employment, and income, potentially resulting in a "low-level equilibrium trap." Here an opening for state fiscal policy is created, as the state can borrow excess, unused savings via running budget deficits, thereby propping up aggregate demand and stimulating private-sector production *without necessarily "crowding out" private investment and pushing up interest rates*.

Keynes dismembered the Classical argument by arguing against the latter's fundamental theoretical axioms (Davidson 2009). First, Keynes rejected the Classical "neutrality of money" axiom, which claimed that changes in the money supply have no effect upon real variables such as output and employment; second, he rejected the "gross substitution axiom," which assumed that price and wage flexibility will automatically generate market-clearing demand; and third, he rejected the "ergodic axiom," which assumes that market actors can use data drawn from the past and present to predict the future. In addition to these critiques of Classical axioms, Keynes introduced his theory of liquidity preference, showing that particularly during (possibly extended) periods of uncertainty concerning the future, market actors can have significant demand for cash (instead of goods and services which are produced). The result: the presence – as the *normal*, "general" state of affairs – of involuntary unemployment.

> The existence of savings in the form of money and other liquid assets breaks the Say's law proposition that supply must create its own demand. The reason why savings are stored in this non-employment-inducing demand for liquid assets is, according to Keynes, the recognition by income recipients that the future is uncertain and that one must protect oneself against unforeseen and unforeseeable contractual commitments and eventualities.
>
> *(Davidson 2009, 54)*

Now, let us recall that Keynes was not a political radical – he was, to the contrary, a staunch defender of capitalism (Sweezy 1982) – but his theory was utilized by social democrats to demonstrate that market outcomes and *equality* could be advanced via determined state intervention into the economy. These developments proved to be very meaningful with respect to the ability of the preferences of the non-propertied to be pursued via the state, a significant advancement of the Dahl democracy criterion. Korpi (1978, quoted in Berman 2006, 184) explicitly emphasizes this political component of Keynesianism: "political power [had become] separated from economic power. . . . Public power [could therefore now be used] to encroach upon the power of capital."

Thus, the Dahlian democracy conditions were advanced by even the more cautiously reformist variants of European social democracy oriented towards increasing equality of opportunity and distributive justice, reducing inequality, and increasing material security: instead of a movement trying to transform capitalist society, we see a party diligently pursuing the material interests of its primary voting constituency. Vertiainen (2001, 44–45), discussing the case of Sweden, explains how Keynesianism served several objectives. First, it involved active political efforts to direct the performance of the capitalist economy more in line with workers' interests; second, it generated high levels of employment; and third, it made feasible more active state provision of public services and welfare. As Moene and Wallerstein (1993) show, the *political* and *institutional* dimensions of social democracy can be summed up by representing the latter (using Scandinavia as an illustration) as a party-union alliance for advancing workers' material interests through parliament via policies associated with the welfare state, active labor market policies, wage leveling, and fiscal policy. On the rare occasions when property rights were targeted, such as the example of the Swedish wage-earner funds (Berman 2006, 197–198; Vertiainen 2001, 32–35), effective countermobilization from capital was successful. Nonetheless, these social democratic efforts realized a significant degree of success in pursuing what Esping-Andersen (1990, 21–23) has famously termed the *de-commodification* of labor-power: providing services as a matter of right and providing non-market sources of income to workers.

The limits to this social democratic strategy have been the subject of neomarxist theories of state intervention in the capitalist economy, calling attention to the contradictions which are inherent to state intervention in a private enterprise, class society. Interestingly, these "contradictions" bear a resemblance to those which neoliberals also came to use as ammunition against interventionist, redistributionist state activities. What Marxists add to Keynes' framework is the perspective of focusing on the state as necessary for "reproducing" capitalism. Following Habermas and Offe (see Przeworski 1990), the key functions of the state in twentieth-century capitalism are to promote the legitimacy of the capitalist system (via the welfare state and redistribution) and to promote economic growth (via correcting market failures and stimulating aggregate demand). The problem, however, is that "legitimation is costly and the cost is expressed in accumulation" (Przeworski 1990, 74), i.e. increased welfare spending and more radical redistribution may result in less private-sector investment (accumulation of capital), while cutting back on welfare spending and directing resources towards the private sector may damage the legitimacy of the capitalist system. This interesting overlap in points of emphasis between neomarxists and neoliberals will become apparent in the next section, as I summarize the central arguments of the latter perspective.

The neoliberal counteroffensive: scaling back the state

There exists almost uniform agreement that the neoliberal political onslaught against social democracy and the latter's contemporary, ongoing era of crisis and decline can be dated from the world economic crisis of the late 1970s and the rise of the political right, which emerged in the midst of a slowdown in rates of economic growth, rising unemployment, and high, persistent rates of inflation (Blyth 2002; Crouch 2011; Harvey 2005). A central component of the neoliberal policy agenda is to enhance "competition," free of political intervention:

> It is based on the idea that the ideal world order should be a "free" and "fair" competition between individuals. This competition is always under threat by groups who try to protect themselves from its rigor and consequences and seek to obtain more than their due share. Public intervention is thus legitimated when it tries to restore the conditions of fair competition and "level the playing field."
>
> *(Amable 2011, 5)*

In the realm of politics, neoliberalism "conceives of the polity as consisting of the individual first and the community second, with legitimate state action extremely limited with regard to community-based demands on the individual" (Schmidt and Thatcher 2013, 7). In political theory, the seminal contributions of Nozick (2001[1974]), as well as the public choice school (Buchanan and Tullock 1962), resonate to this day, all following the lead of Hayek (1943; 1944) and later Chicago school theorists from the discipline of economics.

Milton Friedman's effort to confirm the Classical argument that money is neutral (with effects only upon the price level) and thus combat the Keynesian claim that monetary and fiscal policy can have lasting effects upon real variables such as output and employment was profoundly illustrated by his famous long-run, vertical Phillips curve (Friedman 1968). The scholarly and policy impact of this model cannot be overestimated: it served to discredit activist governmental intervention via fiscal and monetary demand stimulus. Friedman identified a "natural" rate of unemployment, which while sometimes significantly positive, was fundamentally "voluntary," as it reflected *not* the failure of markets but rather market distortions which resulted from *choices* made by actors such as unions (utilizing their monopoly power to inflate the cost of labor) and governments (which create labor market rigidities, distort prices, alter market allocations of resources through taxation and redistribution, and subsidize leisure through generous welfare state provisions). Any activist government attempts to reduce unemployment below this level would prove to be fruitless, instead generating only inflation in the medium run. This is perfectly consistent with the Classical postulates explained in part two of this chapter: given the axiom that markets in a competitive economy maximize output to the full employment level, *any governmental intervention that alters this resource allocation* – or even worse, transfers incomes – causes efficiency losses.

This anti-state perspective was also embodied in the Nordhaus (1974) model of political business cycles, which again blamed self-interested vote-maximizing politicians for willful manipulation of the macroeconomy in order to gain re-election, thereby generating medium-run efficiency costs. These two contributions – the Friedman Phillips curve and models of deadweight costs due to political intervention in the macroeconomy – work together in a persuasively complementary manner, as is exhibited in Keech's (1996) textbook on political economy. More generally, public choice theories of rent-seeking (Buchanan and Tullock 1962; Mueller 2003; Snowdon and Vane 2005) view governments as sources of rents (unearned income), distributed in exchange for political support. This source of deadweight costs is compounded by the waste of resources which takes place as various organized interests compete with each other for political influence via lobbying and campaign contributions.

The implications of these arguments are clear: democracy entails efficiency costs, and certain issues and state activities should be placed outside of democratic influence even if numerical majorities of voters express preferences to the contrary. This has important implications for whether or not Dahl's conditions for democracy are satisfied, as neoliberal voices insist upon the *withdrawal* of the state from intervening in how privately owned productive resources are utilized: markets maximize output and employment and distribute incomes fairly, according to contribution; the state is the problem to the degree to which it alters market allocations of resources and distributions of incomes. Avenues for public pressure upon self-serving politicians must therefore be blocked; even better, certain key policy areas must be removed from politicians' influence altogether. This worldview is clearly manifested in its prescriptions for monetary policy.

The central pillar of the neoliberal prescription for monetary policy, one which has become the almost universal conventional wisdom in macroeconomic policy, is that the central bank should be afforded independence from popularly elected governments. But even if central banks are afforded independence from elected politicians, are not central bankers political beings, subject to pressure from politicians, voters, and citizens, however indirect such influence may be? Furthermore, has not Friedman already shown how monetary policy should *not* be conducted in a manner intended to influence short-term economic variables? As he has stated, leaving room for discretion "enhances the danger that the scope of government will spread from activities that are, to those *that are not*, appropriate in a free society, from providing a monetary framework to *determining the allocation of resources among individuals*" (Friedman 1962, 27, emphasis added). Given these points, the Chicago monetarist school has consistently argued that monetary policy should be conducted according to fixed rules which are clear and transparent. Abel and Bernanke (2007, 553–557) nicely explain the "monetarist case for rules": (1) monetary policy has only transitory effects upon real variables, affecting only the price level in the medium run; (2) given information constraints and the long and variable lagged effects of monetary policy, discretionary policy is fruitless; (3) the best approach is to choose some target of money supply growth and stick to it, regardless of short-term economic fluctuations; and (4) for this to work in practice, market actors must conclude that central bankers will credibly commit themselves to such principles. In this respect, precommitment and reputation are essential. One way of advancing such a reputation is through appointing conservative bankers who make it clear that they will prioritize the control of inflation even if it entails higher unemployment, viz., adopt the German model, "where price stability is considered to be the primary objective of the central bank. And, although the central bank can pursue other objectives, this is always conditional on the requirement that their pursuit does not endanger price stability" (De Grauwe 2007, 162).

The component of the neoliberal program concerning the international context cannot be neglected. Recall that the post-war Bretton-Woods international economic order was an important element in the Keynesian framework, as it was designed to control the flow of international capital, thereby avoiding sudden, destabilizing waves of capital flows in and out of national borders. To accomplish this, strict controls on capital were institutionalized, exchange rates were fixed (but adjustable if necessary), and thus governments were free to utilize monetary policy for domestic macroeconomic objectives. Under the Mundell-Fleming model (Cohen 1996; Moses 2000, 2014), a state cannot possess all three of the following: fixed exchange rates, the use of monetary policy for domestic macroeconomic objectives, and the free flow of international capital. Under Bretton-Woods, the latter was sacrificed. Following the breakdown of Bretton-Woods in the early 1970s, exchange rates became flexible, but international capital controls were progressively loosened, eventually removed, and hence monetary policy remained available for macroeconomic goals (Simmons 1999). But Europe was moving rapidly back towards fixed exchange rates, and given the free flow of capital, this mandated giving up democratic control over monetary policy. As Iversen (2001, 267) writes:

> Like the Danish policy reversal in 1982, the pegging of the value of the krona to the ecu in May 1991 was arguably the most important change in Swedish macroeconomic policies since the 1950s. It signaled a *de facto* abandonment of the social democratic commitment to full employment. It had also committed itself to bringing other economic policy goals into line with the pursuit of this strategy, including employment. Fiscal policies were tightened, interest rates increased, and EC membership and participation in the EMS became government policy.

The key factor in the contemporary era of "hyperglobalization" (Rodrik 2011) is the free movement of financial capital across borders, which can be brutally destabilizing. But what Rodrik views as a source of "destabilization" is viewed in the neoliberal ideology as a source of "discipline," yet another useful mechanism for tying the hands of "self-serving politicians" subject to "capture" by organized interests such as labor. This misbehavior of governments is viewed as fundamentally symptomatic of a much deeper problem: the legacy of social democracy and its practice of state intervention into market allocations of resources and distributions of income. Larry Summers (quoted in Rodrik 2011, 86) adds:

> Even as globalization increases inequality and insecurity, it is constantly and often legitimately invoked as an argument against the viability of progressive taxation, support for labor unions, strong regulation and substantial production of public goods that mitigate its adverse impacts.

All of this brings us right back to the political arena, as the neoliberal program has set into play a conflict between the needs of global capital and the ability of domestic politics to give voice to citizens' preferences for public policy – and it is precisely the policies and institutions associated with the postwar Keynesian model, and the preferences of workers and other social democratic constituents which are explicitly targeted by the neoliberal onslaught. Again, following Dahl, these segments of citizens' preferences are explicitly *not* to be "weighed equally." The consequences for democracy are dire:

> Once the rules of the game are dictated by the requirements of the global economy, domestic groups' access to, and their control over, national economic policy making must inevitably become restricted. . . . The hyperglobalization agenda, with its focus on minimizing transaction costs in the international economy, clashes with democracy for the simple reason that it seeks not to improve the functioning of democracy but to accommodate commercial and financial interests seeking market access at low cost. It requires us to buy into a narrative that gives predominance to the needs of multinational enterprises, big banks, and investment houses over other social and economic objectives.
>
> *(Rodrik 2011, 202, 206)*

What historical developments in the late post-war era set these liberal ideas into practical, implementable motion? A variety of studies (Armstrong et al. 1991; Brenner 2006; Frieden 2006; Glyn 2007; Obstfeld 1998) analyze late-twentieth-century global trends and explain in detail the origins and develop of the economic downtown of the late 1970s, focusing on downward trends in the rate of profit, the slowdown in the rate of growth of labor productivity, the growth in wages, the oil crisis, and the fall in the ratio of output to capital. Based upon rich empirical data, they explain the clear slowdown in the rate of profit, which began in the mid-1960s in the rich countries, wherein this "profits squeeze" fundamentally reflected overaccumulation, viz. over-investment. Labor markets became very tight and money wages rose rapidly. Firms were unable to pass these increases on fully in prices because of international competition (Armstrong et al. 1991, 194). The key argument made here is that the increase in labor's organizational strength, state regulation of labor markets, and the security afforded by the welfare state – all legacies of Keynesian social democratic intervention in the market – resulted in this state of affairs. Bowles and Gintis (1986, 60) describe it as follows:

> The combined effort of the growth of the social wage and the generally low levels of unemployment greatly enhanced labor's bargaining power by taking some of the bite out of the employer's threat of job termination. Labor's new bargaining power could not be easily accommodated, however, for price increases by employers were met with losses in market shares due in part to the burgeoning of international competition, especially in the years since the late 1960s. The profit squeeze was considerably tightened in the 1970s, because in most countries labor was strong enough to resist paying in full the cost of the increasingly adverse international terms of trade and the rising price of oil in particular. The result was a rise in labor's share of the national income in virtually every major capitalist country extending from the early 1950s through the mid-1970s.

Sassoon (1996) also calls our attention to the dramatic slowdown in the rate of growth of labor productivity, which failed to keep up with the rate of growth of wages, also contributing to the squeeze on profits. Sassoon goes on to remind us of the key precondition for social democratic policies oriented towards altering the distribution of income: the production of a sufficient *economic surplus*. Overall, the consequences of this crisis, measured in terms of lost output, inflation, unemployment, and a general loss of confidence amongst investors, convinced policy-makers of the "failure of Keynesianism" and the fruitlessness of governmental manipulation of the macroeconomy, the latter best illustrated in the swings of monetary and fiscal policy undertaken in vain attempts to push the rate of unemployment below its "natural" rate. Given the association between such policies and left-of-center governments, all of this rebounded negatively upon social democratic parties and ushered the political right (and/or the adoption of the neoliberal policy prescription by social democratic parties) into government throughout the rich countries of the world. A largely universal reorientation of public policy followed, emphasizing, as Armstrong et al. (1991, Chapter 17) discuss, key components such as tightening monetary policy to increase interest rates and unemployment, fiscal austerity, the reduction of welfare-oriented state expenditure, privatization, tax cuts, and deregulation, particularly of the labor market. The *result* of this reorientation of policy which was perhaps most consequential was massive increases in unemployment. In an article which has been widely cited for decades, Kalecki (1998 [1943], 351) explains that:

> It is true that profits would be higher under a regime of full employment than they are on the average under *laissez-faire*; and even the rise in wage

rates resulting from the stronger bargaining power of the workers is less likely to reduce profits than to increase prices, and thus adversely affects only the rentier interests. But "discipline in the factories" and "political stability" are more appreciated than profits by business leaders.

The democratic advances made by social democracy – the increased weight afforded to the policy preferences of the unpropertied – were placed on the road to ruin under conditions of mass, sustained unemployment and the consequent loss of union and social democratic power. The *political* victory of neoliberalism, riding the wave of neoliberal supremacy in the realm of *ideas* had been achieved across Europe, even in social-democratic strongholds such as Sweden. As Keynes (quoted in Glyn 2001, 4) expressed it, "the task of keeping efficiency wages [wages per unit of output] reasonably stable . . . is a political rather than an economic problem."

Since the 1990s in particular, neoliberal ideas and policies have been incorporated into European social democratic parties to such a degree that on many of the policy dimensions discussed above, there is no significant disagreement with moderate right-of-center parties (Cronin et al. 2011). This chapter's scope does not discuss the peculiarities of the post-2008 era, but it is important to mention that notwithstanding the outpouring of scholarly analyses (Cassidy 2009; Blyth 2013; Krugman 2012; Quiggin 2012; Schlefer 2012) of the "great recession" and how it has "discredited" neoliberal theories and policies, no meaningful alteration in social democratic policy agendas has been initiated, despite the very significant electoral success of the Syriza party in Greece, the electoral emergence of the Podemos party in Spain, the emergence of Jeremy Corbyn as leader of the British Labour Party, and the meaningful challenge posed to Hillary Clinton by Bernie Sanders in the 2016 U.S. Democratic Party presidential primary election. The resurrection of Keynes has not happened. In sum, within the policy realms which involve state intervention into the private realm of productive resource ownership and use – viz., state intervention in the allocation of resources and the distribution of incomes – social democracy as a meaningfully distinct, left political program, has in many important respects ceased to exist since the early 1990s.

Conclusion

It is telling that Przeworski (2001, 320–322) calls the post-1970s period of European social democracy the era of "resignation." This chapter has focused upon the war of ideas, visions, and theories in which – for decades now – (neo)liberalism has won a series of battles over social democracy. The preferences of actors associated with capital have remained prioritized, and democracy, wherein the preferences of all collectivities of citizens – propertied as well as unpropertied – are to be equally weighed by governments, has been degraded. Neomarxist challenges to social democracy, which emphasize the structural constraints placed upon all governments by capital, remain relevant and pinpoint the source of the inherent limits to the advancement of democracy under capitalism.

Further reading

Amable, Bruno. 2011. "Morals and Politics in the Ideology of Neo-Liberalism." *Socio-Economic Review* 9: 3–30.

Dahl, Robert. 1971. *Polyarchy: Participation and Opposition*. New Haven: Yale University Press. Chapter 1: "Democratization and Public Opposition".

Friedman, Milton. 1962. *Capitalism and Freedom*. Chicago: University of Chicago Press. Chapter 2: "The Role of Government in a Free Society".

Lindblom, Charles. 1977. *Politics and Markets: The World's Political-Economic Systems*. New York: Basic Books. Chapter 13: "The Privileged Position of Business".

Key questions for discussion

1   How does capitalism have consequences for the likelihood that Robert Dahl's criteria for a democracy can be satisfied?
2   How does John Maynard Keynes' theoretical model of the economy "fit" well with the politics of social democracy?
3   What are the key manners in which neoliberalism is consistent with classical liberalism and to what degree is the former a revision of the latter?

References

Abel, Andrew B., and Ben S. Bernanke. 2007. *Macroeconomics*. 6th ed. New Jersey: Pearson Prentice Hall. Chapter 8: "Business Cycles," 282–300; Chapter 12: "Unemployment and Inflation," 444–70; Chapter 14: "Monetary Policy and the Federal Reserve System," 550–57; Chapter 15: "Government Spending and Its Financing," 573–600.

Amable, Bruno. 2011. "Morals and Politics in the Ideology of Neo-Liberalism." *Socio-Economic Review* 9: 3–30.

Armstrong, Philip, Andrew Glyn, and John Harrison. 1991. *Capitalism Since 1945*. Oxford: Blackwell.

Berman, Sheri. 2006. *The Primacy of Politics: Social Democracy and the Making Europe's Twentieth Century*. Cambridge: Cambridge University Press.

Bernstein, Eduard. 1993 [1899]. *The Preconditions of Socialism*. Cambridge: Cambridge University Press.

Blaug, Mark. 1996. *Economic Theory in Retrospect*. 5th ed. Cambridge: Cambridge University Press.

Block, Fred. 1977. "The Ruling Class Does Not Rule: Notes on the Marxist Theory of the State." *Socialist Revolution* 33: 7–28.

Blyth, Mark. 2002. *Great Transformations: Economic Ideas and Institutional Change in the Twentieth Century*. Cambridge: Cambridge University Press.

Blyth, Mark. 2013. *Austerity: The History of a Dangerous Idea*. Oxford: Oxford University Press.

Bobbio, Norberto. 1989. *Democracy and Dictatorship: The Nature and Limits of State Power*. Minneapolis, MN: University of Minnesota Press.

Bowles, Samuel, and Herbert Gintis. 1986. *Democracy and Capitalism: Property, Community, and the Contradictions of Modern Social Thought*. New York: Basic Books.

Brenner, Robert. 2006. *The Economics of Global Turbulence*. London. Verso.

Buchanan, James M., and Gordon Tullock. 1962. *The Calculus of Consent*. Ann Arbor: University of Michigan.

Cassidy, John. 2009. *How Markets Fail: The Logic of Economic Calamities*. London: Penguin.

Cohen, Benjamin J. 1996. "Phoenix Rising: The Resurrection of Global Finance." *World Politics* 48 (January): 268–96.

Cohen, Joshua, and Joel Rogers. 1983. *On Democracy: Toward a Transformation of American Society*. New York: Penguin.

Cronin, James, George Ross, and James Schoch, eds. 2011. *What's Left of the Left*. Durham: Duke University Press.

Crouch, Colin. 2011. *The Strange Non-Death of Neoliberalism*. Cambridge: Polity.

Dahl, Robert. 1971. *Polyarchy: Participation and Opposition*. New Haven: Yale University Press.

Davidson, Paul. 2009. *The Keynes Solution: The Path to Global Economic Prosperity*. Basingstoke: Palgrave Macmillan.

De Grauwe, Paul. 2007. *Economics of Monetary Union*. 7th ed. Oxford: Oxford University Press.

Esping-Andersen, Gøsta. 1985. *Politics Against Markets: The Social Democratic Road to Power*. Princeton: Princeton University Press.

Esping-Andersen, Gøsta. 1990. *The Three Worlds of Welfare Capitalism*. Princeton: Princeton University Press.

Frieden, Jeffrey A. 2006. *Global Capitalism: Its Fall and Rise in the Twentieth Century*. New York: Norton.

Friedman, Milton. 1962. *Capitalism and Freedom*. Chicago: University of Chicago Press. Chapter 2: "The Role of Government in a Free Society".

Friedman, Milton. 1968. "The Role of Monetary Policy." *American Economic Review* 58 (1): 1–17.

Glyn, Andrew. 2001. "Aspirations, Constraints, and Outcomes." In *Social Democracy in Neoliberal Times*, ed. Andrew Glyn. Oxford: Oxford University Press, 1–20.

Glyn, Andrew. 2007. *Capitalism Unleashed: Finance, Globalization, and Welfare*. Oxford: Oxford University Press.

Harvey, David. 2005. *A Brief History of Neoliberalism*. Oxford: Oxford University Press.

Hayek, Friedrich A. 1972 [1944]. *The Road to Serfdom*. Chicago: University of Chicago Press.

Hayek, Friedrich A. 1980 [1943]. *Individualism and Economic Order*. Chicago: University of Chicago Press.

Iversen, Torben. 2001. "The Choices for Scandinavian Social Democracy in Comparative Perspective." In *Social Democracy in Neoliberal Times*, ed. Andrew Glyn. Oxford: Oxford University Press, 253–275.

Kalecki, Michał. 1998 [1943]. "Political Aspects of Full Employment." In *Collected Works of Michal Kalecki, Volume 1, Capitalism: Business Cycles and Full Employment*, ed. Jerzy Osiatyński. Oxford: Clarendon Press, 347–56.

Keech, William R. 1996. *Economic Politics*. Cambridge: Cambridge University Press.

Kitschelt, Herbert. 1999. "European Social Democracy between Political Economy and Electoral Competition." In *Continuity and Change in Contemporary Capitalism*, ed. Herbert Kitschelt et al., Cambridge: Cambridge University Press, 317–345.

Knoop, Todd A. 2008. *Modern Financial Macroeconomics: Panics, Crashes, and Crises*. Oxford: Blackwell.

Korpi, Walter. 1978. *The Working Class in Welfare Capitalism*. London: Routledge.

Krugman, Paul. 2012. *End this Depression Now!* New York: W.W. Norton.

Lindblom, Charles. 1977. *Politics and Markets: The World's Political-Economic Systems*. New York: Basic Books.

Luxemburg, Rosa. 1970 [1900]. "Reform or Revolution." In *Rosa Luxemburg Speaks*. New York: Pathfinder Press, 33–90.

Moene, Karl Ove, and Michael Wallerstein. 1993. "The Decline of Social Democracy." In *The Economic Development of Denmark and Norway since 1870*, ed. Karl Gunnar Persson. Brookfield, VT: Edward Elgar, 385–403.

Moses, Jonathon. 2000. *Open States in the Global Economy: The Political Economy of Small-State Macroeconomic Management*. Basingstoke: Palgrave Macmillan.

Moses, Jonathon. 2014. "Political Capital: The Shrinking Realm of Autonomous Economic Policy." (unpublished).

Mueller, Dennis C. 2003. *Public Choice III*. Cambridge: Cambridge University Press.

Munck, Gerardo L. 2001. "The Regime Question: Theory Building in Democracy Studies." *World Politics* 54 (1), 119–144.

Nordhaus, Robert. 1974. "The Political Business Cycle." *Review of Economic Studies* 42: 169–90.

Nozick, Robert. 2001 [1974]. *Anarchy, State, and Utopia*. Malden, MA: Wiley-Blackwell.

Obstfeld, Maurice. 1998. "The Global Capital Market: Benefactor or Menace?" *Journal of Economic Perspectives* 12 (4): 9–30.

Poggi, Giovanni. 1978. *The Development of the Modern State: A Sociological Analysis*. Stanford: Stanford University Press.

Polanyi, Karl. 1944. *The Great Transformation: The Political and Economic Origins of Our Times*. Boston: Beacon Press.

Przeworski, Adam. 1985. *Capitalism and Social Democracy*. Cambridge: Cambridge University Press.

Przeworski, Adam. 1990. *The State and the Economy Under Capitalism*. London: Harwood Academic Publishers.

Przeworski, Adam. 2001. "How Many Ways Can be Third?" In *Social Democracy in Neoliberal Times: The Left and Economic Policy Since 1980*, ed. Andrew Glyn. Oxford: Oxford University Press.

Przeworski, Adam. 2010. *Democracy and the Limits of Self-Government*. Cambridge: Cambridge University Press, 312–333.

Przeworski, Adam, and Michael Wallerstein. 1988. "Structural Dependence of the State on Capital." *American Political Science Review* 82: 11–29.

Przeworski, Adam, Michael E. Alvarez, José Antonio Cheibub and Fernando Limongi. 2000. *Democracy and Development: Political Institutions and Well-Being in the World, 1950–1990*. Cambridge: Cambridge University Press.

Quiggin, John. 2012. *Zombie Economics: How Dead Ideas Still Walk Amongst Us*. Princeton: Princeton University Press.

Rodrik, Dani. 2011. *The Globalization Paradox: Why Global Markets, States, and Democracy Can't Coexist*. Oxford: Oxford University Press.

Sassoon, Donald. 1996. *One Hundred Years of Socialism*. New York: The New Press.

Schlefer, Jonathan. 2012. *The Assumptions Economists Make*. Cambridge, MA: Harvard University Press.

Schmidt, Vivian A., and Mark Thatcher. 2013. "Theorizing Ideational Continuity: The Resilience of Neo-Liberal Ideas in Europe." In *Resilient Liberalism in Europe's Political Economy*, ed. Vivian A. Schmidt and Mark Thatcher. Cambridge: Cambridge University Press, 1–50.

Schumpeter, Joseph A. 1942. *Capitalism, Socialism and Democracy*. New York: Harper & Row.

Simmons, Beth A. 1999. "The Internationalization of Capital." In *Continuity and Change in Contemporary Capitalism*, ed. Herbert Kitschelt, Peter Lange, Gary Marks and John D. Stephens. Cambridge: Cambridge University Press, 36–69.

Snowdon, Brian, and Howard R. Vane. 2005. *Modern Macroeconomics: Its Origins, Development and Current State*. Cheltenham, UK: Edward Elgar. Chapter 10: "The New Political Macroeconomics".

Streeck, Wolfgang. 2014. "How Will Capitalism End?" *New Left Review* 87: 35–64.

Sweezy, Paul M. 1987 [1982]. "Listen, Keynesians!" In *Stagnation and the Financial Explosion*, ed. Harry Magdoff and Paul M. Sweezy. New York: Monthly Review Press, 39–49.

Tilton, Timothy A. 1979. "A Swedish Road to Socialism: Ernst Wigforss and the Ideological Foundations of Swedish Social Democracy." *American Political Science Review* 73 (2): 505–20.

Vertiainen, Juhana. 2001. "Understanding Swedish Social Democracy: Victims of Success?" In *Social Democracy in Neoliberal Times: The Left and Economic Policy Since 1980*, ed. Andrew Glyn. New York: Oxford University Press, 31–52.

Wolin, Sheldon S. 2004. *Politics and Vision: Continuity and Innovation in Western Political Thought*, 2nd ed. Princeton: Princeton University Press.

7

THE SUSTAINABILITY OF EUROPEAN WELFARE STATES

The significance of changing labour markets

Johannes Andresen Oldervoll and Stein Kuhnle

Introduction: crisis, resilience, sustainability

The modern welfare state is a European invention (Flora 1986), and nowhere else is it more comprehensive – although with substantial internal variations – in terms of both social risk and population coverage. In discussing the viability of advanced welfare states, it is also appropriate to remind ourselves that almost ever since the beginnings of the modern welfare state, which we can reasonably date to Bismarck's social insurance program in the 1880s, it has been claimed that it is in crisis (Alber 1988).[1] It may be instructive to have this perspective in mind when assessing the current 'state of the welfare state' and prospects for its future. The future of the welfare state is not only about economics, but it is also about politics in all its aspects: political participation, inclusion, representation, ideas, political cleavages, political culture, and system of governance.

Pierson (1994) was probably the first author to make an explicit note of the observation that developed welfare states seem to be surprisingly resilient. He referred to the experience of the United Kingdom under Thatcher and the United States under Reagan, and tried to explain why they, despite their election campaign promises and mobilized electoral support, did not have much success rolling back the welfare state. European governments in Scandinavia and on the Continent have been less enthusiastic about propagating retrenchment. It is rarely seen as a vote-winner, and if retrenchment has been considered necessary for the future sustainability of the welfare state, then governments have generally tried to construct broader political compromises for reforms (e.g. for pension systems and health care, which are the heavy posts in the welfare state budgets). Given the apparent resilience of European welfare states, another, less gloomy, perspective on the evolution, consolidation, reconstruction, and future of the welfare state has been conveyed, exemplified by the book *Survival of the European Welfare State* (Kuhnle 2000). In the concluding chapter the editor stated that survival is possible and likely, as well as desirable, not least according to the majority of European voters. European welfare states were assessed to be strong in terms of popular and government support, but it was envisioned that the state's role was likely to become less dominant: "The state is likely to play a relatively less dominant role in the future social Europe given large, economically well-off middle classes which may demand exit options, choice and differentiated services" (Kuhnle 2000: 235).

The challenges pointed to 15 years ago are still present, and – in many European countries – they have been aggravated by the global economic crisis that erupted in 2008. One of the new challenges that has become more apparent after the European Union's enlargement from an EU-15 to EU-28 since 2004 is the unresolved social policy implications of the free movement of labour and citizens within an increasingly diverse union (see Cappelen 2016, this volume) and of the dramatic increase of refugees and asylum seekers from the Middle East and North Africa in the wake of the Arab Spring in 2010. Both challenges illustrate that the future of European societies hinges on European-wide solutions. A pressing question is whether these solutions are forthcoming.

Sustainability is a many-faceted concept in the context of welfare state research, and it may take on a number of meanings depending on analytical vantage points or the policy domains under consideration. In broad terms, 'sustainability of the welfare state' refers to the capacity of European national welfare states to absorb the challenges of demographic change resulting from generally and persistently low fertility rates, the concomitant ageing of populations, of economic viability, of labour market changes, and of political support and legitimacy. Glennerster (2010) suggests that we can distinguish among three main sources of sustainability: (1) *fiscal*, which relates to demography, composition of the population, including migration, and citizens' ability and willingness to pay the taxes needed to maintain the welfare state; (2) *political*, which in our opinion relates to the social division of welfare, expectations towards the state, and political priorities in general where welfare increasingly has to compete with other issues, e.g. climate change, environment, energy, and security; and (3) *moral*, which may be related to the social division of welfare and concerns the willingness or preferences to maintain solidaristic, redistributive institutions and policies. This chapter focuses on a limited aspect of the sustainability challenge. Space does not allow a comprehensive comparison of major social policy areas across time and space. Such overviews would highlight demographic challenges, such as ageing populations combined with low fertility rates, and more-or-less successful pre-emptive reforms in pensions and health. We shall focus on what we consider to be a crucial factor for assessing the future sustainability of the welfare state, namely trends of more or less politically induced changes in the labour market governance in different parts of Europe – in different 'welfare regimes' (Esping-Andersen 1990; Hall and Soskice 2001).

Sustainability fundamentally depends, of course, not only on citizens' preferences for maintaining a substantial public responsibility for welfare, but also on the state of the economy and tax basis, which again is dependent upon demographic trends, international economic fluctuations, and the state and functioning of the labour market. In the conclusion, we shall briefly comment on normative and political implications of labour market changes in European countries and the role of the EU. More specifically, what problems do the different growth regimes within the Eurozone pose, and what are the implications for the future of European welfare states of EU- or EU/International Monetary Fund (IMF)-sanctioned deregulation of employment rights at the national level?

European welfare states in a global perspective

Public social expenditures as a percentage of gross domestic product (GDP) and social expenditures per capita do not tell us the full story of the population coverage, quality, or generosity of welfare schemes. Nor do such statistics inform us about general access to and social distribution of cash benefits and benefits-in-kind. But such statistics represent indicative measures of the size and overall cost of the welfare state, and thus of political priorities. Over-time data indicate the extent of stability of welfare state efforts. European countries, with few exceptions, spend more, in relative and absolute terms, on "welfare" broadly defined, than do the countries of the rest of the world (Organisation for Economic Co-operation and Development [OECD] Social Expenditure Database).

Although welfare state sustainability is often reduced to the subject of tax burdens and international competitiveness, it would be a great mistake to disregard the welfare-enhancing and political and economic-stabilizing effects of highly developed welfare states (e.g. Kvist et al. 2012; Morel et al. 2012), nor welfare states' impact on societies' international competitiveness (Hall and Soskice 2001). Developed welfare states are results of a combination of political mobilization, preferences, will and power, and economic affordability. Welfare states may not only guarantee extensive social rights of citizens, but they may also in general be conducive to political and social stability, trust ('social capital'), economic growth and, not least, access to social security and income protection in times of economic crisis (Kuhnle 2013). While the welfare state appears to be globalizing – as the state takes on a greater welfare role in emerging economies and newly industrializing countries – the current size of most European welfare states in itself is, rightly or wrongly, often considered a major challenge to sustainability in a more open international, global economy. In a context of demographic change, changing labour markets (e.g. atypical work, short-term contracts, rapid turn-over) and family structures (e.g. growth of single-person households and lone parenthood) are developments that imply new social risks and new demands for social protection (Morel et al. 2012).

European welfare states are also, uniquely in the world, confronted with a rather new challenge within a socially and economically unequal Europe 31, wherein citizens can move freely to seek employment, be eligible to social benefits on a non-discriminatory basis, and to portable social security rights, and to live on their pensions in a country other than that of their origin. We shall not deal with this particular challenge, with very uncertain social and political implications, for national welfare states (see Cappelen 2016, this volume).

Sustainable welfare states, employment, and solidarity

Since the publication of Esping-Andersen's (1990) *Three Worlds of Welfare Capitalism*, scholars have tended to think of individual welfare states as representatives of a small number of more general welfare state regimes, models, or families. Often, the central dividing line is drawn between a relatively egalitarian Northern and Continental European capitalism and the inegalitarian, Anglophone capitalism found in the United States and the United Kingdom (cf. Hall and Soskice 2001). Traditionally, the advanced and encompassing welfare states of Continental and Northern Europe have been coupled with densely regulated labour markets governed through a combination of protective labour market policy and legislation, and encompassing collective bargaining arrangements (Iversen and Soskice 2001). On the output side, these institutional configurations have been associated with the effective adjustment of wage increases to prevailing macroeconomic conditions, stable and long-term employment relationships, low rates of poverty, wage compression, and a host of other outputs that have rendered equity and efficiency compatible in the European context (Thelen 2009: 472).

During the *trente glorieuses* of the industrial welfare state, most Western European societies witnessed steady economic growth and full employment. As the industrial era drew to a close, however, Europe's social market economies came under mounting pressures, emanating both from without and within. In the midst of the economic turmoil of the 1970s and '80s, many advanced welfare states experienced weak job creation, high and persistent unemployment, and soaring social expenditures brought on by industrial restructuring and the maturation of welfare state commitments (Pierson 1998; Scharpf 2000). In explaining Europe's disappointing employment performance, many observers pointed to some of the defining features of European welfare capitalism, and especially the panoply of protective welfare and labour market arrangements that are typical of European labour markets (cf. Lindbeck 1994; Siebert 1997). Unemployment benefits, they argued, provide negative work incentives and prolong unemployment spells, while solidaristic wage policies and high minimum wages price low-skilled labour out of the market. Moreover, restrictive employment protection laws reduce firms' willingness to hire workers, particularly in times of economic decline (IMF 2003: 125). In short, the institutions that had lent an egalitarian tenor to European labour markets in the past now resulted in mass labour market exclusion.

According to many observers, advanced welfare states were faced with the challenge of reconciling population ageing and the maturation of welfare state commitments with the post-industrial employment transition (e.g. Pierson 1998; Esping-Andersen 1999). In Iversen and Wren's (1998) formulation, the post-industrial transition confronted political economies with the 'trilemma of the service economy' (see also Scharpf 1997, 2000; Esping-Andersen 1999). In the face of rapidly declining manufacturing employment, European policy-makers struggled to simultaneously attain service-sector employment growth, wage solidarity, and budgetary restraint. In so far as the service sector tends to be characterized by lower productivity gains than manufacturing, employment growth could be pursued by abandoning wage solidarity or by expanding public sector employment (Iversen and Wren 1998). The remaining alternative was to tolerate stagnant or even falling employment. Broadly speaking, the three alternatives corresponded to the paths taken by the Anglophone, Scandinavian, and Continental European market economies, respectively. Over the course of the 1970s and 1980s, the Nordic countries met growing female labour supply through rapid public-sector expansion – thus ensuring large employment gains without sacrificing wage solidarity (Huber and Stephens 2000: 328). By contrast, the response offered by most Continental and Southern European welfare states to surging unemployment was to actively limit the supply of labour. Through a combination of early retirement schemes and eased access to disability pensions, governments sought to remove older and less productive workers from the labour markets (Boeri et al. 2001: 21; Hemerijck and Eichhorst 2010: 6).

Scholars were in broad agreement that advanced welfare states were producing unsustainable labour market outcomes, particularly the Continental and Southern 'male breadwinner' models (cf. Esping-Andersen 1999; Scharpf 2000). As the turn of the millennium drew nearer, however, it was clear that many advanced welfare states appeared to have endured difficult decades with their welfare state arrangements more or less intact. Despite the 'irresistible forces' of population ageing, welfare state maturation, and deindustrialization, welfare states had proven to be durable. In accounting for welfare state persistence in the face of massive challenges, Pierson (1998: 552) emphasized institutional inertia and the difficulty of sustaining broad electoral coalitions in favour of drastic welfare state reform. The erection of welfare programmes tends to produce support coalitions, prepared to mobilize against proposals to remove or alter *their* welfare schemes (Pierson 1994: 29–30). Others looked beyond the electoral arena for sources of institutional resilience. In their seminal formulation, Hall and Soskice (2001) dismissed the notion that protective welfare and labour market arrangements were hampering European competitiveness. These institutions, they argued, are instead at the root of European firms' competitive edge in global markets. European employers, they argued, depend heavily on workers' willingness to invest in firm- and industry-specific skills. Because investments in specific skills raise workers' risk exposure, employees are in need of a safeguard against job loss (e.g. dismissal protection) and/or adequate compensation in the event of unemployment (e.g. unemployment insurance) (Estevez-Abe et al. 2001: 146–147). In so far as social security and protective labour market arrangements fulfil a number of functions that employers cannot easily pursue, and because whole ensembles of institutional solutions are mutually interlocked through institutional complementarities, the institutional frameworks found in European social market economies had proven particularly durable (Mares 2001: 185–187).

Twenty years ago, students of welfare state diversity tended to cast their discussions of the viability of advanced welfare states against the dismal prediction of universal convergence on American levels of welfare provision – a 'race to the bottom' spurred on by the breakdown of the Bretton Woods system of fixed exchange rates, the emancipation of capital from the strictures of capital controls, and the broader unravelling of the 'embedded liberalism' of the post-war era (cf. Iversen and Wren 1998; Pierson 1998; Scharpf 2000; Hall and Soskice 2001; Alvarez 2016, this volume). Within this perspective, welfare state sustainability fundamentally refers to whole regimes' capacity to retain their institutional distinctiveness vis-à-vis Anglophone liberalism. In recent years, scholars have come to recognize that Hall and Soskice (2001) set too high a threshold for meaningful change. Scholars are increasingly arguing that egalitarian capitalism – for a host of reasons – has proven less durable than was suspected. Where Hall and Soskice (2001) sometimes appear to labour under the assumption that the alternative to German political economic governance is American liberalism, more recent scholarship has emphasized how new inequalities can arise within the context of a densely regulated European political economy (cf. Maurin and Postel-Vinay 2005; King and Rueda 2008; Palier and Thelen 2010). Europe, it is argued, has found its very own brand of inegalitarian capitalism – one premised on the unequal distribution of welfare state and labour market protection.

European welfare states between dualization and 'flexicurity'

As previously stated, the previous generation of scholarship on welfare state and production regime diversity tended to set their discussions against the projection of universal convergence on a single, liberal, and inegalitarian model of post-industrial capitalism. Today, the formal organization of European labour markets and welfare states remains as distinct from the United States as ever before. Yet, according to many observers, the traditional distinction between European egalitarianism and the flexible inegalitarianism of Anglophone capitalism is reaching its maturation date (cf. Maurin and Postel-Vinay 2005; King and Rueda 2008; Baccaro and Howell 2011). While European societies are unlikely to embrace American institutional solutions, the densely regulated market economies of Northern and Continental Europe are often found to change in ways that produce new inequalities at the periphery of previously encompassing welfare state and labour market arrangements. This process – and one that has served as a focal point in recent debates on welfare state and labour market change – is frequently referred to as *dualization* (cf. Emmenegger et al. 2012). At present then, the issue of sustainability does not revolve around the capacity of welfare states to weather challenges with their institutional solutions more-or-less intact, but whether and when welfare states are capable of pursuing adjustment pathways that can retain the solidaristic accent of European welfare and labour market arrangements. The question, then, is not so much whether welfare states can survive per se, but whether egalitarian capitalism can.

Against scholars who see European institutions undergoing a functional convergence on liberal institutional arrangements (cf. Baccaro and Howell 2011), other students of welfare state diversity argue that Europe's welfare and labour market regimes are traversing distinct institutional pathways, premised on institutional resources inherited from the past and the coalitional dynamics that they have given rise to (cf. Hall and Thelen 2010). The central contention is that some political economies have institutional legacies that give rise to new inequalities, whereas others are capable of making more radical adaptations of the institutional landscape in pursuit of egalitarian solutions. According to Thelen (2012: 149–150), the containment of dualization is predicated on regimes' capacity to balance the interests of service-sector and manufacturing-sector employers and employees. Where the latter dominates the former, dualization is a likely outcome. In Continental Europe, employer associations continue to be dominated by manufacturing interests, and trade unions have a weak presence in the service sector (Thelen 2012: 152–154). Here, powerful manufacturing interest group coalitions have joined forces with some service-sector employers in pursuing a segmentalist reform pathway bent on easing protection for some groups of workers, while maintaining protective arrangements for core workers (Martin and Thelen 2007: 5). In Scandinavian societies, by contrast, trade unions are heavily feminized and retain a strong foothold in services due to their large, service-oriented welfare states (Martin and Thelen 2007: 5). This, it is argued, has prevented manufacturing firms from externalizing the costs of flexibility to service-sector workers. In the presence of vocal, strongly organized service-sector workers, Scandinavian policy-makers have pursued an integrated approach to post-industrial labour market mobility, the most visible policy result of which is a strong, cross-partisan commitment to a highly enabling, active labour market policy repertoire (Häusermann & Palier 2008; Thelen 2012: 146–147). In a sense, then, Scandinavia's strongly gendered labour markets are said to have staved off the segmentalist reform impulse.

A central contention in this literature is that Continental Europe has exchanged mass labour market exclusion for growing insider-outsider divides within the employed population, whereas Scandinavian societies have drawn upon their institutional heritage and devised something akin to a post-industrial Rehn-Meidner model (cf. Rehn 1987; Häusermann and Palier 2008).[2] As a result, Continental European labour markets are characterized by growing insider-outsider divides, whereas Scandinavian labour markets are not (Thelen 2012). In the upcoming sections, we investigate the proposition that dualization is an adjustment pathway that is unique to Southern and Continental European welfare states, with an emphasis on two central policy domains: job security regulation and unemployment insurance.

Job security and contractual segregation in Europe

Labour law has long been considered a crucial discriminant between the European 'social market economies' and the Anglophone liberal market economies, where the managerial prerogative to dismiss is – by comparison – more-or-less unbridled. In many European societies, open-ended employment contracts are associated with a number of legally enshrined rights, most importantly the protection against unjustified dismissals. Job security regulation has long been said to limit labour market flexibility, but mounting pressures on European labour market regulation have failed to translate into full-blown labour market deregulation. European labour law has not proven completely resistant to change, however. Many countries have undertaken significant job security reforms, but these efforts have largely targeted restrictions on the use of temporary employment contracts – so-called *two-tier* labour market reforms (Emmenegger 2015: 103–105).[3] This strategy is often said to have eased pressures on open-ended employment contracts by providing employers with new means of flexibility by enabling the emergence of employment forms that are not covered by the legal protection afforded to workers on open-ended contracts (Marx 2012: 706). In this sense, recent labour market reforms have opened up a European 'job security gap', ensuring that workers – depending on their form of employment – are facing very different levels of risk exposure (Maurin and Postel-Vinay 2005).

Table 7.1 provides tentative evidence on labour market dualization in Europe – the coincidence of strong legal protection of open-ended contracts and a large segment of workers on temporary contracts, whose access to open-ended contracts is limited (cf. Marx 2012: 706). As can be seen in column one, temporary employment is a pervasive phenomenon, but its incidence varies greatly. Among the Nordic countries, both Norway and Denmark make relatively little use of temporary contracts. In Denmark, this can probably be attributed to its relatively liberal definition of fair dismissal (Emmenegger 2011: 272). In Norway, where employers' access to dismissal is tightly regulated, restrictions on the use of temporary contracts are likely to have played a role (Svalund 2013: 124). In Sweden and Finland, by contrast, temporary employment is widespread. Indeed, judging by the incidence of temporary employment alone, their labour markets appear to be as segmented as those in Germany and France (cf. Maurin and Postel-Vinay 2005; Palier and Thelen 2010), and far more so than in Austria, Belgium, and Luxembourg. Poland and Slovenia aside, temporary employment appears not to be widely used in Eastern Europe.

The incidence of temporary employment provides an imperfect approximation of labour market dualization. Importantly, similar levels of temporary employment may mask large differences in temporary workers' likelihood of landing an open-ended contract. Moreover, the relative unemployment risk associated with temporary employment is likely to vary both across time and space. Bearing in mind that the available data cover the crisis years (2007–2012), Table 7.1 provides measures of relative unemployment risk (third column) and upward contractual mobility for temporary workers (fourth column).

TABLE 7.1 The extent of labour market dualization in 25 European societies

	Share of temporary workers		Relative risk of unemployment	Annual transition to permanent contract
	2000	2014		
Denmark	9,7	8,5	3,6	26
Finland	16,3	15,5	4,5	28,2
Iceland	7,9[a]	13,4	3,3	44,3
Norway	9,5[a]	7,9	3,9	45,4
Sweden	15,8	17,5	6,0	40,4
Austria	8	9,1	3,2	45,3
Belgium	9,1	8,7	6,1	37,4
France	15,2	15,8	5,4	12,3
Germany	12,7	13	5,3	35,6
Luxembourg	5,3	8,2	7,2	36,7
Netherlands	13,7	21,5	3,2	21,2
Greece	13,5	11,7	3,4	19,1
Italy	10,1	13,6	5,0	24,1
Portugal	19,9	21,4	4,0	23,7
Spain	32,2	24	4,3	18,6
Czech Republic	8,1	10,2	3,5	36,2
Estonia	3	3,2	5,0	55,0
Hungary	7,1	10,8	4,0	44,1
Latvia	6,7	3,3	3,1	46,0
Lithuania	4,4	2,8	4,5	47,1
Poland	5,8	28,4	4,6	24,2
Slovakia	4,8	8,9	3,3	47,6
Slovenia	13,7	16,7	5,1	37,7
Ireland	5,9	9,3	3,1	44,1
United Kingdom	7	6,4	4,2	56,0

Source: Eurostat Labour Force Survey for data on incidence of temporary contracts; Eurostat EU–SILC database for data on labour transitions by type of contract (ilc_lvhl32).

Notes: Relative risk of unemployment refers to temporary workers' risk of being unemployed a year on, compared to permanent workers. Annual transition to permanent contracts refers to the share of temporary workers who reported being employed on a permanent basis the following year. Both figures are averaged over the years 2006 to 2013.

[a]Figures on incidence of temporary employment drawn from closest available year (2003).

Unsurprisingly, temporary employment contracts are associated with a much higher risk of unemployment than are open-ended contracts. Some qualifications are in order, however, in so far as the figures do not control for other, perhaps equally or more salient sources of unemployment risk (e.g. age, educational level, occupation, health). It is also important to note that the figures in column three do not reflect workers' likelihood of *experiencing* unemployment over the course of the year, but rather the likelihood of them reporting being unemployed a year on, compared to permanent workers.[4] The table nonetheless indicates that temporary contracts carry a disproportionate unemployment risk, and this appears to hold true across diverse job security regimes. This should not come as a surprise, because the signifying feature of temporary contracts is that they are easily or automatically terminated. This being so, the question is whether temporary workers are able to escape to the relative security of open-ended employment (see Table 7.1, column four).

In France, Portugal, and Spain, temporary workers exhibit very low rates of transition to open-ended contracts. In Portugal and Spain, low rates of transition coincide with particularly high rates of temporary employment. The same holds true in Finland, the Netherlands, and Poland – all countries in which temporary contracts are widely employed and where workers on open-ended contracts enjoy strong job security provisions (Emmenegger 2011: 345). In these countries, contractual segregation appears to be especially pronounced. The Netherlands is particularly interesting in this regard, in so far as it is often portrayed as a paragon of flexicurity (European Commission 2007: 37). Elsewhere in Europe, and particularly in Austria, Norway, the Baltics, and the Anglophone societies, temporary workers enjoy rates of contractual mobility that are considerably higher. Among these countries, however, Austria and Norway are the only ones to combine relatively strong job security legislation for workers on open-ended contracts with relatively high rates of contractual mobility into permanent jobs. Interestingly, Swedish temporary workers report relatively strong upward contractual mobility.

The figures in Table 7.1 largely corroborate the proposition that many Southern and Continental European countries are characterized by a pronounced labour market dualization. It is worth noting, however, that some Continental European societies – Austria, Belgium, and Luxembourg – appear to have steered clear of deep contractual segregation, at least for the time being. A second prevailing wisdom – namely, that the Nordic countries have avoided this adjustment pathway – deserves to be adjusted somewhat. There is little to suggest that these countries have chosen more encompassing adjustment pathways in the field of job security regulation (see also Svalund 2013). Norway, the only Nordic country that does not compensate strict employment protection with a high incidence of temporary employment, has recently relaxed its regulation of temporary employment contracts – 30 years after Sweden took its first regulatory steps towards a two-tier labour market (Emmenegger 2015: 111). Only time will tell if the reform will translate into more pronounced contractual segregation.

If we accept the notion that labour market dualization does not map neatly onto the diversity of European welfare state regimes, it may nonetheless be the case that Nordic dualism is distinct from Continental European dualism, which in turn may be distinguishable from Southern European dualism and so on. This, clearly, is a multi-dimensional question, and one that relates to all facets of workers' employment relationships (e.g. pay, working-time, leave), as well as access to welfare state services. A key question is whether some welfare states are better equipped to deal with the concentration of labour market risks that contractual segregation entails. In other words, do welfare states tend to ameliorate or simply reflect the unequal allocation of risks in post-industrial labour markets? In the upcoming section, we look at income replacement for the unemployed.

Against dualization? Unemployment insurance and social assistance systems

Have European unemployment insurance systems kept pace with the heightened employment volatility implied by the erosion of standard employment relationships? At present, evidence remains patchy, but preliminary findings suggests that the answer is no (Immervoll and Scarpetta 2013: 9).[5] According to a report presented to the European Commission, coverage appears to be falling in most European countries, and the temporarily employed are particularly at risk of being ineligible for benefits receipt (Matsaganis et al. 2014: 22–23). Evidence from France and Germany suggests that an increasing share of unemployed workers fall beyond the reach of the standard unemployment insurance systems (Clegg 2007; Palier and Thelen 2010; Clegg 2011: 40; Seeleib-Kaiser et al. 2012: 164–165). This pattern is found elsewhere as well. In the Nordic countries, available evidence suggests that a significant and growing share of the unemployed fail to qualify for earnings-related unemployment benefits. According to Lorentzen et al. (2014: 49), the coverage of the Norwegian earnings-related unemployment declined from 74 per cent of all unemployed workers in 1989 to 60 per cent in 2010. In Sweden, coverage fell from 66 per cent in 1999 to 49 per cent in 2009. Today about 90 per cent of unemployed Swedes under the age of 25 fail to qualify for earnings-related unemployment benefits (Lorentzen et al. 2014). In Finland, coverage was initially far lower (48 per cent in 1989) and had fallen to 41 per cent by 2008 (Lorentzen et al. 2014). In short, the unemployed are increasingly failing to qualify for unemployment benefits – a change that falls under the radar of studies of welfare state generosity and stratification (cf. Esping-Andersen 1990).

The comparative welfare state literature has paid much attention to unemployment insurance systems and far less to means-tested social assistance systems (but see Clasen and Clegg 2011). Nelson (2013) investigates developments in the adequacy of social assistance transfers – that is, whether social assistance levels are set above the European poverty threshold (60 per cent of median income) – in 28 European societies between 1990 and 2008. The study uncovers significant cross-country variation, but in idealized terms, the Northern welfare states have more generous minimum income provisions than do their Continental counterparts, whose social assistance benefits are in turn more generous than in Southern Europe, and far more generous than in Central and Eastern Europe (Nelson 2013: 396). The most important observation to emerge from this study, however, is that the generosity of social assistance transfers has declined considerably and more-or-less continuously over the last 25 years, regardless of the welfare state regime under consideration (Nelson 2013: 396).

In the past, students of welfare state diversity have tended to focus on two properties of extant unemployment insurance systems: their generosity (the net replacement rate) and their degree of status maintenance (i.e. the distributive accent of the insurance scheme) (cf. Esping-Andersen 1990). These are still important properties of extant regimes, but our guiding intuition is that generosity matters little if the unemployed fail to qualify for receipt. As argued by Clegg (2007: 599), the expansion of atypical forms of employment – and particularly temporary employment – has meant that more workers struggle to attain eligibility for earnings-related unemployment insurance. In so far as workers' labour market biographies continue to diverge from the employment biographies for which unemployment insurance systems were designed, declining coverage can only be prevented through social policy reform that addresses widening welfare gaps. A widespread contention in the broader welfare state literature is that outsider-friendly reform is difficult to enact, in so far as most workers – the insiders – benefit from growing welfare and labour market segmentation (cf. Rueda 2005). The upcoming section investigates the implications of labour market dualization for the political sustainability of central welfare state arrangements.

Labour market dualization and popular welfare state support

By now, there is widespread agreement that recent decades have witnessed a widening schism between workers on relatively secure, open-ended contracts and workers in fixed-term or otherwise insecure forms of employment (cf. Rueda 2005; Palier and Thelen 2010; Emmenegger et al. 2012). In the following section, we investigate whether current theoretical and empirical work in the field of social policy preferences and partisan support would lead us to expect a re-calibration of welfare state provision or an intensification of labour market and welfare state dualization (cf. Rueda 2005).

A number of studies have long since demonstrated that popular welfare state support is strongly influenced by the distribution of risk and income in society (cf. Rehm et al. 2012). The allocation of both risk and income, in turn, are heavily influenced by the design of welfare state and labour market institutions. In so far as labour market and welfare state dualization influences the distribution and the intensity of social risks, these twin processes are liable to exercise an impact on popular welfare state support. A prominent theory – the insider-outsider theory of social policy – holds that European labour forces should be sub-divided into two groups of workers: (1) insiders, who benefit from restrictive dismissal protection rules and generous welfare state provision, and (2) outsiders, who are disproportionately exposed to the risk of unemployment. These two groups, it is argued, hold preferences that are largely irreconcilable (Rueda 2005: 66).

As we have seen, contractual status appears to matter both for workers' exposure to unemployment and their rights vis-à-vis the welfare state. This observation lends some credence to the proposition that these workers derive different levels of protection from extant labour market and welfare state institutions. Rueda (2005: 65) argues that insiders and outsiders differ in their preferred level of dismissal protection. In so far as strict dismissal protection acts as a barrier to entry for the unemployed and an obstacle to upward contractual mobility for temporary workers, outsiders may be expected to prefer the relaxation of job security regulations. Moreover, and as we have seen, temporary workers are disproportionately exposed to unemployment and less likely to be in receipt of earnings-related unemployment benefits. Insiders, by contrast, are both less likely to experience unemployment and more likely to satisfy the criteria for unemployment benefits receipt (Matsaganis et al. 2014: 22–23). In regards to the provision of income security for the unemployed, too, insiders and outsiders are liable to hold divergent preferences. Being adequately insured, insiders should not be expected to support measures to broaden the coverage of extant insurance systems, in so far as this would either lead to increased costs or reduced generosity (Boeri et al. 2001: 41). According to David Rueda (2005: 62), this presents Social Democratic parties with a dilemma, in so far as the pursuit of an encompassing reform agenda runs counter to the interests of their core constituency – the insiders. Fearing insider defection, Social Democrats will prefer to alienate outsiders through the pursuit or maintenance of policies that are clearly insider-biased. Outsiders, then, should be expected to be less supportive than insiders of Social Democratic parties.

Research on the determinants of attitudes toward job security regulation remains scarce, but available evidence does not appear to support Rueda's (2005) insider-outsider argument. Svalund et al. (2016) investigate whether insiders and outsiders differ in their attitudes toward dismissal protection in Finland, Norway, and Sweden. As we have seen (Table 7.1), temporary employment is both more widespread and considerably more durable in Sweden and Finland. For this reason, we would expect attitudinal differences to be more pronounced in these countries than in Norway, where temporary employment is more transitory. The authors find no sign of this – indeed, they find no statistical support for the proposition that temporary workers are more supportive of labour market deregulation than are workers on open-ended contracts (Svalund et al. 2016: 14–15). Similarly, Guillaud and Marx (2014) leverage a French proposal to combine open-ended and temporary employment contracts into a single, more flexible type of employment contract (*contrat travail unique*). They found that temporary workers were no more enthusiastic than workers on open-ended contracts about the proposal (Guillaud and Marx 2014: 1182). This finding is interesting, in so far as French temporary workers have a relatively low propensity to escape into the relative security of open-ended employment (see Table 7.1). Importantly, the authors find that the unemployed and the self-employed were significantly more supportive of the single-employment contract (Guillaud and Marx 2014: 1182). As stated, insider-outsider theory also leads us to expect attitudinal differences between insiders and outsiders in terms of income protection for the unemployed. Indeed, studies *do* tend to find that temporary workers and the unemployed are more supportive of income transfers for the unemployed (Marx and Picot 2013; Guillaud and Marx 2014; Marx 2014). In regards to the question of whether outsider-friendly reform in the domain of unemployment insurance is likely, the studies offer relatively few conclusions. To our minds, they demonstrate that workers who are more exposed to risk are also more keen on insurance, a finding that simply reinforces general conclusions from the literature on the determinants of welfare state support (cf. Rehm et al. 2012).

There is some evidence that temporary workers differ from workers on open-ended contracts in terms of social policy preferences. To what extent do these differences appear to affect the voting behaviour of outsiders as compared to insiders? Emmenegger (2009) finds that temporary and permanent workers do not differ in their support for Social Democratic parties, and against Rueda's (2005: 65) supposition that the unemployed will be particularly critical of Social Democratic parties, he finds that the unemployed are the most reliable supporters of Left parties. In a pooled analysis of cross-national survey data, Marx (2014: 146–149) finds no significant effect of contract type on support for Social Democratic ('old left') parties, but does find that European temporary workers are significantly more likely to support 'new left' parties than are workers on open-ended contracts. Similarly, Marx and Picot (2013: 172) find that German atypical workers are more likely to favour 'new left' parties whose social policy platforms cater to disadvantaged workers, particularly on the issues of minimum pay, temporary contracts, and the accessibility of unemployment benefits and pensions (Marx and Picot 2013: 168). Support for the Social Democratic party appears not to be affected by contractual status, however. Importantly, none of the studies find that workers in non-standard employment are more likely to abstain from voting than are workers on open-ended contracts (Marx and Picot 2013: 175; Marx 2014: 145).

The Euro-crisis: imposed labour market reform and democratic legitimacy

Studies of capitalist and welfare state diversity have tended to focus on institutional differences between the coordinated economies of Northern and Continental Europe, on the one hand, and the liberal political economies of the United Kingdom and the United States, on the other hand (cf. Hall and Soskice 2001). Moreover, students of welfare state and production regimes have tended to pay relatively little attention to the European Union and the ever-closer integration of European societies. With the emergence of the European sovereign debt crisis, the interaction between European-wide institutions and institutional differences between Southern and Northern Europe have been brought squarely into the research agenda. Within the institutionalist literature, scholars tend to reject the notion that the crisis resulted from fiscal profligacy at the periphery of an otherwise responsible core. Instead, prominent observers emphasize the fact that countries entered the monetary union with divergent institutional capacities, particularly in the domain of collective wage setting (Scharpf 2011, 2013; Hancké 2012; Hall 2012).

The European response to this crisis of institutional incompatibility has been to impose austerity and internal devaluation – the process of driving down wages and prices in order to bring the real exchange rate in line with trading partners – upon debtor countries. The severity of these measures has resulted in escalating social misery in a number of debtor countries. In Greece and Spain, unemployment remains in excess of 20 per cent, and in other debtor countries unemployment is sitting at very high levels (OECD 2015: 266). Moreover, draconian austerity measures have resulted in a strong reduction in Southern European welfare states' capacity to absorb social risks at a time of deepening social crises. The broader austerity strategy pursued in European debtor countries aims to enhance fiscal sustainability and external competitiveness through internal devaluation and drastic budget cuts, including cuts in pensions and benefits schemes, wages, and public-sector jobs (Crespy and Menz 2015: 762–763). While the sovereign debt crisis is ostensibly of a fiscal origin, the need to restore competitiveness – most importantly, reining in increases in nominal unit labour costs (Hancké 2012: 93) – has also prompted the Troika (the International Monetary Fund, the European Central Bank, and the European Commission) to demand far-reaching changes in debtor countries' labour markets institutions (Schulten and Müller 2013; Hermann 2014). As we shall see, the creditors have taken an overtly deregulatory approach to resolving the crisis of competitiveness. In part, this renewed attention to labour market and wage-setting institutions has been channelled through EU-level agreements, but the Troika's most significant reform instrument has come in the form of conditionalities imposed on crisis-struck nations in return for 'bailouts', as prescribed in their respective Memoranda of Understanding (MoU) (Barnard 2012: 98). The MoUs represent unprecedented interventions into national social and labour market policy, as well as collective bargaining arrangements. Reflecting the Troika's focus on fiscal consolidation and competitiveness, demands that promote downward wage flexibility – particularly through public-sector wage freezes and cuts, reductions in national minimum wages, and unemployment insurance replacement rates – have been particularly pronounced (Schulten and Müller 2013: 181).

According to many observers, the Southern countries' difficulties stem from their weaker capacity to coordinate wage bargaining across their economies. The uneven distribution of institutional resources resulted in a divergence within the Eurozone, where creditor countries have had the institutional capacity – rather than the moral aptitude – to keep wage increases in line with productivity increases and price growth below the European inflation average, whereas Southern societies have not (cf. Hancké 2012). In so far as the debtor countries' dwindling competitiveness stems in large part from a failure to control wages, it is not surprising that the Troika has targeted wage-setting institutions in their quarterly MoUs (Schulten and Müller 2013: 188–189). Somewhat surprisingly, however, the Troika appears to labour under the assumption that a decentralized wage-setting system would be more successful in keeping debtor countries' real exchange rates in line with trading partners (Scharpf 2013: 13). Instead of seeking to bolster Southern capacity for wage coordination, the Troika appears intent on reducing these countries' capacity for centralized wage agreements. In Greece, Portugal, and Spain, for instance, the Troika demanded the abandonment of the favourability principle, thus permitting employers to deviate unfavourably from the terms set in collective agreements (Hermann 2014: 120). Moreover, the Troika's list of demands has often included measures to reduce the coverage of collective agreements (Schulten and Müller 2013: 198). Needless to say, this amounts to a strong reduction in trade union involvement in the setting of workers' wages and working conditions. It remains unclear, however, what is to be gained from these interventions. While there are good reasons to assume that decentralization will permit higher levels of wage inequality, which may in turn bolster employment (cf. Kahn 2011: 106), there is perhaps less reason to believe that a decentralized wage-bargaining system will be more successful in containing wage growth in the event of economic recovery and growth (cf. Scharpf 2013: 13). By reducing the impact of collective agreements, decentralization should give policy-makers fewer channels to affect future wage developments.

The Troika has also pursued other supply-side reforms in an attempt to render debtor countries' labour markets more flexible. Importantly, the Troika has demanded the relaxation of rules governing the dismissal of workers (Barnard 2012: 111–112; Hermann 2014: 5–6). According to some observers, dismissal protection reform may reduce barriers to entry for the unemployed and lower the threshold into ʼpermanent employment contracts for the temporarily employed (Kahn 2011: 104). Spain, in particular, has long been marked by an extremely high prevalence of very durable temporary contracts (see Table 7.1), so dismissal reform may be justified with reference to the distribution of labour market risks. That being said, the Troika's lists of demands have often included reforms that render temporary contracts more attractive and potentially more durable (Hermann 2014: 5–6). The effect, then, may simply be to reduce the security enjoyed by workers on open-ended contracts, with limited effect on extant labour market divisions.

In the past, the loss of competitiveness now faced by many Southern European societies would have been resolved through a relatively painless external devaluation of the national currency (Hall 2012: 359). By joining the currency union, societies have effectively abandoned this adjustment pathway, and they are now left with painful internal devaluations as the sole lever of adjustment in the face of weakened competitiveness. As argued by Fritz Scharpf (2011), the impossibility of pursuing external devaluation in the face of dwindling competitiveness places democratic institutions under considerable strain. Specifically, the Euro regime presumes that democratically elected, national policy-makers must shoulder the full burden of legitimating externally imposed austerity and internal devaluation (Scharpf 2011). This has proven difficult in practice, and recent events illustrate that Southern European citizens have limited control over policy decisions that have a large impact on their social citizenship rights. As demonstrated by Armingeon et al. (2016: 10–11), austerity has provoked a dramatic increase in political disenchantment in the crisis-struck nations. Northern and Continental European citizens' satisfaction with democratic institutions appears to be far less affected by the crisis. In effect, then, the European debt management is imposing great uncertainty on a large portion of its citizenry in return for uncertain gains and with stark implications for political citizenship in an increasingly divided Europe.

Towards segmented welfare states in a divided Europe?

Millennial scholarship was concerned with the identification of threats to welfare state sustainability and the exploration of why welfare state retrenchment had proven exceedingly difficult to achieve. In the European context, dramatic liberalization – understood as the privatization of social risks – was considered both unlikely and undesirable (Pierson 1998; Hall and Soskice 2001). Recent trends have, to an extent, confirmed these authors' predictions, while revealing a number of blind spots along the way. Perhaps most dramatically, most researchers were unprepared for a situation in which – admittedly large – failures of institution building at the European level would open up the door for sweeping and democratically dubious reforms in a number of European societies (cf. Scharpf 2013).

Elsewhere, changes that have been far less dramatic have received much scholarly attention. In the past, research into welfare state diversity has tended to be informed by a number of antinomies, between regulation, protection, security, and inequality on the one hand, and market, flexibility, insecurity, and inequality on the other hand (cf. Thelen 2012). Increasingly, scholars argue that non-market-based solutions and dense labour market regulation give rise to new inequalities in European – and particularly Southern and Continental European – labour markets. Two-tier labour market reforms have left dismissal protection intact for the majority of workers, while engendering the emergence of a sizable segment of workers whose contracts are not subject to the same – or even some – level of protection (Maurin and Postel-Vinay 2005). As we have seen, labour market changes have also reduced welfare states' capacity to insure against common forms of social risk, not least unemployment.

Disregarding debates as to the impact of temporary work on aggregate employment, it can be argued that many European countries have reached a more viable balance between labour market participation and welfare state provision (cf. Hemerijck and Eichhorst 2009). These changes have come at a price, however.

Scholars have tended to argue that Continental European institutions have given rise to coalitional dynamics that have been conducive to segmentalist or inegalitarian reform strategies (Palier and Thelen 2010). Owing to the encompassing nature of Scandinavian trade unions and the composition of service-sector employment, these societies have pursued more encompassing adjustment pathways (Thelen 2012). As we have seen, however, some Nordic countries are characterized by strong contractual segregation. A pressing question, then, is whether some welfare states have proven more effective in absorbing the heightened concentration of unemployment risk implied by the emergence of temporary employment. This issue is yet to be adequately resolved, not least because scholars have been slow to investigate the actual coverage of extant unemployment insurance systems and their interplay with subsidiary income replacement schemes (but see Clasen and Clegg 2011).

To our minds, today's welfare states appear inadequately equipped to deal with the emergence of post-industrial social risks. At present, those who are most heavily exposed to the risk of unemployment are also most heavily at risk of poverty in the event of unemployment. Unemployment insurance, it would seem, is increasingly taking on the characteristics of an insider privilege as opposed to a social citizenship right. It is possible to envision a recalibration of extant welfare state institutions that would strike a more outsider-friendly balance between accessibility and generosity, but we know relatively little about the potential for encompassing reform. David Rueda (2005) argues that insider–outsider divides narrow the scope for encompassing reform. The fact that crucial components of Rueda's (2005) arguments have been lent little support by recent studies does not leave us much wiser regarding the politics of outsider-friendly reform, however (cf. Marx and Picot 2013; Marx 2014). Given that welfare states and labour markets are producing stronger insider–outsider divides, Rueda's (2005) contention that policy-makers will tend to favour the status quo over outsider-friendly reform is still fairly appealing, but we may not need an insider–outsider model of politics in order to make sense of this phenomenon. In order to close observed welfare gaps between insiders and outsiders, it will almost certainly be necessary to construct broad coalitions in support of encompassing welfare state reform. Only time will tell if, when, and where the conditions for outsider-friendly reform are likely to be met.

The Troika's management of the debt crisis dampens hopes of the European Union leading the charge against labour market dualization and increasing social insecurity. More importantly, however, the European Union – which has a very weak capacity to engender input-oriented democratic legitimacy – appears to be demolishing debtor countries' institutional capacity to engender both input- and output-oriented democratic support. The Euro crisis, then, has long since been shadowed by a crisis of legitimacy and a crisis of political disenchantment, particularly in debtor countries (cf. Armingeon et al. 2016). The consequences of these political developments will almost certainly be felt in upcoming years, and the question is how it will change European societies and the European Union itself.

Further reading

Armingeon, Klaus, Kai Guttmann and David Weisstanner (2016) 'How the Euro divides the union: The effect of economic adjustment on support for democracy in Europe', *Socio-Economic Review* 14(1): 1–26.

Emmenegger, Patrick, Silja Häusermann, Bruno Palier and Martin Seeleib-Kaiser (2012) 'How we grow unequal', in Patrick Emmenegger, Silja Häusermann, Bruno Palier and Martin Seeleib-Kaiser (eds.), *The Age of Dualization: The Changing Face of Inequality in Deindustrializing Societies.* Oxford: Oxford University Press, pp. 3–26.

Scharpf, Fritz (2011) 'Monetary union, fiscal crisis and the preemption of democracy', *MPIfG Discussion Paper No. 11/1.*

Key questions for discussion

1 What does dualization of the labour market mean?
2 Why do Southern European countries appear to experience greater challenges than Northern European countries to welfare state sustainability?
3 What are possible political consequences for the future of European welfare states of EU or EU/IMF-sanctioned deregulation of employment rights at the national level?

Notes

1 The concept of 'welfare state' was, however, hardly in use, and if it was, with a different, less 'positive', connotation than is common in Europe today (Petersen and Petersen 2013).
2 Sweden's Rehn-Meidner approach to industrial policy was premised on the absence of restrictive employment protection legislation, a solidaristic wage policy that served as a taxation of inefficient labour utilization and, finally, generous unemployment benefits coupled with an active manpower approach to unemployment designed to facilitate high geographic and inter-industrial labour mobility (Erixon 2010).
3 For instance, easing or lifting restrictions on permissible grounds for temporary employment; easing or lifting restrictions on maximum number of renewals; easing or lifting restrictions on the duration of temporary employment, and so on.
4 The figures will also reflect unemployed workers' propensity to escape from unemployment.
5 Although widely used datasets on unemployment insurance systems include information on the share of the employed population covered by unemployment insurance, they do not include information on the share of unemployed workers actually in receipt of earnings-related unemployment benefits. See Lyle Scruggs' Comparative Welfare Entitlements Dataset (www.cwed2.org) and Korpi and Palme's Social Citizenship Indicator Project.

Bibliography

Alber, Jens (1988) 'Is there a crisis of the welfare state? Cross-national evidence from Europe, North America, and Japan', *European Sociological Review* 4(2): 181–207.

Alvarez, Michael E. (2016) 'The Struggle Between Liberalism and Social Democracy', in Y. Peters and M. Tatham (eds.), Democratic Transformations in Europe: Challenges and Opportunities. Abingdon: Routledge, pp. 99–119.

Armingeon, Klaus and Lucio Baccaro (2012) 'Political economy of the sovereign debt crisis: The limits of internal devaluation', *Industrial Law Journal* 41(3): 254–275.

Armingeon, Klaus, Kai Guttmann and David Weisstanner (2016) 'How the Euro divides the union: the effect of economic adjustment on support for democracy in Europe', *Socio-Economic Review* 14(1): 1–26.

Baccaro, Lucio and Chris Howell (2011) 'A common neoliberal trajectory: The transformation of industrial relations in advanced capitalism', *Politics and Society* 39(4): 521–563.

Barnard, Catherine (2012) 'The financial crisis and the Euro Plus Pact, a labour lawyer's perspective', *Industrial Law Journal* 41(1): 98–114.

Boeri, Tito, Axel Boersch-Supan and Guido Tabellini (2001) 'Would you like to shrink the welfare state? The opinions of European citizens', *Economic Policy* 32(4): 7–50.

Cappelen, Cornelius (2016) 'Intra-EU Migration and the Moral Sustainability of the Welfare State', in Y. Peters and M. Tatham (eds.), *Democratic Transformations in Europe: Challenges and Opportunities*. Abingdon: Routledge, pp. 143–162.

Clasen, Jochen and Daniel Clegg (2011) *Regulating the Risk of Unemployment: National Adaptations to Post-Industrial Labour Markets in Europe*. Oxford: Oxford University Press.

Clegg, Daniel (2007) 'Continental drift: On unemployment policy change in bismarckian welfare states', *Social Policy and Administration* 41(6): 597–617.

Clegg, Daniel (2011) 'France – Integration versus Dualisation', in Jochen Clasen and Daniel Clegg (eds.), *Regulating the Risk of Unemployment: National Adapations to Post-Industrial Labour Markets*. Oxford: Oxford University Press, pp. 34–54.

Crespy, Amandine and Georg Menz (2015) 'Commission entrepreneurship and the debasing of Social Europe before and after the crisis', *Journal of Common Market Studies* 53(4): 753–768.

Emmenegger, Patrick (2009) 'Barriers to entry: Insider/outsider politics and the determinants of job security regulations', *Journal of European Social Policy* 19(2): 131–146.

Emmenegger, Patrick (2011) 'Job security regulations in Western democracies: A fuzzy set analysis', *The European Journal of Political Research* 50(3): 336–364.

Emmenegger, Patrick (2015) 'The politics of job security in Western Europe: From drift to layering', *Politics and Society* 43(1): 89–118.

Emmenegger, Patrick, Silja Häusermann, Bruno Palier and Martin Seeleib-Kaiser (2012) *The Age of Dualization: The Changing Face of Inequality in Deindustrializing Societies*. Oxford: Oxford University Press.

Erixon, Lennart (2010) 'The Rehn-Meidner Model in Sweden: Its rise, challenges and survival', *Journal of Economic Issues*, 44 (3): 677–715.

Esping-Andersen, Gøsta (1990) *The Three Worlds of Welfare Capitalism*. Princeton: Princeton University Press.

Esping-Andersen, Gøsta (1999) *Social Foundations of Postindustrial Economies*. Oxford: Oxford University Press.

Estevez-Abe, Margarita, Torben Iversen and David Soskice (2001) 'Social Protection and the Formation of Skills: A Reinterpretation of the Welfare State', in Peter Hall and David Soskice (eds.), *Varieties of Capitalism: The Institutional Foundations of Comparative Advantage*. Oxford: Oxford University Press, pp. 145–183.

European Commission (2007) *Towards Common Principles of Flexicurity: More and Better Jobs through Flexibility and Security*. Luxembourg: Office for Official Publications of the European Communities.

Flora, Peter (ed.) (1986) *Growth to Limits: The Western European Welfare States since the Second World War – Volume I*. Berlin: de Gruyter.

Glennerster, Howard (2010) "The Sustainability of Western Welfare States", Ch. 47 in Francis G. Castles, Stephan Leibfried, Jane Lewis, Herbert Obinger and Christopher Pierson (eds.), *The Oxford Handbook of the Welfare State*. Oxford: Oxford University Press, pp. 689–702.

Guillaud, Elvire and Paul Marx (2014) 'Preferences for employment protection and the insider-outsider divide: Evidence from France', *West European Politics* 37(5): 1177–1185.

Hall, Peter (2012) 'The Economics and Politics of the Euro Crisis', *German Politics* 21(4): 355–371.

Hall, Peter A. and David Soskice (2001) 'Introduction', in Peter Hall and David Soskice (eds.), *Varieties of Capitalism: The Institutional Foundations of Comparative Advantage*. Oxford: Oxford University Press, pp. 1–71.

Hall, Peter A. and Kathleen Thelen (2010) 'Institutional change in varieties of capitalism', *Socio-Economic Review* 7(1): 7–34.

Hancké, Bob (2012) 'The missing link: Labour unions, central banks and monetary integration in Europe', *Transfer* 19(1): 89–101.

Häusermann, Silja and Bruno Palier (2008) 'The politics of employment friendly welfare reform', *Socio-Economic Review* 6(3): 559–586.

Hemerijck, Anton and Werner Eichhorst (2010) 'Whatever happened to the Bismarckian welfare state? From labor shedding to employment-friendly reforms', *IZA Discussion Paper No. 4085*.

Hermann, Christoph (2014) 'Crisis, structural reform and the dismantling of the European Social Model(s)', *Economic and Industrial Democracy*, 35 (1): 1–18.

Huber, Evelyn and John Stephens (2000) 'Partisan governance, women's employment and the Social Democratic service state', *American Sociological Review* 65(3): 323–342.

Immervoll, Hedwig and Stefano Scarpetta (2013) 'Activation and employment policies in the OECD countries', *IZA Journal of Labor Policy* 1(9): 1–20.

International Monetary Fund (2003) 'Unemployment and labor market institutions: Why reforms pay off', in *World Economic Outlook*. Washington, DC: International Monetary Fund, pp. 129–150.

Iversen, Torben and David Soskice (2001) 'An asset theory of social policy preferences', *American Political Science Review* 95(4): 875–893.

Iversen, Torben and Anne Wren (1998) 'Equality, employment and budgetary restraint: The trilemma of the service economy', *World Politics* 50(4): 507–546.

Kahn, Lawrence M. (2010) 'Employment protection reforms, employment and the incidence of temporary jobs in Europe: 1996–2001', *Labor Economics* 17(1): 1–15.

Kahn, Lawrence M. (2011) 'Labor market policy: A comparative view on the costs and benefits of market flexibility', *Journal of Policy Analysis and Management* 31(1): 94–110.

King, Desmond and David Rueda (2008) 'Cheap labour: The new politics of "bread and roses" in industrial democracies', *Perspectives on Politics* 6(2): 279–297.

Kuhnle, Stein (2013) "The Global Economic Crisis and Implications for Social and Employment Policy in the EU", in Richard Youngs (ed.), *A New Context for EU-Korean Relations*. Madrid, Spain: Fride, pp. 41–50.

Kuhnle, Stein (ed.) (2000) *Survival of the European Welfare State*. London: Routledge.

Kvist, Jon, Johan Fritzell, Bjorn Hvinden and Olli Kangas (2012) *Changing Social Equality: The Nordic Model in the 21st Century*. Bristol: The Policy Press.

Lindbeck, Assar (1994) 'The welfare state and the employment problem', *The American Economic Review* 84(2): 71–75.

Lorentzen, Thomas, Anna Angelin, Espen Dahl, Timo Kauppinen, Pasi Moisio and Tapio Salonen (2014) 'Unemployment and economic security for young adults in Finland, Norway and Sweden: From unemployment protection to poverty relief', *International Journal of Social Welfare* 23(1): 41–51.

Mares, Isabella (2001) 'Firms and the Welfare State: When, Why and How Does Social Policy Matter to Employers?', in Peter Hall and David Soskice (eds.), *Varieties of Capitalism: The Institutional Foundations of Comparative Advantage*. Oxford: Oxford University Press, pp. 184–213.

Martin, Cathie Jo and Kathleen Thelen (2007) 'The state and coordinated capitalism: Contributions of the public sector to social solidarity in postindustrial societies', *World Politics* 60(1): 1–36.

Marx, Paul (2012) 'Labour market dualization in France', *European Societies* 14(5): 704–726.

Marx, Paul (2014) 'Labor market risks and political preferences: The case of temporary employment', *European Journal of Political Research* 53: 136–159.

Marx, Paul and Georg Picot (2013) 'The party preferences of atypical workers in Germany', *Journal of European Social Policy* 23(2): 164–178.

Matsaganis, Manos, Erhan Ozdemir and Terry Ward (2014) 'The coverage of social benefits', *European Commission – Employment, Social Affairs and Inclusion Research Note 9/13*, 1–39.

Maurin, Eric and Fabien Postel-Vinay (2005) 'The European job security gap', *Work and Occupations* 32(2): 229–252.

Morel, Natalie, Bruno Palier and Joakim Palme (eds.) (2012) *Towards a Social Investment State?* Chicago: University of Chicago Press.

Nelson, Kenneth (2013) 'Social assistance and EU poverty thresholds 1990–2008: Are European welfare systems providing just and fair protection against low income?', *European Sociological Review* 29(2): 386–401.

OECD (2015) *Employment Outlook 2015*. Paris: OECD Publishing.

OECD Social Expenditure Database (SOCX). http://www.oecd.org/social/expenditure.htm

Palier, Bruno and Kathleen Thelen (2010) 'Institutionalizing dualism: Complementarities and change in France and Germany', *Politics & Society* 38(1): 119–148.

Petersen, Jorn Henrik and Klaus Petersen (2013) 'Confusion and divergence: Origins and meanings of the term "welfare state" in Germany and Britain 1840–1940', *Journal of European Social Policy* 23(1): 37–51.

Pierson, Paul (1994) *Dismantling the Welfare State? Reagan, Thatcher, and the Politics of Retrenchment.* Cambridge: Cambridge University Press.

Pierson, Paul (1998) 'Irresistible forces, immovable objects: Post-industrial welfare states confront permanent austerity', *Journal of European Public Policy* 5(4): 539–560.

Rehm, Phillip, Jacob Hacker and Mark Schlessinger (2012) 'Insecure alliances: Risk, inequality, and support for the welfare state', *American Political Science Review* 106(2): 386–406.

Rehn, Gösta (1987) 'State, economic policy and industrial relations in the 1980s: Problems and trends', *Economic and Industrial Democracy* 8(1): 61–79.

Rueda, David (2005) *Social Democracy Inside Out – Partisanship and Labor Market Policy in Advanced Industrialized Democracies.* Oxford: Oxford University Press.

Scharpf, Fritz (1997) 'Employment and the welfare state: A continental dilemma', *MPIfG Working Paper No. 97/7.*

Scharpf, Fritz (2000) 'The viability of advanced welfare states in the international economy: Vulnerabilities and options', *Journal of European Public Policy* 7(2): 190–228.

Scharpf, Fritz (2011) 'Monetary union, fiscal crisis and the preemption of democracy', *MPIfG Discussion Paper No. 11/1.*

Scharpf, Fritz (2013) 'Political legitimacy in a non-optimal currency area', *MPIfG Discussion Paper No. 13/15.*

Schulten, Thorsten and Torsten Müller (2013) 'A New European Interventionism? The Impact of the New European Economic Governance on Wages and Collective Bargaining', in David Natali and Bart Vanhercke (eds.), *Social Developments in the European Union 2012.* Brussels: European Trade Union Institute, pp. 181–214.

Seeleib-Kaiser, Martin, Adam Saunders and Marek Naczyk (2012) 'Shifting the Public-Private Mix: A New Dualization of Welfare', in Patrick Emmenegger, Silja Häusermann, Bruno

Palier and Martin Seeleib-Kaiser (eds.), *The Age of Dualization: The Changing Face of Inequality in Deindustrializing Societies*. Oxford: Oxford University Press, pp. 151–175.

Siebert, Horst (1997) 'Labor market rigidities: At the root of unemployment in Europe', *Journal of Economic Perspectives* 11(3): 37–54.

Svalund, Jørgen (2013) 'Labor market institutions, mobility and dualization in the Nordic countries', *Nordic Journal of Working Life Studies* 3(1): 123–144.

Svalund, Jørgen, Antti Saloniemi and Patrik Vulkan (2016) 'Attitudes towards job protection legislation: Comparing insiders and outsiders in Finland, Norway and Sweden', *European Journal of Industrial Relations*. Published online before print, January 27, 2016. doi: 10.1177/0959680115626057

Thelen, Kathleen (2009) 'Institutional change in advanced political economies', *British Journal of Industrial Relations* 47(3): 471–498.

Thelen, Kathleen (2012) 'Varieties of capitalism: Trajectories of liberalization and the new politics of social solidarity', *Annual Review of Political Science* 15: 137–159.

8

INTRA-EU MIGRATION AND THE MORAL SUSTAINABILITY OF THE WELFARE STATE

Cornelius Cappelen

Introduction

In May 2004, eight Central and Eastern European countries (A8) joined the European Union together with Cyprus and Malta, followed by Romania and Bulgaria in January 2007 and by Croatia in July 2013. While cheered by many, these enlargements also brought about numerous concerns, many of which were rooted in the income and wealth differentials between the acceding countries and the EU15. This contribution examines the concern that the post-enlargement escalation of intra-EU migration may adversely affect the legitimacy of the national welfare state. It studies the compatibility of unrestricted intra-EU labor migration and the right that intra-EU migrants have to access the receiving country's welfare state on equal terms with the natives.

Intra-EU labor migrants acquire – through EU regulations – access to the same welfare benefits as natives, which amplify an ever-present tension within the EU: that between market liberalization on the one hand – including the free movement of workers – and social protection on the other hand. We have a situation where Community rules and regulations have partly dissolved state borders in social policy and where EU enlargements expand the potential numbers of social policy claimants (Kvist, 2004). Even though social policy *de jure* is a national prerogative, *de facto* it is not since EU states no longer can choose whom to give social rights: the domain of potential welfare beneficiaries is decided by the uncontrollable flux of intra-EU migrants.

This chapter has the following structure. After the introductory remarks, "The tension between redistribution and migration" examines the moral tension between free labor movement and the national welfare state. "The scope of intra-EU labor migration" presents trends on intra-EU migration, followed by a presentation in "The policy of 'equal social rights'" of the rights that intra-EU immigrants have to access the welfare state on equal terms with natives. In the next section, I present some scenarios in which access of immigrants to welfare benefits can be seen as especially problematic. "Intra-EU labor immigrants" highlights some of the unique features of intra-EU migration that I believe can make people more hostile towards it than other types of migration, and ultimately why it can become the most contentious issue that the EU must face in the coming years. "Intra-EU migration and welfare chauvinism" presents new evidences on welfare chauvinism directed towards intra-EU immigrants, followed by various survey evidences on European identity. The chapter concludes with a discussion of the democratic challenges posed by the combination of open borders and equal access to the welfare state.

The tension between redistribution and migration

Arguably the most fundamental aspect of a nation-state is its claim of territorial jurisdiction over the member citizens (Recchi and Favell, 2009). To be a national citizen implies that borders are in place to protect against "others," rinsing out "unwanted elements" – like a water filter strains out impurities. We welcome heartily the "good" people, those that work hard and play spinelessly – by the rules; not welfare scroungers and the bogus. Modern nation-states, it is said, are bound together not so much by a common legal status as by a set of common values – a set of shared beliefs and ideals expressed through ethnicity, religion, language and other commonalities (Anderson, 2013). Many are sceptical towards "outside" elements that can threaten this tranquil structure.

According to Marshall, the welfare state developed alongside the nation-state (Marshall, 1950). In Western Europe, civil rights were established in the eighteenth century, political rights in the nineteenth century, while the twentieth century saw the formation of social (welfare) rights. And according to Marshall, all of these rights developed in the context of welfare states that granted and protected them.

Several authors (e.g. Marshall, 1950; Esping-Andersen 1990) have stressed that the development of welfare policies – such as softening the impact of unemployment, sickness and distress – was fundamental to political and social stability. And the apparent success of the post-war welfare state – in securing social cohesion – was a strong argument in favor of its continuation. However, it is often emphasized that, in particular, social rights by their nature imply boundaries that distinguish members from non-members. Michael Walzer is perhaps the strongest defender of this view. According to him, "distributive justice presupposes a bounded world within which distribution takes place" (Walzer, 1983: 31). Goods to be divided among individuals have social meanings that are specific to particular communities, and only within their boundaries can conflict be resolved and distributive schemes judged either just or unjust. A political community is probably the closest we can come to a world of common meanings – a "collective consciousness" (Walzer, 1983: 28). To reject political communities' right to distribute the goods of membership is to undermine their capacity to preserve their integrity. It is to condemn them to become nothing more than neighborhoods, random associations lacking any legally enforceable admissions policies.

Drawing on Walzer, Freeman argues that:

> The welfare state is a closed system because a community with shared social goods requires for its moral base some aspect of kinship or fellow feeling. The individuals who agree to share according to need have to experience a sense of solidarity that comes from common membership in some human community. But the concept of membership implies the existence of persons who are not members and who are, therefore, excluded from the process of sharing.
>
> *(Freeman, 1986: 52)*

Of course, we know by now that the EU has changed the way we think of modern nation-states (e.g. Tatham, 2016, this volume). EU states have bounded together and voluntarily relinquished large parts of their sovereign control to a set of common supranational institutions – creating a post-national citizenship within a transnational regional political order (Recchi and Favell, 2009). At the heart of this order lies the principle of free movement of people, goods, services and capital. The freedom of movement and residence for persons in the EU is perhaps the cornerstone of Union citizenship.[1] EU citizens are entitled to look for a job in another EU country, work there without needing a work permit, and stay there even after employment has finished.

The scope of intra-EU labor migration: trends

After the Second World War, migration patterns in Europe were primarily characterized by emigration to North America, South America and Australia (Castro-Martín and Cortina, 2015). Gradually, however, Europe became increasingly popular as a destination for labor and post-colonial migrants, mainly driven by the high demand for labor. The first large migratory movements from southern European countries to the more industrialized northwestern European countries began in the 1950s (Castro-Martín and Cortina, 2015). Reasons for these movements were a combination of the tremendous economic expansion, due to reconstruction of the economies of Northern European countries, coupled with serious labor shortages (Dustmann and Frattini, 2011). While former colonial powers like France and the UK drew mainly on their former colonies to satisfy demands for unskilled labor, other countries, like Germany, Austria or the Scandinavian countries, actively recruited workers predominantly from the southern peripheries of Europe (Dustmann and Frattini, 2011). The oil crisis in the early 1970s put an end to the so-called guest worker programs, and labor migration consequently declined sharply.

The next population movement was initiated in the late 1980s by a liberalization of Soviet policy and accelerated by the fall of the Berlin Wall in 1989. Most significant was the movement of Ethnic Germans from Eastern Europe and the former

Soviet Union to Germany. In 1990 alone, more than 397,000 Ethnic Germans came to Germany from Eastern Europe and the former Soviet Union (Dustmann and Frattini, 2011). The collapse of Soviet rule in the early 1990s led to a new wave of migration, targeting not only Northern Europe but also Southern European countries. This wave of migration ebbed towards the end of the 1990s, when the Balkan conflicts ended.

The latest movements in Europe can be characterized as being purely internal, triggered by the expansion of the EU towards the former Easter European countries. For the first time, intra-EU migration rose sharply. It is motivated primarily by large differences in the labor market opportunities and earnings.

In 2013, 17.3 million Europeans lived in a member state other than the one in which they were born, accounting for 3.5 per cent of the total EU population and for 34 per cent of the total migrant population in the EU (Eurostat Statistics Database, 2014). This is a substantial increase from 2003, when the number was 1.3 per cent.[2] If we go back farther in time, the number of Europeans living in another EU country was about 5.5 million in 1990.

Intra-European migrants comprise an important share of the population in many European countries, often accounting for half of all migrants in the country (based on citizenship), and in some countries, such as Luxembourg, Cyprus, Ireland, Malta, Belgium or the Netherlands, they even outnumber non-EU foreign citizens (Eurostat Statistics Database, 2014). The effects of the eastward enlargements of 2004 and 2007 are clearly visible, not only in the overall figures but also when it is considered that the two largest national groups in the EU mobile population were those of Romania and Poland. Thus, the origin and spatial distribution of intra-EU immigrants across Europe is not balanced. In 2013, half of the intra-EU immigrants were from the new member states that joined the EU in 2004 (Eurostat Statistics Database, 2014). The largest numbers of EU citizens that lived in another EU country in 2013 were from Romania (2.3 million), Poland (1.8 million) and Italy (1.1 million). The top five countries of destination were Germany, Spain, the United Kingdom, France and Italy.

It should be stressed that the phenomenon of intra-EU labor mobility is likely to be underestimated since short-term EU mobile citizens are not included in the population statistics and household surveys, which mainly catch long-term residents (more than one year) (Juravle et al., 2013). Furthermore, surveys point to increasing mobility intentions in countries that have been hardest hit by the economic crisis, especially among young people (Eurobarometer 77, 2012). To illustrate, Gallup polls for 2008–2010 indicate that 19 per cent of Greeks aged 15 and older would like to move to another country permanently if they had the opportunity (Karantinos, 2013). A survey published by *Le Figaro* newspaper in April 2013 showed that half of 18–34-year-olds in France wished to live in another country (Gineste, 2013). The Spanish Barometer conducted by the Sociological Research Centre in February 2012 found that 64 per cent of the sample surveyed in Spain considered living abroad a positive experience, with an even higher percentage of young people viewing emigration favorably (Gonzalez and Kirzner, 2013). A recent Eurobarometer poll showed that of all the rights associated with European citizenship, respondents are most familiar with their right to free movement: 88 per cent are aware that a citizen of the EU has the right to reside in any member state of the Union (subject to certain conditions).[3] Furthermore, the reality now is that many intra-EU immigrants choose to stay rather than to return home, and that they have formed networks in their new countries that allow for ease of movement from one country to the other (Friberg, 2012). In other words, there are established migration communities within (many) EU states that facilitate migration for any particular migrant group.

Thus, much evidence indicates that intra-EU immigrants are going to continue to move throughout the Union. In this context, it should be stressed that early on the right to free movement of people was not a general right to all but rather the free movement of *workers*, which was deemed necessary to help build the single market. Over time, however, the concept has grown to include the right of workers to bring their families, to access training and avoid discrimination (Johns, 2014). This freedom to move within the EU to find employment and eventually become a permanent resident of receiving countries has developed in a piecemeal fashion after some initial loosely defined fundamental freedoms (Johns, 2014). Prior to the enlargement in 2004, intra-EU migration was relatively low and stable and also did not provoke much debate.

The policy of "equal social rights"

The organization of welfare in the EU continues to be primarily a national pre-rogative. Throughout the decades of European integration, welfare policies have been one of the few policy areas where national governments have usually resisted integration, not least because of the electoral importance of most social programs, but also due to the compulsory nature of social policies, which enhances loyalty and solidarity within national states (Ferrera, 2005). Thus, the integration of national welfare regimes into a fully fledged "European" model is not likely to happen in the foreseeable future.

However, even though the design of welfare policies continues to be a national prerogative, coordination of the various (national) welfare regimes does happen at the EU level (to ensure that people have social security coverage and do not lose rights when exercising their right to free movement in the EU). Ensuring the right of social security when the right of freedom of movement is exercised has been one of the major concerns for the EU. To achieve this, social security measures – the rules on social security regulation (SCR) – have been adopted, which prevent EU citizens who are working and residing in a member state other than their own from losing some or all of their social security rights (Regulations 883/2004 and 987/2009). The SCR contains three main principles:

1   Intra-EU labor immigrants have the same rights and obligations as the nationals of the country where they work (and are covered). This is known as the principle of equal treatment or non-discrimination, and it implies that intra-EU immigrants have access to the same welfare benefits as natives.

2   When intra-EU immigrants claim a benefit, their previous periods of insurance, work or residence in other European countries are taken into account if necessary.

3   If they are entitled to a cash benefit from one country, they may generally receive it even if they are living in a different country. This is known as the principle of exportability.

The tension alluded to in the introductory remarks now becomes apparent: on the one hand, we have the liberal ideal of free movement of people, but on the other hand, we have the ideal of the *national* welfare state. In the words of Freeman (1986), the welfare state is "inward looking," seeking to take care of its own, and its ability to do so is premised on the assumption that "outsiders" can be kept at distance. But this is no longer possible in a world erased of borders and with supranational regulations requiring outsiders to be granted full access to the welfare state. EU states cannot any longer claim (full) territorial jurisdiction over the citizens that live within their borders, since EU citizens can in any given member state claim equal treatment to that of natives in (close to) every dimension of work and public life. A particular fear is that the protection offered by the "equal rights" regulations goes too far and that member states with the highest level of social protection have to pay disproportionately favorable benefits to people who are covered by them (Cornelissen, 2013).

The economic disparities between old and new member states – combined with the scale of recent enlargements – has created grounds for widespread perceptions, particularly in the EU15, of A8+3 migrants as a threat to their labor markets and their welfare systems.[4] To illustrate, in a recent letter to the Irish Presidency, the UK, Germany, Austria and the Netherlands stated their concern to tackle "abuses" of national welfare systems by the social welfare "tourists."[5] Bemoaning the impact on their social welfare systems, the four governments consider that they should have at their disposal legal tools to prevent and fight this kind of fraud.

Some key challenges: empirical evidence

According to Juravle et al. (2013), there are in particular two scenarios in which the access of immigrants to welfare benefits is especially problematic: (1) the *social security magnet* effect, where migrants move to a country to benefit from its generous social security system; and (2) the *social security overuse* effect, where non-active migrants are/become more intensive users of certain social security benefits compared to the natives with similar socio-demographic characteristics, even if they did not initially arrive in the country in order to do so.

One method for testing the validity of the *welfare magnet* hypothesis is by identifying – through surveys – what motivates (intra-EU) migration. The evidences all point in one direction: the main motivation is to work or to find employment (followed by education and family), and thus is not benefit related

(Bonin et al., 2008; Barrett, 2012). However, and as stressed by Juravle et al. (2013), evidence from surveys where self-declaration is required (such as the Eurobarometer) are unlikely to reveal the true intentions of those who are welfare motivated rather than work motivated. To the extent that people do migrate primarily with the intention of claiming benefits, it is likely that self-reports in surveys underreport it due to social desirability responding.

An alternative method to test the *magnet* effect is to study whether or not intra-EU migrants cluster in countries offering the highest welfare benefits. Boeri and Brücker (2005), as an illustration, argue that when the risk of being unemployed is greater for immigrants than for natives, the incentive to migrate increases with the replacement rate of unemployment insurance compensation. However, there is of yet no strong empirical evidence that this is actually the case (De Giorgi and Pellizzari, 2009; Giulietti et al., 2013). When Europeans migrate, they do not choose as their destination countries that offer the most generous welfare benefits.

To date, there is not much evidence supporting the overuse effect either. According to a study by Barrett and Maître (2011), welfare receipts for EU-born migrants are equal or less to those for natives (controlling for personal characteristics, such as educational attainment and age). Juravle et al. (2013) – in a review of the relevant literature – claim that in those studies that found evidence supporting the "overuse effect" hypothesis, the overall estimated effects are typically small or not statistically significant. In their own empirical examination they found that migrants are less likely to receive disability benefits in most countries studied but more likely to receive unemployment benefits – albeit these differences are statistically significant in only one-third of the countries covered.

Actually, there are reasons to believe that intra-EU immigrants – at least in some countries – are net contributors rather than net receivers. Dustmann and Frattini (2013), focusing on migration to the UK, found that European immigrants who arrived in the UK since 2000 have contributed more than £20bn to UK public finances between 2001 and 2011. Moreover, they have endowed the country with productive human capital that would have cost the UK £6.8bn in spending on education. Over the period from 2001 to 2011, European immigrants from the EU-15 countries contributed 64 per cent more in taxes than they received in benefits. Immigrants from the Central and East European "accession" countries contributed 12 per cent more than they received.[6]

However, it needs to be underlined that welfare states differ. Some are more generous than others, and some are more universal than others. Degree of universality can be especially vital with respect to how natives view the "equal rights" policy. Bonoli (1997) differentiates between Bismarckian and Beveridgean welfare states:

> Bismarckian social policies are based on social insurance; provide earnings related benefits for employees; entitlement is conditional upon a satisfactory contribution record; and financing is mainly based on employer/employee

contributions. In contrast, Beveridgean social policy is characterized by universal provision; entitlement is based on residence and need (or only residence); benefits are typically flat rate and are financed through general taxation.

(Bonoli, 1997: 257)

Clearly, one could expect that in typical Beveridgean welfare states, the immigrants can get full access to the welfare state, often without contributing much because of the universal nature of the various welfare programs. To illustrate, the Norwegian social security system is relatively universal, implying that people with no or only a weak relation to the labor market receive a varied assortment of benefits. For example, the Labor and Welfare Administration in Norway pays child benefits and cash-for-care benefits to children living in other EU countries independent of earnings and contributions, as long as one of their parents work in Norway. With respect to social contribution benefits, these are also relatively universal in Norway because eligibility criteria (i.e. work and contribution requirements) are soft; for example, as long as an EU migrant has worked a minimum of four weeks, she can receive full (and generous) sickness benefits for up to a year, which she can take to another EU country.

Relatedly, the benefit levels in Norway (as in other countries) are connected to the national wage and price level. When fully or relatively universal benefits (conditioned on only a weak relation to the labor market) are exported to low-cost countries, natives can find this unfair (since in purchasing power, the migrants receive comparatively more). Thus, the more universal a welfare system is (as opposed to earnings-based), the more (potentially) contentious is the tension between openness and equal access to welfare, and the more open the system is to potential abuse from immigrants – real or imagined.

Intra-EU labor immigrants: a new type of immigrant

This section highlights some of the unique features of intra-EU migration that I believe can make people more hostile towards it than to other types of migration, and ultimately why it can become the most contentious issue that the EU must face in the coming years.

Prima facie, one would perhaps expect traditional asylum, refugee and family reunification immigration to provoke a higher level of xenophobia or nationalism than labor migration would. First, it has been claimed that people tend to develop positive feelings towards people who share their social categories – e.g. ethnicity, religion, language (the in-group) – and negative feelings towards people who do not (the out-group) (Connor, 1994; Gibson, 2002; Sniderman et al., 2004). Arguably, traditional asylum and family reunification immigrants represent more of an out-group than do intra-EU immigrants, the latter creating (comparatively) less heterogeneity. There might be an "ethnic hierarchy" defined by the degree of resemblance to the in-group (Lubbers et al.,1998). Moreover, it can be argued that intra-EU migrant workers put less pressure on the welfare state (than, for example, asylum immigrants) since many of them remain in the country on a temporary basis, working a lot at the heights of their working careers. As far as the financing of the welfare state is concerned, employment is a blessing, not a burden. Freeman contends for example that:

> [t]emporary migrants are usually male, single, young, and relatively healthy. They arrive as adults, relieving the host country of the costs of raising them from birth to working age. As a whole they have a much higher activity rate and a lowered pendency ratio than the indigenous population. They are much less likely to need or to utilize the various services of the welfare state than are native workers.
>
> *(1986: 58)*

These claims square well with what has been documented about the typical intra-EU labor immigrants earlier in this chapter. Still, and despite the earlier arguments to the contrary, there are reasons to believe that the post-enlargement, intra-EU migration can be more detrimental to (preferences for) social spending than non-Western migration.

Most importantly, perhaps, intra-EU (labor) immigrants possess a form of citizenship immediately upon arrival in the host society (Johns, 2014). They have, as we have seen, rights that are protected and that cannot be violated. This is different from all other types of migration. To illustrate, Ruhs (2013) examined (non-EU) labor migration policies in more than forty countries, as well as policy drivers in major migrant-receiving and migrant-sending states. He found that the design of labor migration policy requires simultaneous policy decisions on (a) how to regulate the number of migrants to be admitted (e.g. through quotas or points-based systems); (b) how to select migrants (e.g. by skill and/or nationality); and (c) what rights to grant migrants after admission (e.g. temporary or permanent residence, access to welfare benefits, and limited or unlimited rights to employment). Ruhs finds that there are tradeoffs in the policies of high-income countries between openness to admitting migrant workers and some of the rights granted to migrants after admission. Insisting on greater equality of rights for migrant workers can come at the price of more restrictive admission policies, especially for lower-skilled workers. In other words, states can deliberately make policy tradeoffs with respect to non-EU immigrants, and thus tailor policies to preferences.

With respect to intra-EU immigrants, EU states cannot make such tradeoffs. Thus, as migrants they have a privileged position resembling that of native-born migrants moving within a country. Actually, intra-EU immigrants are in some areas better protected than within-country immigrants in some countries. To illustrate, rural (labor) immigrants within China overall do not get the same welfare benefits as urban workers, and are as such discriminated against (Huang & Cheng, 2014).

With respect to non-EU migration, negative or xenophobic attitudes towards the out-group can find legislative expression precisely in terms of exclusionary policies or tradeoffs of the type alluded to by Ruhs between the amount of migration, type of migration and degree of social protection. When a state has the authority to make such tradeoffs, xenophobia can be dampened precisely because they can find relief through national legislation. We can call this the "xenophobic relief" mechanism – through which the natives can satisfy discriminatory preferences. When such a relief mechanism is not available, widespread xenophobia is possible. This again can lead to – amongst other – welfare chauvinistic preferences (Cappelen and Peters, 2016), which we shall take a closer look at later.

The detrimental effect that the lack of any "xenophobic" relief mechanism can have on attitudes towards intra-EU immigrants can be enhanced by the rapid change or speed of intra-EU migration since 2004. In arguing this claim, I build on findings by Hopkins (2010), who argues that at least three factors minimize the risk that immigrants pose to the natives' interest: "Immigrants are often unable to vote, and they tend to work in segmented labor markets and live in segregated communities" (2010: 40). Thus, the fact that there are immigrants, either many or few, might not matter too much since they are simply not that visible and lack leverage in the host's political system. The key challenge for theories of racial or ethnic threat, then, is to specify the conditions that lead an out-group to be perceived as threatening. Hopkins argues that in particular two conditions need to be met; there must be an abrupt change in demographic and migration must be politicized: "when communities are undergoing sudden demographic changes at the same time that salient national rhetoric politicizes migration, immigrants can quickly become the targets of local political hostility" (2010: 40). Sudden demographic changes, Hopkins argues, generate uncertainty and attention, and media information about these changes can politicize them in people's minds: "Acting in tandem, local demographics and nationally salient issues can produce anti-immigrant attitudes and outcomes" (2010: 41).

The post-2004 escalation of intra-EU migration satisfies both (necessary) conditions posed by Hopkins. Compared with traditional (and long-standing) asylum and family reunification immigration, the post-enlargement EU migration has been much more abrupt and rapid. Moreover, few phenomena have been as politicized as intra-EU migration during the last decade. Among the many intra-EU migration-related issues that have been politicized, the possibility to export social security benefits has received much attention. Prior to 2004, this issue had neither been politicized nor had it been discussed rigorously in relation to non-Western migration. As underlined, and according to the EU coordination rules, many social security benefits can be exported from one place to another when an EU citizen moves elsewhere in the EU. Since the booming of intra-EU migration, this has been a fear especially in high-income countries, because this export opportunity can make them more attractive than other countries and may therefore generate an influx of migrants who are likely to export benefits outside of the host country (Brochmann and Grødem, 2013).

Intra-EU migration and welfare chauvinism

A large literature has examined the effect that migration has on preferences for (and actual levels of) social spending. In the U.S., migration-induced diversity seems to negatively affect *actual* social spending (James, 1987; Poterba, 1998; Goldin and Katz, 1999; Alesina et al., 2001) as well as preferences for social spending (Gilens, 1995, 1999; Alesina and Glaeser, 2004; Lind, 2007; e.g. Luttmer, 2001; Fullerton and Dixon, 2009).

In Europe, the results are much more mixed than for the U.S. First, there is scant evidence of an association between migration-induced diversity and social *spending* within Europe (e.g. Banting, 2005; Brooks and Manza, 2006). Second, the association between migration and redistribution *preferences* is weak at best (Crepaz, 2006; Finseraas, 2008; Eger, 2009; Mau and Bukhardt, 2009; Senik et al., 2009). However, the association between migration and preferences for social spending in Western Europe may just be different rather than absent. Unease about migration might provoke so-called *welfare chauvinism* rather than whole-sale retrenchment. Welfare chauvinism is the notion that welfare benefits should be restricted to certain groups, usually natives (Andersen and Bjørklund, 1990). A welfare chauvinist does not necessarily want to reduce benefit levels but is instead more concerned about restricting or qualifying immigrants' access to these benefits.

To the best of my knowledge, there has been little research on welfare chauvinism directed towards intra-EU immigrants specifically (Cappelen and Peters, 2016). In what follows I use data generated by the *euandi* (reads: EU and I) to remediate part of this shortcoming.[7] The *euandi* is a transnational Voting Advice Application (VAA) for the 2014 European Parliament Elections. Essentially, VAAs are online applications that compare the policy preferences of users with the position of political parties on the same issues and offer users "voting advice" based on the results of this comparison (Garzia and Marschall, 2014). In order to provide users with information on the extent to which their preferences match the partisan offer, VAA makers have to profoundly engage in party positioning efforts. Different methods have been employed for this purpose so far, largely overlapping with traditional scientific techniques (for a review, see Garzia and Marschall, 2014). The *euandi* used the so-called *iterative* method, consisting of a combination of expert judgement and party self-placement.[8] It encompassed 242 parties across the EU28, and it included 30 statements. Parties were positioned on a five-point Likert scale ranging from "completely disagree" to "completely agree" plus a "no opinion" option. One of the statements read: "It should be harder for EU immigrants working or staying in [your country] to get access to social assistance benefits than it is for [your country's] citizens."

It is possible to give a country's party system an average score on this issue, taking into account the percentage vote the parties received in the 2014 European Parliament Elections. If a party received, for example, 30 per cent of the votes, then its score is weighted 30 per cent. Given this type of weighted average, seven countries have party systems with scores above 3, which indicate that their respective parties at the aggregate strongly are against the "equal social rights" policy. These countries include unsurprisingly the Netherlands, UK, Germany, France and Denmark – all of which have been vocal in the belief that EU immigrants' access to their welfare states should be restricted. More generally, of all the parties coded, around one-third completely agreed with the current policy that it should *not* be harder for EU immigrants to access the receiving country's welfare state. The rest of the parties did not fully agree, ranging from "tend to agree" to "completely disagree." Around one-quarter of all the parties completely disagreed with the equal rights policy.

Thus, welfare chauvinism towards intra-EU immigrants is surprisingly high, and the combination of unrestricted labor migration and equal access to the welfare state is not endorsed by national, political parties in the EU – far from it. In order to realize why, we need to reconsider Freeman's and Walzers' sentiment that the sharing of social goods (e.g. social security) requires for its moral base some aspect of kinship or fellow feeling. The individuals who agree to share have to experience a sense of solidarity that comes from common membership in some human community. It can be questioned whether that feeling is strong enough towards intra-EU immigrants.

As revealed in Figure 8.1, only 26 per cent of Europeans *definitely* feel that they are citizens of the EU (2014 numbers), which is a slight increase from previous years, and 39 per cent feel that they are citizens of the EU to *some extent.*

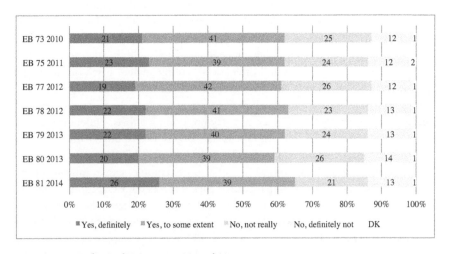

FIGURE 8.1 Feeling of European citizenship

What is striking, however, is that more than one-third of Europeans did not feel that they were EU citizens. This number has been more or less stable since the first time this question was asked (in the Standard Eurobarometer survey in spring 2010).

According to Eurobarometer 77 (2012), a narrow majority of Europeans continue to think that, in terms of shared values, EU member states are close to each other – 49 per cent, while 42 per cent disagree (Eurobarometer 77). Within this majority, 46 per cent say that the member states are "fairly close" and 3 per cent "very close." This sense of closeness has declined somewhat since this question was asked in the Eurobarometer 69 survey of spring 2008 (49 per cent now, compared with 54 per cent then). There are significant differences among the new member states, in which a clear majority of respondents say that the member states are close in terms of values (59 per cent), and the EU15 countries, where they are more measured (47 per cent, against 45 per cent). Overall, it is tempting to conclude that in terms of shared values, EU member states are not overly close to each other.

Furthermore, when the Eurobarometer asked Europeans in 2014 if migration of people from other EU states evokes positive or negative feelings, 41 per cent answered that it invokes negative feelings, while 52 per cent answered that it invokes positive feelings (Figure 8.2). Considering that free mobility within the EU is one of its pillars, 41 per cent negativity is a staggeringly high number. True, the results are even more depressing in the case of immigration from outside the EU: this evokes positive feelings for around one-third of Europeans (35 per cent) and negative feelings for a majority (57 per cent). Still, it is not in the "spirit" of the EU that

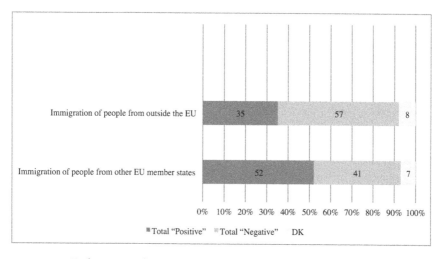

FIGURE 8.2 Feelings toward immigration

41 per cent of Europeans have negative feelings towards people with whom they share (EU) citizenship.

Conclusions

One can question whether the aforementioned feelings of shared values or EU citizenship are strong enough to base a "shared" welfare state on.[9] According to David Miller (1995), national identity is fundamental in sustaining a viable welfare state: "Social justice will always be easier to achieve in states with strong national identities" (1995: 96). National identity creates first of all a sense of sympathy for co-nationals, but also a sense of trust that is the precondition for individuals to act on their sympathy.

It is far from obvious that a European identity has been developed in which individuals residing in Europe consider the EU as identical to their political, social, cultural and economic norms and values (for a deeper exploration of this issue, see Knutsen, 2016, this volume). This can then help explain the high level of welfare chauvinism in Europe. As a matter of empirical observation, there seems to be no (clear) European *demos* – not a people and not a nation. Neither the subjective element (the sense of shared collective identity discussed above) nor objective conditions (such as shared language, religion, history) are sufficiently satisfied for EU countries to unconditionally open their welfare states to other EU citizens – or so it could be argued.

From a democratic perspective, the tension between openness to labor migration and access to welfare rights is unfortunate. The tradeoff between openness and rights is no longer one that is done at the national level, but rather it is dictated from supranational institutions: no such tradeoffs can be done. Taking into account how contentious the tradeoff between openness and access to the welfare state is for many countries, a growing and long-standing discontent with how the EU performs is a possible result.

The quality of democracy can be measured precisely by looking at the output of a political process – the legislation and regulations that emerge from it – and asking ourselves whether the voters get what they want and whether their policy preferences are reflected in the output (Crombez, 2003). The level of welfare chauvinism among political parties in the EU alluded to earlier indicates that this type of democratic deficit is relatively high concerning the "equal rights" policy (Dahl, 1998).

A main feature of the openness/welfare rights tradeoff is that it affects countries differently. To illustrate, some countries are net receivers of intra-EU immigrants, while others are net senders. Furthermore, member states have different labor markets and different welfare policies. In countries with universal policies, one could – as argued – speculate that the "equal rights" policy is much more contentious than in countries where benefits to a larger extent are earnings-based, since migration potentially is more expensive for them (everything else being equal). In other words, the combination of open borders and equal access to the welfare state can be seen as fair from some countries' perspectives but unfair from others'.

At the time of writing, intra-EU migration stimulates outbursts of reactionary, political activity. It has given the political right material with which to appeal to voters and to bash the left. As EU states continue to face economic disorder, we witness a growth of radical right parties, which oppose new migration and reject cultural diversity within a state (e.g. Mudde, 2013; Bjånesøy and Ivarsflaten, 2016, this volume). Historically, most of the frustration is directed towards Muslims and other clearly identifiable minority groups, but after the EU enlargements in 2004, venom or frustration is now also directed towards intra-EU immigrants (Johns, 2014). As argued by Knutsen (in this volume, 2016: 29), the increased electoral appeal of radical right parties may be "taken as a sign that something is not working in the interaction between the national and supranational level".

If the tension between openness and equal access to welfare continues to pose challenges and to spur venom, several policy options are available. One is for universal welfare states to become more earnings-based and/or to make eligibility criteria stricter, so as to decrease the risks – imagined or not – of welfare tourism or other types of abuse, as well as to help lower the fiscal costs of migration. From a democratic perspective, this solution is unfortunate since it would affect natives as well as immigrants (see Oldervoll and Kuhnle, 2016, this volume, on the rise of labor and welfare dualism). It would be an unwanted response to a problem caused by supranational decision making (see also Bay et al., 2013).

A second solution is to work with the EU in restricting either the free flow of labor or the rights that immigrants have to access the welfare state on equal terms with natives. The former seems impossible since the right to free movement of workers is one of the pillars of the single market. It is the right most closely associated with EU citizenship and arguably the EU's most positive achievement. Still, the freedom of movement was a big part of, for example, the British debate in the May 2014 European elections. The United Kingdom Independence Party (UKIP), which is hostile to the EU, came first, winning 24 seats. Previously it had 13 members in the European Parliament.

Agreeing on (some) restrictions on the welfare rights of intra-EU immigrants is not implausible. The problem with this solution, however, is that the equal rights to welfare are in place precisely to make it easier for workers to move within the EU. It would create a dual labor market, with natives in the "primary" sector enjoying a full set of welfare rights and intra-EU immigrants in the "secondary" sector enjoying fewer rights. Arguably, it would decrease the feeling of a shared European identity and citizenship and ultimately weaken the EU. However, as the recent Brixton negotiations have made clear, the EU can be flexible when dealing with the issue of immigrants' access to benefits. The UK (which has recently decided to leave the EU) negotiated a seven-year term for the emergency brake to restrict EU migrants in the UK claiming in-work benefits. Furthermore, the UK negotiated child benefit payments indexed to the cost of living for children living outside the UK for all new arrivals to the UK, extending to all workers from 1 January 2020.

Further reading

Dustmann, C., & Frattini, T. (2013). The Fiscal Effects of Immigration to the UK. *CReAM DP, 22*, 13.
Freeman, G. P. (1986). Migration and the Political Economy of the Welfare State. *Annals of the American Academy of Political and Social Science, 485*, 51–63. doi: 10.2307/1045440

Key questions for discussion

1 Why would we expect immigration to have a negative effect on attitudes towards the welfare state?
2 What are possible politically acceptable solutions to the welfare state challenge posed by intra-EU immigration, and how can we encourage intra-EU labour migration without losing support for social policies?
3 Should labour immigrants have access to the same welfare benefits as natives? Argue your position.

Notes

1 Today, the free movement of persons is mainly governed by Directive 2004/38/EC on the right of EU citizens and their family members to move and reside freely within the territory of the member states.
2 A standard measure of the rate of intra-EU mobility is the cumulative flow of migration from one EU member state to another in a given year, relative to the size of the EU population.
3 Flash Eurobarometer 365, 2013.
4 As a consequence, a policy instrument – transitional arrangements – was adopted that allowed member states to maintain restrictions on the cross-border mobility of labor from the new EU countries. This (potentially) delayed the migrant flow between new and old member states for up to seven years.
5 Letter to Mr. Alan Shatter, Minister for Justice and Equality (Republic of Ireland), President of the European Council for Justice and Home Affairs, May 2013.
6 They performed three types of analysis. First, based on survey information from the UK Labor Force Survey (LFS), they assessed the probability of different immigrant groups receiving benefit payments or tax credits and living in socially provided housing. Second, they considered the total population of immigrants who resided in the UK in each year between 1995 and 2011, distinguishing between immigrants from countries that are not part of the European Economic Area (EEA) and immigrants from EEA countries, and then computed their net fiscal contribution in each of these years (by assigning individuals their share of cost for each item of government expenditure and identifying their contribution to each source of government revenues). Third, they performed the same analysis but for all immigrant cohorts who arrived in the UK since 2000 over the period between 2001 and 2011.
7 The *euandi* VAA was developed by the European University Institute (EUI) in Florence, Italy, in close collaboration with the Berkman Center for Internet and Society at Harvard University and in cooperation with LUISS University in Rome.

8 Expert coding and party self-placement are carried out independently, but the respective results are subsequently compared in order to introduce a control mechanism. All texts that are taken into account by the expert coders are made publicly available, so that each coding choice remains transparent and verifiable at any point. At the same time, the inclusion of parties in the process reduces the bias inherent to expert placing of small and new parties, which are likely to know more about themselves than expert coders usually do. For a detailed analysis of the party positioning used by the *euandi*, see Garzia et al. (2015).

9 See e.g. Scharpf (1999) for an exploration of this issue.

References

Alesina, A., & Glaeser, E. (2004). *Fighting Poverty in the US and Europe: A World of Difference.* Oxford: Oxford University Press.

Alesina, A., Glaeser, E., & Sacerdote, B. (2001). *Why Doesn't the US Have a European-Style Welfare System?* National Bureau of Economic Research Working Paper Series, No. 8524.

Andersen, J. G., & Bjørklund, T. (1990). Structural Changes and New Cleavages: The Progress Parties in Denmark and Norway. *Acta Sociologica, 33*(3), 195–217. doi: 10.1177/000169939003300303

Anderson, B. (2013). *Us and Them? The Dangerous Politics of Immigration Control.* Oxford: Oxford University Press.

Banting, K. G. (2005). The Multicultural Welfare State: International Experience and North American Narratives. *Social Policy & Administration, 39*(2), 98–115. doi: 10.1111/j.1467-9515.2005.00428.x

Barrett, A. (2012). Welfare and Immigration: Migration Policy Centre (MPC) Research Report 2012/07. European University Institute, Robert Schumann Centre for Advanced Studies.

Barrett, A., & Maître, B. (2011). *Immigrant Welfare Receipt across Europe.* IZA Discussion Paper, No. 5515.

Bay, A. H., Finseraas, H., & Pedersen, A. W. (2013). Welfare Dualism in Two Scandinavian Welfare States: Public Opinion and Party Politics. *West European Politics, 36*(1): 199–220.

Bjånesøy, L. L., & Ivarsflaten, E. (2016). Right-Wing Populism. In Y. Peters & M. Tatham (eds.), *Democratic Transformations in Europe: Challenges and Opportunities.* Abingdon: Routledge, pp. 33–50.

Boeri, T., & Brücker, H. (2005). *Migration, Co-Ordination Failures and EU Enlargement (No. 1600).* IZA Discussion Papers.

Bonin, H., Eichhorst, W., Florman, C., Hansen, M. O., Skiöld, L., Stuhler, J. L., . . . & Zimmermann, K. F. (2008). *Report No. 19: Geographic Mobility in the European Union: Optimising its Economic and Social Benefits (No. 19).* Institute for the Study of Labor (IZA).

Bonoli, G. (1997). Classifying Welfare States: A Two-Dimension Approach. *Journal of Social Policy, 26*(3), 351–372.

Brochmann, G., & Grødem, A. S. (2013). Migration and welfare sustainability: The case of Norway. *Europe's Immigration Challenge: Reconciling Work, Welfare and Mobility.*

Brooks, C., & Manza, J. (2006). Why Do Welfare States Persist? *Journal of Politics, 68*(4), 816–827. doi: 10.1111/j.1468-2508.2006.00472.x

Cappelen, C., & Peters, Y. (2016). *Intra-EU Migration and Welfare Chauvinism.* Working Paper, UiB.

Castro-Martín, T., & Cortina, C. (2015). Demographic Issues of Intra-European Migration: Destinations, Family and Settlement. *European Journal of Population, 31*(2), 109–125.

Connor, W. (1994). *Ethnonationalism: The Quest for Understanding.* Princeton, NJ: Princeton University Press.

Cornelissen, Rob – in Guild, E., Carrera Nunez, S., & Eisele, K. (2013). *Social Benefits and Migration: A Contested Relationship and Policy Challenge in the EU.* Brussels: Centre for European Policy Studies, pp. 82–111.

Crepaz, M. M. L. (2006). If You Are My Brother I May Give You a Dime! Public Opinion on Multiculturalism, Trust, and the Welfare State. In K. G. Banting & W. Kymlicka (eds.), *Multiculturalism and the Welfare State: Recognition and Redistribution in Contemporary Democracies.* Oxford: Oxford University Press, pp. 92–117.

Crombez, C. (2003). The Democratic Deficit in the European Union Much Ado about Nothing? *European Union Politics, 4*(1), 101–120.

Dahl, R. A. (1998). *On Democracy.* New Haven: Yale University Press.

De Giorgi, G., & Pellizzari, M. (2009). Welfare migration in Europe. *Labour Economics, 16*(4), 353–363.

Dustmann, C., & Frattini, T. (2011). Immigration: The European Experience. Centro Studi Luca d'Agliano Development Studies Working Paper, No. 326.

Dustmann, C., & Frattini, T. (2013). The fiscal effects of immigration to the UK. *CReAM DP, 22,* 13.

Eger, M. A. (2009). Even in Sweden: The Effect of Immigration on Support for Welfare State Spending. *European Sociological Review,* 26(2): 203–217. doi: 10.1093/esr/jcp017

Esping-Andersen, G. (1990). *The Three Worlds of Welfare Capitalism.* Oxford: Polity Press.

Eurobarometer, S. (2012). 77, Spring 2012. Public Opinion in the European Union (first results).

Eurostat Statistics Database. (2014). http://ec.europa.eu/eurostat/data/database

Ferrera, M. (2005). *The Boundaries of Welfare: European Integration and the New Spatial Politics of Social Protection.* Oxford: Oxford University Press.

Finseraas, H. (2008). Immigration and preferences for redistribution: An empirical analysis of European survey data. *Comparative European Politics,* 6(4), 407–431.

Freeman, G. P. (1986). Migration and the Political Economy of the Welfare State. *Annals of the American Academy of Political and Social Science, 485,* 51–63. doi: 10.2307/1045440

Friberg JH (2012) The 'Guest-Worker Syndrome' Revisited? *Nordic Journal of Migration Research* 2(4): 316–324.

Fullerton, A. S., & Dixon, J. C. (2009). Racialization, Asymmetry, and the Context of Welfare Attitudes in the American States. *Journal of Political and Military Sociology,* 37(1), 95.

Garzia, D., & Marschall, S. (eds.). (2014). *Matching Voters with Parties and Candidates: Voting Advice Applications in a Comparative Perspective.* Colchester: ECPR Press.

Garzia, D., Trechsel, A., & De Sio, L. (2015). Party Placement in Supranational Elections An Introduction to the Euandi 2014 Dataset. Party Politics, 1354068815593456.

Gibson, R. K. (2002). *The Growth of Anti-Immigrant Parties in Western Europe* (Vol. 3). Lewistown, NY: Edwin Mellen Press.

Gilens, M. (1995). Racial Attitudes and Opposition to Welfare. *The Journal of Politics,* 57(4), 994–1014. doi: 10.2307/2960399

Gilens, M. (1999). *Why Americans Hate Welfare: Race, Media, and the Politics of Antipoverty Policy.* Chicago: University of Chicago Press.

Gineste, S. (2013). Geographical labour mobility in the context of the crisis: France. European Employment Observatory

Giulietti, C., Guzi, M., Kahanec, M., & Zimmermann, K. F. (2013). Unemployment Benefits and Immigration: Evidence from the EU. *International Journal of Manpower, 34*(1), 24–38.

Goldin, C., & Katz, L. F. (1999). Human Capital and Social Capital: The Rise of Secondary Schooling in America, 1910–1940. *Journal of Interdisciplinary History, 29*(4), 683–723. doi: 10.1162/002219599551868

Gonzalez-Gago, E., & Kirzner, M. S. (2013). Geographical labour mobility in the context of the crisis: Spain. European Employment Observatory.

Hopkins, D. J. (2010). Politicized Places: Explaining Where and When Immigrants Provoke Local Opposition. *American Political Science Review, 104*(1), 40–60. doi: 10.1017/S0003055409990360

Huang, Y., & Cheng, Z. (2014). Why Are Migrants' Not Participating in Welfare Programs? Evidence from Shanghai, China. *Asian and Pacific Migration Journal, 23*(2), 183–210.

James, E. (1987). The Public/Private Division of Responsibility for Education: An International Comparison. *Economics of Education Review, 6*(1), 1–14. doi: http://dx.doi.org/10.1016/0272-7757(87)90028-8

Johns, M. (2014). *The New Minorities of Europe: Social Cohesion in the European Union.* Lanham, MD: Lexington Books.

Juravle, C., Weber, T., Canetta, E., Fries-Tersch, E., & Kadunc, M. (2013). A Fact Finding Analysis on the Impact on the Member States' Social Security Systems of the Entitlements of Non-Active Intra-EU Migrants to Special Non-Contributory Cash Benefits and Healthcare Granted on the Basis of Residence. Final Report Submitted by ICF GHK in Association with Milieu Ltd. DG Employment, Social Affairs and Inclusion via DG Justice Framework Contract.

Karantinos, D. (2013), Geographical labour mobility in the context of the crisis: Greece. European Employment Observatory.

Knutsen, T. (2016). A Re-Emergence of Nationalism as a Political Force in Europe? In Y. Peters & M. Tatham (eds.), *Democratic Transformations in Europe: Challenges and Opportunities.* Abingdon: Routledge, pp. 13–32.

Kvist, J. (2004). Does EU Enlargement Start a Race to the Bottom? Strategic Interaction among EU Member States in Social Policy. *Journal of European Social Policy, 14*(3), 301–318.

Lind, J. T. (2007). Fractionalization and the Size of Government. *Journal of Public Economics, 91*(1–2), 51–76. doi: http://dx.doi.org/10.1016/j.jpubeco.2006.09.006

Lubbers, M., Scheepers, P., & Wester, F. (1998): Ethnic Minorities in Dutch Newspapers 1990–5. *Patters of Criminalization and Problematization, Gazette, 60*(5), 415–431.

Luttmer, E. F. P. (2001). Group Loyalty and the Taste for Redistribution. *Journal of Political Economy, 109*(3), 500–528. doi: 10.1086/321019

Marshall, T. (1950). *Citizenship and Social Class.* Cambridge: Cambridge University Press.

Mau, S., & Burkhardt, C. (2009). Migration and Welfare State Solidarity in Western Europe. *Journal of European Social Policy, 19*(3), 213–229. doi: 10.1177/0958928709104737

Miller, D. (1995). *On nationality.* Oxford: Oxford University Press.

Mudde, C. (2013). Three Decades of Populist Radical Right Parties in Western Europe: So What? *European Journal of Political Research, 52*(1), 1–19.

Oldervoll, J. A., & Kuhnle, S. (2016). The Sustainability of European Welfare States: The Significance of Changing Labour Markets. In Y. Peters & M. Tatham (eds.), *Democratic Transformations in Europe: Challenges and Opportunities.* Abingdon: Routledge, pp. 120–142.

Poterba, J. M. (1998). Demographic Change, Intergenerational Linkages, and Public Education. *The American Economic Review, 88*(2), 315–320. doi: 10.2307/116940

Recchi, E., & Favell, A. (eds.). (2009). *Pioneers of European Integration: Citizenship and Mobility in the EU.* Cheltenham, UK: Edward Elgar Publishing.

Ruhs, M. (2013). *The Price of Rights: Regulating International Labor Migration.* Princeton: Princeton University Press.

Scharpf, F. W. (1999). *Governing in Europe: Effective and Democratic?* Oxford: Oxford University Press.

Senik, C., Stichnoth, H., & Van der Straeten, K. (2009). Immigration and Natives' Attitudes Towards the Welfare State: Evidence from the European Social Survey. *Social Indicators Research, 91*(3), 345–370. doi: 10.1007/s11205-008-9342-4

Sniderman, P. M., Hagendoorn, L., & Prior, M. (2004). Predisposing Factors and Situational Triggers: Exclusionary Reactions to Immigrant Minorities. *American Political Science Review, 98*(1), 35–49. doi: 10.1017/S000305540400098X

Tatham, M. (2016). Multi-Jurisdictional Politics: State Adaptation and Mixed Visions of Democracy. In Y. Peters & M. Tatham (eds.), *Democratic Transformations in Europe: Challenges and Opportunities.* Abingdon: Routledge, pp. 269–293.

Walzer, Michael. 1983. *Spheres of Justice: A Defense of Pluralism and Equality.* New York: Basic Books.

9

DISPLACING POLITICS

The state of democracy in an age of diffused responsibility

Yvette Peters

Over the course of time, many developments and changes occurred and have altered the contours of the political system. Although the rise of democracy in the world has been cause for optimism (indeed, this is an improvement for basic human welfare, as also Warren emphasizes (2002)), some scholars are nonetheless concerned with the health of contemporary democracies. They have even expressed a more pessimistic outlook on the future of democracy (e.g. Linz, 2000; Mair, 2005; Pharr, Putnam, & Dalton, 2000). Even though threats to democracy worldwide seem to be less imminent (Dahl, 1998; Linz, 2000), it has been argued that democracies are threatened from *within*.

Central to this concern has been the changed attitudes and behavior of citizens in many of the advanced industrial societies. People's confidence in key political institutions has declined (e.g. Pharr & Putnam, 2000); people are increasingly reluctant to participate in the political process as indicated by the decline in voter turnout, party membership, and other mainstream political activity (Dahl, 2000; Dalton & Wattenberg, 2000; Li & Marsh, 2008; Mjelde & Svåsand, 2016); and socio-economic inequality in electoral participation has increased (Armingeon & Schädel, 2015). People seem to have become disaffected and alienated with their democracy (Linde & Dahlberg, 2016). These developments are cause for concern. Both political support and political involvement are necessary in order to sustain a healthy democracy – *specifically*, democracies need the endorsement and the input of their citizens in order to self-sustain (see e.g. Dahl, 2006 [1956]; Dalton, 2004; Norris, 1999; Ostrom, 2000). It is thus argued that democracy is heading towards a crisis; people seem to be taking themselves out of the democratic equation, which is leading to "a notion of democracy that is being steadily stripped of its popular component – a notion of democracy without a demos" (Mair, 2005, 1).

On the other hand, some scholars point to a different trend. They argue that although people seem to be less trustful towards their political leaders and governments and tend to turn out to vote less, they are far from withdrawing themselves from the political process. Due to modernization processes, citizens in advanced industrial societies not only have access to higher levels of education, have a higher income and easier access to information, but they also tend to have changed values and different ways of manifesting those values (discussed in e.g. Dalton, 2005; Inglehart, 1977; Stolle, Hooghe, & Micheletti, 2005). People who are involved in the more recent avenues of participation are often younger and are more concerned with issues pertaining to the environment, inclusion of minorities, self-expression, equality, and human rights (Dalton, Van Sickle, & Weldon, 2009; Norris, Walgrave, & Van Aelst, 2004; Stolle et al., 2005). People seem to be involved in politics, though differently – it might be argued that patterns of participation have changed, but democracy is not necessarily in crisis (see also Peters, 2016 for how these developments may further threaten democracy).

At the level of the political system, too, there have been changes; the political system has undergone several modifications and sometimes bigger shifts. Today's democratic political system looks rather different than it did some decades ago. Democratic governments have attempted to shape up their bureaucracies to be more efficient in providing goods to citizens (e.g. Suleiman, 2003); several countries have introduced or extended elements of direct democracy (e.g. Butler & Ranney, 1994; Scarrow, 2003); and there have been a number of often local-level initiatives with deliberative decision-making (e.g. Fung & Wright, 2003). In part as a response to demands of more democracy (Dalton, Scarrow, & Cain, 2003), governments have tried to improve democracy. Although these changes to the democratic system have been discussed at length, studies often focused on the (theoretical) aspects of one of those developments without connecting them to other aspects related to changes in the political system. Moreover, these studies often neglect to tie in the discussion about the two participatory trends and the related evaluation of the current state of democracy (see also Peters, 2016; Peters, forthcoming).

In this chapter I will try to add to this debate by discussing the health of democracy, considering different perspectives. Moreover, I will try to include in this debate some systemic changes that may have affected the health of democracy. My aim is to take some further steps in the evaluation of the state of democracy today, in light of empirical systemic changes in a range of democracies.

This chapter will proceed as follows. I first describe in what ways many of the European democracies have changed systematically – the selection of these changes has been made according to their common occurrence among many older democracies. This section will merely describe relatively common trends and show how democracy has diffused its political power over the last three decades. Second, I discuss two implicit assumptions of democracy that complement Dahl's five necessary conditions. I continue with a discussion on what the diffusion of responsibilities could mean and what implications they may have for contemporary democracy based on Dahl's necessary conditions outlined in the introduction to this book

(Peters & Tatham, 2016). This discussion focuses on three aspects: citizenship and community; the link between citizen demands and political decisions; and the democratic constitution with the limitations it poses on freedom. I conclude with a general overview of the argument and discuss how some of the changes may encourage the increase of democratic quality.

Changing political systems

Over time democratic states have altered their appearance. The political system has changed – whether this has been the case because of 'big' changes in institutions (such as the change in the electoral system in Italy, Japan and New Zealand; the change in the executive role in Israel; and additions of international institutions such as the European court of Human Rights), or because of more gradual changes. Many of the gradual changes have, however, resulted in real change (Streeck & Thelen, 2005), and those altogether have altered the political system of democracies. Here, I discuss and illustrate some, often gradual, changes within European democracies. Although many of the developments had already started well before the 1990s, I focus on the period after 1990 so as to include all or most European countries for that period.

One such general trend that has occurred is privatization. As part of the broad reform agenda of new public management, many countries aimed at reducing waste and improving efficiency by either selling state enterprises or sourcing out the provision of public goods (for a description and discussion of some of these trends, see Ansell & Gingrich, 2003a; Suleiman, 2003). Historically, there has always been some kind of mix of publically and privately owned enterprises, and the exact composition between those varies among countries and over time (Megginson & Netter, 2001). In the last few decades, however, this balance seems to have tipped more in favor of the private sector, with governments privatizing and outsourcing previously public goods and services such as telecommunications, public transport, and pension and health care. Figure 9.1 illustrates the general decrease of government enterprises and investment or, in fact, an increase of private enterprises and investment, indicating an increase in economic freedom in the world (Gwartney, Lawson, & Hall, 2014). Countries have been given a score between zero and ten, where countries with more government-investment or more state-owned enterprises received lower ratings.[1] Figure 9.1 shows that there is substantial variation among countries in terms of the level of privatization as well as the way that the trend has developed. Especially many of the East European countries (e.g. Bulgaria, Hungary, and Romania) show a rather steep increase in privatization after the break-up of the Soviet Union (although for some countries, data is not available for the beginning of the 1990s). An increase is somewhat less prominent for some of the West European countries, with some countries even showing a slight decline. Considering that they are likely to have started privatizing earlier, they tend to hover in the upper half of the scale throughout, as for example Belgium, Denmark, Portugal and the UK illustrate. The variation aligns with the idea that new public management is a broad

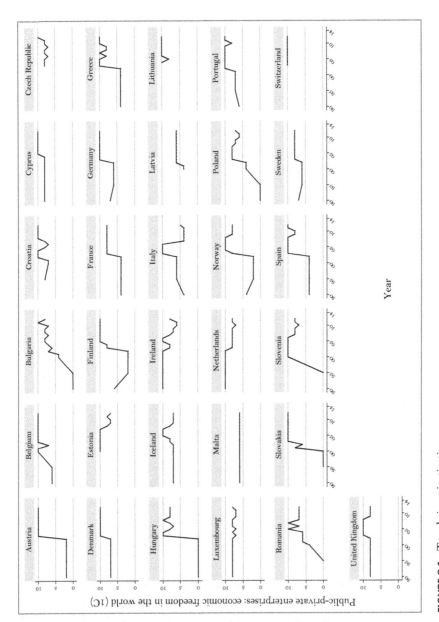

FIGURE 9.1 Trends in privatization

Data source: The Economic Freedom in the World Dataset (see Gwartney et al., 2014)

reform agenda, which has been interpreted and implemented in different ways and at different speeds throughout the world (Hood, 1991; Kettle, 2006). Overall, however, it is clear that many democracies have fewer state-operated enterprises and investments. Indeed, only Estonia, Ireland, and the Netherlands decreased privatization levels, but these countries also started with very high values, and the decrease still leaves them with high levels of privatization. The development of state-operated enterprises supports the notion that democracies have increasingly reallocated tasks concerning the provision of public goods (see also Levi-Faur, 2005).

Second, in an attempt to make policy outcomes better, governments appear to have created an increasing number of non-majoritarian institutions, meaning those institutions that are not directly subject to popular control and have some grant or specialized public authority (Thatcher & Stone Sweet, 2002). It has been argued that the number of this type of institutions has increased and that they can be substantially independent (see e.g Gilardi, 2008; Hanretty & Koop, 2013; Majone, 2001; Thatcher & Stone Sweet, 2002). Focusing on the independence of regulatory agencies, scholars have shown that many (European) countries have delegated authority to such non-majoritarian institutions in areas as diverse as pharmaceuticals, environment, and competition, among others (see e.g. Hanretty & Koop, 2013; Jordana et al., 2011; Majone, 1996). Jordana et al. (2011) have looked at the trend in the number of institutionalized expertise agencies, and they show that more and more countries have created non-majoritarian institutions in various areas. Figure 9.2 reflects their data for Europe – they looked at the existence of regulatory agencies in fifteen fields of policy. This implies that the maximum score a country can receive on the basis of this data is fifteen, and the minimum is zero. The number of regulatory agencies does not in itself indicate the level of independence that these institutions have, but it nonetheless indicates a broad trend of delegation. Figure 9.2 illustrates that the number of these agencies in Europe has increased, and again underlines both the differences and similarities between the West and the East. While the increase in the number is largest for the East European countries (e.g. Czech Republic and Slovakia), West European countries often experienced the change somewhat earlier as they already had a substantial number of regulatory agencies in 1990 (e.g. Germany, France, and Norway). Figure 9.3 further illustrates the difference in the trend of creating regulatory agencies between East and West Europe, by comparing the yearly average of the number of newly created regulatory agencies. It shows that the East accelerated more between 1990 and 2007 than did the West, although Figure 9.2 shows that around 2010 all European countries had a similarly high number of regulatory agencies.

A third development is decentralization (e.g. Ansell & Gingrich, 2003b; Hooghe, Marks, & Schakel, 2010). Decentralization can be thought of as improving the efficiency in the provision of public goods, where a market-like discipline on taxation would motivate people to choose whether they want more public provisions or less taxation. From this perspective, decentralization can also be seen as a measure that fits in the new public management paradigm (Ansell & Gingrich, 2003b). Another argument that is often used in order to move authority or responsibilities to lower

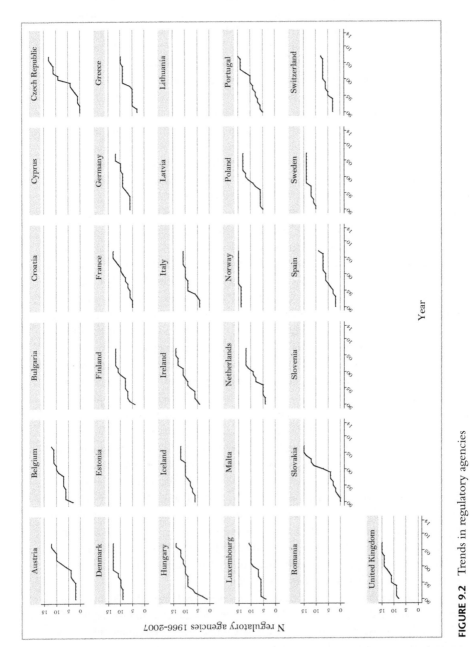

FIGURE 9.2 Trends in regulatory agencies

Data source: Jordana et al. (2011)

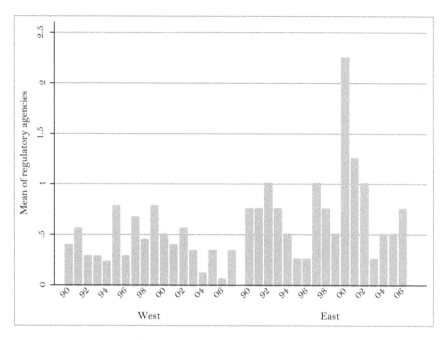

FIGURE 9.3 Average yearly number of newly created regulatory agencies in West and East Europe

Data source: Jordana et al. (2011)

levels of government is that it brings government closer to the people and allows people to participate more directly in politics. People's involvement may be easier when government is in closer reach, and they may find the step to participate smaller if they have a sense of belonging to the community (Ansell & Gingrich, 2003b; Tatham, 2016). This development is further detailed elsewhere in this book (Tatham, 2016).

Furthermore, scholars have observed trends in globalization over the last decades. Globalization has been discussed extensively and has been the subject of numerous studies. It further needs to be noted that this concept has multiple dimensions. Whereas it is often seen as a market-induced process rather than a policy-induced process, states too have a role in the globalization process (e.g. Stevis & Boswell, 2008). Figure 9.4 illustrates patterns of change in such upward delegation of authority – the measure is a combination of political, economic and cultural globalization. It indicates that no country shows an overall decline. It is, in fact, striking that all countries show an increased level of globalization. While there is variation in levels and speed of change, overall globalization as measured at the country level has increased over time, and uniformly so.

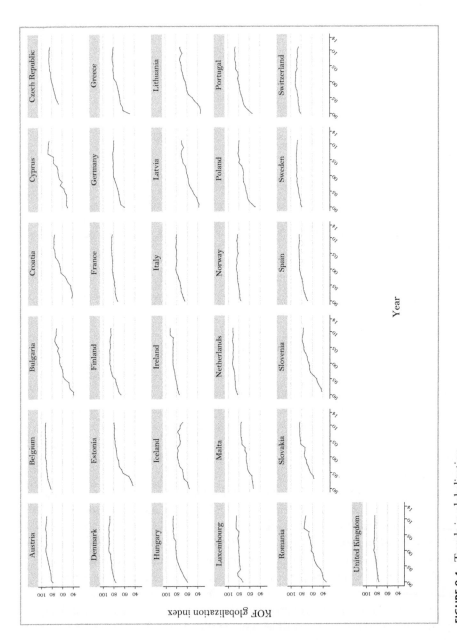

FIGURE 9.4 Trends in globalization

Data source: KOF Globalization index

Lastly, it has been argued that there has been a gradual increase in direct democracy, suggesting a form of 'delegation' to the citizens. The concept of direct democracy has received increasing attention over the years, and it is argued that the usage of national referendums has increased (e.g. Gallagher, 1996).[2] The institutionalization of elements of direct democracy in a comparative way has, however, received somewhat less attention and appears to be less widespread than the previously discussed trends. It needs to be noted that, as Scarrow (2003) showed, many of the institutional changes have taken place at the local level of government. This may fit the logic for reform that is proposed for decentralization as well (the democratic accountability reform agenda, and possibly the neo-liberal one). In addition, there is variation among countries in their national level measures for direct democracy. However, it is also clear that few countries offer all or most types of direct democracy tools to their citizens, with Switzerland being one clear exception. A number of countries still do not offer any possibility to participate directly (e.g. Germany), though many democracies do provide some. Although at a national level we can hardly speak of a general trend towards more direct democracy, including the various instruments that have been used at the local level suggests that elements of direct democracy have been increasingly implemented over the last few decades.

These general patterns of change, although not exhaustive, illustrate that the role of the government concerning *governance* has changed over time. Whereas the government used to be responsible for most or many policy decisions, a number of these responsibilities have now been moved to other areas. Pierre and Peters argue that governance entails four activities[3] and that the role of the government in providing governance could (theoretically) range from being the main or even sole actor to being no actor at all (Pierre & Peters, 2005). Based on the changes in the political system as described above, the role of the government in governance has reduced and seems to be moving *towards* the model of governance where the government is no actor. Figure 9.5 illustrates this changed

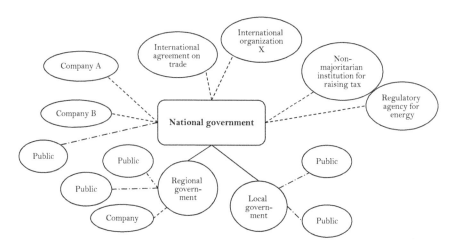

FIGURE 9.5 Displacing politics: the diffusion of political responsibilities

role of the government schematically (see also Peters, forthcoming). Political responsibilities and authority have moved away from the central government to a variety of other actors. Whereas a few decades ago the government had a relatively substantial role in governance, the role of the government in governance is now reduced. This also implies that other actors have gained political power. This can be (as Figure 9.5 reflects) citizens who now have more power to make decisions, but it can also be a company that is now in charge of providing, for example, public transport. So the diffusion of political responsibilities does not 'merely' mean a reduction of responsibilities of the government, but it actually implies an increase and strengthening of the number of political centers in a political system. State authority seems to have been displaced, and command and control is reallocated to different actors.

The notion that governance is now more arranged along multiple centers seems to refer to the notion of polycentricism (but see also McGinnis & Ostrom, 2012; Ostrom, Tiebout, & Warren, 1961). This may be correct to the extent that a number of decision-making centers are more or less independent from each other, but there are some differences as well between the concept and the current situation. For one, it is generally the government that decides to privatize, outsource, or decentralize an issue – for a certain good there may be competition between two or more companies, but here, the government retracts (to some extent) from that good. There does not seem to be so much of an overarching coordination of the complexity of centers, with overlapping jurisdictions and competing communities. Moreover, beyond devolving powers to the local or regional levels of government, in practice there does not seem to be so much focus on differing scales for different public goods, something that was quite important in the theory of polycentrism – different public goods should be dealt with at their appropriate scale, and this does not automatically match the scale of a municipality or region but there could be overlap (see also Hooghe & Marks, 2003). So although the current situation seems to resemble the idea of polycentrism, it may miss some crucial aspects. I will return to this topic in the last section.

The situation of diffused authority also seems to indicate *depoliticization* (Flinders & Buller, 2006) – the idea that politicians try to make elements of governing more indirect, or attempt to convince people that the government cannot be reasonably held responsible for some issues or even policy fields. Reasons for such actions may stem from increased complexity in politics and/or the refusal to be held accountable for certain decisions. Governments now appear to be responsible for a relatively smaller range of issues – they seem to limit their role to 'steering' and have largely delegated the 'rowing' (Levi-Faur, 2005). This notion of an increasingly indirect representative government (steering, not rowing) refers largely to the outsourcing of the provision of public goods to the private and international spheres (and possibly to non-majoritarian institutions), not to lower levels of government or the public per se. Those former shifts seem to pose problems to the democratic states, as is elaborated below.

Democracy and democratic principles

Democracy as a concept has been discussed thoroughly over time, and there are many different perspectives on it. Different people argue for different forms of democracy (e.g. direct or deliberative democracy), and also disagree on whether democracy is actually the most preferred form of organizing society, as Dahl shows in his *Democracy and Its Critics* (1989). Democracy is, however, one form of collective decision-making that ensures at least some minimal level of political equality for the members/citizens of the democratic association/state. Dahl (1989, 1998) formulated five necessary conditions for a democratic process – four to assure political equality and one referring to *who* should be politically equal. These conditions have been discussed in the introductory chapter (Peters & Tatham, 2016). This chapter also underlines that Dahl's concept of democracy is an ideal type which may never be reached empirically in full (and reaching it may not be truly desirable either).

There are, however, some further implicit assumptions in Dahl's concept of democracy. Two of those (discussed in Dahl, 1989) are also central to the evaluation of democracy presented here. The first is the assumption that something like 'a people' actually exists with which to build a democracy. What makes, for example, the citizens of France and Italy distinct, and why should they have separate political units? Why is this autonomy often strongest at the level of the nation-state and not, for example, at the local or regional level? Even with Dahl's criteria for the political unit, this issue concerning the boundaries and legitimacy of a political unit is complex and not straightforward in practice, as the example of Catalonia and Spain clearly shows. So, even this very basic requirement that comes with democracy can cause tensions in practice. Even though this requirement is generally tricky, it seems to have come under pressure even more in the last few decades. As will be discussed below, the described real-world developments seem to challenge citizenship and the justifications for a political community – the nation-state as a political community seems to be eroding to some extent. This is discussed in the "Citizenship" section below.

Second, it is sometimes argued that while democracy focuses on the *process* of decision-making, the output of the process may also be important and should be taken into account. Democracy focuses mostly on the way that decisions are reached, in that political equality is a main requirement. This is the core of democracy exactly, and a shift in focus on output legitimacy would lead to questions of who would be wise enough to make decisions on what is desirable for a community, or whether minorities may be ignored if the measure would ensure the best outcome for the community *generally*. An association is judged on its process when it is considered to be democratic, not on whether the output is desirable. This does not mean that the output does not matter (see also Dahl, 1989, p. 5). In the "Political Institutions" section below, I will consider in what ways the developments as described above have affected the decision-making concerning the political equality of its members. I look at the *input side* of the process (members' communication of their preferences to the government and their weights); the aspect of transparency for the actual *process* of decision-making (so that at least all members can check whether their voices are weighed equally); and I will look at the *output side* of the decision-making (to what extent are public goods public, and do members have 'equal' access to them?).

In short, the five necessary requirements for democracy as proposed by Dahl are also cause for difficulties and tensions in practice. It seems to be very difficult to ensure all five requirements to the fullest, and it may indeed be the case that from that perspective, we have not observed democracy yet. The countries that we call democratic may merely be on their way towards becoming full democracies. However, in addition to these almost inherent difficulties, a number of changes or developments (as described above) seem to cause additional concerns for democracy in practice. I will expand on those below. First, I try to deal with the assumption of the existence of 'a people' and argue that this assumption has become increasingly under pressure in a society that has ever-more consumers for citizens. Further, I discuss how citizens are included in the decision-making process and deal with input, transparency and the output of decision-making – this section thus deals generally with the legitimacy of the democratic state. Political equality is specifically important here. And lastly, the issue of who governs and political equality are combined. Even though it is generally accepted that the majority makes decisions, these decisions should not affect the political equality of the members of society, and in that perspective we need to be careful that contemporary democracies do not transform into either the tyranny of the majority or of the minority.

Implications for democracy

The different trends that have occurred over time in many of the European democracies seem to point at a diffusion of policy-making responsibilities. Practically, this means that the government has 'appointed' other instances or groups to take care of the decision-making and/or the provision of 'public' goods. This can mean that, whereas the state usually arranged public transport, this is now largely taken over by the private sector; or whereas the parliament would usually decide on matters of the ratification of international treaties, the electorate is now asked to 'decide' on that;[4] or while the government would be responsible for the regulation of the provision of energy, new regulatory agencies have taken over this responsibility; or whereas governments would normally decide on their economic policies (with or without the influence of economic experts), appointed European expert officials now give directions on economic policies and goals. For example, monetary policy in the Eurozone is now decided by the European Central Ban (ECB) in Frankfurt, implying a lack of sovereignty, even on paper. Especially concerning the provision of goods that have been moved to the private sector, to the international level, and in some respects also to non-majoritarian institutions, people have less than the initial indirect (representative) influence on the outcomes of policies. Private good provisions are supposed to be more efficient and maybe even better, trying to fine-tune the offer better to the wishes of citizens. When sold or outsourced to the private sector, public goods would be subject to market forces and would therefore be better aimed at individual demands – but also within the government, changes were implemented so that the government could provide (measurable) better outputs. At the same time, citizens become part of a bigger international community, where their preferences and wishes need to be weighed and included into a much bigger pool of preferences and wishes. Governments are sometimes put into awkward positions when dealing with international and national interests.

Citizenship and the need for community

This development seems to indicate that governments have increasingly become political markets (partly deliberately, and most likely partly accidentally). They have moved some things that used to be public goods to the private market: here some public goods provision has become subject to market functioning. These developments were reactions to both existing (efficiency/waste) problems with the public goods provision, as well as to calls for more democracy. But also other issues have become more demand-and-offer related. Some issues that are important now go beyond borders: for example, environmental issues (see also Talbot, 2016), the violation of human rights, or the working conditions of people in other countries. These issues are more difficult to address because they are more international, but they have become even more difficult to access for people through regular institutionalized channels. In all, it has become very difficult for states to listen to their people's concerns related to international issues and even harder to actually act according to them. This is because states have delegated a number of issues, due to the international liberalization (and the therefore more limited state power versus private companies) and due to constraints that the international community poses (which comes with international commitments and the need for support of other nations in order to be able to act internationally).

Those changes may also have consequences for the role of citizens. For where the alterations seem to have led to a political marketplace, where different sellers offer 'public' goods, citizens seem to be increasingly considered as consumers or clients (see e.g. Fountain, 2001). Based on some of the changes that governments have made over the years, it seems that states have started to view their citizens more and more as consumers, and citizens may have started behaving accordingly. At the start of this chapter, I already pointed at one indication of this: people's political behavior has changed over the last few decades. Generally, they seem to be less involved in more regular and institutionalized forms of political participation but more in alternative forms of participation (see also Peters, forthcoming). This involvement (most particularly political consumerism – boycotts and buycotts) is generally more issue-based, more reactive to occurrences (more ad-hoc), and in some cases also more individual. People act more in isolation and less as a community, they pick and choose their issues, and they seem to like the more individual acts of participation – they somehow appear to have changed their political behavior to resemble consumers in a political landscape.

An additional observation that may point at the transformation of citizens to consumers is the decline in people's trust in political institutions, government and politicians, and their seemingly weaker involvement in voluntary institutions. The reason that some scholars are somewhat worried about these developments is that social capital is supposed to bring good things, things that are important to a good or well-functioning democracy. Norris, for example, highlights that associations "provide solutions to community problems, an alternative mechanism of governance, and a training ground for democracy" (Norris, 2002). Involvement in voluntary organizations would foster more trust and the capacity to work together, and would promote the relationships that are core to the civil society. With that, it will help to provide a just and stable democracy (Putnam, 2000). The involvement in associations does not only bring certain positive outcomes to the individual, but also seems to help in building a community on which a good democracy can be built. Trust and involvement in associations seem to provide both private and public goods, and to foster some core conditions for the creation of collective goods (e.g. collaboration, coordination and cooperation) (Putnam, 1993, 2000).

When considering the changes to the political system as discussed above, it may not be surprising that people act more individualistically, their feelings of cohesion and community weaken, and their trust in different elements related to the government declines. When the government moves responsibilities and competencies away to often less accountable units, and shows *and* promotes a behavior that generally resembles actors on a marketplace, it may not be surprising that people start behaving as such, that people lose trust in political institutions, and that communities break down into smaller groups and individuals.

The decline or disintegration of society is a problem for the governability of the state. Although it must be noted that this is a possible problem for any type of state, it may be particularly problematic for democratic states. Democracies need the support of their citizens in order to maintain; if people get too distrustful and dissatisfied with state operations, the political system will break down. This is especially the case when that system is based on the incorporation of its citizens, as is the case for democracies. In these systems it is assumed that people will voluntarily comply with their laws, but if people do not trust the system, or do not feel a common sense of belonging, these laws will be more likely broken (e.g. tax evasion). Democracies are able to function without too much use of violence *because* they rely on legitimacy (Dalton, 2004). When a democratic system has diffused its decision-making or executing power in such a way that people are increasingly forced to act like consumers, and where people cannot hold their government responsible for bad decisions or practices, it is increasingly difficult to maintain legitimacy. When people act more individualistically and act as consumers in the political sphere, and are less connected to other citizens in order to have a common identity, common problems and mutual 'acceptance' as to have a reason to make up a political unit, a democratic state becomes unsustainable. Community and trust are two core conditions on which a democratic government can be built, and when these start to disappear, both the state and the democratic government will do so, too.

Linking citizens and the state: political institutions

A second issue that arises when considering the diffused authority of democratic governments and the changed citizenry is how citizens' preferences are dealt with. It is sometimes argued that current situations are more complex than before, but also that the demands of citizens are more diverse (e.g. Dalton et al., 2003). Additionally, the government has relocated some issues – demand and offer now regulate service and service provision in certain areas, for example. In other areas, when policies or services are rather housed by non-majoritarian institutions or globalization, citizen influence may be more difficult. In short, citizen influence on policies and public goods provision has changed for certain issues. In this section, I discuss how these developments affect political equality – in output, process and input of citizens.

When public goods are moved to the private sphere, citizens have consumer tools in order to influence the provision of those goods. By buying or not buying goods, by choosing some goods over another, citizens can have influence over the companies that produce the products. They might demand them to be produced in more environmentally friendly ways, may desire higher-quality products, or may find that they should be sold by salespersons who have specific characteristics. When they are not happy with the product or provider, citizens can choose another, and with that they influence this private sphere – somewhat similar to how they can influence the public sphere in politics. This, however, brings a problem for democracy: this citizen influence, as well as the service or product itself, is not necessarily equal. For one, it is possible that a previously public service is now not equally accessible for all. It may mean that some people are excluded from the service because they live too remotely or have a physical handicap, for example. This thus makes the 'public' good less public. Delegation to the private sphere, therefore, could foster *output inequality* (see also Peters, 2016). Companies do not have to adopt the same democratic rules that a democratic country has, and therefore, there is no or less of a safeguard against the violation of such rules.

Furthermore, the unequal wealth of citizens also translates into unequal influence on the private sector that provides the previously public goods. Citizens who have a higher income have almost automatically more influence in a market setting because the providers are likely to be profit-driven. What is more, a relatively small but wealthy group can strongly influence the services and goods that are provided by private companies, without there being much safeguard against the content of the preferences of this group. They may prefer, for example, particularly good or frequent public transport in some areas, making it relatively costly for the provider to offer the same service to all citizens. With such incentives to alter public goods, a minority can easily determine the provision of these goods. Ultimately, private companies are more interested in maximizing profits than they are in weighting people's preferences equally. The result is then reduced *input legitimacy* (the possibility to voice preferences due to financial constraints) and *process legitimacy* (the equal consideration and weight of preferences, but also the transparency and accountability of decisions) (see Peters, 2016).

In addition, when issues are moved not to the private sphere but towards the international arena or non-majoritarian institutions, people may again have fewer and different ways of accessing these issues. Often these instances are not directly accountable to citizens, even though they make decisions for them. People might still be able to access the issues through their elected national governments, but influence is relatively limited nonetheless, especially when governments have delegated some of their decision-making. One way of voicing preferences and participating politically concerning these moved issues is through demonstrations or protests, but also here the inclusion of these voices seems to threaten political equality, since they would not give each citizen one voice on this one specific issue (Peters, 2016). Again, democratic principles are put under pressure. People are either not fully included in the decisions, are part of such a substantial group that their individual voice cannot convey enough specificity (see e.g. Dahl, 1994), or their wishes are not included equally (where some people's voices outweigh those of others). It has thus become increasingly difficult to incorporate people's preferences in a democratic way in governing the country. The consequences are problematic for democracy, since some people have more input than others.

Limiting popular influence: the (democratic) constitution

The inequality in input, output and process as discussed above results in a problematic situation for democracies concerning who makes public decisions. People have unequal influence on decisions when public issues are dealt with in a private sphere. The voice of more-affluent citizens seems to weigh more than that of less-affluent citizens, and not just in this private sphere (see e.g. Peters & Ensink, 2015; Rosset, Giger, & Bernauer, 2013). But also the attempts to influence policies in the hands of international organizations or non-majoritarian institutions through protest activity leads to inequality, with active citizens[5] having more weight than non-active citizens. These developments thus make certain groups more influential so that they can (indirectly) make decisions for the population – whether this group represents a majority or not. Put differently, it becomes increasingly possible that minorities set public policies. When such policies concern specifically the protection of minorities or the safeguarding of political equality of all citizens, democracy is not under threat. But when it relates to policies beyond that, key democratic principles are violated. When in addition the government has delegated decision-making power, it may be increasingly difficult for governments to maintain responsibility (Mair, 2009); it has become increasingly challenging to ensure equality and the protection of citizen rights.

To illustrate the point of minority rule, which could lead to (at least) democratic friction, Baek (2010) provides a good example concerning the 2002 Walmart boycott. Walmart had promoted itself by claiming that it was a 'good' company as it did not discriminate on the basis of sexual preference. Not agreeing with this form of the equality principle, as it would represent a sin, a group of orthodox Christians and moral conservatives reacted to this statement by calling for a boycott against Walmart (it was not mentioned what the reaction from the company was). Consumerism does thus not necessarily promote equality or democratic values more widely. Furthermore, it is very difficult to actually correct for the promotion of inequality, worsening the problem, because a company cannot always afford to (or want to) apply democratic principles to its conduct, but at the same time the state cannot always interfere satisfactorily. It would be very difficult for the state and/or the judicial system to prevent a boycott as described above. The one thing it could do is to force the private sphere to behave according to certain principles through regulation. But especially with a government that has changed, is responsible for fewer issues, and that does more steering than rowing, it may not always be easy to do this, especially when public support for the government is low (see also Peters, 2016).

Discussion: rethinking democracy in practice

Although the core institutional set-up has not changed in a widespread manner, democratic political systems have changed in their structure. As we have seen, these shifts have mainly been changes in the role of the government in providing governance. The government has delegated decision-making in a number of issues and areas to other actors, in such a way that there now appear to be a number of different centers that have gained political responsibilities. A number of the changes have been discussed above as causing problems for democracy; even though democracy in practice will not match up to its theoretical version, the alterations to the political system have caused even further difficulties and tensions for the maintenance of democracy. As discussed above, some of the developments are causing serious problems, and they need to be addressed somehow in order to maintain democratic political systems. There are, however, also some developments (outlined above) that may have some potential for strengthening democracy. These developments, notably decentralization and the increase in the institutionalization of direct democracy, have not yet been discussed in relation to democracy here, and they may be part of a solution to the problems of democracy. In the following paragraphs, I point out some avenues for change and discuss some important ideas that have been elaborated on elsewhere, to counter the problems outlined above.

Considering the changes that have taken place in many democratic countries, and that those imply that there has been a shift in the role of the government in governance, the search for solutions may be organized around the different models of governance (Pierre & Peters, 2005). Governance is now provided by a multitude of actors, and although the government still plays a role, it has become more limited. We may have ended up in something like the 'Dutch governance school' model of governance, where the government is just one of the actors involved and society may play a powerful role in that it can organize itself to avoid the power of the state (Pierre & Peters, 2005). This is Pierre and Peters' fourth model out of five; model number one sees the government as the main actor, and model number five considers the government as almost non-existent in governance. Steps to improve or strengthen democracy may be arranged along this scale of involvement of the government in governance.

First, we could imagine moving one model back, where the government plays a bigger role but leaves space for other actors to be responsible for some elements. This would require some re-nationalization in that certain issues or areas would again become part of the government's responsibilities. Issues that are now in the hands of private companies, international organizations, but also in those of non-majoritarian institutions may be brought back under the range of issues that the government deals with. This step may relieve some pressure for democracy in that people would be considered more equally than before with regards to the input, process and output of the decisions concerning public goods. Moreover, when this political equality is improved again, there are fewer chances that either minorities or majorities tyrannize – both because of the increased political equality and because of a stronger government that can act to counter such occurrences. Even though those issues might not be resolved immediately by some re-nationalizing (especially in political systems where money plays a big role in politics, e.g. party funding), they may be less imminent than they seem now. However, the disintegration of the political community (discussed above) is not solved by this step. People are not automatically involved again in politics, and people do not automatically trust political institutions or politicians more. This may still be problematic, and the image that the political system and the politicians have may have different (additional) reasons. For one, the way that politics is reported in the media, as well as the general availability of information, has changed. But also, as mentioned, politicians now have to deal with more and more complex issues, and this is not automatically resolved by re-nationalization.

One way to possibly deal with this under a bigger role of the government is to decentralize political authority, and this is one of the things that we have seen concerning the developments over the last decades. This would allow the government to distribute core tasks among different parts of itself and at the same time bring government closer to the people. This may to some extent allow the government to target the needs and wishes of its citizens better, and it could help in promoting feelings of community at least at the lower levels. Following this line of thought and including the aim of efficiency in public goods provision, we could also imagine reforms in the direction of polycentrism (McGinnis & Ostrom, 2012; V. Ostrom et al., 1961). As discussed above, the current political system might point already in this direction, but by increasing the government's role and maybe providing more coordination, the idea of polycentrism could be seen as a partial solution to the current problems with democracy. Of course, this would then again cause certain tensions (e.g. concerning the competition between wealthier and poorer districts), but especially with more governmental oversight, these may also be remedied.

A second area of solutions could be found when we consider democracies in the current model of governance – the Dutch school model, which leaves only a relatively small role for the government. Even though the current situation seems to cause problems for democracy, there may be some remedies within this model. One of the avenues here would be to install more or new oversight institutions. Pierre and Peters (2005) argue that with a reduced role of the state, there is a lack of overview and accountability. When institutions are installed to monitor and correct the conduct of companies and non-majoritarian/international organs, political equality (as well as the input, process and output legitimacy) could be better safeguarded. Moreover, if the minimal state would succeed in better monitoring, but also clearer structuring the current political system (the government could communicate better who is responsible), then it may even convince people to be less skeptical of political institutions and politicians. Moreover, if the government could strengthen its role in coordination, it may even foster stronger communities – even though that may not be a national community feeling, people may rather cluster together on the basis of local areas or political issues. Alternatively, or in addition to this, the judicial system could be stronger. This would, just like the oversight institutions, help to protect individual rights and political equality. Moreover, if this system can act efficiently, people may actually feel more protected and may therefore trust the political system more. Whether these claims are true should, however, be tested beforehand.

Other possibilities here could again include solutions at a lower level of government. Graham Smith (2009) discusses a number of democratic innovations that could work to improve democracy in involving people more directly (though all have stronger and weaker points). For example, mini-publics, where a body of citizens is selected by random sampling to discuss a certain issue, could give advice (or even make a decision) on that issue. These types of democratic innovations may work especially well at a lower level of government and could add elements of democracy to the current state of affairs. The government may in that sense be supplemented by the views and insights of citizens, who then also have more control and responsibility.

Lastly, some possible solutions come with a further reduction of the role of the government – Pierre and Peters' governance model five, where the government's role is minimal. A change like this would mean that the government would move even more decision-making responsibilities to alternative actors. One avenue along this move would be to give more responsibilities to the people. Following the empirical trend in more institutionalization of direct democracy, many decisions could actually be taken by the citizens of a democratic state. This can be done at different levels of governance, where people can put issues on the agenda and then decide on them themselves. In this scenario, there would still be something of a minimal government that deals with certain day-to-day tasks, but it also could help to coordinate and facilitate the functioning of democracy. Moreover, it would be very important, again, to have a strong judicial system that enforces political equality and protects the individual rights of citizens.

An alternative, but also shifting more responsibilities to citizens, would be something along the lines of what Archon Fung (2004) discussed as empowered participatory democracy. Here, citizens of a community are directly involved in the conduct and type of provision of public goods (e.g. police), but they are at the same time supported by an overarching body that can compare the performance of different communities on an issue and can also provide help and advice. At a larger scale, issues could be dealt with separately and communities are each involved hands-on, while overarching coordination bodies (per issue) could make sure other communities can improve on the basis of the good performance of other communities. This empowered participatory democracy on a national scale sounds to some extent like a form of polycentrism, though with more emphasis on the direct involvement of citizens.

These types of solutions of course come with new problems. Especially when this would be implemented at a large scale, it will require a lot of work for citizens. They would need to be involved in several decisions and issues, would have to vote or deliberate on a variety of topics, and would need to collect a fair amount of information in order to make a minimally informed decision. In practice, this may therefore not work so well. One issue here is also the scale of democracy – both direct democracy and empowered participatory democracy may work better at a lower level of government, or with a smaller community altogether. Moreover, there may be some possibilities for a division of labor, where people could choose an issue to 'specialize' on, and different groups of citizens would decide on different issues.

All in all, a number of reforms are possible in order to strengthen or improve the current state of democracy, even though there is not one clear solution. It does seem to be clear, however, that the developments that have occurred over the past few decades have put increased pressure on democracy, and in order to prevent a crisis of democracy, we need to look for alternative institutional structures.

Further reading

Dalton, R. J., Scarrow, S. E., & Cain, B. E. (2003). New Forms of Democracy? Reform and Transformation of Democratic Institutions. In B. E. Cain, R. J. Dalton & S. E. Scarrow (Eds.), *Democracy Transformed? Expanding Political Opportunities in Advanced Industrial Democracies* (pp. 1–20). Oxford: Oxford University Press.

Levi-Faur, D. (2005). The Global Diffusion of Regulatory Capitalism. *The Annals of the American Academy of Political and Social Science, 598*(1), 12–32.

Mair, P. (2005). Democracy Beyond Parties. *Paper 05'06*, http://repositories.cdlib.org /csd/05-06.

Key questions for discussion

1   What does the author mean by displacing politics, and how can this be conceptualized?
2   What do the institutional reforms have to do with the changes that have been observed in citizen participation?
3   Why does the author argue that the shift in public tasks from the government to the private sphere or non-majoritarian institutions could be harmful for democracy?

Notes

1 Based on data from the Economic Freedom in the World Dataset: see Gwartney et al. (2014) for a more detailed description of the data.
2 Although it is also noted that the initial increase is not necessarily due to the increased use all over the world, but rather the increased use in a few countries such as Ireland, Italy and Switzerland.
3 Which are (1) articulating a common set of priorities for society – goals, (2) coherence – the goals should be consistent and coordinated, (3) steering – the way the goals are attained, through e.g. regulation, and (4) accountability – people should be able to hold the actors that are responsible for governance responsible.
4 As was, for example, the case in the Netherlands in 2005 (see www.C2D.ch).
5 These citizens may be active for a variety of reasons: because they are specifically against a decision, have a very strong preference (against the decision), have the means to actually be active, are more involved in politics generally, etc. The point being that a big protest does not necessarily reflect the ideas of the majority of citizens.

References

Ansell, C., & Gingrich, J. (2003a). Reforming the Administrative State. In B. E. Cain, R. J. Dalton & S. E. Scarrow (Eds.), *Democracy Transformed? Expanding Opportunities in Advanced Industrial Democracies* (pp. 164–191). Oxford: Oxford University Press.

Ansell, C., & Gingrich, J. (2003b). Trends in Decentralization. In B. E. Cain, R. A. Dahl & S. E. Scarrow (Eds.), *Democracy Transformed? Expanding Political Opportunities in Advanced Industrial Democracies* (pp. 140–163). Oxford: Oxford University Press.

Armingeon, K., & Schädel, L. (2015). Social Inequality in Political Participation: The Dark Sides of Individualisation. *West European Politics, 38*(1), 1–27. doi: 10.1080/01402382.2014.929341

Beak, Y. M. (2010). To Buy or Not to Buy: Who Are Political Consumers? What Do They Think and How Do they Participate? *Political Studies, 58*, 1065–1086.

Butler, D., & Ranney, A. (1994). *Referendums in the World; The Growing Use of Direct Democracy.* Basingstoke: The MacMillan Press LTD.

Dahl, R. A. (1989). *Democracy and Its Critics.* New Haven: Yale University Press.

Dahl, R. A. (1994). A Democratic Dilemma: System Effectiveness versus Citizen Participation. *Political Research Quarterly, 109*(1), 23–34.

Dahl, R. A. (1998). *On Democracy.* New Haven: Yale University Press.

Dahl, R. A. (2000). A Democratic Paradox? *Scandinavian Political Studies, 23*(3), 246–251.

Dahl, R. A. (2006 [1956]). *A Peface to Democratic Theory.* Expanded Edition. Chicago: The University of Chicago Press.

Dalton, R. J. (2004). *Democratic Challenges, Democratic Choices: The Erosion in Political Support in Advanced Industrial Democracies.* Oxford: Oxford University Press.

Dalton, R. J. (2005). The Greening of the Globe? Cross-National Levels of Environmental Group Membership. *Environmental Politics, 14*(4), 441–459.

Dalton, R. J., Scarrow, S. E., & Cain, B. E. (2003). New Forms of Democracy? Reform and Transformation of Democratic Institutions. In B. E. Cain, R. J. Dalton & S. E. Scarrow (Eds.), *Democracy Transformed? Expanding Political Opportunities in Advanced Industrial Democracies* (pp. 1–20). Oxford: Oxford University Press.

Dalton, R. J., Van Sickle, A., & Weldon, S. A. (2009). The Individual-Institutional Nexus of Protest. *British Journal of Political Science, 40*, 51–73.

Dalton, R. J., & Wattenberg, M. P. (2000). Unthinkable Democracy; Political Change in Advanced Industrial Democracies. In R. J. Dalton & M. P. Wattenberg (Eds.), *Parties without Partisans; Political Change in Advanced Industrial Democracies* (pp. 3–16). Oxford: Oxford University Press.

Flinders, M., & Buller, J. (2006). Depoliticisation: Principles, Tactics and Tools. *British Politics,* *1*, 293–318.

Fountain, J. E. (2001). Paradoxes of Public Sector Customer Service. *Governance, 14*(1), 55–73.

Fung, A. (2004). *Empowered Participation. Reinventing Urban Democracy.* Princeton: Princeton University Press.

Fung, A., & Wright, E. O. (2003). *Deepening Democracy.* London: Verso.

Gallagher, M. (1996). Conclusion. In M. Gallagher & P. V. Uleri (Eds.), *The Referendum Experience in Europe* (pp. 226–252). London: Macmillan.

Gilardi, F. (2008). *Delegation in the Regulatory State: Independent Regulatory Agencies in Western Europe.* Cheltenham, UK: Edward Elgar Publishing.

Gwartney, J., Lawson, R., & Hall, J. (2014). Economic Freedom of the World: 2014 Annual Report: Fraser Institute.

Hanretty, C., & Koop, C. (2013). Shall the Law Set Them Free? The Formal and Actual Independence of Regulatory Agencies. *Regulation & Governance, 7*(2), 195–214. doi: 10.1111/j.1748-5991.2012.01156.x

Hood, C. (1991). A Public Management for All Seasons? *Public Administration, 69*, 3–19.

Hooghe, L., & Marks, G. (2003). Unraveling the Central State, but How? Types of Multi-Level Governance. *American Political Science Review, 97*(2), 233–243.

Hooghe, L., Marks, G., & Schakel, A. H. (2010). *The Rise of Regional Authority: A Comparative Study of 42 Democracies.* London: Routledge.

Inglehart, R. (1977). *The Silent Revolution: Changing Values and Political Styles Among Western Publics.* Princeton: Princeton University Press.

Jordana, J., Levi-Faur, D., & i Marín, X. F. (2011). The Global Diffusion of Regulatory Agencies: Channels of Transfer and Stages of Diffusion. *Comparative Political Studies, 44*(10), 1343–1369.

Kettle, D. F. (2006). Public Bureacracies. In R. A. W. Rhodes, S. A. Binder & B. A. Rockman (Eds.), *The Oxford Handbook of Political Institutions* (pp. 366–384). Oxford: Oxford University Press.

Levi-Faur, D. (2005). The Global Diffusion of Regulatory Capitalism. *The Annals of the American Acedemy of Political and Social Science, 598*(1), 12–32.

Li, Y., & Marsh, D. (2008). New Forms of Political Participants: Searching for Expert Citizens and Everyday Makers. *British Journal of Political Science, 38*, 247–272.

Linde, J., & Dahlberg, S. (2016). Democratic Discontent in Times of Crisis? In Y. Peters & M. R. Tatham (Eds.), *Democratic Transformations in Europe: Challenges and Opportunities* (pp. 72–95). Abingdon: Routledge.

Linz, J. J. (2000). Democratic Political Parties: Recognizing Contradictory Principles and Perception. *Scandinavian Political Studies, 23*(3), 252–265.

Mair, P. (2005). Democracy Beyond Parties. *Paper 05'06*, http://repositories.cdlib.org/csd/05-06.

Mair, P. (2009). *Representative versus Responsible Government.* MPIfG Working Paper 09/8. Max Planck Institute for the Study of Societies, Cologne.

Majone, G. (1996). *Regulating Europe.* London and New York: Routledge.

Majone, G. (2001). Nonmajoritarian Institutions and the Limits of Democratic Governance: A Political Transaction-Cost Approach. *Journal of Institutional and Theoretical Economics, 157*, 57–78.

McGinnis, M. D., & Ostrom, E. (2012). Reflections on Vincent Ostrom, Public Administration, and Polycentricity. *Public Administration Review, 72*(1), 15–25.

Megginson, W. L., & Netter, J. M. (2001). From State to Market: A Survey of Empirical Studies on Privatization. *Journal of Economic Literature, 39*(2), 321–389.

Mjelde, H. L., & Svåsand, L. (2016). Party Decline? In Y. Peters & M. R. Tatham (Eds.), *Democratic Transformations in Europe: Challenges and Opportunities* (pp. 51–71). Abingdon: Routledge.

Norris, P. (1999). Introduction: The Growth of Critical Citizens? In P. Norris (Ed.), *Critical Citizens; Global Support for Democratic Governance* (pp. 1–29). Oxford: Oxford University Press.

Norris, P. (2002). *Democratic Phoenix: Reinventing Political Activism.* Cambridge: Cambridge University Press.

Norris, P., Walgrave, S., & Van Aelst, P. (2004). Who Demonstrates? Anti-State Rebels, Conventional Participation, or Everyone? *Comparative Politics, 37*(2), 189–206.

Ostrom, E. (2000). The Future of Democracy. *Scandinavian Political Studies, 23*(3), 280–283.

Ostrom, V., Tiebout, C. M., & Warren, R. (1961). The Organization of Government in Metropolitan Areas: A Theoretical Inquiry. *American Political Science Review, 55*(4), 831–842.

Peters, Y. (2016). Hollower Democracy? Studying the Consequences of a Changing Demos. In W. C. Müller & F. C. Bértoa (Eds.), *Party Politics and Democracy in Europe: Essays in Honour of Peter Mair* (pp. 197–212). Abingdon: Routledge.

Peters, Y. (forthcoming). *Diffused Democracy, Displaced Governance, and Political Participation.* Abingdon: Routledge.

Peters, Y., & Ensink, S. J. (2015). Differential Responsiveness in Europe: The Effects of Preference Difference and Electoral Participation. *West European Politics, 38*(3), 577–600. doi: 10.1080/01402382.2014.973260

Peters, Y., & Tatham, M. R. (2016). The Transformation of Democracy. In Y. Peters & M. R. Tatham (Eds.), *Democratic Transformations in Europe: Challenges and Opportunities* (pp. 1–9). Abingdon: Routledge.

Pharr, S. J., & Putnam, R. D. (Eds.). (2000). *Disaffected Democracies; What's Troubling the Trilateral Democracies.* Princeton, NJ: Princeton University Press.

Pharr, S. J., Putnam, R. D., & Dalton, R. J. (2000). Introduction: What's Troubling the Trilateral Democracies? In S. J. Pharr & R. D. Putnam (Eds.), *Disaffected Democracies. What's Troubling the Trilateral Countries?* (pp. 3–29). Princeton: Princeton University Press.

Pierre, J., & Peters, G. B. (2005). *Governing Complex Societies. Trajectories and Scenarios.* Basingstoke: Palgrave Macmillan.

Putnam, R. D. (1993). *Making Democracy Work: Civic Traditions in Modern Italy.* Princeton, NJ: Princeton University Press.

Putnam, R. D. (2000). *Bowling Alone: The Collapse and Revival of American Community.* New York: Simon & Schuster.

Rosset, J., Giger, N., & Bernauer, J. (2013). More Money, Fewer Problems? Cross-Level Effects of Economic Deprivation on Political Representation. *West European Politics, 36*(4), 817–835.

Scarrow, S. E. (2003). Making Elections More Direct? Reducing the Role of Parties in Elections. In B. E. Cain, R. J. Dalton & S. E. Scarrow (Eds.), *Democracy Transformed? Expanding Political Opportunities in Advanced Industrial Democracies* (pp. 44–58). Oxford: Oxford University Press.

Smith, G. (2009). *Democratic Innovations. Designing Institutions for Citizen Participation.* Cambridge: Cambridge University Press.

Stevis, D., & Boswell, T. (2008). *Globalization and Labor: Democratizing Global Governance.* Lanham: Rowman & Littlefield Publishers, Inc.

Stolle, D., Hooghe, M., & Micheletti, M. (2005). Politics in the Supermarket: Political Consumerism as a form of Political Participation. *International Political Science Review, 26*(3), 245–269.

Streeck, W., & Thelen, K. (2005). Introduction: Institutional Change in Advanced Industrial Political Economies. In W. Streeck & K. Thelen (Eds.), *Beyond Continuity. Institutional Change in Advanced Industrial Political Economies* (pp. 1–39). Oxford: Oxford University Press.

Suleiman, E. (2003). *Dismantling Democratic States*. Princeton: Princeton University Press.

Talbot, F. (2016). Climate Change Mitigation. In Y. Peters & M. R. Tatham (Eds.), *Democratic Transformations in Europe: Challenges and Opportunities* (pp. 209–230). Abingdon: Routledge.

Tatham, M. R. (2016). Multi-Jurisdictional Politics: State Adaptation and Mixed Visions of Democracy. In Y. Peters & M. R. Tatham (Eds.), *Democratic Transformations in Europe: Challenges and Opportunities* (pp. 269–293). Abingdon: Routledge.

Thatcher, M., & Stone Sweet, A. (2002). Theory and Practice of Delegation to Non-Majoritarian Institutions. *West European Politics, 25*(1), 1–22.

Warren, M. E. (2002). What Can Democratic Participation Mean Today? *Political Theory, 30*(5), 677–701.

PART 3

Governing beyond and below the state

10

TERRORISM, COUNTERTERRORISM, AND DEMOCRACY

Jan Oskar Engene

Introduction

Terrorism has attracted public attention and been high on the political agenda of advanced democracies for decades. Whether separatist or nationalist, as found in the Basque Country, Corsica, or Northern Ireland, revolutionary in the struggle to topple capitalist states, right-wing extremist, such as the 22 July attacks in Norway in 2011, or internationally jihadist, as exemplified by the 9/11 al-Qaeda attacks in the U.S., followed by large-scale attacks in Madrid in 2004 and London in 2005, terrorism is often seen as an increasing threat to society. In particular, terrorism is often presented as a challenge to democracy, or democracies, in that non-democratic perpetrators target democratic societies by taking advantage of their openness, freedom, and rule of law. Democracies are then portrayed as especially vulnerable and more exposed than other regimes to terrorism.

This chapter will review the literature in terms of how the relationship between terrorism and democracy has been conceptualized, and survey what empirical basis has been found to support the suggested relationships. In such a discussion, it would be necessary to look at terrorism in democratic versus non-democratic regimes, but also to investigate the category of democracy to see whether there might be institutional variation within democracies that could explain why some democracies are more exposed to terrorism than other democracies are (thresholds of representation, inclusiveness, etc.). Furthermore, the chapter will raise the question of the effect of terrorism on democracy in terms of civil and political liberties, asking whether the challenge to democracy comes not from terrorism but from efforts to fight terrorism, counterterrorism.

Data sources on terrorism: domestic and international

In the literature there is a long-standing distinction between international terrorism, simply defined as terrorist attacks involving citizens or the territory of two or more states, and domestic terrorism, attacks taking place within a country and involving only its own inhabitants. International terrorism may also be labelled *transnational*, whereas the term *internal* is sometimes also used for domestic terrorism (in this chapter, the terms *international* and *domestic* will be used). For a long time, international terrorism was considered more important compared to the type of terrorism where perpetrators attacked their fellow nationals. International terrorism affected several states, became an issue in international relations, and was put on the international political agenda, especially from the late 1960s onwards. This distinction also affects data on terrorism. Data sources on terrorism, the major ones listed in Table 10.1, differ in geographical and time coverage, as well as in the type of terrorism covered: domestic terrorism or international terrorism.

TABLE 10.1 Major datasets on terrorism

Data set	Type of terrorism covered	Geographical coverage and time coverage	Number of events/ coding units	Availability
ITERATE – International Terrorism: Attributes of Terrorist Events (International Terrorism Data Center, 2015)	International terrorism	Global, 1968–2014	13,087 attacks (1968–2007)	Proprietary, available at cost
RDWTI – RAND Database of Worldwide Terrorism Incidents (RAND, 2015)	International terrorism, from 1998 onwards international and domestic terrorism	Global, 1968–2009	+40,000 incidents	Online
GTD – Global Terrorism Database (National Consortium for the Study of Terrorism and Responses to Terrorism (START) 2015b)	Domestic and international terrorism	Global, 1970 onwards (except 1993)	140,000 attacks (August 2015)	Online
TWEED – Terrorism in Western Europe: Events Data (Engene, 2007)	Domestic terrorism	18 West European countries, 1950–2004	11,026 events	Online
Domestic Terrorist Victims – DVT (de la Calle & Sánchez-Cuenca, 2011a)	Domestic terrorism	18 West European countries, 1965–2005	4,955 killings	Online

The first data sources on terrorism that appeared, such as the ITERATE dataset or the RAND chronology, were concerned with international terrorism. Then, as later on, datasets relied on open news sources for information on incidents (for an overview of data sources for terrorism research, see Bowie & Schmid, 2011). Later datasets such as TWEED (Engene, 2007) and DVT (de la Calle & Sánchez-Cuenca, 2011a) focused on domestic terrorism, though for a limited number of countries in Western Europe. In addition to the major datasets mentioned in Table 10.1, some additional datasets have been discontinued and gone offline. This applies to the Worldwide Incidents Tracking System (WITS), once maintained by the U.S. government organization National Counterterrorism Center (NCTC) and covering international and domestic terrorism globally from 2004 to early 2012. The RAND Terrorism Chronology Database covering international terrorism from 1968 to 1997 has been incorporated into the RAND Database of Worldwide Terrorism Incidents (RDWTI). RAND data was also included in the MIPT Terrorism Knowledge Base, once made available online by the National Memorial Institute for the Prevention of Terrorism (MIPT) in the U.S.

Though much attention has been devoted to the threat of international terrorism, researchers now acknowledge that domestic terrorist attacks are far more frequent than international attacks (Enders, Sandler & Gaibulloev, 2011, p. 320). According to Bowie and Schmid (2011, p. 337) about 85 per cent of terrorist attacks are *not* international. Nevertheless, the first datasets on terrorism were limited to international terrorism, a fact that has set its mark on the literature, creating an "international terrorism bias," in the words of Sánchez-Cuenca (2014, p. 395).

The newest and increasingly predominant dataset, the GTD, includes both types of terrorist attacks, and in August 2014 variables to distinguish domestic from international attacks were added to this dataset. Applying a more differentiated approach than the traditional domestic–international dichotomy, LaFree, Dugan and Miller (2015) identify different types of international terrorism in the GTD data. Distinguishing among attacks that are *logistically* international, *ideologically* international, or *indeterminately* international, they find that a total of 16.81 per cent of attacks from 1970 to 2012 fall into any of the international types of terrorism (LaFree, Dugan & Miller, 2015, p. 160). Furthermore, a decline in these kinds of international terrorism is observed over time. Logistically international terrorism, what probably comes closest to the traditional or common understanding of international terrorism as a type of terrorism in which perpetrators cross international borders to execute attacks, reached a maximum of 15 per cent of the total number of attacks in the mid-1970s, compared to 2–3 per cent in the period from 2004 to 2012 (LaFree, Dugan & Miller, 2015, pp. 166–167). However, it should be noted that attacks by nationalist minority groups, such as those based in Corsica or Northern Ireland, have been classified as logistically international, even though the attacks were carried out in the state to which those regions belong. In other words, attacks that were

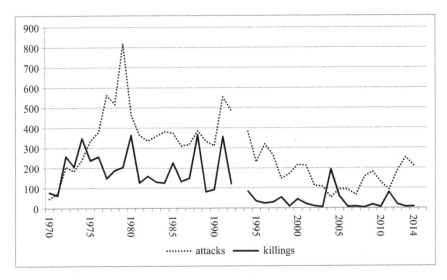

FIGURE 10.1 Number of domestic and international terrorist attacks and killings by year, 1970–2014, in current Europe 31 countries according to the Global Terrorism Database

National Consortium for the Study of Terrorism and Responses to Terrorism (START) (2015a)

Note: Data was drawn from GTD for countries now forming Europe 31, using strict criteria in defining terrorism and filtering on GTD's three criteria so that only events that meet all three have been included, that is, "The act must be aimed at attaining a political, economic, religious, or social goal", "There must be evidence of an intention to coerce, intimidate, or convey some other message to a larger audience (or audiences) than the immediate victims", and "The action must be outside the context of legitimate warfare activities." (National Consortium for the Study of Terrorism and Responses to Terrorism (START), 2015b, p. 9). Unsuccessful attacks and cases coded as ambiguous have been excluded. Data is missing for 1993. GTD data collection methodology has changed over time and the compilers warn that "users should note that differences in levels of attacks before and after January 1, 1998, before and after April 1, 2008, and before and after January 1, 2012 may be at least partially explained by differences in data collection" (National Consortium for the Study of Terrorism and Responses to Terrorism (START), 2015c).

traditionally and commonly understood as domestic may have inflated these figures on international terrorism.

In Figure 10.1, data has been culled from the GTD for the current 31 European countries this book mainly addresses. A strict definition of terrorism has been used, excluding unsuccessful attacks and ambiguous cases. The data covers both domestic and international terrorism. As can be seen from Figure 10.1, both the total death toll from terrorism as well as the frequency of attacks was higher in the first part of the time period covered. Whereas the total death toll from terrorism varied between 100 and 200 people killed annually most years between 1970 and the early 1990s, since 1994 the lethality of terrorism has dropped to below 100 people per year, and mostly below fifty, towards the end of the time period. Exceptions exist, such as the year 2004, when jihadist attacks on commuter trains in Madrid drove the death toll upwards to close to 200 that year, or in 2011, when the Oslo and Utøya attacks in Norway, which claimed a total of seventy-seven lives, contributed to a combined death toll that was much higher than for the preceding or following years.

In the first part of the period covered in Figure 10.1, sustained terrorist campaigns connected with minority nationalism (as opposed to majority nationalism discussed in Knutsen, 2016, this volume) fed both the total number of attacks and the total death toll. The conflicts in Northern Ireland and the Basque Country in particular contributed to terrorist lethality, but additional territorial tension in Corsica and elsewhere also contributed to the frequency of attacks. With adaptation by states in terms of decentralization and regional autonomy (cf. Tatham, 2016, this volume) on the one hand, and the Good Friday agreement in Northern Ireland in 1998 on the other hand, a number of ceasefires followed by the declaration of "definitive cessation of armed activity" by Euskadi Ta Askatasuna (ETA) in 2011, and even the abandonment of armed struggle by the National Liberation Front of Corsica (FLNC), the source that once fueled the flames of terrorism in Europe has largely been cut off.

Along with terrorism related to minority nationalism, domestic terrorism from the extreme right and the extreme left was at a high level in the 1970s and 1980s, as illustrated by the high number of active groups on the extreme right in Italy and France, as well as the activities of the Red Army faction in Germany and the Red Brigades in Italy (Engene, 2004). In addition, international terrorism from a wide range of sources, including Palestinian and Armenian groups, also contributed to making the 1970s and 1980s the decades of terrorism in Europe. However, by 9/11, a global turning point, terrorism had for some years been at an historically low level in Europe. With some prominent exceptions, it has remained so, though much attention is still devoted to the threat of jihadist terrorism in Europe.

The composite origin of terrorism also contributes to explain some of the peaks seen in the first part of the data series. In 1974 the death toll from terrorism in Europe 31 exceeded 300. The bombing of an airliner by the People's Front for the Liberation of Palestine (PFLP), with the loss of eighty-eight lives contributed to this, along with ten or more lives claimed by bombs placed by the Basque group ETA in Spain, the Ulster Volunteer Force (UVF) and the Irish Republican Army (IRA) in Ireland and the United Kingdom, and the Black Order in cities in Italy. In 1980, the Bologna railway station bombing, killing eighty-five people (the GTD records seventy-six), contributed to driving up the death toll, along with the bomb placed at the Oktoberfest in Munich by a neo-Nazi, claiming thirteen lives. For 1980, the GTD also records an attack in London, with thirty-seven lives lost in a nightclub fire. One may question, however, why this event has been included in the dataset, as it does not seem that the Denmark Street fire was a terrorist attack. A single attack, the bomb that brought down Pan Am flight 103 over Lockerbie in the United Kingdom, with 270 lives lost, explains most of the death toll for the peak in 1988. The following peak in 1991, however, is driven by events in Croatia during the war in the then-dissolving Yugoslavia, illustrating the general problem that insurgency, guerilla campaigns, and civil war spill over into the dataset (de la Calle & Sánchez-Cuenca, 2011b; Berkebile, 2015). In one case, the dataset records 180 people killed in an assault by Serb militants on a police station in Croatia in July 1991. While spillover from other types of violence may be a greater problem with data for countries outside of Europe 31, another event recorded in the dataset for 1991 and driving up the death toll for that year, is another false positive, a supposed attack by Croat militia on a school in the city of Vukovar with forty-one children killed. However, this "attack" is a piece of Serb war propaganda (Somerville, 2012, p. 82). Both this attack and the Denmark Street fire of 1980 have been coded in the dataset as unambiguous cases of terrorism. The number of attacks increases towards the end of the period covered in Figure 10.1, but as data-gathering methodology changed from 2012, the increase may at least in part be explained by this change.

Democracy, dictatorship, and terrorism

Early studies of the relationship between democracy and terrorism tended to treat the regime variable dichotomously, contrasting democracies to authoritarian systems. Limited systematic data was available, the ITERATE dataset, focusing on international terrorist attacks, being the main data source for quantitative studies. Democracies, as modern, industrialized societies, offer a number of permissive causes of terrorism in that general social and political conditions that make terrorism more likely are present. Crenshaw (1981) identified these as modernization, industrialization, and urbanization, which have created complex, increasingly vulnerable societies with a wide range of possible targets for terrorists, along with better means of transportation and increasingly sophisticated means of communication that have made it easier to conduct acts of terrorism. Early studies on the relationship between terrorism and democracy emerged during the Cold War pitting (mostly) democracies in the West against an authoritarian Soviet bloc. Theories and explanations of why democracies were more exposed than their authoritarian antagonists to terrorism concentrated on what Chenoweth (2013, pp. 360–364) identifies as structural explanations pointing to the role of institutional environments in the democracy–terrorism link. On the one hand, these explanations focus on civil liberties in democracies as causes of terrorism, but on the other hand, they point to the role of free media in creating incentives for terrorism.

With the publication of Schmid and de Graaf's volume *Violence as Communication: Insurgent Terrorism and the Western News Media* (1982), the relationship between a free press, such as that existing in liberal democracies, and terrorism came into focus. Terrorists take advantage of the fact that independent news media give attention to their acts of violence and thereby to their existence and political message. The publicity explanation (Chenoweth, 2013, pp. 362–363) suggests that a key feature of liberal democracies – freedom of the press – creates incentives for terrorists to target democracies. Free media provides terrorists with publicity and the means to spread their message. However, as Chenoweth points out, the explanation does not hold empirically. Many countries with media freedom, such as advanced democracies, experience no or low levels of terrorist violence. What then can explain the variation of levels of terrorism among countries that share a common characteristic, that of media freedom? Furthermore, over time and with the new technology, the publicity explanation may have become less relevant, Chenoweth (2013, p. 363) suggests. With the rise of the Internet and spread of social media, there is no longer any need for terrorists to go to a democracy with free media to commit acts of violence that are guaranteed coverage. This can be done from home.

It has also been suggested that the observed association between democracy and terrorism is really just found because terrorist attacks are underreported in authoritarian regimes (Chenoweth, 2013, pp. 363–364). Democracies are open and have a free press in which violent opposition is reported, and datasets on terrorism usually rely on this kind of news reporting. In authoritarian regimes, media censorship is in place and violent opposition and terrorist attacks may not be reported in their own countries, and thus never come to the attention of the media sources used to compile data on terrorism.

On further dimensions, democracy entails open societies of a kind that make it easier for terrorists to commit acts of violence. Wilkinson (1977, p. 102f) argued this is because of several central principles of democratic polities: democracy is based on the rule of law, freedom of expression and association, and the principles of freedom and openness triumph over the impetus of the state apparatus to maintain order. Inhabitants in democracies are allowed to express dissident opinions and organize themselves accordingly, even in opposition to democracy. Government use of force to maintain law and order is defined, limited by law, and under the check of independent courts. Those preparing for, or involved with, preparing acts of terrorism thus enjoy a certain protection from the state and may take advantage of the freedom and openness offered by a democratic society to commit their acts of violence.

Explaining why terrorism is more prevalent in democracies by pointing to civil liberties is an explanation that focuses on opportunity structures (Chenoweth, 2013, pp. 360–362). Democracies are targets of terrorism because democracies are committed to human rights and civil rights, and they guarantee freedom of movement, association, and expression. Furthermore, democracies are self-restraining, which means that there are strict limits to repression of opposition and strict rules as to judicial persecution. The argument is then that all of this freedom provides opportunities for terrorists and lowers the cost of terrorism in democracies. Democracies are more open for terrorists; in fact, they are victims of their own openness.

In an early study covering the post–World War II period until 1987, Eubank and Weinberg (1994) argued there was a clear link to be found between democracy and terrorism measured as the presence of terrorist groups. Terrorist groups were less likely to be found in authoritarian systems and more likely to be found in democracies. They also concluded that the presence of terrorist groups was not affected by type of democracy (stable, insecure, partial) or type of authoritarian system (limited, absolute) (Eubank & Weinberg, 1994, p. 314). Using event data on international terrorism, Weinberg and Eubank later concluded that international terrorist attacks are substantially more likely to occur in democratic political systems than in other political regimes, but that regime change exposed countries to more terrorism (Weinberg & Eubank, 1998). Using a different dataset on international terrorism (ITERATE), Eubank and Weinberg (2001) found that international terrorist attacks occurred most often in stable democracies.

Although it is a popular explanation, also outside academia, Chenoweth (2013, p. 363) concluded the civil liberties explanation lacks empirical support. Studies have progressively turned their attention towards a more fine-grained categorization of regime types than the democracy–dictatorship dichotomy, and interest in the role of political institutions in explaining variations in levels of terrorism has increased.

Based on data from the GTD for the period from 1970 to 1997, and using initially an eight-category classification of regimes, distinguishing among democracies, partial democracies, factionalized democracies, partial autocracy, autocracy, and transitioning states, with failed states and states under occupation in addition, Chenoweth (2013, pp. 357–360) found support for a curvilinear relationship between regime type and terrorism. Domestic terrorism is likely to occur in economically poorer democracies, in transition to democracy, and with "internally inconsistent institutions." Less domestic terrorism is found in authoritarian regimes and advanced democracies (Chenoweth, 2013, p. 356).

Institutions, types of democracy, regime age, and terrorism

Attention has been directed to institutional design within states to find explanations of variation in the levels of terrorism. These explanations point to institutions that regulate access to the political system, institutions that regulate representation and power distribution.

One such institution is the electoral system, with its threshold for representation that might make it easier or more difficult for opposition groups to gain access and representation in key institutions. Some studies find that countries with proportional representation electoral systems are less exposed to terrorism than are countries using majoritarian electoral systems. Investigating how democracy affects international terrorism, based on data for 119 countries covering the 1975 to 1997 period, Li (2005) found that democratic participation in a country reduces the occurrence of international terrorist attacks, whereas government constraints increases the occurrence. Moreover, Li found that countries using proportional representation experienced a lower number of international terrorist attacks than did countries using majoritarian or mixed electoral systems.

This conclusion was based on data for international terrorism. However, results from studies on the relationship between electoral systems and domestic terrorism are contradictory. Whereas some studies find that countries with proportional representation electoral systems are less exposed to terrorism, the literature is far from conclusive on this point (Chenoweth, 2013, p. 365). Studying domestic terrorism in relation to institutions promoting proportionality, support has also been found for the opposite effect: "The presence and greater degrees of proportionality are significantly associated with greater levels of domestic terrorism when ethnic fractionalization within a given society increases. Moreover, domestic terrorism increases as the number of small parties represented in the legislature increases" (Foster, Braithwaite & Sobek, 2013, p. 541).

We may also hypothesize that other characteristics of political systems may influence the level of terrorism, such as type of party system, presidential versus parliamentary forms of government, or federalism, unitary government, or regional autonomy. Concerning the latter relationship, Frey and Luechinger (2004, p. 513) argued that "strengthening decentralized decision-making in the polity and economy provides disincentives for terrorist attacks." On the other hand, using MIPT Terrorism Knowledge Base data on domestic terrorism for 100 countries from 1998 to 2004, Dreher and Fischer (2011, p. 225) found that local *political autonomy* had no impact on domestic terrorism, but that *expenditure decentralization* is associated with lower levels of domestic terrorism.

Still others argue that the overall type of democracy – consensus versus majoritarian democracy – matters. Studying Western Europe for the period from 1985 to 2010, Qvortrup (2012) found that domestic terrorist attacks are more frequent in political systems of the majoritarian type compared to consensus democracies. Consensus institutions in a political system correlate negatively with levels of terrorist attacks. Exclusion of minorities through disproportionality tends to create situations in which higher levels of domestic terrorism are found. In a broader study of thirty-six democracies, which, in addition to nineteen West European countries, also includes advanced democracies such as Canada, Australia, New Zealand, the U.S., and democracies elsewhere in the Americas, Africa, Asia, and Oceania, Qvortrup and Lijphart (2013) concluded that majoritarian democracies are far more at risk than consensus democracies of fatal domestic terrorist attacks. Terrorism is here understood as domestic and organized; that is, fatal attacks on fellow citizens carried out by groups, and operationalized as a dummy variable counting whether or not a country experienced a fatal domestic terrorist attack. Democracies differ in the opportunities they present for political influence, and this is related to the level of fatal domestic terrorism (Qvortrup & Lijphart, 2013).

There is indication that how well established a democracy is may influence how exposed it is to terrorism. Regime longevity or age may play a part. An early indication of this was found by Eyerman (1998). Studying international attacks for 154 states in the period from 1968 to 1986, Eyerman found that new democracies were more exposed than either established democracies or non-democracies, though established democracies were less likely to experience international terrorism compared to non-democracies.

With better data encompassing both domestic and international terrorism, Piazza (2013) studied the effect of regime age or longevity on levels of terrorism. Finding that terrorism is less common in dictatorships compared to other regime types, Piazza concluded that dictatorships, regardless of age, have a capacity for reducing levels of terrorism that democratic regimes only achieve at a late age (Piazza, 2013, p. 261). However, young democracies are more exposed than old democracies to terrorism, demonstrating the effect of the longevity of the democratic regime on terrorism.

From this, the hypothesis that the older and more established a democracy gets, the less of a challenge terrorism will be can be derived. For regimes in transition to democracy and for newly formed democracies, the prospects are grimmer. Such regimes may be at serious risk. Examples of this are also found in the recent political history of Europe 31 countries. The third-wave democracies of Spain, Portugal, and

Greece all experienced terrorist campaigns early on after transition to democracy (Engene, 2004, pp. 126–134, 147–156). The exposure to terrorism in a process of democratization and the risk of backlash is perhaps best illustrated by the case of Spain. The intensity of terrorism, in the form of killings by the Basque separatist group ETA, increased markedly after the death of the dictator Franco in late 1975, only to increase year by year as liberalization was followed by round-table negotiations, agreement on the road to democracy, free elections, and a new constitution, in the end provoking hardliners from the ranks of the old regime to attempt a coup d'état in early 1981. On the other hand, the collapse of communism and transition to democracy in what is now the Central and Eastern European member countries of the EU largely did not produce sustained terrorist campaigns, though regime change was violent in Romania, and Lithuania, Slovenia, and Croatia were affected by violence and war in the breakdown of the larger states they had been part of.

Grievances

Chenoweth (2013, p. 369) argues that institutional explanations have more to do with political access than with democracy as such. Alternatively, political explanations focusing on grievances people or groups have may help explain the occurrence of terrorism. Typically, such grievances have to do with political underrepresentation or some form of discrimination, either political or economic.

The argument is that democracies are able to sustain legitimacy, which is needed to avoid terrorism. This is done by respecting fundamental human rights and by promoting economic, political, and ethnic equality. This explanation would lead us to expect that democracies are less prone to experience terrorist attacks and that regimes with no respect for human rights or less promotion of economic, political, and ethnic equality will tend to be more exposed to terrorism. However, pointing to the contrary, territorial or ethnic conflict may increase terrorist violence also in democracies that do respect human rights and promote equality, which can also be the case in in authoritarian regimes with similar conflicts.

Kurrild-Klitgaard, Justesen, and Klemmensen (2006) did an analysis of international terrorism and political rights and civil liberties for the period 1996 to 2002 using ITERATE data on international terrorism, though it might have been better to test these factors on data on domestic terrorism. They found that political rights and civil liberties were negatively related to the generation of international terrorists. Furthermore, there was a negative relationship to be found between political rights and the occurrence of international terrorist attacks, but a non-linear relationship between civil liberties rights and the occurrence of international terrorist attacks. Investigating the economic discrimination of minority groups and domestic terrorism, Piazza (2011) found that countries which discriminate against minorities economically experience higher levels of domestic terrorism, a finding that also holds when accounting for the level of economic development. De la Calle and Sánchez-Cuenca (2012) found that terrorism tends to occur in richer countries, though not in the very richest countries.

Conflicting findings – conceptual issues

Testing assumptions on the relationship between democracy and terrorism has produced a collection of confusing or contradictory findings, some based on international terrorism, some on domestic terrorism, and others on both, with limited possibilities for generalization. Faced by the challenge of summing up a review of the literature, Chenoweth concluded that concerning the period between 1968 and 1997, domestic terrorism was more likely in "relatively poor and transitioning democracies with internally inconsistent institutions" compared to both advanced democracies and authoritarian regimes Chenoweth (2013, p. 356). Higher levels of terrorism are associated with democratic regimes with "low levels of legitimacy, poor human rights practices, intermediate levels of political and economic development, and unresolved conflict among ethnic or political groups" (Chenoweth, 2013, p. 356).

Furthermore, concerning the distinction between domestic and international terrorism, Chenoweth concluded that advanced democracies were targeted by international terrorism originating in authoritarian regimes in cases when democratic countries had a record of military interference in other countries, resulting in higher levels of terrorism (2013, pp. 356–357).

Disagreement on the question of definition has long plagued research on terrorism, and the conceptual issue is far from settled (Schmid, 2011, pp. 39–98; de la Calle & Sánchez-Cuenca, 2011b; Sánchez-Cuenca, 2014). Terrorism is a concept strongly influenced by its use in politics, as a normative term and a label used for particularly objectionable acts or reprehensible adversaries. As Hoffman notes, in such a situation,

> virtually any especially abhorrent act of violence perceived as directed against society – whether it involves the activities of anti-government dissidents or governments themselves, organized-crime syndicates, common criminals, rioting mobs, people engaged in militant protest, individual psychotics, or lone extortionists – is often labelled "terrorism."
>
> *(Hoffman, 2006, p. 1)*

The term is applied to events ranging from genocide and atrocities of civil wars to political assassinations of presidents. For those who collect data, the risk is that non-state violence of most kinds ends up in the dataset, with violence from guerrilla groups engaged in civil war inflating the data (Sánchez-Cuenca, 2014, p. 596). Furthermore, terrorism is measured in many ways. In some studies terrorism may be measured by frequency, typically attack counts that treat small attacks resulting in no damage or deaths equally to attacks causing great damage and tens or hundreds of deaths. Alternatively, terrorism may be measured based on lethality (killings) or by some organizationally based indicator (i.e. number, longevity of groups, campaigns).

Testing hypotheses on data either on domestic and/or on international terrorism may have contributed to the conflicting findings. International terrorism, attacks involving perpetrators or victims of one or more country, is a particularly difficult category. There are at least three different levels of internationality. If we distinguish between attacks carried out in the perpetrator's home country versus attacks carried out abroad, and on the other hand distinguish between attacks victimizing the perpetrator's own countrymen versus attacks directed at foreigners, we get a fourfold set of categories. Whereas domestic terrorist attacks fit into the category where perpetrators attack their own countrymen within the borders of their own country (1), international terrorism can take three forms: (2) attacks on foreigners in a perpetrator's home country, (3) attacks on a perpetrator's fellow countrymen abroad, and (4) attacks where perpetrators go abroad to attack foreigners. While the last category (4) may be seen as undisputedly international, categories (2) and (3) are somewhere in between. Category (2) may arise not only by intent, but also coincidentally when one victim among many turned out to be foreign, so that this category may be seen as a variant of domestic attacks. It may also be argued that attacks in category (3) could be a continuation of domestic terrorism on abroad. The domestic-international distinction may be more problematic than usually realized, and it may be questioned whether or when international terrorism should be used for testing the hypothesis, and if actually done, operationalized in what way. One point of view is that the category of international terrorism "lacks theoretical foundations" (Sánchez-Cuenca, 2014, p. 595).

Sánchez-Cuenca (2014, p.5 93) argues that because of conceptual issues, which also influence datasets and data quality, less is known about terrorism compared to other forms of political violence. One reason, already mentioned, is the data situation. In general there is far more interest in using existing datasets on terrorism than in contributing to the effort of collecting, maintaining, and improving data or produce new datasets. Compilation and maintenance of event data on terrorism is time and resource demanding, especially if the focus is global and the dataset is to be kept up to date on a regular basis. Many, especially early, studies used the ITERATE dataset. After the GTD appeared, this has become the most popular dataset. Chenoweth (2013, p. 371) notes that even with the GTD dataset, the data availability for research on terrorism is more limited than is the case for other types of conflict. While data on war is available back to the early 1800s, datasets on terrorism are much more limited, none extending farther back than 1950. Nevertheless, the availability of new and larger datasets will not necessarily solve the fundamental problems facing research on terrorism. Especially since 9/11, and a new wave of research, there has been a tendency to escape conceptual issues by unquestioning reliance on existing datasets, though the conceptual issues apply in force to these too. As Sánchez-Cuenca points out, "the biases that these databases may have, are transferred to the substantive findings of the literature" (Sánchez-Cuenca, 2014, p. 595).

Another approach is to look at the self-reporting of terrorism by advanced democracies. The European Union police agency Europol publishes an annual report containing a retrospective overview of terrorism and counterterrorism efforts in the EU member states, based on what the governments of these states report. Data is available from 2006 onwards.

As can be seen from Table 10.2, never more than eleven of the EU27/EU28 countries have reported to have been affected by terrorism (domestic and international) in

TABLE 10.2 Terrorist attacks in EU member states, 2006–2014, as reported by Europol

	2006	2007	2008	2009	2010	2011	2012	2013	2014
Austria	1	1	6	6	2	0	0	0	0
Belgium	1	0	0	0	0	0	2	0	1
Bulgaria	–	0	0	0	0	0	2	0	0
Croatia	–	–	–	–	–	–	–	0	0
Cyprus	0	0	0	0	0	0	0	0	0
Czech Rep.	0	0	0	0	1	0	0	0	0
Denmark	0	1	0	0	2	4	0	0	0
Estonia	0	0	0	0	0	0	0	0	0
Finland	0	0	0	0	0	0	0	0	0
France	294	267	147	95	84	85	125	63	52
Germany	13	20	0	0	0	1	0	0	0
Greece	25	2	14	15	21	6	1	14	7
Hungary	0	0	0	4	0	0	0	0	0
Ireland	1		2	0	0	0	0	0	0
Italy	11	9	9	3	8	5	11	7	12
Latvia	0	0	0	0	0	0	0	0	0
Lithuania	0	0	0	0	0	0	0	0	0
Luxembourg	0	0	0	0	0	0	0	0	0
Malta	0	0	0	0	0	0	0	0	0
Netherlands	0	0	0	0	0	0	0	0	0
Poland	1	0	0	0	0	0	0	0	2
Portugal	1	2	0	0	0	0	0	0	0
Romania	–	0	0	0	0	0	0	0	0
Slovakia	0	0	0	0	0	0	0	0	0
Slovenia	0	0	0	0	0	0	0	0	0
Spain	145	279	263	171	90	47	54	33	18
Sweden	0	0	0	0	1	0	0	0	0
UK	5	2	74	*	40	26	24	35	109
Total	498	583	515	294	249	174	219	152	201
Number of countries reporting activity	11	9	7	7*	9	7	7	5	7
Total EU membership	25	27	27	27	27	27	27	28	28

– Country was not an EU member state in this year.

*For 2009, the UK did not report the number of failed, foiled, and completed attacks according to Europol criteria, though the TE-SAT report makes clear such attacks had in fact occurred.

Covers domestic as well as international terrorism.

Year 2006: Completed attacks. From 2007 onwards: failed, foiled, and completed attacks. No failed, foiled, and completed attacks reported, then assumed to be 0.

Source: Annual TE-SAT reports, Europol.

any given year from 2006 onwards, even when counting failed and foiled attacks in addition to those actually carried out. Typically, West European member states have attacks to report, usually the larger states of France, Spain, and the UK, with frequent, and usually smaller, attacks from separatist, national minority groups. Only exceptionally do newer member states in Central and Eastern Europe report anything. Taking into account that most of the attacks reported originated in regional conflicts, were small in scale, and most often resulting in no deaths, it is hard to conclude that advanced democracies such as the EU member states are particularly challenged by terrorism. Terrorist attacks do happen in these countries, occasionally on a large scale, but the problem appears limited compared to the levels of terrorist violence experienced elsewhere. Drawing on GTD data, the Institute for Economics and Peace (2014, p. 35) observed that for the 2000 to 2013 period, 7 per cent of terrorist attacks and 5 per cent of deaths resulting from terrorism worldwide occurred in Organisation for Economic Co-operation and Development (OECD) countries, with eight out of thirty-four OECD member countries experiencing lethal attacks in 2013. Chenoweth (2013, pp. 357, 372) concludes that the pattern of terrorism may have shifted since 11 September 2001, observing that terrorism appears to be moving from democracies to non-democracies – that is, partial autocracies or countries under military occupation.

Counterterrorism and democracy

In the wake of the attacks in the U.S. on 11 September 2001, advanced democracies find themselves in a situation in which the protection of societies against terrorists has become a prominent political issue. While not based on an argument for the total replacement of democracy by the rule of guardians, to use the terms of Robert A. Dahl (1998), advanced democracies increasingly witness policy developments introducing measures aimed at guarding society and democracy from its terrorist enemies. While this may be regarded as responsibility, governments trying to protect their citizens, counterterrorist policies may also involve redefining the boundaries of accepted political involvement. Citizens call for protection and find responsive governments. Those in authority sometimes argue the necessity of guarding society against enemies of democracy, terrorists, even if this entails encroaching on some of the fundamental principles otherwise seen as essential for democracy, in the perspective of Dahl (1998). New countermeasures aimed at curtailing terrorism may then have consequences for such principles as the right to discuss and deliberate, the opportunity to obtain information relevant for policy decisions, including alternatives, and for the protection of minorities and their integration in the political system influencing the inclusiveness of political systems.

Though there are cases where young democracies broke down or where processes of democratization were reversed in situations where countries faced terrorism, resulting in military coups or the establishment of dictatorships (Weinberg, 2011, pp. 31–33), this seems unlikely to happen in advanced or established democracies.

However, early on in the literature on terrorism, it was realized that government response to terrorism might pose a threat to democracy as well: "If the government is provoked into introducing emergency powers, suspending habeas corpus, or invoking martial law, it confronts the paradox of suspending democracy in order to defend it" (Wilkinson, 1974, p. 109). In his discussion of strengths and weaknesses of democracies confronted by terrorism, Schmid (1992) emphasized that, in the end, terrorism and counterterrorism are a struggle for legitimacy. He argued that for democracies, it is more important to maintain legitimacy than to gain short-term victories through succumbing to the temptation to employ immediate counter-measures to crack down on terrorism.

The terrorist attacks in the U.S. on 11 September 2001 moved the fight against terrorism towards the top of the political agenda, not only in the U.S. but also in many other countries. Though the Bush administration launched a War on Ter-ror to be fought by military means, the struggle against terrorism has also been intensified in the civilian sector, through changes in penal codes, intelligence gath-ering, and policing. In international organizations such as the United Nations, the European Union, and the Council of Europe, states have agreed on international standards in the struggle against terrorism and adopted partly binding obligations. As a consequence, new measures against terrorism have been adopted in many countries. Though several countries that experienced terrorist campaigns from the 1970s and through the 1980s had already adopted temporary or permanent legal measures aimed at fighting terrorism (Haubrich, 2003), post-9/11 countries that had no previous exposure to terrorism have adopted new measures (Nordenhaug & Engene, 2008).

The post-9/11 developments represent a change of paradigm in fighting ter-rorism from reactive measures towards increasingly pre-emptive measures (Husabø, 2005). Traditional criminal justice, dominating the pre-9/11 struggle against ter-rorism, would pursue terrorists after the fact of the crime; that is, after the terrorist attack was a fact. In light of the catastrophic consequences of 9/11, and high casu-alty attacks like those in Madrid on 11 March 2004 and in London on 7 July 2005, a reactive response to terrorism is increasingly seen as insufficient, because this approach could not prevent deadly terrorist attacks from happening. As a conse-quence of what was seen as the threat of "new terrorism," a shift towards preventing and pre-empting terrorism may be observed. Many of the new measures adopted by liberal democracies governed by the rule of law aim at preventing terrorism from happening by granting police and intelligence agencies more powers of investiga-tion in cases of suspected terrorist plots, but also through the criminalization of activities connected to terrorism in a wider sense than direct participation in the execution of terrorist attacks. Financing, instigation, recruitment, and other sup-port activities have been criminalized, together with preparation to commit acts of terrorism.

Some of the measures adopted by liberal democracies are controversial because they potentially transgress the border of what is considered acceptable within polities governed by the rule of law, with respect for fundamental civil and political rights. Two such basic principles are the presumption of innocence and the right to fair trial. According to the first principle, no one is to be considered guilty of any crime unless prosecution can build a substantiated case against a person. Suspicion alone is generally not enough to jail people. According to the other principle, the case must be presented before an impartial court, with the defendant having the right of legal representation.

Detention of terrorist suspects without trial is one of the most controversial policies in the struggle against terrorism, because these principles are set aside. Some liberal democracies have a long-standing history of using such measures, originating in attempts to handle domestic terrorism. The United Kingdom and the conflict in Northern Ireland is a case in point. In the UK, the maximum period authorities may detain terrorism suspects without trial has been extended step by step. Currently, authorities may hold suspects for up to twenty-eight days. Previously, proposals asked parliament to extend the limit to forty-two days or even ninety days of detention (both were defeated). No other advanced democracy grants authorities such extensive periods of detention in cases of suspected terrorism. In Australia the maximum period police may hold suspects is twelve days, in Ireland seven days, France six days, Spain five, Italy four, Denmark and Norway three, and the period in Germany, New Zealand, and the U.S. is two days (Russell, 2007, p. 9).

In several countries, the period for which police may hold suspects before presenting them before a court is the same for all types of crime, and no special measures are in place for suspected terrorism. While a draconic measure like detention might be exceptional, in several countries policies in line with the pre-emptive model of counterterrorism implies the criminalization of activity associated with terrorism, or even opinions, as in the case of instigation and glorification of terrorism. Increased powers in terms of communication control (e.g. phone tapping, control of email and other electronic communication, etc.) and surveillance are granted to investigative agencies. The threshold of criminalization is lowered, moving criminalization into areas that are usually protected by the principles of freedom of association or freedom of speech. Identity control is reinforced, and limits may be placed on public access to public places or buildings. Counterterrorism may have far-reaching consequences also in advanced democracies.

Whether targeted at specific groups, especially immigrants or members of suspicious groups or networks, or applying to all inhabitants in general, post-9/11 a convergence of counterterrorism measures has been observed. Among EU member states, peer review processes were set in motion in the area of counterterrorism and other fields of internal security (Bossong, 2012). Though Neumayer, Plümper, and Epifanio (2014) did not find support for a process of ever stricter counterterrorism measures leading to all states adopting the strictest possible policies, they nevertheless concluded that states must take into account the counterterrorism policies adopted by states in their peer group.

The pressure to adopt new legislation or adjust existing legislation is not only made through the coordinating efforts of the European Union, which in 2002 adopted a framework decision that introduced a common definition of terrorism to help harmonize the definition of terrorist offences in all EU states. United Nations Security Council resolution 1373, adopted within two weeks of the 9/11 attacks in 2001, obliges all UN member states to implement legislation that criminalizes terrorist activity, prohibits support of terrorism, especially financial support, and denies safe haven to terrorists, as well as requiring all UN member states to cooperate in fighting terrorism. A Counter Terrorism Committee was appointed to oversee member country implementation.

Based on a study of OECD countries, Lehrke and Schomaker (2014) concluded that the convergence of domestic counterterrorism regulations was mainly driven by international networks that promote learning, working in particular following an increase in the level of the international terrorism threat. Though moving in the same direction of tightening counterterrorism efforts, advanced democracies differ in how long down that road they have travelled. Pokalova (2015) concludes that before 9/11 counterterrorist legislation was adopted by countries faced with terrorist groups, but that after 9/11 previous counterterrorism legislation led to the adoption of new legislation, and that countries taking part in the War on Terror did so too. In a study of twenty liberal democracies in the period from 2001 to 2008, Epifanio (2011) found that all of them had strengthened counterterrorist legislation, though the scope of change varied. While countries such as the United Kingdom and the U.S. adopted counterterrorist measures on a broad range affecting civil rights for citizens in general, as well as suspects and immigrants, legislation was more cautious in other countries, such as in Scandinavia, or in Canada or Switzerland.

Conclusion

Although terrorist attacks, occasionally on a large scale, happen even in advanced democracies, it does not appear that such regimes are more exposed to terrorism in comparison to other regimes. There is indication of an inverted U-shape relationship between regime type and levels of terrorism: the more established democracies get, the less exposed to terrorism they are. This is a trait that advanced democratic regimes share with the most authoritarian regimes that maintain a level of control that suppresses opposition, both violent and nonviolent. Regimes somewhere between advanced democracies and authoritarian regimes, whether partial democracies, partial autocracies, or in some stage of transition, are exposed to more terrorism. At the same time, such regimes may be vulnerable and at risk from the negative consequences of terrorism and efforts to counter terrorism. Seen from the perspective of counterterrorism, advanced democracies with a high capacity of counterterrorism are those less at risk. Nevertheless, policies and measures to prevent terrorism may intrude on established principles of rule of law and of civil and political rights that are central to democracy. In this way terrorism and counterterrorism influences the development of democracy, even among the most advanced in this group of regimes, though it would be going too far to conclude that democracy is at risk from either.

Further reading

de la Calle, Luis & Sánchez-Cuenca, Ignacio (2011) What we talk about when we talk about terrorism. *Politics & Society*, 39(3), pp. 451–472.

Qvortrup, Matt & Lijphart, Arend (2013) Domestic terrorism and democratic regime types. *Civil Wars*, 15(4), pp. 471–485.

Wilkinson, Paul (2011) *Terrorism versus democracy: The liberal state response*, 3rd edition. Abingdon: Routledge. Chapter 6: "Law-Enforcement, Criminal Justice and the Liberal State", pp. 75–100.

Key questions for discussion

1   Terrorism is a controversial concept, with discussion and disagreement on how to define the term. How may this controversy influence datasets, empirical analysis, and ultimately conclusions drawn about terrorism?
2   Some argue that institutions, institutional design, or models of democracy may explain why countries are more or less exposed to terrorism. In a deeply divided society, what kind of institutions could help reduce the risk of groups turning to terrorism?
3   In countering terrorism, democratic governments are sometimes warned that hard-line responses and repression might constitute an overreaction that actually poses a more serious threat to democracy than that coming from terrorist attacks. Discuss this warning and consider whether all democracies are equally at risk from overreaction.

References

Berkebile, R.E. (2015) What is domestic terrorism? A method for classifying events from the global terrorism database. *Terrorism and Political Violence*, pp. 1–26.

Bossong, R. (2012) Peer reviews in the fight against terrorism: A hidden dimension of European security governance. *Cooperation and Conflict*, 47(4), pp. 519–538.

Bowie, N.G. & Schmid, A.P. (2011) Databases on terrorism. In Schmid, A.P. ed. *The Routledge handbook of terrorism research*. London: Routledge, pp. 294–340.

Chenoweth, E. (2013) Terrorism and democracy. *Annual Review of Political Science*, 16, pp. 355–378.

Crenshaw, M. (1981) The causes of terrorism. *Comparative Politics*, 13(4), pp. 379–399.

Dahl, R.A. (1998) *On democracy*. New Haven: Yale University Press.

de la Calle, L. & Sánchez-Cuenca, I. (2011a) The quantity and quality of terrorism: The DTV dataset. *Journal of Peace Research*, 48(1), pp. 49–58.

de la Calle, L. & Sánchez-Cuenca, I. (2011b) What we talk about when we talk about terrorism. *Politics & Society*, 39(3), pp. 451–472.

de la Calle, L. & Sánchez-Cuenca, I. (2012) Rebels without territory: An analysis of nonterritorial conflicts in the world, 1970–1997. *Journal of Conflict Resolution*, 56(4), pp. 580–603.

Dreher, A. & Fischer, J.A.V. (2011) Does government decentralization reduce domestic terror? An empirical test. *Economics Letters*, 111(3), pp. 223–225.

Enders, W., Sandler, T. & Gaibulloev, K. (2011) Domestic versus transnational terrorism: Data, decomposition, and dynamics. *Journal of Peace Research*, 48(3), pp. 319–337.

Engene, J.O. (2004) *Terrorism in Western Europe explaining the trends since 1950*. Cheltenham: Edward Elgar.

Engene, J.O. (2007) Five decades of terrorism in Europe: The TWEED dataset. *Journal of Peace Research*, 44(1), pp. 109–121.

Epifanio, M. (2011) Legislative response to international terrorism. *Journal of Peace Research*, 48(3), pp. 399–411.

Eubank, W. & Weinberg, L. (1994) Does democracy encourage terrorism? *Terrorism and Political Violence*, 6(4), pp. 417–463.

Eubank, W. & Weinberg, L. (2001) Terrorism and democracy: Perpetrators and victims. *Terrorism and Political Violence*, 13(1), pp. 155–164.

Eyerman, J. (1998) Terrorism and democratic states: Soft targets or accessible systems. *International Interactions: Empirical and Theoretical Research in International Relations*, 24(2), pp. 151–170.

Foster, D.M., Braithwaite, A. & Sobek, D. (2013) There can be no compromise: Institutional inclusiveness, fractionalization and domestic terrorism. *British Journal of Political Science*, 43(3), pp. 541–557.

Frey, B.S. & Luechinger, S. (2004) Decentralization as a disincentive for terror. *European Journal of Political Economy*, 20(2), pp. 509–515.

Haubrich, D. (2003) September 11, anti-terror laws and civil liberties: Britain, France and Germany compared. *Government and Opposition*, 38(1), pp. 3–27.

Hoffman, B. (2006) *Inside terrorism*, revised and expanded edition. New York: Columbia University Press.

Husabø, E.J. (2005) The implementation of new rules on terrorism through the pillars of the European Union. In Husabø, E.J. & Strandbakken, A. eds. *Harmonization of criminal law in Europe*. Oxford: Hart Publishing, pp. 53–78.

Institute for Economics and Peace (2014) *Global Terrorism Index 2014*. [Internet]. Available from: http://www.visionofhumanity.org/sites/default/files/Global%20Terrorism%20 Index%20Report%202014_0.pdf [Accessed 18 November 2014].

International Terrorism Data Center (2015) *Vinyard Software: Mission Statement*. [Internet]. Available from: http://vinyardsoftware.com/ [Accessed 29 June 2015].

Knutsen, T. (2016) A Re-Emergence of Nationalism as a Political Force in Europe? In Peters, Y. & Tatham, M. eds. *Democratic Transformations in Europe: Challenges and Opportunities*. Abingdon: Routledge, pp. 13–32.

Kurrild-Klitgaard, P., Justesen, M.K. & Klemmensen, R. (2006) The political economy of freedom, democracy and transnational terrorism. *Public Choice*, 128(1–2), pp. 289–315.

LaFree, G., Dugan, L. & Miller, E. (2015) *Putting terrorism in context: Lessons from the global terrorism database*. London: Routledge.

Lehrke, J.P. & Schomaker, R. (2014) Mechanisms of convergence in domestic counterterrorism regulations: American influence, domestic needs, and international networks. *Studies in Conflict and Terrorism*, 37(8), pp. 689–712.

Li, Q. (2005) Does democracy promote or reduce transnational terrorist incidents? *The Journal of Conflict Resolution*, 49(2), pp. 278–297.

National Consortium for the Study of Terrorism and Responses to Terrorism (START) (2015a) *Global Terrorism Database*. [Data File]. Available from: http://www.start.umd. edu/gtd [Accessed 30 June 2015].

National Consortium for the Study of Terrorism and Responses to Terrorism (START) (2015b) *Global Terrorism Database: Codebook: Inclusion Criteria and Variables: June 2015*. [Internet]. Available from: http://www.start.umd.edu/gtd/downloads/Codebook.pdf [Accessed 30 June 2015].

National Consortium for the Study of Terrorism and Responses to Terrorism (START) (2015c) *Frequently Asked Questions*. [Internet]. Available from: http://www.start.umd. edu/gtd/faq/ [Accessed 30 June 2015].

Neumayer, E., Plümper, T. & Epifanio, M. (2014) The 'peer-effect' in counterterrorist policies. *International Organization*, 68(1), pp. 211–234.

Nordenhaug, I. & Engene, J.O. (2008) *Norge i kamp mot terrorisme.* Oslo: Universitetsforlaget.

Piazza, J.A. (2011) Poverty, minority economic discrimination and domestic terrorism. *Journal of Peace Research*, 48(3), pp. 339–353.

Piazza, J.A. (2013) Regime age and terrorism: Are new democracies prone to terrorism? *International Interactions: Empirical and Theoretical Research in International Relations*, 39(2), pp. 246–263.

Pokalova, E. (2015) Legislative responses to terrorism: What drives states to adopt new counterterrorism legislation? *Terrorism and Political Violence*, 27(3), 474–496.

Qvortrup, M.H. (2012) Terrorism and political science. *British Journal of Politics and International Relations*, 14(4), pp. 503–517.

Qvortrup, M. & Lijphart, A. (2013) Domestic terrorism and democratic regime types. *Civil Wars*, 15(4), pp. 471–485.

RAND (2015) *RAND Database of Worldwide Terrorism Incidents.* [Internet]. Available from: http://www.rand.org/nsrd/projects/terrorism-incidents.html [Accessed 29 June 2015].

Russell, J. (2007) *Terrorism pre-charge detention: Comparative law study.* London: Liberty.

Sánchez-Cuenca, I. (2014) Why do we know so little about terrorism? *International Interactions: Empirical and Theoretical Research in International Relations*, 40(4), pp. 590–601.

Schmid, A.P. (1992) Terrorism and democracy. *Terrorism and Political Violence*, 4(4), pp. 14–25.

Schmid, A.P. (2011) The definition of terrorism. In Schmid, A.P. ed. *The Routledge handbook of terrorism research.* Abingdon: Routledge, pp. 39-98.

Schmid, A.P. & de Graaf, J. (1982) *Violence as communication: Insurgent terrorism and the western news media.* London and Beverly Hills: SAGE.

Somerville, K. (2012) *Radio propaganda and the broadcasting of hatred: Historical development and definitions.* Basingstoke: Palgrave Macmillan.

Tatham, M. (2016) Multi-jurisdictional politics: State adaptation and mixed visions of democracy. In Peters, Y. & Tatham, M. eds. *Democratic Transformations in Europe: Challenges and Opportunities.* Abingdon: Routledge, pp. 269–293.

Weinberg, L. (2011) *Democracy and terrorism: Friend or Foe?* London and New York: Routledge.

Weinberg, L.B. & Eubank, W.L. (1998) Terrorism and democracy: What recent events disclose. *Terrorism and Political Violence*, 10(1), pp. 108–118.

Wilkinson, P. (1974) *Political terrorism.* London: Macmillan.

Wilkinson, P. (1977) *Terrorism and the liberal state.* London: Macmillan.

11

CLIMATE CHANGE MITIGATION

Friederike Talbot

Introduction

Emitted greenhouse gases (GHGs) accumulate in the atmosphere and trap some of the sun's heat, which makes life on Earth possible. But since the industrial revolution, GHG emissions have increased drastically – thus less and less of the sun's heat can escape – resulting in climate change or global warming.[1] While precise predictions are difficult to make, if left unmitigated, the rise of the average temperature of Earth's atmosphere and oceans will soon have severe negative effects for the planet and its inhabitants. These include loss of habitat due to desertification or sea level rise, decrease in water resources in many already dry areas and a reduction in the food supply due to a decrease in the length of growing seasons and suitable area for agriculture in many parts of the world. Furthermore, incidences and severity of storms, floods and droughts are likely to increase (see IPCC 2013).

In order to mitigate these effects, we need to minimize the warming of the globe: precise temperature goals are controversial and range from around one to three degrees Celsius (see Hansen et al. 2008), but all of them require a significant reduction of global GHG emissions in the near future. This poses a unique political challenge to the world as a whole, as well as to Europe and its individual countries in particular. The first part of the chapter briefly presents and discusses important characteristics of this challenge, as well as some empirical and theoretical trends regarding responses to climate change in Europe. The second part is devoted to a more theoretical discussion of the relationship between climate change and democracy. It addresses the degree to which climate change poses unique problems and/or opportunities to democracy per se, as well as how democratic systems might thrive or fail in responding to this tremendous threat.

Empirical and theoretical trends regarding climate change in Europe

In order to critically discuss empirical and theoretical trends in Europe 31[2] regarding climate change, we need to keep in mind that it posits a unique problem for various reasons, which are outlined in the following sections.

First and foremost, the fact that the issue is hard to see makes it difficult to adequately address. Unlike other environmental problems – where a specific action leads to a specific problem, which can be measured and observed in a certain space and time – climate change's cause and projected effects are spatially and temporally disconnected from one another (see Loske 1997). The effect is not limited to any location and is unrelated to where the GHGs were emitted in the first place. The cumulative effect of years of increasing GHG emissions will lead to further global warming in the future, making it harder to mobilize for the cause of fighting climate change. This is a typical phenomenon of future discounting, where – since the dangers of global warming are not yet visible in daily life everywhere – people are not motivated to do anything concrete about them. But if we wait until the dangers become more visible, action will come too late (Giddens 2009). Additionally, future problems are easily superseded by actual or even perceived problems in the present, which reduces climate change's perceived urgency in daily life even further.

Although precise predictions about future impacts are difficult to make, some effects of climate change (such as changes in the atmospheric composition, global average temperatures and ocean conditions) can already be observed (see IPCC 2013). And it is apparent that not all countries are equally at risk. Its effects are predicted to vary widely by geographic location, which means that climate change – while being a global problem – does not pose an equal threat to all.

While some sectors and regions (for instance, Southeast Asia and Africa) are particularly vulnerable, others will likely be less affected and might even see limited potential benefits (see IPCC 2014b). In general, industrialized countries tend to not face a high risk of severe negative impacts, while the developing world is considered most affected (see, for instance, Germanwatch 2014b), because climate vulnerability varies according to geographic as well as economic factors. Most European countries tend to be both geographically fortunate as well as being more capable of dealing with these challenges, but there is already variation of climate-related impacts within the region, as Figure 11.1 shows.

These graphs show annual impacts of weather-related loss events (such as storms, floods, heat waves,[3] etc.) for the years 2004, and 2006 to 2013.[4] We can see some dramatic incidences in individual years in some countries, leading to deaths and financial losses. For instance, in the UK in 2013, 775 people (1.21 per 100,000 inhabitants) died due to weather-related events, in Latvia 45 people (1.96 per 100,000) died in 2006, and in Poland 437 people died in the years 2009 and 2010 (1.16 per 100,000 inhabitants for both years combined). Similarly, there are a few instances in which individual countries have experienced losses in GDP. However, despite these more or less isolated incidences, the region as a whole has not suffered

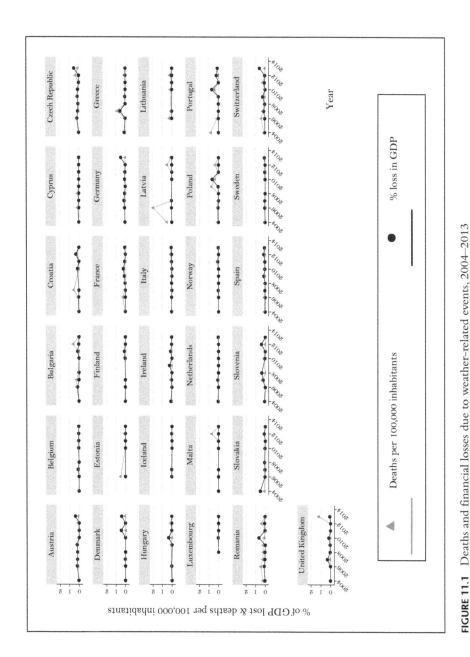

FIGURE 11.1 Deaths and financial losses due to weather-related events, 2004–2013

Data source: Germanwatch's Climate Risk Index (2006b, 2007c, 2008b–2014b)

significantly due to weather-related losses (yet). This is especially apparent if we compare it with the losses of the countries that were most affected in the year 2013: in the Philippines, 6,479 people (6.65 per 100,000 inhabitants) and in India 7,437 people (0.6 per 100,000 inhabitants) are recorded to have died due to weather-related events alone. And Cambodia suffered a 3.24 per cent loss of gross domestic product (GDP).

We need to keep in mind that these trends are not predictions for future impacts and can only serve to indicate that some climate-related losses can already be observed, and that their distribution is uneven. Also, this data does not indicate vulnerabilities to climate change effects other than weather-related losses, such as sea level rise (which will also worsen the impact of storms, as well as being a destructive force in and of itself), and which will particularly affect coastal regions and islands (such as the Netherlands, the UK, Ireland, Italy, Malta, etc.). However, we can conclude that some comparatively minor impacts of climate change can already be observed, even in the not-particularly-vulnerable European countries.

We also need to keep in mind that climate change has no regard for national borders, and different regions within countries, as well as different economic sectors, can be affected differently. Furthermore, different individuals in the same region can be differently at risk as well. Social inequalities shape vulnerability to climate change (see IPCC 2014b). And just as, for instance, environmental health problems disproportionately affect poor minorities in the U.S. (see, for instance, Chambers 2007), the impact of global warming is predicted to be worst for poor and marginalized people, particularly in the global South (see Kaijser & Kronsell 2014). This point will become relevant in the discussion of climate change and democracy later on.

In addition to the unequal distribution of climate vulnerability – which makes the issue more urgent for some and less for others – we also need to keep in mind that not all countries are equally responsible for the occurrence of climate change. Due to varying emission levels and emission periods, not all countries feel equally responsible to contribute to climate change's solutions. Paradoxically, there is an imbalance between the most-developed countries that are most responsible and largely not particularly vulnerable and many less-developed countries with much smaller per capita emissions and a shorter historical period of emitting GHGs, which are very vulnerable to climate change.

We can see that – largely because of various levels of vulnerability and responsibility – not all countries might feel equally committed to tackling the issue of global climate change. However, its effects can only be mitigated if everyone – or at least a large number of countries (and people) – contribute. Otherwise, countries that do reduce their emissions have to bear the short-term costs of doing so potentially without benefiting from actually achieving their long-term goal. Thus, they might end up bearing the cost of reduction in addition to the cost that climate change poses to them. Conversely, a country that chooses to do nothing to reduce its emissions could still benefit from other countries' efforts without having to bear any of the associated costs. In this way it is a prime example of the "free rider" problem, in which the benefits to any individual nation are not directly linked to the contribution of that nation to reducing GHG emissions, creating an incentive for nations to "free ride" on the efforts that other nations have taken (see Grundig 2009; Pavlov 2010). This collective action problem requires global action, and thus calls for international regulations or agreements which reduce the fear of "free riding."[5] International efforts by nation-states, however, are not the only response to climate change, as local efforts and urban politics play a promising and increasingly larger role in tackling the issue (see Barber 2013), as they can, for instance, promote public transport and thus increase energy efficiency tremendously for large groups of people. In addition to these local developments, national and international efforts are still very relevant if we are to prevent the worst effects from happening.

The following section looks at some empirical as well as theoretical trends to the question of how Europe 31 is tackling the issue of climate change, as well as why that might be the case. In Figure 11.2, we see annual GHG emissions for each European country between the years 1990 and 2012. All 31 countries are so-called Annex I countries (certain parties to the Kyoto Protocol), and thus they have committed themselves to specific emission reduction goals[6] (i.e. a decrease of around 5 per cent[7] compared to the base year 1990[8] in the period between 2008 and 2012), as well as to regularly report emission inventories to the United Nations Framework Convention on Climate Change (UNFCCC) Secretariat (basis of the data shown).

The most apparent observation from these graphs is that the emission levels vary tremendously among the different countries. For instance, Germany – while having a clear downward trend – has much higher emissions than any other European country. Unsurprisingly, countries with stronger economies tend to emit more than ones with weaker economies, with France, Germany, Italy, Poland, Spain and the UK being the largest GHG emitters among this group.[9] In Figure 11.3, we can more clearly see the emission trends for each country.

The majority of European countries have decreased their emissions from 1990 levels. Only 10 out of 31 countries have increased, with Cyprus and Malta having the highest percentage increase (around 53 per cent and 58 per cent, respectively). Six countries have decreased their emissions by more than 40 per cent. All countries combined decreased their emissions by around 19 per cent in this 22-year period. Although this seems like a positive development, we are still far from reaching the goal of reducing the levels of GHGs emitted sufficiently to prevent the worst of climate change. As mentioned in the first section, precise predictions about possible future scenarios are impossible and are often controversially disputed. However, according to the Intergovernmental Panel on Climate Change's (IPCC)[10] newest assessment report (IPCC 2014a), in order to maintain warming below two degrees Celsius, we need to reduce anthropogenic GHG emissions by 40 per cent to 70 per cent by the year 2050 compared to 2010 levels. That is about 1 to 2 per cent each year. Considering that the emission trends of several developing countries are increasing, an even larger reduction might be needed from European countries with consolidated economies to make up for it. Thus, while it appears that some successes have been achieved, much more needs to be done to tackle the issue at hand.

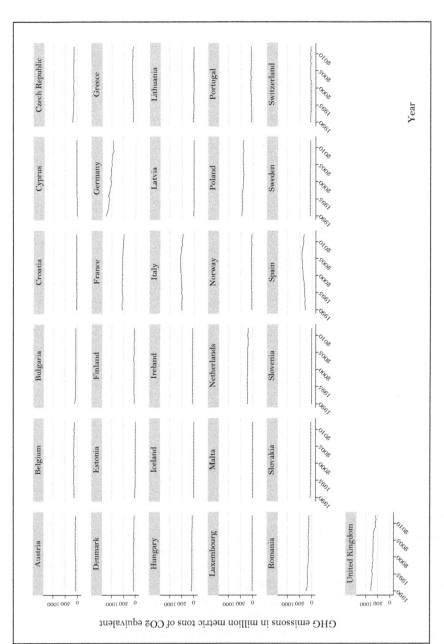

FIGURE 11.2 Greenhouse gas emissions, 1990–2012

The levels of greenhouse gas emissions shown exclude Land Use Change and Forestry (LUCF), which are changes in levels of greenhouse gases that are attributed to land-use change activities (for instance achieved through forest management).

Data source: CAIT Climate Data Explorer 2015

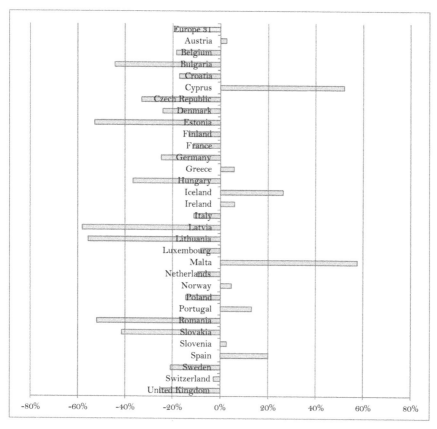

FIGURE 11.3 Percentage growth in greenhouse gas emissions, 1990–2012

Again emission reductions due to Land Use Change and Forestry (LUCF) are excluded.

Data source: CAIT Climate Data Explorer 2015

What might make us even less optimistic about hitting crucial emission targets is the fact that much of the observed emission reduction in the region can be attributed to economic factors, rather than political effort. In particular, reductions among formerly socialist countries are often seen as a by-product of their economic development and are thus considered "accidental" (see Oberthür & Ott 2000) or a "hot air" effect (Kemfert 2002). Their economies' transition from central to market economies led almost inevitably to an economic contraction, which in turn led to reduced emissions (see Grubb 2004). The European Commission (2011) names the decline in energy-inefficient heavy industry and the overall restructuring of the economy in the late 1980s and 1990s as the main reasons for the decrease in emissions in Eastern European member states. Similarly, the world financial crisis of 2008 led to a decrease in emissions, which was especially visible in Italy, Ireland, Germany, Spain and the UK. This might lead us to question the extent to which we actually affect GHG emissions politically or whether it is all just a by-product of economics. This question is somewhat theoretically dividing: in fact, according to the neoliberal tradition of advocating for free trade – due to the free market's supposed superiority over state regulation (see Friedman 1953) – an argument can be made that (environmental) standards increase when per capita income increases, which in turn is favoured by free trade (see Anderson 1998). According to this view, political intervention would only disrupt the inevitable development towards protecting the environment. Whether or not one agrees with this view, economic development and performance on mitigating climate change are linked in various ways: First, economic developments directly affect GHG emissions. Second, how clean an economy is to start with affects how costly or difficult it is for that country to further decrease emissions. Countries whose economies are more inefficient have more "low-hanging fruit" to pick (see Popp 2010), and thus have an easier time reducing their emissions than do countries with already relatively clean economies. Third, economic pressure can sometimes create incentives to save energy or to use more efficient technologies, which in turn leads to a decrease in emissions. Fourth, the economic situation of a country and its standard of living of individuals can also be seen as having an effect on the social values in a society. It appears that a certain standard of living is necessary for people to move from materialist (i.e. giving priority to economic growth) to post-materialist values (i.e. placing emphasis on the quality of life, such as environmental protection) (Inglehart & Abramson 1994; Inglehart 1995).

However, all this should not lead us to conclude that political efforts do not matter. On the contrary, while economic development affects climate performance dramatically and while there sometimes are economic incentives to act, political solutions are needed to meet emission reduction targets and mitigate the worst of climate change.[11]

In Figure 11.4, we see a rating of countries' national and international climate change policies.[12] These two policy grades range from 1, for best possible policy, to 5, for worst possible policy (with decimals in between).

We can see that no countries' national climate policies are graded as being particularly good. The best national climate policy grade is 1.9 for Denmark in the year 2013. Furthermore, in most cases, countries' national climate change policies were graded worse than their behaviour within international climate negotiations. While in many countries national and international policies are rated similarly, there is variation both within countries and over time. Germany, the United Kingdom and Norway have shown particularly good international efforts, but their national policies are somewhat lagging. On the other side, several countries perform poorly both nationally and internationally, with Italy and Romania's climate policy performance being particularly poorly rated. A full discussion of why countries might be performing the way they are goes beyond the scope of this chapter, but this data helps to illustrate how these cases fit or contradict theoretical expectations.

A number of theoretical perspectives have been used to attempt to explain why some countries are better than others at politically tackling the challenge of climate change. For the purpose of review, we can distinguish these broad types of theoretical viewpoints: those that focus on rational state interests, on the effects of political

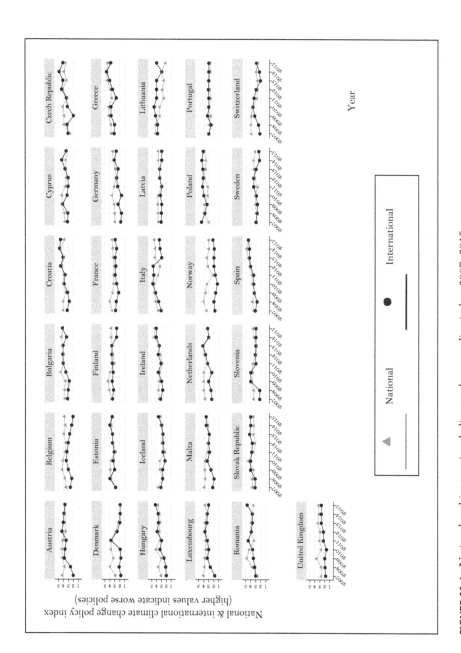

FIGURE 11.4 National and international climate change policy index, 2007–2015

Data source: Germanwatch's Climate Change Performance Index (2006a, 2007a, 2007b, 2008a–2014a)

systems, and on the influence of public opinion. The following is not meant to serve as an exhaustive review of all relevant theory, but rather to give an introductory overview.

As described previously, not all countries are equally at risk due to climate change. This fact might easily lead to the assumption that not all countries are equally motivated to tackle the issue, but rather that countries will only act if they have a lot to gain. Furthermore, countries' cost of fighting climate change varies according to geographic and economic factors. Thus, they would have different cost-benefit analyses and accordingly different priorities and policy preferences regarding climate change mitigation. The focus on rational state interests views climate change as a rational choice problem, where on one side of the scale are the benefits to a country of successful action and on the other hand are the costs of such action (see, for instance, Sprinz & Vaahtoranta 1994; Dolsak 2001).[13]

Based on this type of rational choice analysis, we would expect that Europe's most vulnerable countries would have better climate policies as they would have the most to benefit from mitigation, while Europe as a whole does not have high incentives for acting as it is not particularly vulnerable. However, the performance of Europe's most vulnerable countries (as indicated by weather-related losses in recent years) appears to vary significantly (e.g. while the UK's climate policy performance is among the best, Poland's climate policy is among the worst).

Regarding the cost of climate action, several factors could be taken into account. For instance, for economies that are already comparatively clean, further emission reductions are more costly than they are for economies that are more inefficient to start with. Additionally, countries' climatic and geographic features can influence their abatement costs. Countries that have many sunny days per year, for instance, can adopt an energy plan that relies heavily on solar power. Another such factor is whether a country benefits from exporting fossil fuels, and thus climate action could mean that it would have to forgo valuable revenue. (This would likely have less of an impact on a country's national climate action and more on its position for international negotiations.) The majority of European countries are not significant exporters of fossil fuels, but Norway and the Netherlands are among the world's top ten exporters of natural gas,[14] and after Norway, the UK is Europe's second largest exporter of crude oil (CIA's World Factbook 2013). The region's three largest coal exporters between the years 2008 and 2012 have been the Czech Republic, the Netherlands and Poland (U.S. Energy Information Administration 2015). According to rational choice assumptions, we would expect these countries to have poor climate policies, but again their performance varies significantly. While Poland and the Czech Republic do have poor climate policies, the UK and Norway are doing well. Based on these inconsistencies it seems that European countries' climate policy performance cannot be fully explained by this type of rational choice analysis.

These different rational state interests are not the only conclusion of a rational choice analysis of the climate crisis. A different perspective, for instance, arrives at the conclusion that climate action is always the rational course of action globally because the benefits of action outweigh the cost of not acting (and dealing with significant losses) in the long run. Furthermore, arguments are made that climate action creates significant new business opportunities (e.g. new markets for low-carbon technologies) and is thus a pro-growth strategy (see, for instance, Stern 2006).

This alternative rational perspective points to some difficulties with the theoretical assumptions of rational climate interests. Cost-benefit analyses vary tremendously depending on who is considered to be the rational agent: the world as a whole, a group of states (such as the EU as a whole), individual states, or maybe even rational actors within a state (such as voters or politicians). Similarly, a different rational conclusion might be drawn depending on the time span employed. Furthermore, it is very difficult to accurately calculate the costs and, even more so, the benefits of climate action (as precise predictions about the future are impossible).

Contrary to the rational choice school of thought, new institutionalism believes that political systems matter as institutions exert a significant influence on political decision-making processes. Thus, policy outcomes are not just simply driven by the interest of rational actors (whoever they are). This could mean that states' capacities to tackle the climate problem depend on their political structure and institutions (i.e. that some political systems might be better suited to dealing with this type of problem).

One such institutional difference is the number of veto points in a political system (see Immergut 1990, 1992; Tsebelis 1995, 1999). Veto points indicate the number of opportunities for vetoing legislative proposals within the process of policy-making, and thus can serve as an indicator of how difficult it is to pass legislation in a given country. While this theory was initially applied mainly for explaining social policy-making, a number of scholars have applied it to environmental policy issues as well (for instance, see Zito 1998 or Haverland 2000). This would mean that countries with a bicameral legislature (i.e. where legislative proposals have to pass two chambers) are less likely to pass climate policies, simply because their legislative process contains more obstacles. Looking at the European countries, we see that some unicameral countries, such as Denmark and Norway, have comparatively better national climate policies. However, if we look at Germany and the UK (which both have strong second chambers),[15] we see that their comparatively good performance does not match the theoretical expectations. Furthermore, such a simplistic veto-point analysis is unable to explain changes in performance over time (a dynamic veto-point approach that takes political configurations into account might be better suited here).

In addition to rational state interests and institutional constraints on policy-making, public opinion is another influential factor for climate change performance. Public opinion on climate change is important for climate performance in multiple ways: it is necessary to get the public and businesses on board in order to put policies into place (see Giddens 2009), to increase the probability of compliance with such policies, and because politicians need to meet citizens' preferences to some degree in order to get re-elected (see Stadelmann-Steffen 2011). Thus, public opinion influences policy change directly and via influencing election outcomes (see Stimson et al. 1995).

Actions like the "People's Climate March" on 21 September 2014 in New York City (which about 400,000 people attended) and the corresponding events in 162 countries (see Alter 2014) show a general trend of public concern for the issue of climate change around the world. According to the Special Eurobarometer on Climate Change in 2013 (European Commission 2014), half of all Europeans[16] thought that climate change is one of the world's most serious problems. On a scale from one to ten indicating how serious of a problem climate change is at the moment – where one means "not at all a serious problem" and ten means "an extremely serious problem" – Europeans on average rate it a 7.3, indicating that they view it as a rather serious issue. However, besides this broad general concern, there are of course also regional differences: for instance, there is a large range of the proportion of people who view climate change as the most serious problem, ranging from at least 70 per cent in Austria, Denmark, Germany and Sweden to less than 40 per cent in countries like the Czech Republic, Bulgaria, Estonia, Latvia, Poland, Portugal and Romania. And we see that in 2013 both Denmark and Germany had relatively good national climate policy scores (2.3 and 2.9, respectively), while all of the other countries mentioned above performed worse. However, there is a wide range of scores from Portugal (at 3.0) to Bulgaria (at 4.2), and both Austria and Sweden, where public opinion viewed climate change as quite important, scored poorly (at 3.7 and 3.4, respectively). Thus, public opinion is not in itself sufficient to explain differences in policy outcomes. The general trends of public concern for climate change are paradoxically mismatched with the comparative unpopularity of possible policy options aimed at mitigating it, such as wind farms, etc. The general concern often does not turn into specific political demands and subsequent responses in Europe (or the rest of the world).

To summarize the trends in Europe 31, we have seen that the region as a whole is not very vulnerable to climate change, but there are differences among the countries. Furthermore, we have seen that the European countries are reducing their GHG emissions, albeit not fast enough. Finally, climate policy performance varies tremendously within the region, but none of the countries' performance is particularly good.

Regarding the theoretical viewpoints mentioned (rational state interests, institutional differences in policy-making or the influence of public opinion), we saw that none can, by themselves, serve to explain the variation in countries' climate change mitigation efforts. While all of them provided some insight into some cases, none of them was able to explain the entire pattern. Understanding what determines countries' performance in this area remains an interesting area for future research.

Democracy and climate change

After discussing these empirical and theoretical trends regarding climate change, this last part of the chapter discusses the question of the extent to which climate change poses a challenge to democratic systems.

The following discussion is oriented along Dahl's principles of democracy, as they have been previously introduced in this book. To briefly revisit these principles, Dahl (1998: 37–38) introduces necessary conditions which determine whether a decision-making process can be considered democratic. The first four ensure political equality, while the last one defines who should be considered as politically equal. These conditions are (1) *effective participation* (equal opportunities for all members of a community to make their views regarding a policy known to one another); (2) *voting equality* (equal and effective opportunity to vote regarding a policy for every member); (3) *enlightened understanding* (equal and effective opportunities for all members to learn about relevant alternative policies and likely consequences, within reasonable time limits); (4) *control of the agenda* (members have the exclusive opportunity to decide what matters are put on the political agenda); and (5) *inclusion of adults* (all or most permanent adult residents should have full citizenship rights).

This section will first show how far the reality of our democracies fails to meet these conditions in full, especially regarding the issue of climate change. Second, it will look at why Dahl's requirements might not go far enough for ensuring democratic debates and policy-making in regards to climate change. And third it will question whether climate change might be an intrinsically undemocratic problem which cannot be addressed adequately with democratic tools.

As mentioned above, Dahl's requirements are ideal type conditions which are already not met by real-world democratic nations, in Europe or elsewhere. As we will see below, none of the five conditions is entirely fulfilled, especially regarding climate change. Maybe most obviously the first and second conditions (effective participation and voting equality) are violated in Europe's modern-day democracies. In representative democracies, members' opportunity to deliberate policy preferences among one another and to vote on each issue individually can never be fully met. But particularly in regards to climate change, our modern-day democracies have an especially bad track record, as some voices in society are always louder than others. In representative democracies, interest groups attempt to influence policy-making via lobbying or through influencing public opinion on a matter. However, there appears to be an intrinsic imbalance in resources and opportunity to make their political voice heard between different interest groups. Dunlap and McCright (2011), for instance, name various groups of climate change deniers (their focus is the United States), such as the fossil fuel industry, contrarian scientists and conservative media and politicians. A common reason for denial is of an economic nature (particularly apparent for the fossil fuel industry). While the authors do not want to go so far as to proclaim that organized climate change denial has been the sole factor in the United States' reluctant environmental positions, they state that deniers' campaigns have played a crucial role in blocking environmental legislation. So we see that anti-environmental regulation voices can make themselves heard well. On the other side, people who are particularly vulnerable to climate change are often (socially, economically, culturally, politically, institutionally or otherwise) marginalized (see IPCC 2014b), and thus they are most likely to have far fewer resources and less opportunity to participate equally in the political debate. While climate change is an issue that the majority of people in Europe care a lot about, particular policies (stricter carbon taxes, wind farms in prosperous residential areas, etc.) often get blocked by sectional interest groups.

Additionally, effective political participation and voting equality regarding climate change gets undermined in another manner entirely when legal procedures attack democratically legitimized decisions. This was the case in May 2012, for example, when the Swedish energy company Vattenfall filed a request for arbitration against Germany at the International Centre for the Settlement of Investment Disputes (ICSID), because of the country's decision to phase out nuclear energy (see IISD 2012).

Just as the first and second conditions are not fully met by European democracies, neither are any of the other three. The third one (enlightened understanding) is particularly difficult to ensure in our increasingly complex world, especially for such a difficult issue as climate change. Furthermore, the fourth condition (control of the agenda) gets violated because which political issues are worth consideration in democracies is the result of agenda-setting battles where different members of society have different resources and opportunities to participate (see, for instance, Birkland 2007). Dahl's last condition (inclusion of adults) is increasingly challenged by growing numbers of immigrants who do not have citizenship rights and are thus not politically equal. This trend will likely increase in the future, when Europe can expect a greater influx of immigrants and refugees due to climate-related disasters around the world. In short, none of Dahl's conditions are really fully met in modern-day representative democracies, especially in regards to climate change.

The following section discusses how Dahl's conditions are not sufficient to ensure a democratic process for dealing with climate change. First, because his underlying assumption of community membership, as well as his fifth condition, fail to address crucial aspects of climate change. If only members of a certain community have the right to deliberate on policy ideas, cast votes or control the political agenda, then we miss an important aspect of the nature of climate change. As we saw above, the European countries are not particularly vulnerable to climate change and will likely not have to deal with much of its worst effects in the near future. Thus, it could be very reasonable for European citizens to not put climate change on the political agenda in their countries or to vote against substantial policy changes. This would have tremendous effects for the rest of the world, which is more affected by climate change and which depends on Europe to act on the issue (as it is one of the largest emitters of GHGs and because of the aforementioned free-rider problem). This thought challenges the notion that there are naturally given or otherwise justified communities with exclusive membership rights, which can and should decide upon all of their 'own' political issues by themselves. It becomes more apparent that, in our globalized world, international problems increasingly challenge the notion of nation-states, which are an underlying assumption for all of Dahl's conditions.

In an ideal world we would expect democracies to tackle the issue of climate change aggressively as informed citizens – whose preferences are shaped by civic beliefs and scientific knowledge – would pressure them to do so (Barber 2013). However, the fact that this is not the case might not point to a failure of democracy but rather to a failure of nation-states (Barber 2013, 2014). Barber finds that nation-states inherently cannot deal with the ever-increasing number of issues that surpass nations and cross borders (from climate change to issues regarding economic markets or terrorism).[17] In his view, antiquated nation-states are incapable of meeting these new challenges, and he calls for us to "globalize democracy or democratize globalization." His proposal is that we need to change our focus away from nation-states towards cities. This might seem counter-intuitive at first, as it appears that the problem stems from an already too small focal point, which excludes too many relevant actors and issues. However, he argues that cities – particularly in regards to climate change – have the capacities to be effective on both local urban as well as global scales through international urban networks (such as 'Energy Cities' or 'Climate Alliance' etc.). Barber views cities' potential for successful action in the facts that the majority of people in the world live in cities, particularly in the developed world, and that cities thus also generate the majority of GHG emissions. Thus, while being responsible for much of the occurrence of the problem, due to high urban population density, cities can significantly and more easily contribute to solutions, for instance by investing in public transport. Finally, many cities are located near water and are thus particularly vulnerable to sea level rise. Furthermore, due to shortage in urban space, people cannot easily relocate. Both of these facts contribute to cities seeing the urgency of climate action more quickly than whole nations.

Whether or not we agree that local urban efforts are the only serviceable approach to climate change, Barber's argumentation nicely shows us the inherent difficulty of nation-states. It appears that there is a danger in nation-state democracies that either the tyranny of the majority fails to protect vulnerable minorities or that too many sectional interests block important action that many members of a community are willing to take. The question remains how big a political community is reasonable and how to draw a line on inclusion and exclusion. In regards to climate change, it appears to make sense to both strengthen local efforts – exactly for the reasons put forward by Barber – as well as to widen the focus to a more global frame in order to ensure that people who need to act on climate change, even though it does not affect them tremendously, cannot just ignore the rest of the world, who depend on their action.[18]

However, Dahl's underlying assumption of 'a people' who get to establish a political community based on (natural or otherwise defined) membership is not the only point where the democratic principles put forward do not adequately address the issue of climate change. As already mentioned above, we can also question his fifth condition (inclusion of adults): climate change is mainly a matter regarding our future. Thus, in order to adequately tackle the issue, we need to employ a very long-term focus, for the benefit of upcoming generations. While it seems unreasonable to suggest that children be considered equal members of a political community with full citizen rights, we need to hear their views and ensure that their interests are taken into account, especially in regards to climate change. Children are already more vulnerable to climate change (particularly in the global south), and our political decisions mostly affect their future (see Gibbons 2014), as they have many more years in which they might need to live with climate change's worst effects if we do not act now. In order for climate change decisions to be fully democratic, we need to orient ourselves along an intergenerational contract (see Burke 1790). Of course, we can only hypothesize what our children's and future generations' political interests will be, but one can reasonably assume that a wish to live on a planet that continues to support them is among them. It would be undemocratic to make decisions that clearly go against future generations' interests.

In sum, this criticism goes hand in hand with Dahl's assumption of 'a people' and 'natural' nation-states: it is most likely not reasonable to completely open up citizen rights to every person, in every location, regardless of age. Restrictions of political membership are necessary in order for a political community to function. However, we do need to figure out how to take the interests of people outside of our political community (whether based on locality or generation) into account in our decision-making processes, at least when our policies affect them as much as they do in regards to climate change. If we are not the bearer of the burden, then it seems unreasonable and also undemocratic that we should get to seal the fate of others.

The above discussion leads us to question the degree to which climate change can be tackled appropriately in a democracy or whether an issue of this urgency is maybe inherently undemocratic. Democracies' ability to tackle climate change is subject to debate, for instance because election cycles do not allow for the long-term planning necessary for climate policies. Loske (1997) suggests that politicians who put a strong emphasis on issues regarding the future tend to not be rewarded but rather to be punished by the electorate. Additionally, future problems are easily superseded by actual or even perceived problems in the present. Shearman and Smith (2009) argue that in order to adequately address the issue, some authoritarian action might be necessary. The following theoretical considerations lead us to wonder whether climate change might be a challenge that democratic systems are incapable of addressing.

While some small portion of scientists dispute the existence of climate change, the overwhelming majority agrees that it is a real phenomenon that can already be observed to some extent, that it is at least partially anthropogenic, and that policy options could mitigate the worst-case scenarios (Dolsak 2001). In this sense, climate change's existence is not an issue that we can vote or deliberate opinions on but rather an objectively given fact. We can only choose whether we care about the future and the environment, whether we want to take the risk that future generations will have to deal with the consequences of our inaction, and what actions to take, if we choose to act. However, both our ability to democratically debate *whether* we want to respond, as well as *how* we want to respond are severely limited, as argued below. Democracies (according to Dahl and many other theorists) are defined by characteristics of decision-making processes. Democratic states need to be responsive to their citizens and act according to stated preferences, but with an extremely urgent issue such as climate change, we might wonder whether we can really afford to always act democratically. What if citizens just decide that they do not care enough about climate change to adopt any of the many unpopular policy options, but rather that they just want to 'see what happens' and not take any action. The result here is potentially disastrous and could in the long run lead to the demise of the human species. Is that really a decision we are allowed to make? Can we really take such a tremendous future risk based on our democratic principles? The urgency of the issue, the size of the potential threat and the huge risk we are dealing with might mean that voting to not act is not an option. And if that is the case, the question becomes whether the debate is still fully democratic if we exclude one policy option (inaction) entirely. And even our ability to debate the remaining policy options is severely limited, as climate change is an extremely complex issue, which brings us back to the impossibility of meeting Dahl's third condition (enlightened understanding). The fact that climate scientists have come up with various different scenarios with different likelihoods, that they dispute what our reduction goals should be, or what appropriate policy options are to get us there, shows that the issue requires a level of specialized knowledge that is inaccessible to the average layperson (or politician for that matter). Thus, climate change requires us to rely on the rule of experts to some extent, rather than allowing for democratic deliberation by all members of a community. However, this need to rely on science comes with another great danger. We should not commit the fallacy of blindly trusting climate experts without any deliberation, both because science has a history of getting it wrong and because there are also power dynamics within sciences that make the attempt to objectively observe truths problematic.

In sum, we can say that climate change poses a challenge to democracy and democratic nation-states, mainly because of its objective urgency and threat, its future-oriented and international nature, and its call for expert rule rather than popular deliberation. In addition, climate change is an issue which makes obvious the degree to which European democracies fail to completely fulfil any of Dahl's democratic requirements and where improvements in the democratic process might be needed. If we look back at the track record of climate change (especially vulnerability as well as responses), we can only hope that we are able to adequately address the issue in time.

Further reading

Bernauer, T. (2013). Climate Change Politics. In: *Annual Review of Political Science* 16, pp. 421–448.

Dolsak, N. (2001). Mitigating Global Climate Change: Why Are Some Countries More Committed Than Others? In: *Political Studies Journal* 29 (3), pp. 414–436.

Harrison, K. & Sundstrom, L.M. (2007). The Comparative Politics of Climate Change. In: *Global Environmental Politics* 7 (4), pp. 1–18.

Key questions for discussion

1 In what ways might democracies be ill-suited to addressing the issue of climate change?
2 What challenges does the free-rider problem pose to international cooperation on the issue of climate change mitigation?
3 What are the challenges to addressing climate change when looked at from an ethical, a social, or a pragmatic perspective?

Notes

1 The terms *climate change* and *global warming* are used interchangeably in this chapter, referring to the same phenomena.
2 Europe 31 includes the European Union's 28 member states plus Switzerland, Iceland and Norway.
3 While these events are not solely caused by climate change, their severity and the chances of their occurrence are likely to increase further in the future due to climate change (see IPCC 2014b).
4 This data was not available for 2005, and individual data points are missing for various countries in different years.
5 A prime example of such an international attempt has been undertaken by the *United Nations Framework Convention on Climate Change (UNFCCC)*, an international environmental treaty first signed by countries in 1992 with the objective of stabilizing greenhouse gas concentrations in the atmosphere. While the convention is legally non-binding and does not contain mandatory limits on emissions, it provides for updates that do. The principle update is the Kyoto Protocol. It has been signed by all Europe 31 countries – in addition to some others – by which they have committed themselves to certain greenhouse gas reduction goals.
6 The greenhouse gases in question are carbon dioxide (CO_2), methane (CH_4), nitrous oxide (N_2O), fluorocarbons (PFCs), hydrofluorocarbons (HFCs) and sulfur hexafluoride (SF_6).
7 The actual emission targets range from an 8 per cent decrease to some countries being allowed to increase by 10 per cent.
8 Some countries (especially formerly socialist Eastern European countries) have baseline years other than 1990.
9 It should be noted that these emission levels are not measured on a per capita basis, and as such total emission output is strongly linked to the size of the countries' populations.
10 The Intergovernmental Panel on Climate Change (IPCC) is a scientific intergovernmental body sponsored by the United Nations.
11 The policy options that might facilitate the achievement of this goal are manifold and include the introduction of a price on carbon (for instance through a carbon tax or some kind of cap and trade system), state funding for research on clean energy and energy efficiency, consumer subsidies to reduce the costs of environmentally friendly technology (for instance for the purchase of hybrid vehicles or solar panel installation), the elimination of subsidies for fossil fuels, weathering and energy efficiency laws for housing, and requirements for products to indicate their energy consumption to customers, among many others.
12 This index consists of annually collected data in the form of expert evaluation via questionnaires. Country-specific experts grade the energy, traffic, construction and industry policies in order to assess the countries' national climate policy. Furthermore, they grade countries' political action in climate negotiations and in other international conferences (for more information, see Germanwatch 2015).
13 One factor to keep in mind here is that attempting to reduce greenhouse gases is not the only strategy available to countries: climate change can be tackled through mitigation (i.e. preventing the worst of climate change) and/or through adaptation (preparing for

the changes to come), and for individual countries it might be more rational to invest in adaptation rather than mitigation.

14 It should be noted that although natural gas is, relatively speaking, cleaner than other fossil fuels, it still accounts for a large percentage of anthropogenic greenhouse gas emissions.

15 See, for instance, VanDusky-Allen and Heller (2014: 732) for the case of the UK having a strong second chamber.

16 Here this only refers to the 28 European Union member states and does not include Switzerland, Iceland and Norway.

17 See also in this volume Engene, Jan Oskar. "Terrorism, Counterterrorism, and Democracy." In Peters, Y. and Tatham, M. (eds.), *Democratic Transformations in Europe: Challenges and Opportunities*. Abingdon: Routledge, pp. 189–208.

18 See also in this volume Tatham, Michaël. "Multi-Jurisdictional Politics: State Adaptation and Mixed Visions of Democracy." In Peters, Y. and Tatham, M. (eds.), *Democratic Transformations in Europe: Challenges and Opportunities*. Abingdon: Routledge, pp. 269–294.

Bibliography

Alter, C. (2014, September 21st). Hundreds of Thousands Converge on New York to Demand Climate-Change Action. In: *Time* – Available at: http://time.com/3415162/peoples-climate-march-new-york-manhattan-demonstration/

Anderson, K. (1998). Environmental and Labor Standards: What Role for the WTO? In: Anne O. Krueger (Ed.): *The WTO as an International Organization*. Chicago, London: University of Chicago Press, pp. 231–255.

Barber, B. (2013). *If Mayors Ruled the World: Dysfunctional Nations, Rising Cities*. New Haven: Yale University Press.

Barber, B. (2014). Democracy of Sustainability? The City as Mediator. In: *Minding Nature* 7 (1), pp. 11–19.

Bernasconi-Osterwalder, N. and Hoffman, R.T. (2012). The German Nuclear Phase-Out Put to the Test in International Investment Arbitration? Background to the New Dispute Vattenfall v. Germany (II). Winnipeg, MB: IISD.

Birkland, T.A. (2007). Agenda Setting in Public Policy. In: F. Fischer, G.J. Miller, and M.S. Sidney (Eds.): *Handbook of Public Policy Analysis: Theory, Politics, and Methods*. Boca Raton, FL: CRC Press, Taylor & Francis Group, pp. 63–78.

Burke, E. (1790). *Reflections on the Revolution in France, and on the Proceedings in Certain Societies in London Relative to that Event. In a Letter Intended to Have Been Sent to a Gentleman in Paris*. London: J. Dodsley in Pall Mall.

CAIT Climate Data Explorer. (2015). Washington DC: World Resources Institute. Available online at: http://cait.wri.org

Central Intelligence Agency. (2013). *The World Factbook 2013*. Washington, DC: Author.

Chambers, S. (2007). Minority Empowerment and Environmental Justice. In: *Urban Affairs Review* 43 (1), pp. 28–54.

Dahl, R.A. (1998). *On Democracy*. New Haven: Yale University Press.

Dolsak, N. (2001). Mitigating Global Climate Change: Why Are Some Countries More Committed Than Others? In: *Political Studies Journal* 29 (3), pp. 414–436.

Dunlap, R. & McCright, A. (2011). Organized Climate Change Denial. In: John Dryzek, Richard Norgaard, and David Schlosberg (Eds.): *The Oxford Handbook of Climate Change and Society*. Oxford, New York: Oxford University Press, pp. 144–160.

Engene, Jan Oskar. (2016). Terrorism, Counterterrorism, and Democracy. In: Y. Peters and M. Tatham (Eds.): *Democratic Transformations in Europe: Challenges and Opportunities*. Abingdon: Routledge, pp. 189–208.

European Commission. (2011). *Progress towards Achieving the Kyoto Objectives*. Brussels. Report from the Commission to the European Council.

European Commission. (2014). Special Eurobarometer 409: Climate Change Report. November – December 2013. TNS Opinion & Social.

Friedman, M. (1953). *Essays in Positive Economics*. Chicago: University of Chicago Press.

Germanwatch. (2006a). The Climate Change Performance Index 2006. Burck, J., Bals, C., Treber, M. and Avram, R. Berlin & Bonn: Germanwatch e.V.

Germanwatch. (2006b). Global Climate Risk Index 2006. Weather-related loss events and their impacts on countries in 2004 and in a long-term comparison. Anemüller, S., Monreal, S. and Bals C. Berlin & Bonn: Germanwatch e.V.

Germanwatch. (2007a). The Climate Change Performance Index 2007. Burck, J., Bals, C. and Beck, M. Berlin & Bonn: Germanwatch e.V.

Germanwatch. (2007b). The Climate Change Performance Index 2008. Burck, J., Bals, C., Beck, M. and Rüthlein, E. Berlin & Bonn: Germanwatch e.V.

Germanwatch. (2007c). Global Climate Risk Index 2008. Weather-related loss events and their impact on countries in 2006 and in a long-term comparison. Harmeling, S. Berlin & Bonn: Germanwatch e.V.

Germanwatch. (2008a). The Climate Change Performance Index 2009. Burck, J., Bals, C. and Ackermann, S. Berlin & Bonn: Germanwatch e.V.

Germanwatch. (2008b). Global Climate Risk Index 2009. Weather-Related loss events and their impact on countries in 2007 and in a long-term comparison. Harmeling, S. Berlin & Bonn: Germanwatch e.V.

Germanwatch. (2009a). The Climate Change Performance Index 2010. Burck, J., Bals, C. and Rossow, V. Berlin & Bonn: Germanwatch e.V.

Germanwatch. (2009b). Global Climate Risk Index 2010. Who is most vulnerable? Weather-related loss events since 1990 and how Copenhagen needs to respond. Harmeling, S. Berlin & Bonn: Germanwatch e.V.

Germanwatch. (2010a). The Climate Change Performance Index 2011. Burck, J., Bals, C. and Parker, L. Berlin & Bonn: Germanwatch e.V.

Germanwatch. (2010b). Global Climate Risk Index 2011. Who Suffers Most From Extreme Weather Events? Weather-related Loss Events in 2009 and 1990 to 2009. Harmeling, S. Berlin & Bonn: Germanwatch e.V.

Germanwatch. (2011a). The Climate Change Performance Index 2012. Burck, J., Bals, C. and Bohnenberger, K. Berlin & Bonn: Germanwatch e.V.

Germanwatch. (2011b). Global Climate Risk Index 2012. Who suffers most from extreme weather events? Weather-related loss events in 2010 and 1991 to 2010. Harmeling, S. Berlin & Bonn: Germanwatch e.V.

Germanwatch. (2012a). The Climate Change Performance Index 2013. Burck, J., Hermwille, C. and Krings, L. Berlin & Bonn: Germanwatch e.V.

Germanwatch. (2012b). Global Climate Risk Index 2013. Who suffers most from extreme weather events? Weather-related loss events in 2011 and 1992 to 2011. Harmeling, S. and Eckstein, D. Berlin & Bonn: Germanwatch e.V.

Germanwatch. (2013a). The Climate Change Performance Index 2014. Burck, J., Marten, F. and Bals, C. Berlin & Bonn: Germanwatch e.V.

Germanwatch. (2013b). Global Climate Risk Index 2014. Who suffers most from extreme weather events? Weather-related loss events in 2012 and 1993 to 2012. Kreft, S. and Eckstein, D. Berlin & Bonn.

Germanwatch. (2014a). The Climate Change Performance Index 2015. Burck, J., Marten, F. and Bals, C. Berlin & Bonn: Germanwatch e.V.

Germanwatch. (2014b). Global Climate Risk Index 2015. Who suffers most from extreme weather events? Weather-related loss events in 2013 and 1994 to 2013. S. Kreft, D. Eckstein, L. Junghans, C. Kerestan & U. Hagen. Berlin & Bonn: Germanwatch e.V.

Germanwatch. (2015). The Climate Change Performance Index: Background and Methodology. Burck, J., Hermwille, L. and Bals, C. Berlin & Bonn: Germanwatch e.V.

Gibbons, E. (2014). Climate Change, Children's Rights, and the Pursuit of Intergenerational Climate Justice. In: *Health and Human Rights* 16 (1), pp. 19–31.

Giddens, A. (2009). *The Politics of Climate Change.* Cambridge: Polity Press.

Grubb, M. (2004). The Economics of the Kyoto Protocol. In: W. Owen and N. Hanley (Eds.): *The Economics of Climate Change.* London: Routledge, pp. 143–189.

Grundig, F. (2009). Political Strategy and Climate Policy: A Rational Choice Perspective. In: *Environmental Politics* 18 (5), pp. 747–764.

Hansen, J., Sato, Mki., Kharecha, P., Beerling, D., Berner, R., Masson-Delmotte, V., Pagani, M., Raymo, M., Royer, D.L., and Zachos, J.C. (2008). Target Atmospheric CO2: Where Should Humanity Aim? In: *Open Atmospheric Science Journal* 2, pp. 217–231.

Haverland, M. (2000). National Adaptation to European Integration: The Importance of Institutional Veto Points. In: *Journal of Public Policy* 20 (1), pp. 83–103.

Immergut, E. (1990). Institutions, Veto Points, and Policy Results: A Comparative Analysis of Health Care. In: *Journal of Public Policy* 10 (4), pp. 391–416.

Immergut, E. (1992). *Health Politics: Interests and Institutions in Western Europe.* Cambridge: Cambridge University Press.

Inglehart, R. (1995). Public Support for Environmental Protection: Objective Problems and Subjective Values in 43 Societies. In: *Political Science and Politics* 28 (1), pp. 57–73.

Inglehart, R. & Abramson, P. (1994). Economic Security and Value Change. In: *The American Political Science Review* 88 (2), pp. 336–354.

IPCC. (2013). Summary for Policymakers. In: T.F. Stocker, D. Qin, G.-K. Plattner, M. Tignor, S.K. Allen, J. Boschung, A. Nauels, Y. Xia, V. Bex, and P.M. Midgley (Eds.): *Climate Change 2013: The Physical Science Basis. Contribution of Working Group I to the Fifth Assessment Report of the Intergovernmental Panel on Climate Change.* Cambridge, United Kingdom and New York, NY, USA: Cambridge University Press, pp. 3–29.

IPCC. (2014a). *Climate Change 2014: Synthesis Report. Summary for Policy Makers. Contribution of Working Group I, II and III to the Fifth Assessment Report of the Intergovernmental Panel on Climate Change.* [Core Writing Team, Pachauri, R.K. and Meyer, L.A.]. IPCC, Geneva, Switzerland.

IPCC. (2014b). Summary for Policymakers. In: C.B. Field, V.R. Barros, D.J. Dokken, K.J. Mach, M.D. Mastrandrea, T.E. Bilir, M. Chatterjee, K.L. Ebi, Y.O. Estrada, R.C. Genova, B. Girma, E.S. Kissel, A.N. Levy, S. MacCracken, P.R. Mastrandrea, and L.L. White (Eds.): *Climate Change 2014: Impacts, Adaptation, and Vulnerability. Part A: Global and Sectoral Aspects. Contribution of Working Group II to the Fifth Assessment Report of the Intergovernmental Panel on Climate Change.* Cambridge, United Kingdom and New York, NY, USA: Cambridge University Press, pp. 1–32.

Kaijser, A. & Kronsell, A. (2014). Climate Change through the Lens of Intersectionality. In: *Environmental Politics* 23 (3), pp. 417–433.

Kemfert, C. (2002). Global Economic Implications of Alternative Climate Policy Strategies. In: *Environmental Science and Policy* 5, pp. 367–384.

Loske, R. (1997). *Klimapolitik. Im Spannungsfeld von Kurzzeitinteressen und Langzeiterfordernissen.* Marburg: Metropolis-Verlag.

Oberthür, S. & Ott, H. (2000). *Das Kyoto-Protokoll. Internationale Klimapolitik für das 21. Jahrhundert.* Opladen: Leske & Budrich.

Pavlov, Y. (2010). How Rapid Should Emission Reduction be? A Game-Theoretic Approach. In: *Natural Resource Modeling* 23 (4), pp. 251–267.

Popp, D. (2010). Innovation and Climate Policy. In: *Annual Review of Resource Economics* 2 (1), pp. 275–298.

Shearman, D. & Smith, J.W. (2009). *The Climate Change Challenge and the Failure of Democracy.* Westport, Connecticut & London: Praeger.

Sprinz, D. & Vaahtoranta, T. (1994). The Interest- Based Explanation of International Environmental Policy. In: *International Organizations* 48 (1), pp. 77–105.

Stadelmann-Steffen, I. (2011). Citizens as Veto Players: Climate Change Policy and the Constraints of Direct Democracy. In: *Environmental Politics* 20 (4), pp. 485–507.

Stern, N. (2006). *Stern Review: The Economics of Climate Change.* Cambridge: Cambridge University Press.

Stimson, J.A., Mackuen, M.B., & Erikson, R.S. (1995). Dynamic Representation. In: *The American Political Science Review* 89 (3), pp. 543–565.

Tatham, Michaël. (2016). Multi-Jurisdictional Politics: State Adaptation and Mixed Visions of Democracy. In: Y. Peters and M. Tatham (Eds.): *Democratic Transformations in Europe: Challenges and Opportunities.* Abingdon: Routledge, pp. 269–294.

Tsebelis, G. (1995). Decision Making in Political Systems: Veto Players in Presidentialism, Parliamentarism, Multicameralism and Multipartyism. In: *British Journal of Political Science* 25 (3), pp. 289–325.

Tsebelis, G. (1999). Veto Players and Law Production in Parliamentary Democracies: An Empirical Analysis. In: *American Political Science Review* 93 (3), pp. 591–608.

U.S. Energy Information Administration. (2015). *International Energy Statistics: Total Coal Exports.* Washington, DC: Author.

VanDusky-Allen, J. & Heller, W.B. (2014). Bicameralism and the Logic of Party Organization. In: *Comparative Political Studies* 47 (5), pp. 715–742.

Zito, A. (1998). Comparing Environmental Policy-Making in Transnational Institutions. In: *Journal of European Public Policy* 5 (4), pp. 671–690.

12

MINORITY RIGHTS UNDER MAJORITY RULE

LGB rights in Europe

Vegard Vibe

> Democracy does not simply mean that the views of the majority must always prevail:
> a balance must be achieved which ensures the fair and proper treatment of minorities
> and avoids any abuse of a dominant position.
>
> *Baczkowski and others v. Poland (2007)*

On 22 May 2015, Ireland witnessed a historic moment. For the first time, a majority in a national referendum had voted in favor of same-sex marriage.[1] It was a massive victory, as the pro-same-sex marriage campaign received 62 per cent of the votes. This is a remarkable achievement in many ways and a testament to the increasing acceptance and tolerance of LGB people[2] across Europe 31. Later in the same year, the European Court of Human Rights (ECtHR) issued a landmark judgment in *Oliari and others v. Italy* (2015), where Italy was found violating the right to privacy (article 8 of the European Convention on Human Rights [ECHR]) for not providing formal recognition of same-sex relationships. The ECtHR had previously ruled that not providing civil unions to gays and lesbians when providing them to heterosexuals violated the convention (*Vallianatos and others v. Greece* 2013), but in *Oliari* a violation of the ECHR for not providing any type of recognition of same-sex relationships irrespective of whether an option of civil unions existed for heterosexuals was found for the first time. These decisions and developments stand in stark contrast to (1) current anti-LGB developments in other parts of the world, (2) the continuous constitutional prohibition of same-sex marriage found in many Eastern European countries, and (3) the recent history of political homophobia in Europe 31, illustrated both in the prejudice with which sexual minorities were met within national settings and the ways in which homosexual demands were treated in the early jurisprudence of the ECtHR.

This chapter focuses mainly on how minority rights are secured under a system of democratic majority rule. This is seen in the context of another phenomenon, namely the increasing judicialization of politics or the process by which non-majoritarian institutions increasingly are making decisions that have traditionally been made by institutions that are more directly under democratic control (Hirschl 2008).[3] The chapter asks whether courts are becoming more involved in the protection of sexual minority rights throughout Europe 31. I thus focus on how European democracies have solved the challenge of minority protection in the context of increasing judicialization. This chapter will proceed as follows: following a brief discussion of minority rights and the role of courts, I look at how LGB rights have evolved in Europe since the end of the Second World War. Then, I discuss the ways in which courts have been involved in the development of LGB rights, with a focus on ECtHR data on the number of cases decided, their admissibility and the win/loss ratio, with a brief discussion of ECtHR jurisprudence on same-sex marriage. I focus on the ECtHR because it has increasingly developed into a sort of constitutional court exercising (weak) judicial review (Bates 2010). Moreover, comparable and complete data for national courts is not readily available.

With the change in public opinion over the past years, it may be seen as far-fetched to argue that, in today's Europe 31, sexual minorities cannot find adequate protection within the political channels and thus are in need of judicial protection. Indeed, as the case of Ireland shows, the majority is capable of securing the protection of minority rights. However, there are at least three reasons why it is still interesting to discuss judicial protection for the LGB minority. First, as will be shown, the comprehensive legal framework that serves to protect sexual minorities is a fairly recent invention and not one that is universally shared. Second, sexual minorities are still today being discriminated against due to prejudice, as evidenced by the uproar in France following the marriage equality law enacted by parliament in 2013. Third, many different types of minorities face similar challenges. As such, this chapter may be seen as a case study of minority rights protection in Europe, and the cases that it speaks to is the broad range of minorities (sexual, religious, ethnic, linguistic, etc.) that can be found throughout Europe 31.

One may distinguish among at least three types of minorities that are in need of various degrees of protection. First, democratic elections by definition produce regular political minorities. They require a basic type of protection, especially securing them an equal chance of one day becoming the majority again. These are called topical minorities (Waldron 2006: 1403). A second type is ascriptive minorities, who can be identified by some inherent feature (such as race or religion). They are more vulnerable as it is unlikely that they will ever be in majority, demographically speaking. Moreover, the nature of their minority status is inherent in the sense that they cannot simply change it. A third and final type of minority are insular and discrete minorities (as first highlighted in Justice Stone's classic footnote four in *United States v. Carolene Products*). In addition to being ascriptive, these minorities are also despised by the majority, disconnecting them from society (Hart Ely 1980). For a very long period, LGB people belonged to this category. They were (and are still in many countries) the focus of hate crimes, political homophobia and scapegoating. However, with their increasing recognition – politically, socially and culturally – LGB people in Europe today may seem to have moved out of this category. This chapter is a discussion of this trend towards greater recognition, from being a despised and insular minority to being allowed to marry on par with others. This is not to say that sexual minorities in Europe do not face hatred, injustices or discrimination, but they have made enormous legal progress in just a few decades.

When the majority's prejudice is reproduced through legislation infringing upon the rights of the minority, it would be foolish to believe, some would contend, that the very same institution that enacted these laws would strike them down for not respecting minority rights (as defined in a constitution or human rights' treaty). Therefore, a separate institution is needed to enforce rights protection. Since judges are thought to be more independent from majority concerns, courts have often been trusted with this task. The role of courts is the discussion to which I turn now.

The counter-majoritarian difficulty

The protection of minorities is intimately linked to the discussion of what role courts should play in society and whether they should have the right to overturn legislation emanating from the legislative branch. The first part of this discussion will primarily examine American literature, but I will also show that this is relevant in Europe 31. Central to this debate is the notion that in a democracy the popular will should prevail (mediated through elections). All definitions of democracy encompass the idea that the people should decide. Dahl (1998) has called this the popular preference-policy congruence, in which to a certain extent at least, the policies of the polity should reflect the preferences of the populace. In some definitions, majority rule is the *only* component of democracy (Schumpeter 1975, Svensson 2009). This in theory gives rulers the right to, and even the obligation to, rule according to what the majority decides, even if this infringes upon minority rights. However, recognizing that this could lead to severe injustices, a central concern going back to the founding of the American constitution has been how to secure minority rights and avoid the "tyranny of the majority". This was heavily debated by James Madison in the Federalist Papers at the end of the eighteenth century. He was concerned that one day the property-owning elite would be in minority and therefore stripped of entitlements (Dahl 2006: 31).[4] He was adamant that the tyranny of the majority had to be curbed by some counter-majoritarian measure, most often through judicial review. Madisonian democracy crucially involves a compromise between majorities and minorities. This balancing has been termed the counter-majoritarian difficulty, and it centers around how judicial review is compatible with democracy (Bickel 1962). The perhaps most adamant defender of judicial review has been Ronald Dworkin (1996), who argues that justices, based on a moral reading of the constitution, are supposed to engage in judicial review.

John Hart Ely (1980), one of the most influential American legal scholars, held that it is legitimate for the court to engage in judicial review to keep the political channels open for participation and in the protection of insular minorities, whose status makes them vulnerable to unfair treatment in the other political channels. Others have argued that judicial review is legitimate when it helps to lower the stakes of politics and avoid driving "salient, productive groups away from engagement in pluralist politics" (Eskridge 2005: 1293).

Many theorists have been more skeptical. The arguments against judicial review can be divided into two related strands: one focusing on the lack of favorable outcomes, meaning the relative inability of courts to provide minority protection; and the other on the inherent lack of democratic legitimacy courts enjoy. The outcome-related criticism focuses on the lack of real impact that decisions have had on the protection of minorities, with critics arguing that there is insufficient evidence that courts actually protect minority rights effectively (Tushnet 1999, Rosenberg 2008). Critics have especially focused on *Brown v. Board of Education*, which spelled the end of school segregation in the Southern states of the United States, and *Roe v. Wade*, which legalized abortion, for not living up to expectations. Waldron (2006) identifies the lack of favorable outcomes as one of two main criticisms against judicial review and argues that nothing indicates that courts will protect rights better than legislatures. He also criticizes judicial review for being inherently undemocratic. The process through which a decision is made is generally more democratic in a legislature than in the courtroom, due to the inherent unaccountability of appointed judges. Still, Waldron (2006) acknowledges that, in some cases, where his assumptions do not hold, judicial review may play a role, especially when the legislative channel is dysfunctional. This is especially true in the protection of insular minorities for whom the political process is clearly inadequate. However, this does not mean that protection should necessarily come through the judicial system, as judges may be equally prejudiced against minorities. Another related argument comes from the backlash literature. Due to the lack of legitimacy, significant advances made through the judiciary may serve only to energize a counter-movement (Klarman 2005).

European debates

These debates from the U.S. context are also relevant in the European context. In France, there has been a continuous battle between the primacy of the majority, exemplified through the legislature (general will), and minority rights, protected through judicial review (constitutionalism). According to Stone Sweet (2002: 85), legislative statutory supremacy was long unquestionable. Under the Fifth Republic, the constitutional council was never intended to have any form of power of constitutional review. However, after 1971, it has gradually increased in importance and now has strong constitutional powers.

Also other parts of Europe, including the Nordic countries, have seen extensive debates on the merits of judicial review and the judicialization of politics, following an increase in the power of courts over the past few years (Hirschl 2011). Stone Sweet (2002: 78) writes that there has been a "deep political hostility toward judges" in Europe for the past 200 years, and that a main effort of the "Kelsenian" constitutions of continental Europe has been to secure legislative supremacy. Despite this effort, judicial review appears to be spreading (Hirschl 2011). In relation with the ECtHR, there has also been debate over the legitimacy of the court's judicial review (Føllesdal 2009). The debate is exacerbated by the fact that international judges are seen to be less in touch with the national sensitivities of each country. This debate thus seems to be of concern to many European countries that are included in the study, as well as some of the governing bodies of Europe 31.

Despite conflicting views as to the appropriate extent of judge involvement in politics, it seems that most can agree that there needs to be a check on majorities and that some rights of minorities should be protected. There thus appears to be some agreement that a role exists for courts in the protection of minority rights.

State of LGB rights in Europe today

I will focus on three important policies for the recognition of LGB rights: decriminalization, anti-discrimination measures in the workplace, and same-sex relationship recognition. Following the theory of incremental change (Waaldijk 2001), these are theoretically and empirically linked (Bodnar and Śledzińska-Simon 2014: 221). According to these authors, the development of gay rights will follow a well-known trajectory, which is largely based on the Dutch experience. First, sodomy is decriminalized and age of consent is equaled. Second, various anti-discrimination measures are initiated in the workplace and in housing, and sexual orientation is included in hate crime laws. The final step is related to the recognition of homosexual relationships. Each previous step facilitates the next. Anti-discrimination laws are, for example, unthinkable if homosexual relations are still criminalized. Aloni (2010) contends that one cannot assume that countries take this trajectory, and one can certainly not predict where same-sex marriage will be allowed in the future, based on this theory. With these important reservations in mind, I take the theory of incremental change only as a guide to identify some of the most crucial aspects of LGB rights recognition.[5]

Figure 12.1 illustrates the trends discussed. All countries in the study have repealed anti-sodomy laws. The last region in Europe to decriminalize was the Turkish part of Cyprus in January 2014, making Europe the first region in the world where same-sex sexual practices have been completely decriminalized (Carroll and Paoli Itaborahy 2015). The first country to decriminalize was France in 1791. Following the French Revolution, revolutionaries introduced a new penal code where the prohibition on sodomy had been removed. This does not mean that homosexuality was condoned; rather, it was linked to the revolutionaries' wish to eliminate offenses that were intimately linked with Christian theology and to secularize the penal code. Repression of same-sex relations continued, especially in the

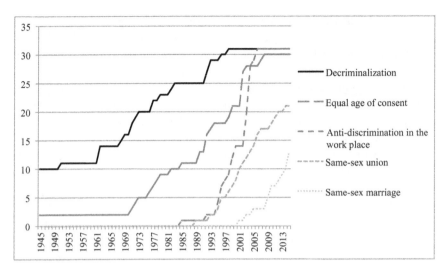

FIGURE 12.1 The three phases of LGB rights in Europe[6]

Source: (Carroll and Paoli Itaborahy 2015)

public place, and the homosexual orientation of offenders was often an aggravating factor leading to harsher sentences (Corriveau 2011: 53–55). Fearful of spillover effects on youth, the medical profession intervened, and many LGB people were sent to asylums. In the years to follow, a range of countries, including Luxembourg (1795), Belgium (1795) and the Netherlands (1811), changed their penal codes adopting variations of the French one. Other countries also decriminalized before the end of the Second World War, including Denmark (1930), Poland (1932) and Sweden (1944). In total, nine of the countries in this study had decriminalized prior to the end of the Second World War.

Modern decriminalization of homosexuality, however, originates historically in at least three distinct periods due to different but related dynamics. The first decriminalization period took place in the 1960s to 1970s through modernizations in civil codes in various countries. In England the Wolfenden Report suggested modernizing the penal code and removing the sodomy law already in 1957. The report was widely cited in numerous countries and led to the Sexual Offences Act of 1967, which legalized homosexual acts between individuals over the age of 21 (Kollman and Waites 2011).[7] Many more countries followed suit, including East and West Germany in 1968 and 1969, Finland in 1971, Norway in 1972 and Malta in 1973. Over a twelve-year period from 1961 through 1973, ten countries decriminalized. This development can especially be linked to broader cultural changes happening in the 1960s, and the development of liberation social movements at the end of the 1960s[8] and beginning of the 1970s demanding more rights (Roseneil et al. 2013). Ayoub (2015) argues that such early adopters are best explained by the strength of national movements.

In the 1980s, a second distinct period arose following the *Dudgeon v. UK* (1981) judgment in the ECtHR, which declared that Northern Ireland's "buggery" law violated the right to privacy of the applicants, as defined in Article 8 of the ECHR. Following this, same-sex sexual relations in private were de facto protected throughout the jurisdiction of the ECtHR. However, it took several more judgments to actually implement this protection, and particularly Cyprus proved resilient, only decriminalizing in 1998 following the judgment in *Modinos v. Cyprus* (1998) by the ECtHR. By the early 1990s, following the demise of the Soviet Union, a spate of new states sought to join the European Community and later the European Union, which forms the third period. This meant adhering to the ECHR as well as the EU charter of human rights. This led many countries, such as Estonia and Latvia in 1992, Lithuania in 1993 and Romania in 1996, to decriminalize. Ireland, as one of the late-comers in Western Europe, decriminalized only in 1993. Formal decriminalization was therefore completed in the countries in question by the end of the 1990s. These late-adopter countries are to a larger degree influenced by international factors, and their adoption of LGB-favorable legislation was to some extent dependent on the degree to which national movements were able to tap into international resources and use international opportunities (Helfer and Voeten 2013, Ayoub 2015).

Decriminalization also relates to the age at which one is allowed to engage in sexual acts and whether this age of consent is different from that for heterosexuals. In many countries same-sex relations were first decriminalized with a higher age of consent for homosexuals. *Dudgeon*, for example, did not touch upon the age of consent, as it deemed that each member state should regulate this matter itself. One had to wait for *Sutherland v. UK* (1997), *L. and V. v. Austria* (2003) and *S.L. v. Austria* (2003) for differing ages of consent to finally be deemed in violation of the ECHR. National courts, notably in Austria (2002), Hungary (2002) and Portugal (2007), also struck down different ages of consents. At the same time, several Eastern European states lowered their ages of consent through changes in their penal code (Estonia 2001; Romania 2001 and Lithuania 2004). In parts of Western Europe this development came many years after the initial decriminalization occurred. Finland, for example, decriminalized same-sex relations in 1971, but only in 1999 did they equate ages of consent. France is in this respect an interesting case. In 1942, the Vichy regime introduced a new penal code in which the age of consent for homosexuals was set at 21, whereas it was 13 for heterosexuals (Corriveau 2011: 105–106). This was part of an effort to turn the country back to its Christian roots in order to rebuild the nation after the humiliating defeat to Germany and to spur population growth (Corriveau 2011: 107). The unequal age of consent remained unchanged until 1974, when it was lowered to 18 and finally equaled in 1982. According to the International Lesbian and Gay Association (ILGA), the only country in Europe in which homosexuals are treated different with regards to age of consent is Greece, where homosexual relations require the participants to be at least 17 years old, whereas heterosexuals can engage in sexual relations at the age of 15 (Carroll and Paoli Itaborahy 2015: 32). The degree to which this is actually enforced is uncertain. According to Frank et al. (2010), the only countries that regressed in Europe during this period were Belgium and Luxembourg, which raised the age of consent in 1965 and 1971, respectively. There is thus an undeniable trend in Europe towards decriminalization of homosexual relations.

Anti-discrimination laws in the workplace have been implemented all over Europe 31 (Carroll and Paoli Itaborahy 2015). The first country to implement anti-discrimination measures in the workplace was France in 1985. In the latter half of the 1990s, a spate of countries followed suit, with ten states recognizing anti-discrimination laws. These were overwhelmingly Western European countries (Slovenia in 1995 and the Czech Republic in 1999 remain the exceptions). In the beginning of the 2000s, more and more countries implemented these measures, and by 2006 all of the countries in the study had legislation banning discrimination of homosexuals in the workplace. The EU has been central in making this a region-wide trend by issuing the European Equality Framework Directive in 2000 (Mos 2014). Courts have also played an important role here, especially the European Court of Justice, which has issued a range of important judgments in terms of labor discrimination (de Waele and van der Vleuten 2011). This highlights the fact that European trends seem to be more important for latecomers than for early adopters (Ayoub 2015).

There has also been increased recognition of same-sex couples in Europe over the past 25 years. Starting with the recognition of same-sex civil unions in Denmark in 1989, many countries followed suit in the years to come, such as the Netherlands in 1991, Norway in 1993, France in 1999, Germany in 2001, etc. The number of countries that currently has or has had same-sex unions grew steadily during the 1990s and beginning of the 2000s. Most of the countries that introduced same-sex unions in the 1990s have later substituted this for same-sex marriage, the only exception being Hungary, which already in 1996 introduced some form of recognition of cohabitation (this was later reformed in 2009, giving more rights to same-sex couples). However, most countries that recognized same-sex unions in the 2000s have yet to implement same-sex marriage. Marriage equality is indeed a new invention. As can be seen from Figure 12.1, all marriage reforms have occurred from the year 2001 and onwards, when the Netherlands, as the first country in the world to do so, recognized same-sex marriage. Since then, and especially from 2009 and onwards, twelve more countries have taken this important step. Italy is (at the time of writing in March 2016) the only remaining country in Western Europe that still has no legal framework for same-sex couples, although there have been extensive debates over introducing a civil union bill in both 2015 and early 2016.

Courts have generally stayed out of the same-sex marriage question, although over the past few years they have increasingly been called upon to adjudicate these matters. The Hungarian Constitutional Court has been amongst the most activist. In 1995, the court said that marriage was between one man and one woman; however, not allowing any legal recognition for same-sex couples amounted to a violation of the equal treatment and human dignity of LGB people (Bodnar and Śledzińska-Simon 2014: 227). In Slovenia, the court has been called upon to review the constitutionality of two referenda that would overrule same-sex legislation emanating from the legislative branch. The constitutional court has narrowly allowed both of the referenda. In France the marriage equality question has mainly remained a political question, but the court has been called upon to clarify the stance of the constitution. Following the unlawful initiation of gay marriages in Bègles in 2004, the Cour de Cassation stated that marriage, as defined in French law, remained between one man and one woman. In 2011, the constitutional council stated that it was up to the legislature to validate same-sex marriage and that not providing it was not against the constitution. In 2013, the council also validated the same-sex marriage law (Reyniers 2014). Italy has also seen its fair share of cases, where the courts have found that homosexual couples are covered by Article 8, deserving of legal recognition. Courts have repeatedly called for the legislature to provide some form of legal recognition of same-sex relationships, but the legislature has refused to do so. This led numerous couples to complain to the ECtHR about a violation of several of their rights in *Oliari* (2015). I will discuss the role of the ECtHR more thoroughly below.

Alongside these developments, we see an opposite trend in parts of Eastern Europe. Increasingly, marriage is defined in the constitution as between a man and a woman. Hungary implemented this ban in 2012, and Croatia held a referendum on whether to amend the constitution in 2013, where the conservatives won an overwhelming victory. The Latvian (since 2006), Polish (since 1997) and Bulgarian (since 1991) constitutions also specifically define marriage as the union of one man and one woman (Bodnar and Śledzińska-Simon 2014). There have also been talks about doing this in Lithuania, and a referendum in Slovakia notably failed because it did not reach the quorum required. Eastern Europe is clearly lagging behind with regards to same-sex recognition. There is more widespread opposition there, with some important exceptions. Thus, on the issue of same-sex relationships, the European consensus is less clear. Bodnar and Śledzińska-Simon (2014) argue that same-sex marriage reforms are dependent on national contexts and that there is little evidence of a "Europeanization effect" here.

Most countries appear to have, legally speaking, reached at least the second stage of the three-phase theory of incremental change, and twenty-two countries in the study have some form of relationship recognition. This is suggestive of the enormous steps taken on LGB rights in the European area. It is the most progressive and LGB-friendly region in the world. Overall, changes have mostly occurred through the legislature. Through changes in penal codes and enactment of new laws, the protection of LGB rights, especially early on, was almost exclusively made through national parliaments. However, from the 1980s and onwards, courts have become increasingly involved, sometimes forcing laggards to adopt more progressive policies. Yet, they have also often deferred to the legislature, arguing that this is a political question to be decided by the majoritarian institutions. Still, important changes have occurred, especially on the European level, where courts have become more assertive, which is the debate to which I turn now.

LGB rights in the ECtHR

In this section I will show how the ECtHR has been involved in this struggle. I will assess the ways in which the court has responded to the LGB issues brought before it and how this response changes over time. The analysis will be three-phased. First, I will discuss the gradual increase in LGB petitions the ECtHR has dealt with. Second, I will analyze data on admissibility and violations. Third, I will discuss ECtHR jurisprudence on marriage equality. All data are diachronic and collected from the Vibe, Langford and Kirkebo (2015) database. First, however, I will briefly present the ECtHR.

The ECHR was created in 1950 and the ECtHR in 1959. Up until then, the only semi-judicial body of the Council of Europe (CoE) was the European Commission on Human Rights (ECoHR). Until 1998, the ECoHR was the first instance of the judicial branch of the CoE. It decided on the admissibility of complaints and referred cases onwards to the ECtHR or to the Council of Ministers (CoM) if they were found admissible. To deal with a large caseload, the ECHR system was reformed with the entry into force of protocol 11 (in late 1998), which eliminated the commission and meant that the court itself would decide on admissibility. The convention was initially thought to serve as an alarm function against totalitarian tendencies in member countries. However, it quickly evolved into what many people have called a veritable bill of rights for Europe with the ECtHR as its constitutional court (Bates 2010: 18–20). The ECtHR has been instrumental in the development of many LGB rights, as shown in the previous section and elsewhere (Helfer and Voeten 2013).

Forty-seven countries are under the court's jurisdiction, including the thirty-one studied in this chapter. The court can be said to exercise weak judicial review in the sense that it can find national legislation or administrative and executive actions to be in violation of the ECHR. However, it cannot scrap the policy from the books as the U.S. Supreme Court can (Waldron 2006). It is up to the CoM to see to the implementation of the court's judgment (Føllesdal 2009). The convention is built on the idea of subsidiarity, which implies that its implementation shall be done at the lowest level possible, meaning in the member states themselves. This can be seen through the exigence that all domestic remedies must be exhausted for the court to consider it. Moreover, the court allows for a certain margin of appreciation in the interpretation of articles in the convention. This margin will traditionally be wider if no European Consensus[9] on the particular issue can be discerned. The convention is to be understood and interpreted as a living instrument which evolves with the time (Bates 2010: 154). This has proved important for many LGB rights issues, as the convention does not explicitly mention sexual orientation as a prohibited ground of discrimination. However, through several judgments, this has been read into the "other" status of Article 14 (*Kozak v. Poland* [2010], for example).

Total cases involving LGB issues in the ECHR system

Figure 12.2 shows the total number of petitions that the ECtHR[10] has been called upon to adjudicate on LGB matters in Europe 31 in five-year intervals since 1950. As can be seen from the graph, there is a clear upward trend starting especially from the beginning of the 1990s. The court averages four to five cases every year on a range of different LGB issues, including decriminalization, age of consent, housing rights, employment rights and same-sex marriage (Johnson 2013). With the enlargement following the fall of communism in Eastern and Central Europe, many new members signed onto the ECHR, and following protocol 11 (in 1998), this has meant a drastic increase in potential petitioners, especially since all new signatories are also required to allow for individual petitions, which was not required before (Bates 2010). The court has thus received a steady increase in applications, with 120,000 petitions pending before the court in 2010 (Bates 2010: 3). This general trend in the increase of LGB cases is thus not unique and closely tracks the general caseload of the court. Although still in a clear minority, conservative actors, who are regularly not thought to mobilize in the same way as progressives, are increasingly using the courts, as exemplified in *Ewedia and others v. UK* (2013). Conservatives are basing their claims on human rights, in a way emulating progressives. This suggests a more dynamic situation in which the balancing between rights (rights to privacy and anti-discrimination on the one hand and the right to freedom of religion on the other) will be decided in the courtroom, as has been the case in the U.S. (Keck 2014). A potential explanation for the great increase in court cases could be that as the court has grown in importance, issued more favorable decisions and the number

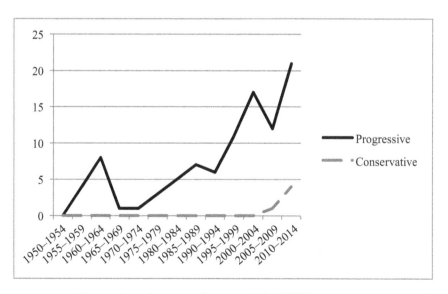

FIGURE 12.2 Progressive and conservative cases in the ECHR system concerning LGB rights claims in five-year intervals

Source: Vibe, Langford and Kirkebo (2015)

of potential litigants increased substantially, especially in countries with deplorable human rights records, the court is perceived as a valuable venue for mobilization by increasingly well-organized movements. This is especially the case when local opportunities are closed off. In these cases, the transnational level can present itself as the only option (Keck and Sikkink 1998).

Outcome of LGB cases before the ECtHR

The first case concerning homosexuality claiming a violation of the ECHR came in 1955 (*W.B. v. Germany* 1955). The ECoHR rapidly dismissed the case, raised by a gay man from Germany, as being manifestly ill-founded, stating that the convention permitted state members to criminalize homosexual relations for the protection of public health and morals (Johnson 2013: 23). All of the seven first cases came from Germany, contesting paragraph 175 of the German penal code, accusing it of being reminiscent of the Nazis and a breach of particularly the right to privacy. Despite this powerful evocation, the court dealt with these cases with extreme brevity. Claims against Austria and the UK were also treated with the same haste by the commission. Again, this is not unique for sexual minorities. Only in 1958 were the first cases deemed admissible, and in 1961 came the first judgment on the merits by the court (Bates 2010: 140). The first LGB case to be deemed admissible by the commission was *X v. United Kingdom* in 1978. This case contested the different age of consent laws in the UK at the time. It was deemed admissible by the commission, but the court sided with the government. In the beginning, therefore, the court does not present itself as an ally to the LGB movement, rather to the contrary. It strengthens the position of national governments and allows them a wide margin of appreciation. The court quite clearly deferred to the national governments on these issues. The fact that so many cases were inadmissible because they were deemed manifestly ill-founded, and thereby decided on the merits at the admissibility stage, is particularly interesting. Although this guideline was intended to keep frivolous and unmerited claims from reaching the court (Zwart 1994), it was also quite clearly a way to keep sensitive moral issues from reaching the court. Although not creating a guiding precedent, the message this sends to the petitioners is quite clear. This first phase, therefore, serves to entrench majoritarian views of homosexuals, highlighting the criticism made by many critics of the unconvincing outcomes of judicial review (Tushnet 1999, Waldron 2006).

As Figure 12.3 shows, the percentage of petitions deemed admissible has increased rapidly, especially from the end of the 1990s. Between 50 per cent and 100 per cent of all LGB petitions are now deemed admissible. The court's view of homosexuality has drastically changed. Increasingly, the court started to view homosexuality as falling more clearly within the ambit of the Convention (Johnson 2013). This is also very much due to the developments at the national level discussed in the previous section, which has shaped the jurisprudence of the court by shaping the European Consensus in a more LGB-friendly fashion, through which the court can narrow the margin of appreciation. Another reason may be that interest groups, lawyers and support structures around these movements have become more professional, and therefore they are more likely to comply with stringent rules of admissibility. Moreover, lawyers know which types of arguments will win. That is why privacy violations are so pervasively evoked; the lawyers know the court's jurisprudence and know which claims they should forward in order for them to be admissible. This is also evidenced in the increased participation of so-called repeat players in the court cases. The fact that a case is admissible does not mean there is a violation; rather, this means that the questions raised by the petition raise substantial issues that should be discussed more thoroughly (and that it has been filed within the appropriate time limit and that domestic remedies have been exhausted). The first successful case in the ECtHR was *Dudgeon v. UK*, which effectively decriminalized homosexuality in Northern Ireland. As can be seen in Figure 12.3, this did not immediately become the fate of all cases concerning homosexuality. Following the first three successful cases in 1981, 1988 and 1993 (all concerning the same issue), it is only by the end of the 1990s and beginning of the 2000s that cases are more readily won. In the beginning, the court was committing what Føllesdal (2009: 294) would call "false positives", which is when a court fails to prevent normatively unacceptable legislative acts. From 1981 until 1997, the court had evolved on its view of homosexuality and proved to be an important ally, but only on one issue (decriminalization) and in relation to one right (privacy). All claims relying on provisions other than Article 8 failed. This was the case until the court/commission opened the door for Article 14 complaints following *Sutherland* (ECoHR) in 1997 and *da Silva Mouta v. Portugal* in 1999. Including sexual orientation in the ambit of Article 14 opened the floodgates for more litigation. Discrimination

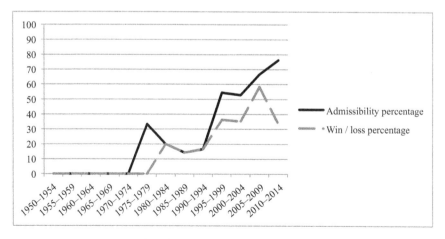

FIGURE 12.3 Percentage of total LGB petitions deemed admissible and percentage of total LGB petitions where the court finds a violation of the ECHR in five-year intervals

Source: Vibe, Langford and Kirkebo (2015)

claims, to a greater extent than privacy claims, could more easily be linked to other LGB issues, including free speech, tenancy, adoption, discrimination in the military and more (Johnson 2013).

It is interesting to note that for a period of time the percentage of won cases tracks perfectly the number of cases deemed admissible. This suggests that for a long time the largest hurdle for plaintiffs was getting through the admissibility process (i.e. the commission). If they could do this, they were basically assured a victory. The discrepancy over the past few years has increased, however, and for the 2010–2014 interval only 43 per cent of cases deemed admissible were won on the merits. The dip that can be seen from 2007 on could be understood in the relative increase in difficult cases to be heard, such as adoption issues and marriage, which pit competing rights claims and issues (freedom of religion and rights of children) against each other. This has put the court under exceeding pressure, both in terms of the number of cases being presented to the court and in terms of the types of issues being presented and high expectations from movements. Still, the overwhelming picture is that the ECtHR is much more welcoming of LGB claims now than it was even just twenty years ago. The court is less likely to defer to national governments and protects LGB rights to a much greater extent. The court, having long avoided the counter-majoritarian difficulty by not enjoining legislatures on LGB issues, is now firmly facing the issue of the democratic legitimacy of its decisions. Nowhere is this more apparent than in the area of marriage equality, which is both the most contentious issue across Europe with regards to LGB rights and one of the areas where the court has yet to take a firm stance.

Marriage equality

The right to marry in the ECHR is anchored in Article 12, which states: "Men and women of marriageable age have the right to marry and to found a family, according to the national laws governing the exercise of this right". The court has yet to find a right for homosexuals to marry. I will here briefly unveil the court's problematic jurisprudence on homosexual relationships.

The first successful judgments only found violations of the right to privacy, arguing that states could not criminalize what people did in their bedrooms. This has been criticized for reinforcing "the social relations of the closet" (Johnson 2013: 212). Likewise, the court did not find a violation of the right to non-discrimination until 1999, even though it had been litigated on since the very beginning. Even with this development, the court did not recognize that homosexual relations were worthy of protection.

The first signs that the court was changing its opinion came in *Goodwin v. UK* (2002), which concerned a transsexual's right to marry as a person in his/her new gender. The court found that the notion of gender in Article 12 could not be restricted to biological criteria and that the meaning of marriage had changed over time. In 2003, in *Karner v. Austria* (2003), the court for the first time upheld a complaint regarding discrimination against a same-sex couple, in this case tenancy rights (Johnson 2015: 60–62). It is also the first time that LGB rights fell within the home section of Article 8.1 of the ECHR, which reads: "Everyone has the right to respect for his private and family life, his home and his correspondence". The next major evolvement came in *Schalk and Kopf v. Austria* (2010), in which a homosexual couple argued that the prohibition to marry amounted to a discrimination of their right to privacy, non-discrimination and right to marry. The court did not find a violation of the convention, but the case is still very important in court jurisprudence, which has led authors like Scherpe (2013) to predict that this case will go down in the court's history as one of the most important rulings. When discussing the potential violation of Article 8, the court argued that homosexual relationships fall within the family-life ambit of Article 8 of the ECHR. The court states that "same-sex couples are just as capable as different-sex couples of entering into stable, committed relationships" (*Schalk and Kopf v Austria* 2010: 22). This puts homosexual and heterosexual relationships on equal footing, and according to Scherpe (2013), it requires countries to have some sort of legal framework recognizing homosexual relationships. Moreover, the court stated that Article 12 does not prohibit same-sex marriage. However, it does not either necessitate it, and the court did not find a violation of the convention. Johnson (2013: 155–158) is very critical of the interpretation of Article 12 and calls it heteronormative. Austria passed a registered partnership act on 1 January 2010, and although one cannot assume any causality between the pending case and the law, it is still interesting to note that the Austrian government argued that the case should be discontinued, as the complaints of the applicants were no longer valid (Johnson 2013: 156).

In *Vallianatos*, which was decided by the Grand Chamber of the ECtHR, Greece was found to have violated Articles 8 and 14 of the ECHR by limiting civil unions only to heterosexuals in their new partnership law from 2008. This was the first time the court had found a violation of the ECHR with regards to same-sex relationships.[11] However, it is a very limited ruling. It concludes that only Lithuania and Greece limit civil unions to heterosexuals. Thus, the main precedent from *Vallianatos* is not that there is a positive obligation to provide same-sex unions, but rather that not doing so while at the same time offering civil unions to heterosexuals is a violation of the convention. In addition to focusing on the European Consensus, the court highlights that national human rights organizations pointed out the discriminatory aspects of the law. We see that the court incrementally increases the rights of homosexuals, basing it on the very specific context of Greece.

This strategy is even more prevalent in the latest decision, *Oliari and others v. Italy* (2015), handed down in July 2015. Three couples complained to an Italian court in 2008 that they were not allowed to marry or enter into any type of legally recognized relationship. The court stated that marriage was between a man and a woman but acknowledged the lack of recognition and urged parliament to come up with a legal framework for homosexuals, which parliament refrained from doing.

The couples complained to the ECtHR, arguing that their right to privacy/family life and right to marry had been violated. The court granted that there had been a violation of the right to privacy, notably because there is "a conflict between the social reality of the applicants, who for the most part live their relationship openly in Italy, and the law, which gives them no official recognition on the territory" (*Oliari v. Italy* 2015: 53). Moreover, the court argued that relationships form an integral part of a person's existence and identity. The court found that while the national government is usually the best entity to assess national interests, the Italian legislature had quite clearly not paid sufficient attention to community interests, exemplified in the findings of Italian courts and overwhelming support among the population for relationship recognition. This seems to follow John Hart Ely (1980) in focusing on the unfair treatment LGB people receive in the political channels. The applicants recall the non-majoritarian functions of courts when they argue that "the court should not be an accountant of majoritarian domestic views" (*Oliari v. Italy* 2015: 28), and further claim that in many countries in Europe that do not recognize homosexual rights, the processes that have led to these outcomes are not worthy of a democratic process. The national choices are based on discriminatory attitudes, which according to John Hart Ely (1980) would suggest that judicial review is clearly warranted here, and as such is not a democratic problem. However, from an LGB rights perspective, the ruling remains problematic. Since it is the specific and changing conditions of Italy that led the court to find a violation, the precedent of this judgment is quite limited, since this is not necessarily applicable to other states. The court also refused to consider the case under Article 14 (non-discrimination) and Article 12 (marriage). It found Article 12 manifestly ill-founded, which is a significant setback compared to *Schalk*. Here we clearly see that the court is struggling with its position relative to that of the popularly elected national government.

The court's jurisprudence on marriage equality is convoluted and highly incremental. It is a way for the institution to keep its legitimacy and not outpace the European Consensus. Although frustrating for movements, one may understand it from an institutionalist perspective as a way of preserving legitimacy and ensuring compliance. One has to take into consideration the broader political context and the chances of compliance and legitimacy (i.e. the judges' opportunity structures). In the case of marriage, which holds such importance in many member states, the legitimacy of the court may appear to be threatened. and marriage appears out of reach (Johnson 2015: 72), especially with countries like Russia having proposed laws that overturn the supremacy of the convention. As the court stated in *Schalk*: "it must not rush to substitute its own judgment in place of that of the national authorities, who are best placed to assess and respond to the needs of society" (2010: 14).

One could interpret the European Consensus as being the instrument by which the democratic legitimacy of the court is upheld. By always keeping within the European Consensus on the matter, the court ensures that its interpretation of the moral issues at hand do not stray far from the legal interpretation of the member states, which at least in theory have been enacted by democratic institutions. However, the problem is that the court has no formal way of gauging this consensus. The finding of a violation in *Goodwin* was, for example, determined partly based on a European Consensus that was far less extensive than that of *Oliari*. As such, the evocation of the European Consensus may appear to be applied arbitrarily, based on the appointed justices' own values, which echoes the input criticism of Waldron (2006) discussed previously. Another issue is that the consensus itself is not based on democratic processes, as argued by the applicants in *Oliari*. Thus, relying on the European Consensus may be misleading for gauging the true meaning of the convention. This merits a further debate, especially in the context of such morally charged issues.

Conclusion

There is an undeniable trend towards greater recognition of LGB rights in Europe 31 today. No country criminalizes homosexuality, and all countries provide some form of anti-discrimination measure. Equally, twenty-two countries provide some form of legal recognition of same-sex relationships, with thirteen of them providing same-sex marriage. This trend of increased minority protection is good news for the state of democracy in Europe 31. There is, however, also an opposite trend which seems to be spreading in Eastern Europe, notably that of constitutionally banning same-sex marriage and prohibiting so-called gay propaganda. These developments suggest that Europe still has some way to go before it can be called a bastion of LGB rights. Most rights have been achieved through the legislative channels, and only quite recently have courts started making a difference. It is a fact, however, that courts are increasingly becoming activated on this issue and handing down more favorable judgments, effectively overturning decisions made by majoritarian institutions. This same trend is prevalent in the jurisprudence of the ECtHR. The court has oscillated between friend and foe of the LGB movement since its inception, and it remains torn on the issue of same-sex marriage. The court seems to be struggling with implementing what is sound jurisprudence on the non-discrimination of homosexuals and a growing European Consensus, against concerns for the legitimacy of their institution and being perceived as too activist. The inherent tension between majority rule and minority rights can be seen in the relative deference of most national courts when it comes to same-sex relationships, and quite clearly when it comes to the ECtHR's jurisprudence on the issue. While more assertive courts may bode well for the future of LGB rights, the inherent tension between minority rights and majority rule means that the court cannot be a panacea.

The massive increase in the use of the ECtHR as an arbiter of national LGB struggles is a testament to a growing legal consciousness among European citizens and the increasing judicialization of politics. Another group that seems to respond is the conservative movement, which is increasingly mobilizing within the ECtHR. Their main claim is that the recent advances in LGB rights, notably same-sex marriage, and changing societies infringe upon their right to freedom of religion, making them the new minority, one that is worthy of increased judicial protection in the face of majority rule. Although this argument has been unsuccessful until now, the caseload stemming from conservatives is likely to increase.

Further reading

Johnson, Paul (2015). "Marriage, Heteronormativity, and the European Court of Human Rights: A Reappraisal." *International Journal of Law, Policy and The Family* 29: 56–77.

Paternotte, David and Kelly Kollman (2013). "Regulating Intimate Relationships in the European Polity: Same-Sex Unions and Policy Convergence." *Social Politics* 20(4): 510–533.

Sommer, U., V. Asal, K. Zuber, and J. Parent (2013). "Institutional Paths to Policy Change: Judicial versus Nonjudicial Repeal of Sodomy Laws." *Law & Society Review* 47(2): 409–439.

Key questions for discussion

1 To what extent have courts provided appropriate protection of sexual minorities in Europe?
2 Can courts go too far in protecting minority rights? If yes, under what circumstances?
3 What other types of minorities are in need of protection in Europe today?

Notes

1 In various other national referenda, the majority has voted against same-sex marriage, notably in Slovenia and Croatia.
2 LGB(T) refers to Lesbian, Gay, Bisexual (Transsexuals). There is some concern with the use of this denomination, both because it does not encompass enough denominations and because it imposes a Western-type view of sexuality. A different term often advocated at the international level is SOGI rights, which means Sexual Orientation and Gender Identity. The rights discussed in this chapter do not concern gender identity, and I will therefore use the narrower LGB acronym.
3 For more details on the rise of non-majoritarian institutions, see Peters (2016), this volume. For a discussion of the relationship between minority rights, the courts, and right-wing populism, see Bjånesøy and Ivarsflaten (2016), this volume.
4 See Alvarez (2016), this volume, for an exploration of how liberal models of democracy have entrenched the rights of this same property-owning elite.
5 I acknowledge that these questions do not fully cover the whole spectrum of rights that LGB people have struggled for, neither do they do justice to the massive changes that have come in a range of related areas. However, due to place constraints, these are the questions that will be the focus of this chapter.
6 The y-axis denotes the number of Europe 31 countries that have implemented the different policies. The number of countries having implemented same-sex unions includes countries that once had civil unions, but where it was abolished following the opening up of same-sex marriage, like in the Scandinavian countries.
7 However, same-sex relations stayed criminalized in Northern Ireland until 1982.
8 Movements in some countries, such as Norway and the UK, started in the 1950s, but it was only by the end of the 1960s and 1970s that they gained real traction, with more organizations being established.

9 When determining whether there has been a violation, the court engages in an analysis of the European Consensus, which involves asserting how the particular issue in question is solved in member countries. If a European Consensus is found, then the margin of appreciation for member states will be more constrained. If there is no discernable European Consensus, then the margin of appreciation is equally wider. There is no formal way of concluding what the European Consensus is, but rather this is up to the court.

10 Before 1998 this includes cases brought before the ECoHR.

11 Greece has (as of March 2016) yet to implement the recommendations.

Bibliography

Baczkowski and others v. Poland (2007). ECtHR.

Dudgeon v. UK (1981). ECtHR.

Ewedia and others v. UK (2013). ECtHR.

Goodwin v. UK (2002). ECtHR.

Karner v. Austria (2003). ECtHR.

Kozak v. Poland (2010). ECtHR.

L. and V. v. Austria (2003). ECtHR.

Modinos v. Cyprus (1998). ECtHR.

Oliari and others v. Italy (2015). ECtHR.

Salgueiro da Silva Mouta v. Portugal (1999). ECtHR.

Schalk and Kopf v. Austria (2010). ECtHR.

S.L. v. Austria (2003). ECtHR.

Sutherland v. UK (1997). ECoHR.

Vallianatos and others v. Greece (2013). ECtHR.

W.B. v. Germany (1955). ECoHR.

X v. United Kingdom (1978). ECoHR.

Aloni, E. (2010). "Incrementalism, Civil Unions, and the Possibility of Predicting Legal Recognition of Same-Sex Marriage." *Duke Journal of Gender Law & Policy* 18(1): 105–161.

Alvarez, M.E. (2016). The Struggle between Liberalism and Social Democracy. *Democratic Transformations in Europe: Challenges and Opportunities.* Y. Peters and M. Tatham. Abingdon, Routledge: 99–119.

Ayoub, P.M. (2015). "Contested Norms in New-Adopter States: International Determinants of LGBT Rights Legislation." *European Journal of International Relations* 21(2): 293–322.

Bates, E. (2010). *The Evolution of the European Convention on Human Rights.* Oxford, Oxford University Press.

Bickel, A. (1962). *The Least Dangerous Branch: The Supreme Court at the Bar of Politics.* New Haven and London, Yale University Press.

Bjånesøy, L. and E. Ivarsflaten (2016). Right-Wing Populism. *Democratic Transformations in Europe: Challenges and Opportunities.* Y. Peters and M. Tatham. Abingdon, Routledge: 33–50.

Bodnar, A. and A. Śledzińska-Simon (2014). Between Recognition and Homophobia: Same-Sex Couples in Eastern Europe. *Same-Sex Couples before National, Supranational and International Jurisdictions.* D. Gallo, L. Paladini, and P. Pustorino. Heidelberg, New York, Dordrecht, London, Springer: 211–247.

Carroll, A. and L. Paoli Itaborahy (2015). *State-Sponsored Homophobia.* Geneva, ILGA.

Corriveau, P. (2011). *Judging Homosexuals – A History of Gay Persecution in Quebec and France.* Vancouver, The University of British Columbia.

Dahl, R. (1998). *On Democracy.* New Haven, Yale University Press.

Dahl, R. (2006). *A Preface to Democratic Theory*. Chicago and London, The University of Chicago Press.

de Waele, H. and A. van der Vleuten (2011). "Judicial Activism in the European Court of Justice – The Case of LGBT Rights." *Michigan State International Law Review* 19: 639–666.

Dworkin, R. (1996). *Freedom's Law*. Oxford, Oxford University Press.

Eskridge, W. (2005). "Pluralism and Distrust: How Courts Can Support Democracy by Lowering the Stakes of Politics." *Yale Law Journal* 114(6): 1279–1328.

Føllesdal, A. (2009). "Why the European Court of Human Rights Might be Democratically Legitimate – A Modest Defense." *Nordisk Tidsskrift for Menneskerettigheter* 27(2): 289–303.

Frank, D. J., B. J. Camp and S. A. Boutcher (2010). "Worldwide Trends in the Criminal Regulation of Sex, 1945 to 2005." *American Sociological Review* 75(6): 867–893.

Hart Ely, J. (1980). *Democracy and Distrust: A Theory of Judicial Review*. Cambridge and London, Harvard University Press.

Helfer, L.R. and E. Voeten (2013). "International Courts as Agents of Legal Change: Evidence from LGBT Rights in Europe." *International Organization* 68(1): 77–110.

Hirschl, R. (2008). "The Judicialization of Mega-Politics and the Rise of Political Courts." *Annual Review of Political Science* 11(1): 93–118.

Hirschl, R. (2011). "The Nordic Counternarrative: Democracy, Human Development, and Judicial Review." *International Journal of Constitutional Law* 9: 449–469.

Johnson, P. (2013). *Homosexuality and the European Court of Human Rights*. Oxon, Routledge.

Johnson, P. (2015). "Marriage, Heteronormativity, and the European Court of Human Rights: A Reappraisal." *International Journal of Law, Policy and the Family* 29: 56–77.

Keck, M.E. and K. Sikkink (1998). *Activists Beyond Borders*. Ithaca and London, Cornell University Press.

Keck, T. (2014). *Judicial Politics in Polarized Times*. Chicago, The University of Chicago Press.

Klarman, M. (2005). "Brown and Lawrence (and Goodridge)." *Michigan Law Review* 104(3): 431–489.

Kollman, K. and M. Waites (2011). United Kingdom: Changing Political Opportunity Structures, Policy Success and Continuing Challenges for Lesbian, Gay and Bisexual Movements. *The Lesbian and Gay Movement and the State: Comparative Insights into a Transformed Relationship*. M. Tremblay, D. Paternotte, and C. Johnson. Surrey, Ashgate, pp. 181–196.

Mos, M. (2014). "Of Gay Rights and Christmas Ornaments: The Political History of Sexual Orientation Non-Discrimination in the Treaty of Amsterdam." *Journal of Common Market Studies* 52(3): 632–649.

Peters, Y. (2016). Displacing politics: the state of democracy in an age of diffused responsibility. *Democratic Transformations in Europe: Challenges and Opportunities*. Y. Peters and M. Tatham. Abingdon, Routledge: 163–186.

Reyniers, P. (2014). Same-Sex Couples in France and Belgium: The Resilient Practice of Judicial Deference. *Same-Sex Couples before National, Supranational and International Jurisdictions*. D. Gallo, L. Paladini, and P. Pustorino. Heidelberg, New York, Dordrecht, London, Springer: 249–262.

Rosenberg, G. (2008). *The Hollow Hope*. Chicago, University of Chicago Press.

Roseneil, S., I. Crowhurst, T. Hellesund, A. C. Santos and M. Stoilova. (2013). "Changing Landscapes of Heteronormativity: The Regulation and Normalization of Same-Sex Sexualities in Europe." *Social Politics: International Studies in Gender, State & Society* 20(2): 165–199.

Scherpe, J. (2013). "The Legal Recognition of Same-Sex Couples in Europe and the Role of the European Court of Human Rights." *The Equal Rights Review* 10: 83–95.

Schumpeter, J. (1975). *Capitalism, Socialism and Democracy*. New York, Harper.

Stone Sweet, A. (2002). "Constitutional Courts and Parliamentary Democracy." *West European Politics* 25(1): 77–100.

Svensson, P. (2009). "Conceptions of Democracy and Judicial Review." *Norsk Tidsskrift for Menneskerettigheter* 27(2): 208–220.

Tushnet, M. (1999). *Taking the Constitution Away from the Courts.* Princeton, Princeton University Press.

Vibe, V., M. Langford and T. Kirkebø (2015). *Sexual and Reproductive Rights Lawfare Database.* Unpublished.

Waaldijk, K. (2001). Small Change: How the Road to Same-Sex Marriage Got Paved in the Netherlands. *Legal Recognition of Same-Sex Partnerships.* R. Wintemute and M. Andenas. Oxford, Hart Publishing: 437–464.

Waldron, J. (2006). "The Core of the Case against Judicial Review." *The Yale Law Journal* 115(6): 1346–1406.

Zwart, T. (1994). *The Admissibility of Human Rights Petitions.* Dordrecht and Boston: Martinus Nijhoff.

13

IS THE EUROPEAN PUBLIC SPHERE GOOD FOR DEMOCRACY?

Hakan G. Sicakkan

From a democracy point of view, a European public sphere with a European demos, which is conscious of its role of overseeing the actions of supranational policy-makers, is desirable in Europe due to the increasing powers of the European Union. The European Union (EU) concedes that a well-functioning European public sphere (EPS) is essential for creating input legitimacy, as there are few other links between its policy-making bodies and citizens.[1] Indeed, with the European Commission in lead, the EU has been striving to create the three key ingredients of an EPS: (1) a European *political center* by introducing supranational decision-making in increasingly more policy areas, (2) a European *civil society* by initiating and sponsoring pan-European networks of civil society organizations, European party groups in the European Parliament, European party federations, and direct elections to the European Parliament, and (3) a pan-European *media space* by standardizing of national media systems, partial regulation of media ownership, and establishment of pan-European media outlets.

These costly efforts of the EU to reach its citizens directly—as opposed to reaching them indirectly via the member states that they are citizens of—testify to the fact that the EU as a new power center is historically unique in its eagerness to willingly subject itself to citizen critique, control, and opposition by introducing on its own initiative the institutions and channels needed to do so.[2] The reason for this is the EU's concern for its own legitimacy and survival in a region of deep-rooted democracies. However, although a public sphere is essential for the functioning of a democracy, are the EU's efforts to create an EPS good for democracy in Europe?

Not only the EU but also research on the development of the EPS has pointed to the democratizing (Fossum and Schlesinger 2007) and legitimizing (Lord and Beetham 2001) role of public spheres. In addition, research has also exposed the integrative (de Beus 2010), meaning-creating (Calhoun 2005), and emancipatory

(Fraser 2007) functions of the public sphere. In fact, the theorists of democracy on the neo-functionalist and cosmopolitan flanks most enthusiastically call for an institutionalized EPS and a transnational public (i.e. a European demos), which can assume the task of holding the supranational power-holders accountable (cf. Eriksen 2005, Habermas 1989). The intergovernmentalist and communitarian wings, on the other hand, do not entirely recognize, nor do they talk much about, the need for an EPS as their proponents regard EU policies as legitimate outcomes of collective decision-making procedures by democratically elected representatives of the member states.

Building on earlier contributions that hold democratization of the EU as the primary end of the EPS, I emphasize here that current approaches to the EPS barely address the "inclusiveness" element of democracy directly. Although this might be seen as a critique from a substantive democracy perspective (Mouffe 1992, cf. Shapiro 1994), the significance of the inclusiveness criterion for democracy can also be illustrated with reference to a procedural democracy perspective: Dahl (1989) specifies five procedural criteria for a regime to be called a democracy: *effective participation, voting equality, enlightened understanding, control of the agenda*, and *inclusiveness*. He seeks equality of opportunity for *all* citizens in the first four criteria (e.g. equal opportunities for participating in political processes, for voicing preferences, for access to information, and for influencing the political agenda). Thus, being *the* foundational idea constituting the other four procedural criteria, inclusiveness is a necessary condition for democracy. This chapter evaluates the democratic value of the EPS with respect to its inclusiveness. It does so by measuring and comparing the inclusiveness of the notions of citizenship mediated in the public sphere by the citizens, national and trans-European and elites, and national media.

Inclusiveness and democracy

Have the EU attempts to create an EPS since the 1970s helped improve European democracy?[3] Departing from the Habermasian notion that the public sphere is a means for citizens to hold the power-holders accountable and that it should, thus, mirror the citizens' views, transform them into public opinion, and transmit this public opinion upwards in the political system, I answer this question by studying the extent to which European citizens' views on citizenship and diversity are mirrored in national media as well as amongst the national and trans-European elites participating in public debates, and whether the totality of these views promote democracy. Thus, I understand inclusiveness in terms of its two dimensions:

> *The first dimension* concerns the extent to which citizens' preferences are mirrored within elite circles and in the national media (i.e. the bottom-up *reach of citizens' views*). Do the citizens' views appear within the elite circles and the media news? Are they suitably included in elite circles and in media? Or

does the multi-level system filter citizens' views in such a way that opinions that dominate in public debates are different from the citizens' views?

The second dimension is about the inclusiveness of the notions of citizenship (i.e. *the content* of the views). This concerns whether the views are inclusive and non-discriminatory and how inclusive citizens (and elites and national media) are in their conceptions of citizenship. Are they willing to see everybody as equal and worthy citizens with the same set of rights and obligations, including gender groups, people with different sexual orientations,[4] native ethnic and religious minorities, immigrant minorities, persons with different ideological persuasions, etc.?

What is the consequence for democracy of a proper mirroring or filtering out of citizen views at the elite levels and in the media? Indeed, the different configurations of inclusive and non-inclusive notions of citizenship and proportional or non-proportional reach of citizen views constitute the key for understanding the democratic contribution of the EU's policies for creating an EPS. In this respect, there are four main scenarios, as depicted in Table 13.1.

In Scenario I, a majority of the citizens have inclusive conceptions of citizenship, and their views are fairly echoed within elite circles and in the media, regardless of whether these views are inclusive or not. This would ideally meet Dahl's inclusiveness criterion. As to Scenario III, we can ask "Is it democratic to exclude citizens' inclusive preferences from the public sphere?" Not only from a procedural democracy perspective, but also from a substantive democracy viewpoint that emphasizes the fairness of the outcomes of the democratic rules, procedures, and institutions for all citizen groups (Fraser 1990, Mouffe 1999, 2002a, 2002b, Young 1990), this would be a straightforward case of undermining democracy (cf. Shapiro 1994 for a middle position).

The remaining two scenarios are the source of intense normative debates about democracy. Scenario II reproduces the classical dilemma that arises when antidemocratic and/or non-democratic political preferences constitute the majority view. Is a system democratic when an anti-democratic majority dominates in the public debates at the expense of the most basic rights of those holding democracy-friendly

TABLE 13.1 Conceptualizing an EPS's contribution to European democracy

| | | *The content of citizens' views of citizenship and diversity* | |
		Inclusive	*Non-inclusive*
The reach of citizens' views into elite circles and media	*Proportionally represented*	**Scenario I** EPS improves democracy	**Scenario II** EPS improves democracy?
	Underrepresented	**Scenario III** EPS does not improve democracy	**Scenario IV** EPS does not improve democracy?

views? Scenario IV raises a similar dilemma, but this time excluding the anti-democratic views from the public sphere: is it democratic to exclude the anti-democratic views from the public sphere "for the sake of democracy"?

From a procedural democracy perspective, whereas Scenario II would be classified as "democratic" because it includes all citizens in the political processes, Scenario IV would be considered undemocratic because it excludes a group of citizens (i.e. those holding non-democratic views). Nonetheless, the unintended outcomes of the procedural democracy approach in these two scenarios would not be intuitively foreseeable – that is, democratic procedures allowing the dominance of anti-democratic political views in the public sphere (Scenario II) and non-democratic procedures promoting democratic political views (Scenario IV). From a substantive democracy perspective, the democraticness of Scenario II cannot be established because it permits anti-democratic or non-democratic preferences to dominate. Scenario IV, on the other hand, may be classified as democratic from a substantive democracy perspective as it promotes inclusiveness, though by excluding anti-democratic views.

In the typology given in Table 13.1, only Scenario I satisfies the requirements of both procedural and substantive perspectives of democracy. The two perspectives also agree that Scenario III is undemocratic. On the other hand, whereas Scenario II is considered democratic only by the procedural approach, Scenario IV is classified as democratic only by the substantive democracy perspective. Today's political struggles about visibility in the public sphere partly concerns inclusiveness as defined by these two disputing perspectives of democracy.

When assessing the second dimension of inclusiveness (i.e. the content-wise inclusiveness of the views themselves), I search for three categories: Europeanists, nation-statists, and nativists. *Europeanists* are those citizens, elites, and media outlets that display the highest degree of inclusiveness in their understandings of citizenship (see also Sicakkan 2016). In their notions of citizenship, they include all sorts of groups, including those which are generated by the processes of globalization and Europeanization, such as second and third country nationals, people with transnational belongings, shifting identities, multiple identities, etc. The Europeanist approach to citizenship also includes the groups that are generated by the historical state- and nation-building processes and those that are left outside by those processes. *Nation-statists*, on the other hand, have the classical understanding of citizenship as the citizenship of a nation-state, whose inclusiveness is limited to the traditional categories that were generated by the historical state- and nation-building processes (e.g. state-bearing groups, previously suppressed or excluded groups like native ethnic and religious minorities, women, sexual minorities, social classes, culture groups, life-style groups, etc.). This approach categorizes people primarily as members of a nation-state and secondarily as sub-community members or other group members. On the other hand, it tends to exclude the groups that are created by the processes of globalization and Europeanization. *Nativists*, finally, understand citizenship in terms of the combination of people's territorial and ethnic origins; that is, only the minority and majority groups that have their territorial origin in a country are recognized as natural citizens of that country. This approach conceptualizes citizenship with a native community perspective, where persons are primarily viewed as members of native communities and secondarily as members of a nation-state.

The above depiction both expands and clarifies what I mean by "inclusiveness" in the public sphere and its relationship with the notions of procedural and substantive democracy. The empirical question that I will answer in this chapter is whether the EPS can be classified within one or more of the four scenarios in Table 13.1; if so, in which one(s)? The answer to this question will constitute the basis for a further discussion of whether the EPS that the EU has been attempting to create contributes to European democracy.

Case selection and data

Most of the data used in this chapter were collected in fifteen European countries within the framework of the EU-funded integrated project EUROSPHERE.[5] The countries are strategically selected in order to ensure that the diversity of political contexts (*liberal democracies, social democracies*, and *post-communist democracies*), different citizenship traditions (*jus soli, jus sangunis, jus domicile*, and their various combinations), different country sizes and wealths, countries belonging to different waves of EU enlargement, and the full variety of the European geopolitical locations (*East, West, North, South*) within Europe 31 are represented in the data material.

As I compare the citizenship and diversity-related views of *individual citizens, national elites, transnational elites*, and the *national media*, let me first clarify who the citizens and the different categories of elites are in the EU multi-level system, and the information sources about their degrees of inclusiveness: citizens, national elites, trans-European elites, European elites, and national media are mutually interacting components and participants of the EPS. Seen through neo-functionalist lenses, European elites are those elites that represent and/or shape the supranational institutions of the EU. Thus, their views are to be discerned in the discourses and actions of the EU's supranational institutions (e.g. the European Commission). Trans-European elites are people in leading positions at Europe-wide networks of civil society (e.g. networks of non-governmental organizations, think tanks, and political parties). Their views are discernible in their discourses and actions at trans-European networks of civil society organizations, whose aim is to constitute an additional, corporate-plural link between citizens and the EU institutions. Finally, national elite views are observed in their activities and discourses in nationwide non-governmental organizations that participate in politics (e.g. political parties, public interest groups, social movement organizations, think tanks, and media).

Thus, the data material covers (a) institutional data about 242 national and European-level organizations actively participating in public debates, (b) individual data obtained from 764 in-depth elite interviews with persons who are in leading positions in these organizations, (c) media content data collected from a sample of approximately 8,500 print and broadcast media news from 73 different national media outlets, and (d) survey data about citizen attitudes to diversity and inclusive citizenship obtained from the European Values Surveys (EVS).

Concerning media content data, five media channels are researched in each country – three newspapers and two television broadcasters, which were selected on the basis of the same criteria in all countries.[6] Also, a standard procedure was followed in all countries when selecting news items for content analysis. The time period covered for each of the selected media actors was 9 May – 10 October 2008. With a significant variation among countries, the total number of the news items coded, from both print and broadcast media, was 8,458. Although the research covered also 12,053 sources (i.e. persons representing themselves or institutions who were cited with direct quotations in the news), they are not analyzed in this chapter as the aim is to depict the media's framings.

Regarding the interview data, the research focuses specifically on those organizations and elites that have high visibility in public debates – representing the most visible mainstream and alternative, contesting discourses and networks. In each of the fifteen European countries, I focus on three political parties (the party leading the government, the main opposition party, and the most visible maverick party), three non-governmental organizations (NGOs) or social movement organizations (SMOs) – civil society organizations that are the most visible and represent the mainstream or alternative discourses – three think tanks (a policy research institute, an academic think tank, and an advocacy think tank), three print media actors (two main-player newspapers and one smaller newspaper that exhibits anti-establishment views), and two broadcast media actors (one public and one commercial TV channel that are main players). At least one of the organizations under each category in each country was selected from amongst the members of a European network. In addition, in order to study the links between the national and European-level civil society, eighteen leaders at eight trans-European networks included three *European political party federations*, three *European networks of NGOs/SMOs*, and two *European networks of think tanks*.

The final sample includes 242 organizations at the member-state level (fifty-six political parties, sixty-seven public interest organizations [NGOs/SMOs], forty-six think tanks, forty-four newspapers, and twenty-nine TV channels, which are spread throughout fifteen European countries), and eight European umbrella organizations that are the trans-European counterparts of these. In terms of both discourse and networking, these exhibit varying degrees of affiliation with or dissociation from European political spaces. Some are contained in national arenas in terms of both discourse and networking; some operate with Europeanizing discourses in trans-European arenas.

The minimum number of interview respondents in each country ($4 \times 3 \times 4 =$ 48) was determined by three factors: (1) the number of the organization types (which is 4 – political party, NGO, think tank, media), (2) the number of organizations' positions in the national political landscape (which is 3 – mainstream, main opposition, maverick/alternative/anti-establishment), and (3) the number of the elite types (which is formal leader, opinion leader, internal opposition leader, sub-group leader). In some organizations where it was not possible to obtain more information by interviewing more people, the saturation point was reached before the planned number of interviews was achieved.

Data about individual citizens come from the EVS's third and fourth waves that correspond to the data collection period and the countries that EURO-SPHERE covered (cf. Klicperová-Baker and Košťál 2012). The material contains attitude data of 25,196 individuals living in the aforementioned fifteen European countries.

Inclusiveness and the European public sphere

Are citizens' views about citizenship and diversity echoed within elite circles at national and European levels? Whose views do national media mirror? In which of the scenerios in Table 13.1 do the answers to these questions place the EU?

In the following sections, I answer these questions by giving comparative delineations of (a) the extent to which citizens' views are reflected within the national elite circles,[7] (b) the extent to which national elites' views are echoed in the trans-European elite circles, and (c) the extent to which national media's framings are inclusive across various countries.[8] The question about the classification of the EU's EPS policies within Table 13.1 is answered through a comparison of the answers to these three questions.

Are citizens' views echoed within the national elite circles?

There is little research on the gap between elites and citizens. Perhaps one of the most significant works done in this area is an article by Hooghe (2003) comparing the gap among the preferences of European elites, national elites, and citizens concerning European integration in thirteen different policy areas. Citizenship and diversity is not one of the policy areas studied by Hooghe in the aforementioned article. In the following, I use results from two separate comparisons of national elite views and individual citizen attitudes, which document that national elites in European countries are consistently more inclusive than individual citizens in their citizenship and diversity views (Klicperová-Baker and Košťál 2016, Klicperová-Baker and Košťál 2012).[9]

The former source reports a statistically significant variation among the fifteen countries as to the gap between the percentage of national elites and percentage of citizens who view diversity positively. However, despite this gap, the general pattern is that the percentage of the national elites who view inclusive citizenship and diversity positively is much higher than the percentage of citizens who view diversity and inclusive citizenship positively, with the exception of Italy and Spain (see Klicperová-Baker and Košťál 2012: 91, table 2). The authors report that acceptance of ethnic diversity among the national elites varies between 16 per cent (Spain) and

84 per cent (Bulgaria) across the fifteen countries, whereas it varies between 7 per cent (Italy) and 92 per cent (Czech Republic) among the citizens. However, in Italy and Spain, the opposite is the case: citizen views favoring diversity and inclusive citizenship are being filtered on the elite level. The authors explain the Spanish and Italian exceptions in relational terms, as an outcome of countries' internal dynamics between the elites and citizens, as follows:

> Disparities between public and elite views seem to mutually influence each other in a converging process. For example, public intolerance of minorities seems to "push" elites toward recognition of the higher relevance of the problem. On the other hand, the recognition of relevance by the elites appears to push the public towards greater tolerance.
>
> *(Klicperová-Baker and Košťál 2012: 100)*

Despite statistically significant variation across the fifteen countries, this shows that 55.5 per cent of the national elites in Europe express inclusive views about diversity and citizenship, whereas the average is 29.6 per cent for citizens. As these findings are directly coupled with the EUROSPHERE data on elite views and the countries covered by EUROSPHERE, this also shows that citizens' views disfavoring diversity are somehow filtered on their way up to the elite circles.

As a supplement to the above-mentioned research, Klicperová-Baker and Košťál have also published results from research covering 44 European countries (Klicperová-Baker and Košťál 2016). Although the operationalizations in the latter research are somewhat different, and completely different methods have been deployed, and although different labels are used, the phenomena studied are the same: acceptance of inclusive citizenship and diversity. This time, the authors define *diversity* in multidimensional terms and use the EVS data to measure the views of both citizens and elites. Based on these, the authors conclude that:

> In some regions, particularly in the European Northwest, democratic mentality was absolutely prevalent. . . . Almost two thirds (64.3%) of the European general public seemed to lean to skeptically non-democratic or anti-democratic mentalities. The democratic character appeared in a minority in the post-communist region, in the post-soviet countries and in the Southeastern Europe. There, nondemocratic mentalities . . . or anti-democratic tendencies . . . were significantly overrepresented. Still, the *vertical (elite) perspective* reassures us that the democratic spirit seems to significantly and reliably prevail (or at least hold plurality) among the European elites and hence may have a stronger influence than sheer numbers suggest.

When *diversity* is defined in multidimensional terms, we do not find any exceptions from the general pattern: in all forty-four countries, including Italy and Spain, the percentage of elites with favoring attitudes towards inclusive citizenship and diversity (55.1 per cent) is consistently higher than the percentage of citizens with favoring attitudes (35.7 per cent).

Are national elites' views echoed within the trans-European elite circles?

The systematically selected 764 national and trans-European elites were encouraged to talk about persons and groups that they see as relevant to their own idea of a diverse society. After the interviewees talked about their own preferences, they were asked to consider whether they would like to include other categories that they were given a list of. The answers were then registered and coded in a common database. Interviews with leaders of national and trans-European level organizations show there are clear differences in organizations' approaches to citizen identity. Although the whole spectrum of views is represented at both levels, the set of views that dominate at each level differs. Based on a statistically significant comparison of the views of the transnational and national elites on diversity and citizenship, it was concluded that:

> 21.8% of the interviewees from national organizations and 52.9% from trans-European organizations *agree on* a globally/transnationally-oriented definition of citizenship. Inversely, 78.2% of national and 47.1% of trans-European elites *agree on* a nation-statist orientation to citizenship. These results show that nationalizing and Europeanizing discourses are spread in both national and trans-European-level organizations, but nation-state orientation is stronger at the national level whereas the transnational/global orientation is stronger at the trans-European level.
>
> *(Sicakkan 2012)*

Thus, the analysis reveals the presence of two distinct discourses: (1) a *Europeanist* discourse and (2) a *nation-statist* discourse. Europeanist discourses include a broad and inclusive definition of common citizen identity, whereas nation-statist discourses are primarily concerned with the categories that are related with the nation-state idea. Both of these discourses are observed within both national and trans-European elite circles. The Europeanist discourse seems to be dominant in the trans-European umbrella organizations, whereas the nation-statist discourse is more common within the national elite circles.

We will do more in-depth comparisons later in this chapter, but when roughly compared with the findings of Klicperová-Baker and Košťál (2012, 2016) about citizens' individual discourses, the findings about the discourses of national and trans-European elites have several implications in relation to the conceptual framework presented in the beginning.

The discursive pattern comprising two dimensions – the Europeanist and nation-statist discourses – that we find amongst the national and trans-European elites is quite similar to that Kilicperová-Baker and Košťál (2012, 2016) observe in connection with the individual citizens. Another important result to note here is that neither the exploratory nor the final analyses in Sicakkan (2012) detect an independent nativist discourse amongst trans-European and national elites. Similarly, Klicperová-Baker and Košťál do not find an independent nativist discourse at the individual level either. That is, the nativist and nation-statist discourses emerge as parts of a broader discourse that merges nation-statist and nativist discourses within the national and trans-European elite circles, whereas anti-democratic and non-democratic discourses are added to these at the citizen level (see the previous section). The discourse dimensions found in the three independent analyses mentioned above are conceptually close and, therefore, comparable.

As expected, a pro-diversity, inclusive, and all-encompassing view on common European citizen identity is adopted by the leaders of the trans-European networks that the EU has set up. Although allegiance to the nation-state citizen identity is strongly echoed among trans-European elites (47.1 per cent), it is also important to highlight that more than one-third of the individual citizens and one-third of the national elites are convinced about the trans-European elites' understanding of common citizen identity as an inclusive, pro-diversity perspective. Europeanizing views' presence within the national elite contexts is moderately high (21.8 per cent), and the similarity between the views of trans-European and national elites about a common European citizen identity may be on the way to becoming encompassing through EU policies.

Discourses of citizenship and diversity in national media

The EUROSPHERE media content data contains information about how newspapers and prime-time news programmes of selected broadcasters depict the belongings and identities of the people that they mention in their news reports.[10] The project team also coded the news items with respect to their main themes[11] and framing perspectives.[12]

In the exploratory stage of the analysis, it was discovered that immigrant and native minorities are made less visible by national media, except when the issue at stake is minority and migration policies. On the other hand, native and immigrant minorities are often mentioned positively when they are mentioned in the news reports. Second, three framing perspectives are detected, which are placed in clear distance from a fourth frame that is all-encompassing and inclusive: (1) a Europeanist perspective depicting different groups as "European citizens", (2) a communitarian framing depicting everybody as members of native communities, and (3) a nation-state framing labeling different people's belongings as nationals of a country (cf. also Sicakkan 2016).

What is interesting here, however, is the fourth type of framing that contains the belonging designations that remain outside the above-mentioned three framing perspectives. The fourth framing resembles the highly diversity-oriented, all-inclusive Europeanist discourses of trans-European elites. However, it excludes and places the

TABLE 13.2 National media discourses of citizenship and diversity

Discourse	Description	Percentage
Nation-statist	News are framed with a national perspective. Individuals are viewed primarily as members of nations and secondarily as members of an immigrant minority.	57.5% (N = 1456)
Europeanist	News are framed with a Europeanist perspective. Persons are primarily viewed as European citizens and secondarily as members of their nations.	27.6% (N = 698)
Nativist	News are framed with a native community perspective. Persons are primarily viewed as native minorities and secondarily as members of a nation.	15% (N = 379)

European, the national, and the community belongings in separate contexts – Europeanist, nation-statist, and communitarian.

The figures about the media discourses reported in Table 13.2 are results from a two-step cluster analysis, the details of which are published elsewhere (Sicakkan 2016). In this analysis, I used the national media's depictions of belongings, news themes, framing perspectives, and reporters and journalists' political attitudes toward the themes in question[13] as clustering variables.

Three discourses are detected: the first two discourses, nation-statist and Europeanist, were also identified in the interviews with national and trans-European elites as well as in surveys of citizens' views. The third discourse, labeled "nativist", is peculiar to media. It did not emerge as a separate discourse in trans-European or national elites' minds, nor in citizens' attitudes. Rather, nation-statist and nativist attitudes were merged as components of broader perspectives. Therefore, in the following comparative analysis, I will merge the nativist and nation-statist dimensions that are observed in national media discourses in order to make the figures comparable across the levels.

Are citizens' views filtered in national and European public spheres?

When comparing the figures from the three above-mentioned studies, it should be remembered that, whereas *national elites from civil society* in Study II comprise only people in leading positions in political parties, public interest groups, social movement organizations, think tanks, and media outlets, *national elites from all sectors* in Study I include also business elites, corporate elites, economic elites, managers, etc. Thus, comparisons across the first two studies should be done with caution. Also, because the two studies are based on separate samples, the results should be read and compared within each study and not across the three studies. On the other hand,

TABLE 13.3 Media discourses of citizenship and diversity in per cent

		Inclusiveness of Citizenship in Europe	
		Europeanist (Inclusive)	Nation-Statist (Non-Inclusive)
Study I **Intra-national Filter**	Citizens	35.7	64.3
	National elites – all sectors	55.1	44.9
Study II **Trans-national Filter**	National elites – civil society	21.8	78.2
	Trans-European elites	52.9	47.1
Study III **Media Filter**	National media	27,5	72,5

each of the two studies in itself measures reliably the under- and overrepresented views of citizens and elites.

Study I in Table 13.3 shows that, among citizens, the percentage of nation-statists is higher than Europeanists (64.3 and 35.7 per cent, respectively), whereas the opposite is the case amongst national elites: the percentage of Europeanists is higher than nation-statist national elites (55.1 and 44.9 per cent, respectively). This means that, at the national level, there is a filtering out of citizens' nation-statist views – that is, they do not quite reach up to the national elite circles in original proportions.

Study II, on the other hand, documents that nation-statist views are further filtered out, and Europeanist views are even more amplified, at the juncture between national and trans-European elite circles. Whereas the nation-statist views constitute almost four-fifths of the national elites, their representation is reduced to less than 50 per cent among the trans-European elites. In contrast, the Europeanist views that is popular among more than one-fifth of the national elites increase to almost 53 per cent among the trans-European elites.

Thus, the general observation in Table 13.3 is that, during dispersion from citizens to national elites, and from national elites to trans-European elites, at each level crossing, nation-statist perspectives are partly filtered out, whereas the proportion of Europeanist perspectives is amplified.[14] Alternatively, if we agree that this Europeanist diffusion is an intended, top-down outcome of the EU's policies aiming to create an EPS, we may also assert that the Europeanist perspective has diffused quite well into both trans-European and national elite circles, but less into the minds of individual citizens and the national media.

When these figures are compared with the proportions of Europeanist (27.6 per cent) and nation-statist views (72.5 per cent) in national media, we can speculate that national media mirror best the discursive pattern among the national elites in civil society (Study II). They mirror the least the discursive pattern within the trans-European elite circles. Thus, it is correct to say that national media tones down the Europeanist views of trans-European elites and the nation-statist views of citizens and national corporate, business, and managerial elites. At the same time, national media follow suit with the perspectives of the national civil society leaders.

Is the European public sphere good for democracy?

Going back to the conceptual framework given in Table 13.1, the main finding is that citizens' nation-statist views do not reach proportionally to the national and trans-European elite. However, national media amplify the nation-statist preferences of citizens beyond their original proportions while modulating the Europeanist views. Furthermore, in the trans-European elite circles of pan-European networks, national civil society elites' nation-statist views are severely filtered out and Europeanist views are amplified. As a consequence, the proportion of Europeanist views is amplified at each level crossing. At the same time, it is important to remember that nation-statist views empirically comprise a strong non-inclusive notion of citizenship and diversity, whereas Europeanist views appear to entail the most inclusive attitudes in the data materials used here.[15]

This picture clearly places the current EPS in Scenario IV in Table 13.1. Moreover, what we read in Table 13.3 also places the national public spheres in Scenario IV since the nation-statist views are filtered out by national elites (Study I) and Europeanist views are modulated by national media (Study III). Scenario IV is the situation where non-inclusive views of citizenship and diversity are excluded from the public sphere. That is, the visibility of non-democratic and anti-democratic views are limited in the public sphere in order to uphold democracy.

The question that is posed in Table. 13.3 in this respect is not whether this kind of an EPS improves democracy (cf. Scenario II in Table 13.1), but *whether it does not improve democracy* (cf. Scenario IV). There is a fundamental difference between the two questions. The former comes from a procedural democracy perspective, which assumes the democratic rules, procedures, and institutions to lead to democratic outcomes for all groups. Therefore, its main question is about whether fair procedures, rules, and institutions improve democracy. The latter is not entrenched in such an assumption and focuses on the outcomes, improving or terminating the rules, procedures, and institutions that do not have the expected democratic outcomes in certain contexts, although they might seem procedurally correct. Whereas the former is based on a deontological thinking, the latter takes its point of departure in consequentialism.

There are two ways of dealing with this fact: labeling it a democratic deficit or arguing that it is democratic to hinder the dominance of anti-democratic views. Based on the procedural democracy perspective, it is possible to state that the observed lack of inclusiveness concerning anti-democratic preferences (or exclusion of non-inclusive views) contributes to the democratic deficit of the EU.

On the other hand, one may also argue that modulating non-inclusive views is not necessarily a democracy problem since many European countries that are rightly recognized as exemplary liberal democracies have been doing the same since World War II, and/or that it is unfair to demand the EU to score higher on a democracy scale than its member states.

My normative take is to adopt a substantive democracy perspective advocating temporary systemic privileges for marginalized groups in contexts of severe structural inequality so that their voices are heard. One such systemic privilege is to make inclusive views more visible in the EPS, including the national and trans-European elite circles and the mass media. If dominance of non-inclusive views is an important factor in justifying and sustaining structural inequalities that result in severe discrimination against certain groups of citizens, then the procedural approach might be deemed too limited in measuring and addressing the inadvertent outcomes of the institutions, procedures, and rules of the democratic game. The concept of output legitimacy concerns the fairness of policy outcomes for all citizen groups, whereas input and throughput legitimacy is about the procedural and institutional aspects.[16] The EU already has a weighty focus on its output and throughput legitimacy in order to compensate for its questionable input legitimacy. However, a pronouncedly ideological entrenchment of the EU's emphasis on output legitimacy in a theory of substantive democracy would serve the goal of democratization more effectively.

Further reading

Eriksen, Erik Oddvar. 2005. An Emerging Public Sphere. *European Journal of Social Theory*, 8(3): 341–363.

Fraser, Nancy. 2007. Transnationalizing the Public Sphere: On the Legitimacy and Efficacy of Public Opinion in a Post-Westphalian World. *Theory, Culture & Society*, 24(4): 7–30.

Koopmans, Ruud and Jessica Erbe. 2004. Towards a European Public Sphere? *Innovation: The European Journal of Social Science Research*, 17(2): 97–118.

Key questions for discussion

1 What are the key features of (a) a national public sphere and (b) a transnational public sphere? How can we observe and measure them?
2 What are the pre-conditions for a common European public sphere to emerge?
3 In what ways can a common European public sphere be part of solutions for the European democratic deficit?

Notes

1 For example, *White Paper on a European Communication Policy* (COM(2006) 35 Final), *European Governance: A White Paper* (COM(2001) 428 Final), and *Plan D for Democracy, Dialogue and Debate* (COM(2005) 494 Final).

2 Certainly, as there are several other areas in which the EU could be more willing to introduce democratic reforms (e.g. making the European Commissioner posts elective) this statement is limited to the EU's approach to the EPS.

3 Two noteworthy EU attempts to create an EPS include (1) the creation of a Europe-wide civil society by initiating and sponsoring trans-European networks of civil society organizations (hereunder networks of NGOs and think tanks) and (2) the creation of a Europe-wide media space by initiating and sponsoring a common European Media (e.g. experiments with new Europe-wide TV channels and TV programmes) and by regulations on audiovisual services.

4 See Vibe (2016) in this volume for an overview of the status of LGB rights in Europe.

5 EUROSPHERE mobilized approximately 140 researchers in seventeen universities and research institutions in sixteen European countries. The project was initiated and led by this author, on behalf of the University of Bergen. The research activities lasted from February 2007 until March 2013. The countries included in this chapter are Austria, Belgium, Bulgaria, the Czech Republic, Denmark, Estonia, Finland, France, Germany, Hungary, Italy, the Netherlands, Norway, Spain, and the United Kingdom. Although data from Turkey is included in the original data material, this country has been excluded from the analyses in this chapter in order to meet this volume's ambition to cover Europe 31 (see also Peters and Tatham's introduction to this volume, 2016). EUROSPHERE publications, codebooks, and the data material are available at http://eurospheres.org.

6 At the first stage, three main players in print media and two (small) print media actors representing/voicing the alternative views were nominated in each country. Concerning broadcast media, two public service news programmes and two commercial news programmes were nominated. That is, a total of nine media actors were nominated in each country. For each country, we finally chose five media actors – three print media and two broadcasters. The final selection was based on a concern for representing the largest possible variation of media types and their approaches to the EU polity. The nominations were based on information in media websites and secondary literature on media's framing of diversity.

7 The comparison between citizen and national elite views is based on results of analyses conducted by Martina Klicperová-Baker and Košťál (2012, 2016 forthcoming). In both of the above-mentioned publications by Klicperová-Baker and Košťál, the research questions were formulated in collaboration with this author as part of the umbrella Eurosphere project.

8 The comparisons of the latter two – the national and trans-European elite views and media framings – are extensions of my analysis results published in Sicakkan (2012, 2016 forthcoming). None of these analyses are replicated here, but their results are built upon in order to answer a different research question in this chapter.

9 See also Knutsen (2016) in this volume for a separate treatment of citizen attitudes to citizenship and diversity over time.

10 The media's depictions of persons'/groups' belongings were coded as (1) depicted as European citizens, (2) as nationals of a country, (3) as residents of a region, (4) as members of a majority group, (5) as members of an ethno-national minority, (6) as members of a gender group – men or women, and (7) as detached individuals.

11 The theme categories into which news items were coded are (1) EU institutions, (2) reform treaty, (3) enlargement, (4) minorities or minority policies, (5) immigration or migration policy, (6) free movement or mobility, (7) gender and gender policy, and (8) constructing Europe and the EU.

12 News items were coded into the following framing perspectives: (1) individual perspective, (2) group/community perspective, (3) local perspective, (4) regional perspective, (5) member state/national perspective, (6) European perspective, (7) global (justice) perspective.

13 The political preferences of journalists (authors of the news) were coded into the following categories: (1) only positive, (2) more positive than negative, (3) more negative than positive, and (4) only negative. This coding was applied to the eight themes mentioned above.

14 Based on indicators of citizen preferences concerning protection of minorities, Bjånesøy and Ivarsflaten (2016), in this volume, find that "PRR [populist radical right wing] voters have a more populist and majoritarian vision of democracy than do voters of other parties". Although these non-inclusive views seem to be translated into party sympathy and, more importantly, turned into votes, the findings in my current chapter document that they fall short of being voiced in equal proportions in the EPS.

15 Leaving aside the rather non-intuitive conceptual links between the categories "Europeanists" and "inclusiveness" on the one hand, and "nation-statists" and "non-inclusiveness" on the other, I rely on the aforementioned empirically uncovered relationships between them.

16 The concern for the balance between input and output legitimacy is the theme of two other articles in this volume. See Tatham's (2016) assessment of multi-jurisdictional politics as a means for the optimal balance between input and output legitimacy. Also see Linde and Dahlberg (2016), who assess the citizen dissatisfaction on input- and output-related aspects of democracy.

References

Bjånesøy, Lise Lund and Elisabeth Ivarsflaten. 2016. Right-Wing Populism. In Yvette Peters and Michaël Tatham (eds.). *Democratic Transformations in Europe: Challenges and Opportunities*, pp. 33–50. Abingdon: Routledge.

Calhoun, Craig. 2005. Constitutional Patriotism and the Public Sphere: Interests, Identity, and Solidarity. *International Journal of Politics, Culture and Society*, 18(3–4): 257–280.

Dahl, Robert. 1989. *Democracy and Its Critics*. New Haven, CT: Yale University Press.

de Beus, J. 2010. The European Union and the Public Sphere: Conceptual Issues, Political Tension, Moral Concerns, and Empirical Questions. In R. Koopmans and P. Statham (eds.). *The Making of a European Public Sphere: Media Discourse and Political Contention*, pp. 13–33. Cambridge: Cambridge University Press.

Eriksen, Erik Oddvar. 2005. An Emerging Public Sphere. *European Journal of Social Theory*, 8(3): 341–363.

Fossum, John Erik and Philip Schlesinger. 2007. The European Union and the Public Sphere: A Communicative Space in the Making? In J.E. Fossum and P. Schlesinger (eds.). *The European Union and the Public Sphere: A Communicative Space in the Making?*, pp. 1–19. London and New York: Routledge.

Fraser, Nancy. 1990. Re-Thinking the Public Sphere: A Contribution to the Critique of Actually Existing Democracy. *Social Text*, 25–26: 56–80.

Fraser, Nancy. 2007. Transnationalizing the Public Sphere: On the Legitimacy and Efficacy of Public Opinion in a Post-Westphalian World. *Theory, Culture & Society*, 24(4): 7–30.

Habermas, Jürgen. 1989. *The Structural Transformation of the Public Sphere: An Inquiry into a Category of Bourgeois Society*, tr. Thomas Burger with Frederick Lawrence. Cambridge MA: The M.I.T. Press.

Hooghe, Liesbet. 2003. Europe Divided? Elites vs. Public Opinion on European Integration. *European Union Politics*, 4(3): 281–304.

Klicperová-Baker, Martina and Jaroslav Košťál. 2012. Ethno-National, Religious, Ideological and Sexual Diversity. *Javnost – The Public*, 19(1): 85–102.

Klicperová-Baker, Martina and Jaroslav Košťál. 2016. Toward Empirical Assessment of European Demos and Public Sphere: Value Orientations of Citizens and Elites. In H.G. Sicakkan (ed.). *Integration, Diversity and the Making of a European Public Sphere*, pp. 183–208. London: Edward Elgar.

Knutsen, Terje. 2016. A Re-Emergence of Nationalism as a Political Force in Europe? In Yvette Peters and Michaël Tatham (eds.). *Democratic Transformations in Europe: Challenges and Opportunities*, pp. 13–32. Abingdon: Routledge.

Linde, Jonas and Stefan Dahlberg. 2016. Democratic Discontent in Times of Crisis? In Yvette Peters and Michaël Tatham (eds.). *Democratic Transformations in Europe: Challenges and Opportunities*, pp. 72–96. Abingdon: Routledge.

Lord, Christoffer and David Beetham. 2001. Legitimizing the EU: Is There a 'Post-Parliamentary Basis' for Its Legitimation? *Journal of Common Market Studies*, 39(3): 443–462.

Mouffe, Chantal. 1992. *Dimensions of Radical Democracy: Pluralism, Citizenship, Democracy*. London: Verso.

Mouffe, Chantal. 1999. Deliberative Democracy or Agonistic Pluralism? *Social Research*, 66(3): 745–758.

Mouffe, Chantal. 2002a. For an Agonistic Public Sphere. In Okwui Enwezor (ed.). *Democracy Unrealized: Documenta 11, Platform 1*, 87–97. Berlin: Hatje Cantz.

Mouffe, Chantal. 2002b. Which Public Sphere for a Democratic Society? *Theoria: A Journal of Social and Political Theory*, 99 (June): 55–65.

Peters, Yvette and Michaël Tatham. 2016. The Transformation of Democracy. In Y. Peters and M. Tatham (eds.). *Democratic Transformations in Europe: Challenges and Opportunities*, pp. 1–10. Abingdon: Routledge.

Shapiro, Ian. 1994. Three Ways to be a Democrat. *Political Theory*, 22(1): 124–151.

Sicakkan, Hakan G. 2012. Trans-Europeanizing Public Spaces in Europe. *Javnost-The Public*, 19(1): 103–124.

Sicakkan, Hakan G. 2016. European State Building, Top-Down Elite Alliances and the National Media. In H.G. Sicakkan (ed.). *Integration, Diversity and the Making of a European Public Sphere*, pp. 75–93. London: Edward Elgar.

Tatham, Michaël. 2016. Multi-Jurisdictional Politics: State Adaptation and Mixed Visions of Democracy. In Yvette Peters and Michaël Tatham (eds.). *Democratic Transformations in Europe: Challenges and Opportunities*, pp. 269–294. Abingdon: Routledge.

Vibe, V. 2016. Minority Rights under Majority Rule: LGB-Rights in Europe. In Yvette Peters and Michaël Tatham (eds.). *Democratic Transformations in Europe: Challenges and Opportunities*, pp. 231–251. Abingdon: Routledge.

Young, Iris Marion. 1990. *Justice and the Politics of Difference*. Princeton, NJ: Princeton University Press.

14

MULTI-JURISDICTIONAL POLITICS

State adaptation and mixed visions of democracy

Michaël Tatham

Introduction

Political systems survive through adaptation. In this respect, democracies in Europe 31 are no different. Even if one looks back no further than the last six decades, change has been both omnipresent and wide-ranging. Many of these changes have been mapped in the preceding chapters, ranging from the decline of parties (Mjelde and Svåsand, 2016) to the liberal challenge to social democracy (Alvarez, 2016), or the transformation of the welfare state (Oldervoll and Kuhnle, 2016).

This chapter focusses on another type of change: the rise of *multi-jurisdictional politics*. The term is used to describe the changing nature of the scale of government as well as its development at different levels and across sectors. Hence, different jurisdictions have varying political authority at multiple levels. Such authority may be shared or it may be exclusive. Jurisdictions may be territorially defined or they may be functionally defined. They may have a narrow policy remit or a broader one. The rise of multi-jurisdictional politics thus describes the emergence of multiple jurisdictions with varying authority and operating at different functional and territorial scales.

In the last half-century, the rise of multi-jurisdictional politics has been driven by two concomitant factors. First, democracies have *decentralised*. They have increasingly empowered their regional level of government and administration. This regional level is highly heterogeneous. Regions can be defined as a territorial level situated between the local and the state levels. This intermediary level is often called by different names in various countries. In the Netherlands, this level of government and administration is called *Provincies*. In Austria it is called *Länder*. Some small countries, such as Malta, Luxembourg, or Cyprus, do not have an intermediate level. Others have two such intermediate levels, which are again differently termed. The French have *régions* and *départements*, while the Italians have *regioni* and *province*.

In some other countries still, the level called 'region' is neither the more powerful nor the more relevant one. Hungary has weak administrative regions but much stronger counties (*Megyék*). Romania exhibits similar characteristics, as its counties (*Judete*) are more powerful than its regions. Despite the diversity of intermediary bodies, a wave of decentralisation reforms has swept through Europe 31 and rendered regional governments and administrations increasingly powerful. Hence, multi-jurisdictional politics has grown from below.

Second, democracies have *supranationalised*. They have gradually empowered organisations and bodies situated above the state. These international organisations (IOs) are just as diverse as the regional authorities described above. Many have a narrow functional remit and are hence task-specific. This is the case, for example, of the International Civil Aviation Organization (ICAO), the International Telecommunication Union (ITU), or the International Criminal Police Organization (INTERPOL). Despite their functionally defined policy remit, these task-specific organisations have broad membership. The ICAO counts 191 countries, ITU 193 and INTERPOL 190.[1] Others have a broader remit. This is often the case for territorially defined IOs, such as the Council of Europe (CoE), the Benelux union, the Nordic Council, or the European Union (EU). These tend to have narrower membership. While the CoE and the EU count forty-seven and twenty-eight member states each, the Nordic Council and Benelux count only five[2] and three, respectively.[3] The multiplication and empowerment of these IOs implies that multi-jurisdictional politics has also grown from above.

These decentralisation and supranationalisation trends contribute to the rise of multi-jurisdictional politics. In this chapter I first map the two trends and then discuss their implications. Indeed, the decentralisation and the supranationalisation of our polities have generated a number of challenges related to policy gridlock, coordination dilemmas, and lack of transparency and accountability. However, they have also provided opportunities related to efficiency, differentiation, and inclusiveness. The chapter discusses both and draws some conclusions as to how the rise of multi-jurisdictional politics has affected the health of democracy in Europe 31.

Mapping trends over time

Decentralisation, or the downward dispersion of powers away from the central state, has generally been spreading across Europe 31. The most striking example of this trend is possibly Belgium, which went all the way from a decentralised unitary state to a federal state with multiple tiers of territorial governance (see the 1970, 1980, 1988–9, 1993–5, 2001–2, and the 2012–4 reforms). Although to some extent an outlier, Belgium is not an isolated case in Europe 31. France, Italy, and Spain have all gone through major territorial reforms. France went from being unitary and centralised to amending its constitution to recognise its decentralised nature (Act I of the decentralisation reform: 1982–6; Act II: 2003–5). Italy has developed into a quasi-federal polity (1948, 1970, 2001). Similarly to France's *régions* and *départements*,

Italy has two levels of regional government: the *province* and the *regioni*. However, while the *départements* and *province* are similar in many respects, the Italian *regioni* differ from the French *régions* in two fundamental ways. First, they are more powerful in terms of their self-government prerogatives and the leverage they have on state politics. Second, they have varying powers as the *regioni a statuto speciale* benefit from greater authority than their *statuto ordinario* counterparts. Spain is similar to Italy in the sense that it is composed of two territorial tiers (the *provincias* and the *comunidades autónomas*) and that its regionalisation has been asymmetrical, distinguishing the historic communities from the non-historic ones. However, its end result has been an ongoing empowerment of regional authorities via continuous renegotiation of their statutes of autonomy since their creation in 1978 (Keating and Wilson, 2009).

Beyond these four cases, a majority of countries in Europe 31 have moderately decentralised their political system. This was often the result of reforms to strengthen existing regional institutions (Denmark, Norway, the Netherlands), to create new territorial tiers – sometimes to fulfil EU cohesion policy requirements (Greece, Ireland, Finland), or as part of a wider independence and democratisation process (Croatia, Czech Republic, Hungary, Lithuania, Poland, Romania, or Slovakia). In these transition periods, EU incentives have sometimes been considered as a factor contributing to the regionalisation processes (Brusis, 2002; Hughes, Sasse, and Gordon, 2004).

The remaining countries fall into one of three categories: (1) they are already federal and can hence hardly decentralise further (Austria, Germany, or Switzerland); (2) reforms have concerned only a small share of the population (Scotland, Wales, and Northern Ireland in the UK, the Azores and Madeira in Portugal); or (3) no decentralisation process has substantially empowered the country's regions (Bulgaria, Cyprus, Estonia, Iceland, Latvia, Luxembourg, Malta, Slovenia). Many of the countries falling into this last category are unlikely to have a regional level in the first place due to their small size. Indeed, the population of Iceland, Luxembourg, or Malta is well below the 600,000 bar, while that of Latvia, Cyprus, Estonia, or Slovenia is below 2.1 million.

These Europe 31 trends are represented in Figure 14.1. The individual graphs are based on data collected by Hooghe, Marks, and Schakel (2010) and represent levels of 'regional authority' for all countries since 1950 or the date the country became independent and democratic. Hooghe et al. define regional authority as composed of self-rule (0–15), understood as 'the capacity of a regional government to exercise authority autonomously over those who live in its territory', and shared rule (0–9), understood as 'the capacity to co-determine the exercise of authority for the country as a whole' (2010: 6). Each of these two dimensions is further broken down into four sub-components. The region's institutional autonomy, policy scope, fiscal autonomy, and independence of representation contribute to self-rule. Meanwhile, a region's national law-making powers, its national executive control, national fiscal control, and national constitutional reform powers contribute to shared rule (2010: 13–31).

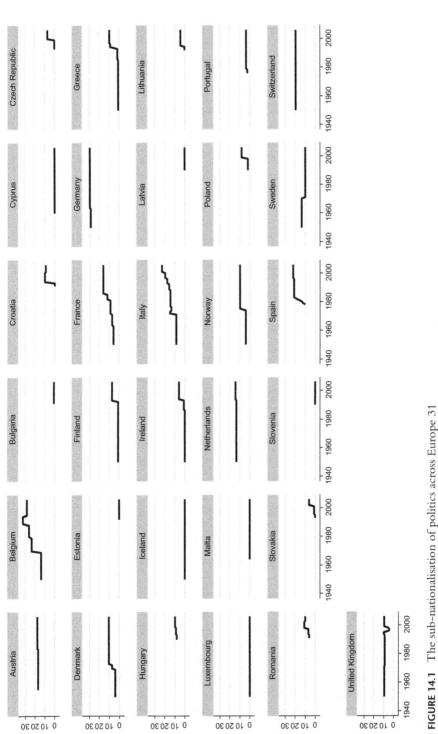

FIGURE 14.1 The sub-nationalisation of politics across Europe 31

Notes: Figures derived from data measuring regional authority collected by Hooghe et al. (2010)

The take-home message from this figure is that unless they are small in size or already highly decentralised, most Europe 31 countries have further decentralised. This applies equally to the twenty-eight EU member states and to the three non-EU states. Indeed, Iceland falls in the category of small and highly centralised countries, together with Cyprus, Estonia, Latvia, Luxembourg, Malta, and Slovenia. Switzerland clusters with the already-federal and regionally stable Austria and Germany. Norway has a similar pattern to other small or medium-sized countries, such as Denmark or the Netherlands, which have gradually strengthened existing territorial tiers of government and administration. Sweden is the only case in Europe 31 to display a drop in aggregate regional authority levels. This is because its 1971 reform – though it widened the *Landstinge*'s policy scope and increased their representation through direct election and choice of their own executives – abolished the upper chamber of the *Riksdag* representing the *Landstinge*, hence wiping out the *Landstinge*'s influence over national politics in terms of law-making, fiscal control, and constitutional reform.

Supranationalisation, or the upward dispersion of powers away from the central state, has also been spreading across Europe 31. Whilst Belgium is the most striking example of decentralisation, the EU is an astonishing illustration of the supranationalisation of Europe 31. Initially formed by a group of six countries seeking cooperation in the fields of coal and steel (1952), the EU has dramatically expanded both territorially and functionally. In July 2013 it welcomed its twenty-eighth member (Croatia), while its Lisbon Treaty (2009) continued the trend of deeper integration in ever-more policy fields. No other supranational organisation in the world has benefited from a higher level of delegation of authority than the EU.

The EU's functional expansion, in terms of both level and depth of integration across policy areas, can be mapped out over time. Figure 14.2 displays data collected by Börzel (2005). She identifies two elements in the integration process. First, the *level* at which authority is located. These levels range from exclusive national competence in a policy field (coded 1), to most competencies at the national level (2), an even split between the national and the EU level (3), most competencies at the EU level (4), and finally exclusive EU competence (5). Second, the *depth* of authority the EU has on the issue in question, irrespective of the level at which the competence is exercised. This includes no EU coordination (0); intergovernmental coordination with no involvement of supranational institutions beyond the European Council (1); intergovernmental cooperation with the involvement of the Commission, consultation of the European Parliament (EP), and limited judicial review by the European Court of Justice (ECJ) (2); joint decision-making with variable EP involvement but full judicial review by the ECJ (3); joint decision-making with cooperation or co-decision with the EP (4); and finally supranational centralisation with no involvement of the Council and EP, but full decisional authority by the Commission or the European Central Bank (ECB), and full ECJ judicial review (5).

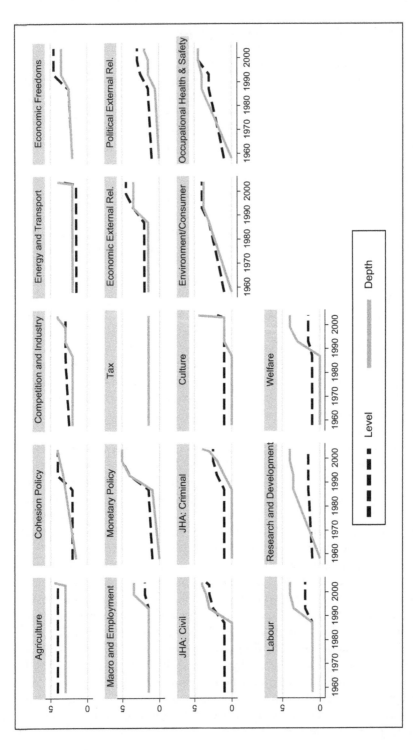

FIGURE 14.2 Level and depth of European integration

Notes: Level and depth across policy areas are derived from data collected by Börzel (2005). The level at which decisions are taken (1–5) varies from exclusive national competencies to exclusive EU competencies. Depth, or the mode by which decisions are taken (0–5), varies from no EU-level coordination to supranational centralisation

The individual graphs for each policy area highlight how integration has been differentiated both across policy fields and over time. In the time period between the Treaty of Rome (1957) and the ill-fated Constitutional Treaty (2004), which served as a template for the Lisbon Treaty (2009), only one policy area has exhibited negligible change: taxation policy. This policy area has remained at a relatively national level (score of 1.5); i.e. somewhere between an exclusive national competence and a mostly national competence, while decisions in the field have been taken in a mode situated between intergovernmental coordination and cooperation (1.5). All other policy fields have displayed variation with a general shift of issues away from the national level and up to the EU level, and increasing powers to supranational institutions such as the Commission, the EP, the ECB, or the ECJ, to the detriment of national governments, as represented in the Council.

While integration has deepened and widened over time in terms of the number of policy areas covered and its decision-taking mode, it has also widened in terms of membership. This means that the degree of supranationalisation of politics in Europe 31 countries has co-varied as the EU both expanded and deepened. Denmark, Ireland, and the UK joined in 1973. They were followed by newly democratic Greece (1981), Spain, and Portugal (1986). A second northern enlargement took place in 1995 with the accession of Austria, Finland, and Sweden. The reunification of Eastern and Western Europe following the fall of the Berlin Wall and the dissolution of the USSR (1989 and 1991) took a first massive step in 2004 with the accession of eight former East European countries (plus two Mediterranean islands). Eastwards enlargement continued in 2007 (Romania and Bulgaria), whilst Croatia is the latest and twenty-eighth member since July 2013.

The territorial expansion of the EU is summarised in Table 14.1 which also highlights the spread of democracy within Europe 31. It can be easily forgotten that many East European countries have only had a quarter of a century's worth of democratic experience, while countries such as Greece, Portugal, or Spain have been democratic for about forty years or less. Table 14.1 also illustrates that though Iceland, Norway, and Switzerland are not formally members of the EU, their involvement in the European project is in many respects similar to that of formal members. While Ireland and the UK opted out of Schengen, all three non-EU states opted in, as early as 2001 for Iceland and Norway and as recently as 2008 for Switzerland. The former two are part of the European Economic Area (EEA). The latter is not, but it is linked to the EU through continuously upgraded bilateral agreements. Despite not being formal members, research has demonstrated a deep implementation of the EU's *acquis* in these three countries and hence a high supranationalisation of their politics, in line with the EU's development (Kux and Sverdrup, 2000; Linder, 2013).

The EU is certainly an outlier in terms of the degree to which states have delegated and transferred authority to it. However, it is part of a wider pattern of expanding supranationalisation of policy-making and decision-taking (Abbott and Snidal, 1998; Keohane, 1982; Lenz, 2012). The EU is far from being the only international organisation of which Europe 31 countries are members. Beyond

TABLE 14.1 Europe 31, democracy, and European integration

Country	Democracy		European integration steps		
	Uninterrupted, according to Boix et al. (2013)	Uninterrupted, according to Doorenspleet (2000)	Membership	Schengen	Eurozone
Austria	1946	1946	1995	1997	1999
Belgium	1894	1949	1952	1995	1999
Bulgaria	1990	1990	2007	Obliged to join	Obliged to join
Croatia	2000	NA	2013	Obliged to join	Obliged to join
Cyprus	1977	NA	2004	Obliged to join	2008
Czech Republic	1993	1990*	2004	2007	Obliged to join
Denmark	1901	1945	1973	2001	Opt-out
Estonia	1991	1991[l]	2004	2007	2011
Finland	1917	1944	1995	2001	1999
France	1946	1969	1952	1995	1999
Germany	1949 (1990)	1949 (1990)	1952 + 1990	1995	1999
Greece	1974	1975	1981	2000	2001
Hungary	1990	1990	2004	2007	Obliged to join
Iceland	1918	1934	No (1994, EEA)	2001	No
Ireland	1922	1923	1973	Opt-out	1999
Italy	1946	1948	1952	1997	1999
Latvia	1993	1991[l]	2004	2007	2014
Lithuania	1992	1991	2004	2007	2015
Luxembourg	1890	1945	1952	1995	1999
Malta	1964	NA	2004	2007	2008
Netherlands	1897	1945	1952	1995	1999
Norway	1900	1945	No (1994, EEA)	2001	No
Poland	1989	1991	2004	2007	Obliged to join
Portugal	1976	1976	1986	1995	1999
Romania	1991	1990	2007	Obliged to join	Obliged to join
Slovakia	1993	1993	2004	2007	2009
Slovenia	1991	1991	2004	2007	2007
Spain	1977	1978	1986	1995	1999
Sweden	1911	1921	1995	2001	Obliged to join
Switzerland	1948	1971	No (1972, EFTA)	2008	No
United Kingdom	1885	1928	1973	Opt-out	Opt-out

Notes: NA = data not available; *Czechoslovakia; [l]still noted as not fully democratic in 1994 by Doorenspleet. EEA = European Economic Area; EFTA = Free Trade Agreement; shaded areas = not EU members.

the Nordic Council, Benelux, CoE, INTERPOL, ITU, or ICAO already mentioned above, these countries also have membership to at least a further thirty-six
IOs. Some of these are well-known and have particularly wide membership, such
as the United Nations (UN), the World Health Organisation (WHO), the World
Trade Organisation (WTO), the International Monetary Fund (IMF), the International Labour Organisation (ILO), or the International Bank for Reconstruction
and Development (IBRD, part of the World Bank). Others have more limited
membership and are to some extent more specialised, such as the European Space
Agency (ESA), the European Organization for Nuclear Research (CERN), the
North Atlantic Treaty Organisation (NATO), or the Organisation for Economic
Co-operation and Development (OECD). Out of seventy-two major world IOs
that Hooghe and Marks (2015) count, I identified forty-two that comprise Europe
31 countries. Figure 14.3 displays these forty-two IOs along with information
about their number of member states and the number of policy areas for which
they have competencies.

Interestingly, the dataset by Hooghe and Marks (2015) also includes a variable
coding an IO's policy scope at its inception. By creating a new, third variable from
these data, one can get a sense of an IO's empowerment – or at least its widening
scope of competence – over time. These new data are represented in Figure 14.4.
While four out of forty-two IOs have seen their policy scope shrink since their
creation, the rest have all expanded. The most striking increases concern the CoE
(see also Vibe, 2016), the Nordic Council, and the UN. The only decreases concern
the ITU, the World Intellectual Property Organisation (WIPO), the ICAO, and the
International Maritime Organisation (IMO). Figure 14.4 reveals that beyond the

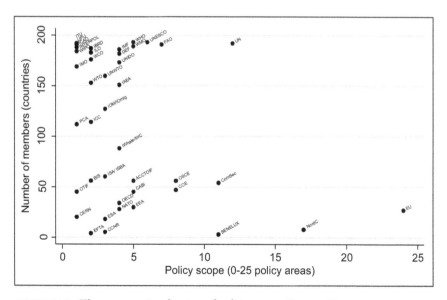

FIGURE 14.3 The supra-nationalisation of politics across Europe 31

Notes: Derived from data collected by Hooghe and Marks (2015).

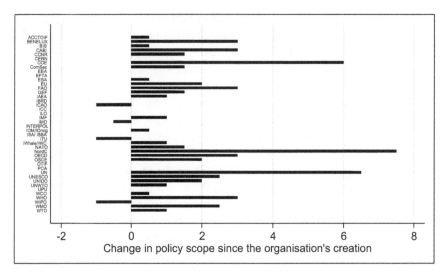

FIGURE 14.4 The growing scope of international organisations over time and across Europe 31

Notes: Derived from data collected by Hooghe and Marks (2015). A unit change represents an increase or decrease by one policy area in the organisation's portfolio since its creation.

EU, the supranationalisation of politics has been growing in Europe 31 as the vast majority of IOs to which they belong have seen their policy scope expand.

Overall, the decentralisation and supranationalisation of politics in Europe 31 has been rather astonishing. The vast majority of these countries have dispersed powers downwards through decentralisation processes, while they have also dispersed powers upwards not only via deepening European integration but also through the expanding scope of the dozens of IOs to which they belong. These processes have been highly differentiated over time and across countries. Some, like France, were founding members of the European project, early members of numerous IOs and have decentralised regularly throughout the last half-century. For others the process is more recent and linked to independence and democratisation processes. The evolution of Spain in the late 1970s and 1980s, or the trajectory of Croatia these last 25 years, illustrate cases of more rapid change. The dual decentralisation and supranationalisation of Europe 31, however, has not been without consequences. These have represented both challenges and opportunities.

Confusion, unaccountability, and stasis: the challenges of multi-jurisdictional politics

The supranationalisation and decentralisation of politics have triggered two main challenges. These relate to modes of decision-taking and issues of accountability and responsibility attribution.

To some extent, the rise of multi-jurisdictional politics has had a disempowering effect on individual Europe 31 countries. This is because, by creating and empowering new sets of players in an expanding number of policy fields, decentralisation and supranationalisation have increased the number of players involved in policy-making. Regarding supranationalisation, when member states decide to pool their sovereignty by forming territorial or functional IOs, they instigate limits to their individual authority in at least one of three ways. They can take decisions by unanimity, hence granting each member a veto right. They can take decisions by majority rule (or super-majority), hence allowing larger groups to outvote smaller ones. Or they can delegate decision-taking to a third party, often in the form of a non-majoritarian, independent body, hence in part relinquishing their authority over outcomes. Supranationalisation can thus generate new sources of policy deadlock by increasing the number of veto players (unanimity rule), while it can disempower individual states through majority or delegated decision-taking. In any case, individual state capacity and autonomy to pursue distinct policy objectives becomes qualified. The proliferation of authoritative policy players, the practice of competence pooling and of third-party delegation have been analysed through various theoretical lenses, ranging from veto player theory (Immergut, 1990; Tsebelis, 2002) to delegation and principal agent theory (Pollack, 1997), path dependence (Pierson, 1996), or multi-level governance (Marks, Hooghe, and Blank, 1996).

The dynamics are somewhat similar regarding decentralisation. As regions have gained increasing shared rule (i.e. 'the capacity to co-determine the exercise of authority for the country as a whole'), they have been able to shape, constrain, and sometimes veto national law-making, bind central government to decisions taken in domestic intergovernmental meetings, negotiate the distribution of national tax revenues, and postpone, amend, or prohibit national constitutional reform. In Europe 31, federal and highly regionalised countries such as Germany, Belgium, Austria, Switzerland, Spain, Italy, or the Netherlands stand out. This is because their regional level has an authoritative say in national politics. Much of the literature has focused on Germany and its bicameral system, which exacerbates gridlock tendencies in the context of party political incongruence (Auel, 2014; Bräuninger and König, 1999). These analyses of Germany's reform logjam (*Reformstau*) and of the challenge of disentangling joint policy-making have been expanded to other federal cases such as Switzerland (Fuglister and Wasserfallen, 2014), Austria (Karlhofer and Pallaver, 2013) and Belgium (Swenden, 2013). They have also been extended to regionalised states such as Spain (Aja and Colino, 2014), Italy (Palermo and Wilson, 2014), the Netherlands (Toonen, 1990), and dramatically asymmetrical states such as the UK (Swenden and McEwen, 2014) and Finland (Hepburn, 2014). They even have a European dimension as the more powerful regions are able to constrain their central government on EU issues too (Tatham, 2011).

If decentralisation and supranationalisation have similar effects in terms of constraining policy change and complicating decision-taking through joint policy-making entanglement, it is not surprising that scholars have drawn parallels between them. Some have sought inspiration from the EU to find new solutions to (some)

Belgian governance problems (Sinardet and Bursens, 2014), while others have examined how Switzerland could provide a governance template for the EU (Lacey, 2014). The likening of decentralisation and surpanationalisation in their gover-nance-impeding effects has perhaps been most striking, however, in scholarship comparing Germany to the EU, starting with Scharpf's work on the joint decision trap (*Politikverflechtung*) (1988; 2006). Scharpf's scholarship has highlighted how issues characterised by high salience and preference heterogeneity among actors lead not only to a joint decision trap in highly decentralised polities (such as Ger-many) and highly supranationalised ones (such as the EU), but also how the EU's institutional architecture has both weakened national capacity for policy-making without enabling it supranationally either. It has weakened national capacity by prohibiting states from using certain policy instruments such as subsidies (for both domestic consumption and exports), import controls (through tariff and non-tariff barriers), currency devaluation or interest rate tweaking. However, as illustrated in Table 14.2, some areas of low national capacity unfortunately overlap with some areas of low EU capacity too, and hence lead to a 'problem-solving gap' (Scharpf, 2006: 855). This gap is especially prevalent in areas such as the taxation of mobile capital and business, macro-economic employment policy, industrial relations or social policy broadly conceived. Later scholarship has since mapped out the EU's various joint decision traps across nine broad policy areas (Falkner, 2011).

Additionally, the rise of multi-jurisdictional politics generates a challenge in terms of responsibility attribution. More colloquially, if everybody is involved, who is responsible? With shared, joint, or blurred competence attribution, accountability becomes less straightforward. This is especially so for citizens who may not have the resources or the inclination to delve into the intricate entanglement of sub-national, national, and supranational policy-making. The confusion around competence and responsibility attribution is as widespread regarding decentralised as it is regarding supranationalised policy-making.

Case study analyses of federal or regionalised systems, such as Canada and Spain, shed some light on this phenomenon. These studies highlight how decentralisation compromises clarity of responsibility for citizens and therefore taints both electoral and democratic accountability. For example, Cutler highlights how overlapping jurisdictions and responsibilities in Canada in the fields of health care and the economy threaten accountability as "the cost of voters' necessary attempts to hack

TABLE 14.2 Fritz Scharpf's 'problem-solving gap'

		EU capacity	
		High	Low
National capacity	High	H/H	H/L
	Low	L/H	L/L

Notes: Derived from (Scharpf, 2006: 855)

their way through the intergovernmental jungle" proves prohibitive (Cutler, 2004: 38). This is worrying, as his study indicates that, on the issue perceived by the electorate as the most salient in election time (health care), 40 per cent of voters were unable to attribute competence responsibility between the provincial and federal levels and hence could (or would) not hold either government to account. Thus, even in election times, with high media coverage and concerning the issue identified as most important by voters (health care), two in five citizens "had good reason to hold a government accountable but failed to do so" (Cutler, 2004: 34). In a later study using panel data, Cutler reached similar conclusions in that voters do not seem to differentiate the different governments' roles across policy issues (Cutler, 2008). Survey evidence indicates that three-quarters of Canadians agree with the statement that "it is often difficult to figure out which government is responsible for what" (Cutler, 2008: 268). Worryingly, interest and attentiveness to politics hardly helped. His study – adequately entitled 'Whodunnit?' – illustrates how the decentralisation of politics represents a major obstacle to voters seeking to electorally reward or punish their governments for policy outcomes.

Similar dynamics apply in Europe 31, with the added challenge that some systems are territorially asymmetrical. This is the case in Spain, where different autonomous communities are governed by different statutes (Keating and Wilson, 2009). This variation reveals that the relationship between clarity of responsibilities and decentralisation levels follows a U-shaped quadratic function as citizens are better able to ascribe responsibility when decentralisation levels are either high or low, but find this more challenging for intermediate levels of decentralisation (Leon, 2011). Similarly to the Canadian case, this relationship is robust to the inclusion of a series of controls evaluating citizens' electoral participation, education, information on regional issues, interest in politics (both national and regional), age, employment status, national/regional identification, party identification, and ideology. Additionally, however, clarity of competence attribution is affected by the length of time citizens have experienced a particular decentralisation arrangement. Through learning processes, citizens are capable of improving their capacity to ascribe responsibilities across multiple levels (Leon, 2012). This is good news for countries characterised by stable settlements. It is more problematic for those where decentralisation has varied over time or is currently undergoing reform. It is then maybe less surprising that decentralisation has failed to generate an increase in political participation across European countries, on dimensions as varied as contacting a politician/government official, signing a petition, wearing a campaign badge, or more simply voting in national elections (Spina, 2014).

If the fragmentation of power induced by decentralisation has diffused responsibility and hampered citizens' ability to ascribe responsibility and, by extension, to hold politicians accountable, one can expect supranationalisation to have had a similar effect. The more so since the supranationalisation process has also been unstable over time, with a generalised strengthening of IOs and a dramatic empowerment of the EU over the last half-century (see Figures 14.2 and 14.4). In the EU's case, the speed of integration, its depth, its institutional complexity and instability, as well as its asymmetrical nature – with some states opting out of arrangements such as the Euro or Schengen – all hamper citizens' ability to allocate policy responsibility and hence accountability. This impairs the feedback loop between policy output and office holding necessary for the functioning of electoral democracy. In such a political system, the basic question of "who's in charge?" then becomes a question of biases and perceptions rather than actual facts. Recent research on the issue highlights the role played not only by a citizen's institutional context (Camyar, 2014) but also by that of 'group-serving biases' such as citizens' support for the EU (Hobolt and Tilley, 2014). Hence, individuals' predispositions about the EU and their own national government affect their attribution of responsibility for outcomes across policy areas. When power becomes fragmented and authority diffused, citizens struggle to identify who is responsible for what. They then resort to beliefs and prejudices as guides in their implementation of the reward–punishment model of electoral accountability.

This is not a welcome development. Accountability and responsibility form the basis of electoral democracy. These principles become trickier to implement in the context of Europe 31, characterised by asymmetrical and time-varying supranationalisation and decentralisation arrangements. As regionalisation and European integration become increasingly differentiated (Keating, 2013; Leuffen, Rittberger, and Schimmelfennig, 2012), traditional models of democracy are put under stress. As Hobolt and Tilley argue, "standard notions of electoral accountability based on performance voting are potentially threatened by the complexity and fluidity of the EU's multilevel system of government" (2014: 811). These results echo concerns expressed in preceding chapters, most notably those of Chapters 5 and 9, which highlight trends of democratic discontent (Linde and Dahlberg, 2016) and the impact of the diffusion of responsibility on Dahl's dimensions of democracy (Peters, 2016).

Efficiency, distinctiveness, and democracy: the compromises of multi-jurisdictional politics

The decentralisation and supranationalisation of politics in Europe 31 poses serious policy-making and accountability challenges. However, despite these challenges, both have successfully spread across Europe 31. Two reasons underlie the success of decentralisation and supranationalisation: the rationalisation of the structure of government on the one hand and increasing demands for self-government on the other. Both flourished and found political space in democracy's slipstream.

It is rather paradoxical if not ironic that, despite the challenge they represent to current models of electoral democracy (see also Peters, forthcoming), the development of decentralisation and supranationalisation processes seems inextricably related to that of democracy. Supranationalisation, as illustrated in Figure 14.3, comes in various guises. Many instances of supranationalisation, however, seek to coordinate economic foreign policies through a selection of instruments. These range from rather minimalist arrangements such as a simple preferential trade agreement, all the way to creating a free trade area, a customs' union, a common market, and finally an economic union, which includes coordinated fiscal and monetary policies. Research mapping dyads of countries in the 1950–2000 period indicates that democracy increases the likelihood of signing *any type* of integration agreement. This tendency becomes more pronounced as the proposed level of integration – from preferential trade agreement to a full-blown economic union – deepens (Mansfield and Milner, 2008). Interestingly, analyses mapping 116 countries over 1960–2007 find that entering even the most minimalistic of supranational arrangement in the form of a free trade agreement also makes democracies last longer and critically reduces the likelihood of authoritarian coups (Liu and Ornelas, 2014). Linked to the fact that many studies suggest that entering such arrangements enhances its members' welfare and that these economic benefits tend to rise with the depth of integration (Lloyd and Maclaren, 2004), thereby benefiting the archetypical median voter (Mansfield and Milner, 2008), this body of research helps to shed light on the concomitant growth of supranational arrangements and democracy worldwide. The two mutually reinforce one another.

If supranationalisation co-varies with democracy, the same is true of decentralisation. Autocracies rarely decentralise. They tend to prefer to concentrate power rather than share it. Democracy does not cause decentralisation, just as decentralisation does not cause democracy (Bergh, 2004; Pius Kulipossa, 2004). However, in Europe 31, democracy does seem to represent a necessary pre-condition for decentralisation to thrive. Just as authoritarian or autocratic regimes are less likely to engage in supranational agreements, these regimes are also less willing to disperse power to territorially defined units of government and administration. Two studies led by Hooghe, Marks, and Schakel have established the link between democracy and decentralisation over time and across countries. The first concerned forty-two democracies, mostly OECD and EU countries, over the 1950–2006 period. They found that democracies are clearly more responsive to pressures for regionalisation (Hooghe et al., 2010: 59). This is because power dispersion will weaken an authoritarian regime, while governments implementing popular decentralisation reforms may be rewarded by their electorate. It is then logical that democratisation processes often generate decentralisation ones. In later work, this time covering eighty countries, including Latin America and South East Asia, over the 1950–2010 period, these scholars find that democracy is strongly related to decentralisation processes over time and across space (Hooghe and Marks, 2016). This is most likely not only because non-democracies dislike sharing power, but also because democracy lowers the costs of political mobilisation for those who wish to have a greater say in the government of their territory.

One can wonder why democracy is conducive to both decentralisation and supranationalisation. Part of the answer is that while power dispersion does not resonate well with autocracy, democratic systems are far more flexible when it comes to their institutional architecture. If the benefits derived from power dispersion are perceived as superior to their costs, then democratic regimes will embrace them for as long as these choices are electorally rewarded. In this sense, democracies are characterised by pragmatism and adaptability.

Discussion about the optimal level at which competencies should be allocated has been rife. However, Hooghe and Marks have highlighted that efficiency gains – in the form of economies of scale, internalising policy externalities, and reducing transaction costs related to coordination – play a crucial role in determining the territorial structure of government for countries as diverse as the United States or Luxembourg (2009a). In their analysis they find that the structure of government seems to be significantly shaped by population levels. The population size of a jurisdiction is hence a key determinant of its structure. It is of course not the only one. However, it comes across as a robust and significant factor. Population levels affect efficiency gains, which in turn affect the structure and level of government. In this respect the structure of local government exhibits the least variation (in terms of policy portfolio allocation) while that of supranational arrangements is more heterogeneous, though dominated by relatively narrowly-defined task-specific organisations (Hooghe and Marks, 2003).

As illustrated in Figure 14.3, the vast majority (i.e. about 78 per cent) of IOs to which Europe 31 countries belong have competencies in five or fewer policy areas. This is in part because IOs often find their source in the management of negative externalities and the solving of common pool issues (Ostrom, Burger, Field, Norgaard, and Policansky, 1999). These interdependencies and functional pressures tend to generate organisations designed to manage specific issues (Mitrany, 1966), in sharp contrast with territorially defined general-purpose jurisdictions such as highly decentralised regional governments, states, or the EU. Caught between functional pressures and territorial factors, regional levels of government exhibit most variation from the prediction generated by the logic of efficiency gains alone (Hooghe et al., 2010).

This is due to non–efficiency-driven demands over the structure of government. While much local government and a majority of IOs are shaped by efficiency logics, the architecture of the regional level has also been shaped by desires for greater self-government. Such desires for autonomy are driven by distinctiveness, which may be ideological, ethnic, linguistic, religious, or cultural. In democratic contexts, however, it has tended to express itself via demands for greater autonomy, crystallised by self-government. Decentralisation may take place in the absence of distinctiveness. However, its presence increases the likelihood that it will take place, hence triggering a departure from patterns shaped by efficiency gains. In this sense, distinctiveness generates governance differentiation that efficiency cannot explain. This is what Hooghe et al. call the 'community' effect (2010). It is embodied in what they later identify as 'Rokkan regions', understood as regions which are peripheral (being distant from the centre in terms of being islands or non-contiguous), linguistically different (when they house a majority of inhabitants who speak a language which is different from that of the parent country), and have a history of independence (in the form of a sovereign state for at least three decades since the High Middle Ages) (Hooghe and Marks, 2016).

While distinctiveness has generated demands for decentralisation, it has also triggered a greater contestation of the supranationalisation of Europe's polity. If citizens still remain today relatively indifferent to the myriad of IOs their country belongs to, the expansion of the EU's powers over more and more policy areas has not gone unnoticed. European integration had been characterised by a 'permissive consensus', further spurred by the continent's economic development of the early 1980s. This changed in the early 1990s with the Maastricht Treaty (1991–2). The following period has been characterised as one of 'constraining dissensus' (Hooghe and Marks, 2009b). Constraining dissensus has manifested itself in a number of ways, such as negative referendum outcomes on Treaty change or on the Euro (Denmark: 1992, 2000; Ireland: 2001, 2008; Sweden: 2003; France: 2005; the Netherlands: 2005) or on membership itself (UK: 2016; Norway: 1972, 1994; Switzerland: 1992 [EEA], 2001 [EU], 2014 [restriction of the free movement of workers]). A yet more striking manifestation has been the rise of Eurosceptic parties, or at the very least parties presenting an ideology incompatible with the stated objective of the EU. These parties cross-cut the left/right and regulated capitalism/market liberalism divides. Their positioning is best captured by the TAN/GAL dichotomy, standing for traditionalist, authoritarian, and nationalist on the one hand (TAN) and green, alternative, and libertarian on the other (GAL). Many of these TAN parties are also populist in nature and express dissatisfaction with the internationalisation of politics as experienced in Europe 31 countries (see also Bjånesøy and Ivarsflaten, 2016). Others are linked to the re-emergence of nationalism and reflect fears and anxieties about immigration and globalisation (Knutsen, 2016).

The greater contestation of European integration is natural. As the EU departed further and further from the template of a functional IO towards a system characterised by deep delegation in a widening area of policy fields (see Figure 14.2), citizens have manifested a greater willingness to engage on EU issues, via the whole repertoire of political mobilisation, from voting for Eurosceptic parties at national and EU elections (Treib, 2014) to demonstrating on EU issues directly in Brussels or in their main capitals (Imig, 2002).

The politicisation and higher saliency of the EU in domestic politics engenders a healthy discussion about the system's architecture and how its link to everyday citizens can be strengthened. It has triggered a debate on what is wrong (and right) about the EU and how it can be bettered (Hix, 2008). The same is true of multi-jurisdictional politics more widely considered. In the face of interdependence, multi-jurisdictionality implies more *joint* decision-making, which renders electoral democracy less straightforward and hence, to some extent, compromises the system's 'input legitimacy'. Input legitimacy, as defined by Scharpf, considers that "political choices are legitimate if and because they reflect the 'will of the people' – that is if they can be derived from the authentic preferences of the members of a community" (1999: 7). This contrasts with an output legitimacy model where "political choices are legitimate if and because they effectively promote the common welfare of the constituency in question" (1999: 7). To a great extent, multi-jurisdictional politics, by blurring responsibility attribution and disrupting electoral democracy through joint decision-making entanglement, has shifted the emphasis of system support towards output legitimacy.

These developments relate well to Easton's work on regime support (1975). He distinguishes between 'affective' and 'utilitarian' sources of support. Affective sources are more diffuse and correlate with an ideological or non-material attachment to a political system. Utilitarian sources are more specific and relate to whether an individual evaluates a given system as materially beneficial. This diptych overlaps well with the arguments made above regarding the role played by efficiency gains and distinctiveness in the development of multi-jurisdictional politics. While one of the drivers of multi-jurisdictional politics lies in efficiency gains (Hooghe and Marks, 2009a), to guarantee its survival it also needs to accommodate desires for distinctiveness. This is usually achieved through electoral politics, but as the link between performance and responsibility is weakened by joint policy-making, multi-jurisdictional politics need to factor in these demands in more creative ways. These then take the shape of differentiated governance, as illustrated by the asymmetric development of the EU and the increasing differentiation of regional governance too (Hooghe et al., 2010; Leuffen et al., 2012). A recent survey of the effect of power dispersion upwards, downwards, and sideways further highlights the inherent tension between actors' quest for autonomy and the acknowledgement of their ineluctable interdependence. The end result is pragmatic: political actors seek to both manage such interdependence and limit it in a process where the optimal equilibrium remains elusive (Jensen, Koop, and Tatham, 2014).

Despite the advent of differentiated governance, utilitarian sources of support (in Easton's terms) are no longer sufficient. As multi-jurisdictional polities expand and deepen, they need sources of support other than output legitimacy – they need to generate greater affective sources of support, most likely by seeking to increase input legitimacy. This process seems to be underway. Regional authorities are increasingly directly elected, and the EU political system has become both more accountable and more politicized through the development of its Parliament: its gradual politicisation, its novel election process (*Spitzenkandidaten*), its growing scrutiny of the Commission, and its new role as co-equal legislator with the Council in Lisbon's 'ordinary' legislative procedure. New instruments, such as the citizenship initiative and the extension of the subsidiarity principle to involve national and regional parliaments, all push in the same direction of greater accountability and clarity of responsibility in Europe 31's institutional quagmire.

Mixed visions of democracy

There are many benefits to multi-jurisdictional politics. The federalist and functionalist literature of the interwar and post-war periods extolls its virtues in terms of solving common pool problems, formalising de facto policy interdependencies (especially for policies displaying high negative externalities), and – perhaps more strikingly – pre-empting the temptation of war by institutionalising interdependence (Burgess, 2000: 25; Mitrany, 1966). This literature, though, was already criticised for the élite-driven, technocratic, and often weakly accountable type of system it promoted. These criticisms remain. It may well be that multi-jurisdictional politics renders armed conflict less likely (Martin, Mayer, and Thoenig, 2012; Vicard, 2012), encourages policy diffusion and best practice sharing through learning, competition, or the spread of common norms (Braun and Gilardi, 2006), stimulates experimentation, differentiation, competition and hence allows for greater citizen choice (Tiebout, 1956; Weingast, 1995), and even contributes to diminish economic inequalities among territories (Sorens, 2014). However, these benefits come at the cost of having to adapt our conception of democracy (Dahl, 1998). In the face of entangled joint-policy-making and blurred responsibility, electoral democracy is challenged. Electoral democracy relies on citizens' capacity to electorally reward or punish office-holders according to policy outcomes. As clarity of responsibility is muddled by multi-jurisdictional politics, electoral democracy is weakened. While electoral democracy is a cornerstone of democracy in Europe 31, the rise of multi-jurisdictional politics should encourage new visions of democracy to complement it (Peters, forthcoming). That, or the distribution of competencies should be sufficiently clarified so as to render vote-casting more appealing to the citizenry.

All is not dark, however, in the age of multi-jurisdictional politics – especially so in Europe 31. Both regional and European elections are becoming increasingly salient and politicised. The second-order nature of these elections is fading with their greater politicisation, their increased relevance as the regional and EU levels are gradually empowered, and the growing practice of holding these elections together – hence boosting turn-out (Schakel and Dandoy, 2014; Schakel and Jeffery, 2012). Combined with citizens' ability to learn – over time – where competencies reside, these are encouraging signs for electoral democracy.

Another encouraging sign resides in the nature of the policy outputs produced by the most multi-jurisdictional polity of all: the EU. In a study comparing the EU and the US, Mahoney finds that the EU's more power-dispersed system is conducive to outcomes characterised by compromise and inclusion, as opposed to winner-takes-all and wealth-driven outcomes in the US Her study on lobbying success found that, in the US,

> more often than not absolute winners dominate clear losers, and on average those winners are the industry. In the EU, the industry wins too but so do citizen groups and foundations. The EU system negotiates compromises which allow more advocates to attain their goals. Ironically, thus, the less democratically accountable system may be more responsive to a broader range of interests.
>
> *(2007: 53–54)*

This is in great part because the private funding model of US electoral politics biases responsiveness in favour of wealthier advocates (i.e. corporations). This is not the case in the EU as a whole, where Mahoney finds that citizen groups, foundations, trade unions as well as elected national governments successfully influence policy outcomes. Consequently,

> EU policymakers that do not face elections and who do not need to fundraise for those elections do not have the same incentives to favour wealthy advocates. As a result, their responsiveness is more balanced, with a wider range of advocate types attaining some level of lobbying success.
>
> *(2007: 52)*

In Dahl's terms (2006), the EU political system comes across as an instance of a Madisonian project which may have achieved greater citizen preference-policy congruence than a more popular or majoritarian models of democracy.

The balanced nature of policy outputs in the EU is undoubtedly good news for Europe 31, not only in terms of output legitimacy (in the shape of greater responsiveness), but also in terms of input legitimacy (in the shape of wider and more equal inclusiveness). To some extent, it is reminiscent of Lijphart's conception of a *consensus democracy*, characterised by power sharing and more balanced and inclusive policies (1999). Multi-jurisdictional politics represent the antithesis of majoritarian democracy, where powers are concentrated and hence clearly attributable, and where office-holders are directly punished or rewarded according to their performance. These systems produce clear winners and losers in terms of both policies and politics. Consensus democracies, however, are characterised by compromise and power-dispersion and produce 'kinder and gentler' policies, for example, in terms of welfare state or foreign aid spending, but also regarding environmental policies or the treatment of the polity's citizens (e.g. death penalty, incarceration rates, women in politics, reduction of economic disparities). That multi-jurisdictional polities share much with consensus democracies may partly account for their development and survival over time.

In line with Dahl's and Lijphart's work, Mahoney's findings give credit to Schmitter's (2000) hope that the supranational mobilisation of a plurality of interests – including regional interest (Tatham and Thau, 2014) – may bring the EU closer to its citizens, and hence help to rekindle them with their polity via more inclusive consultation (Quittkat and Kotzian, 2011). From the perspective of multi-jurisdictional politics, these studies highlight how, as the structure of power has been changing, patterns of interest representation have also had to adapt to the multi-jurisdictional nature of the polity. If electoral democracy has been challenged by the rise of multi-jurisdictional politics and has generated some levels of discontent and disenchantment as a consequence (Linde and Dahlberg, 2016; Peters, 2016), then the increases in output and – more recently – input legitimacy are encouraging. In the longer run, these may generate a shift from more 'utilitarian' to more 'affective' sources of system support (Easton, 1975). In the meantime, however, multi-jurisdictional politics will remain contested and under threat of further reform. While the instability of the current institutional setup may be disconcerting for citizens, its contestation has resulted in improvements in both output and input legitimacy and a better balance between the recognition of functional interdependence and a thirst for autonomy and self-government. As a utopian equilibrium shines on the horizon, multi-jurisdictional politics continues its stubborn and sometimes messy march towards it.

Further reading

Leon, S. (2011) 'Who is Responsible for What? Clarity of Responsibilities in Multilevel States: The Case of Spain', *European Journal of Political Research* 20(1): 80–109.

Marks, G., Hooghe, L. and Schakel, A. (2008) 'Patterns of Regional Authority', *Regional & Federal Studies* 18(2): 167–181.

Scharpf, F. (1988) 'The Joint-Decision Trap: Lessons from German Federalism and European Integration', *Public Administration* 66: 239–278.

Key questions for discussion

1 How can you define multi-jurisdictional politics? How can you illustrate its rise?
2 Why is it that multi-jurisdictional politics seems to correlate with democratization and the sustainability of democracy?
3 If multi-jurisdictional politics hampers electoral democracy, how does it affect input and output legitimacy?

Notes

1 See relevant websites: http://www.icao.int/about-icao/Pages/default.aspx, http://www. itu.int/en/about/Pages/default.aspx, http://www.interpol.int/About-INTERPOL/ Overview [all accessed 31 October 2014]
2 The Nordic Council is an interesting case as it mixes member state and territorial logics. The five countries represented are Denmark, Finland, Iceland, Sweden and Norway. However, Åland, Greenland, and the Faro Islands have their own (smaller) delegations, too.
3 See relevant websites: http://www.coe.int/en/web/about-us/who-we-are, http://www. benelux.int/fr, http://www.norden.org/en/nordic-council/the-nordic-council/member-countries-and-territories [accessed 2 November 2014]

References

Abbott, K. W. and Snidal, D. (1998) 'Why States Act through Formal International Organizations', *Journal of Conflict Resolution* 42(1): 3–32.

Aja, E. and Colino, C. (2014) 'Multilevel Structures, Coordination and Partisan Politics in Spanish Intergovernmental Relations', *Comparative European Politics* 12(4–5): 444–467.

Alvarez, M. E. (2016) 'The Struggle between Liberalism and Social Democracy'. In Y. Peters and M. Tatham (eds.), *Democratic Transformations in Europe: Challenges and Opportunities*, Abingdon: Routledge, pp. 99–119.

Auel, K. (2014) 'Intergovernmental Relations in German Federalism: Cooperative Federalism, Party Politics and Territorial Conflicts', *Comparative European Politics* 12(4–5): 422–443.

Bergh, S. (2004) 'Democratic Decentralisation and Local Participation: A Review of Recent Research', *Development in Practice* 14(6): 780–790.

Bjånesøy, L. L. and Ivarsflaten, E. (2016) 'What Kind of Challenge? Right-Wing Populism in Contemporary Western Europe'. In Y. Peters and M. Tatham (eds.), *Democratic Transformations in Europe: Challenges and Opportunities*, Abingdon: Routledge, pp. 33–50.

Braun, D. and Gilardi, F. (2006) 'Taking 'Galton's Problem' Seriously: Towards a Theory of Policy Diffusion', *Journal of Theretical Politics* 18(3): 298–322.

Bräuninger, T. and König, T. (1999) 'The Checks and Balances of Party Federalism: German Federal Government in a Divided Legislature', *European Journal of Political Research* 36(2): 207–234.

Brusis, M. (2002) 'Between EU Requirements, Competitive Politics, and National Traditions: Re – Creating Regions in the Accession Countries of Central and Eastern Europe', *Governance* 15(4): 531–559.

Börzel, T. (2005) 'Mind the Gap! European Integration between Level and Scope', *Journal of European Public Policy* 12(2): 217–236.

Burgess, M. (2000) *Federalism and European Union: The Building of Europe, 1950–2000*, London: Routledge.

Camyar, I. (2014) 'Institutions, Information Asymmetry and Democratic Responsiveness: A Cross-National and Multi-Level Analysis', *Acta Politica* 49(3): 313–336.

Cutler, F. (2004) 'Government Responsibility and Electoral Accountability in Federations', *Publius: The Journal of Federalism* 34(2): 19–38.

Cutler, F. (2008) 'Whodunnit? Voters and Responsibility in Canadian Federalism', *Canadian Journal of Political Science/Revue canadienne de science politique* 41(3): 627–654.

Dahl, R. A. (1998) *On Democracy*, New Haven: Yale University Press.

Dahl, R. A. (2006) *A Preface to Democratic Theory: Expanded Edition*, Chicago: University of Chicago Press.

Easton, D. (1975) 'A Re-Assessment of the Concept of Political Support', *British Journal of Political Science* 5(4): 435–457.

Falkner, G. (Ed.). (2011) *The EU's Decision Traps: Comparing Policies*, Oxford: Oxford University Press.

Fuglister, K. and Wasserfallen, F. (2014) 'Swiss Federalism in a Changing Environment', *Comparative European Politics* 12(4–5): 404–421.

Hepburn, E. (2014) 'Forging Autonomy in a Unitary State: The Aland Islands in Finland', *Comparative European Politics* 12(4–5): 468–487.

Hix, S. (2008) *What's Wrong with the European Union and How to Fix It*, London: Polity.

Hobolt, S. B. and Tilley, J. (2014) 'Who's in Charge? How Voters Attribute Responsibility in the European Union', *Comparative Political Studies* 47(6): 795–819.

Hooghe, L. and Marks, G. (2003) 'Unravelling the Central State, But How? Types of Multi-Level Governance', *American Political Science Review* 97(2): 233–243.

Hooghe, L. and Marks, G. (2009a) 'Does Efficiency Shape the Territorial Structure of Government?', *Annual Review of Political Science* 12: 225–241.

Hooghe, L. and Marks, G. (2009b) 'A Postfunctionalist Theory of European Integration: From Permissive Consensus to Constraining Dissensus', *British Journal of Political Science* 39(1): 1–23.

Hooghe, L. and Marks, G. (2015) 'Delegation and Pooling in International Organizations', *The Review of International Organizations*, 10(3): 305–328.

Hooghe, L. and Marks, G. (2016) *Community, Scale, and Regional Governance: A Postfunctionalist Theory of Governance, Volume II*, Oxford: Oxford University Press.

Hooghe, L., Marks, G. and Schakel, A. H. (2010) *The Rise of Regional Authority: A Comparative Study of 42 democracies*, Abingdon: Routledge.

Hughes, J., Sasse, G. and Gordon, C. (2004) *Europeanization and Regionalization in the EU's Enlargement to Central and Eastern Europe: The Myth of Conditionality*, Basingstoke: Palgrave Macmillan.

Imig, D. (2002) 'Contestation in the Streets: European Protest and the Emerging Euro-Polity', *Comparative Political Studies* 35(8): 914–933.

Immergut, E. M. (1990) 'Institutions, Veto Points, and Policy Results: A Comparative Analysis of Health Care', *Journal of Public Policy* 10(4): 391–416.

Jensen, M. D., Koop, C. and Tatham, M. (2014) 'Coping with Power Dispersion? Autonomy, Coordination, and Control in Multi-Level Systems', *Journal of European Public Policy* 21(9): 1237–1254.

Karlhofer, F. and Pallaver, G. (2013) 'Strength through Weakness: State Executive Power and Federal Reform in Austria', *Swiss Political Science Review* 19(1): 41–59.

Keating, M. (2013) *Rescaling the European State: The Making of Territory and the Rise of the Meso*, Oxford: Oxford University Press.

Keating, M. and Wilson, A. (2009) 'Renegotiating the State of Autonomies: Statute Reform and Multi-Level Politics in Spain', *West European Politics* 32(3): 536–558.

Keohane, R. O. (1982) 'The Demand for International Regimes', *International Organization* 36(02): 325–355.

Knutsen, T. (2016) 'A Re-Emergence of Nationalism as a Political Force in Europe?'. In Y. Peters and M. Tatham (eds.), *Democratic Transformations in Europe: Challenges and Opportunities*, Abingdon: Routledge, pp. 13–32.

Kux, S. and Sverdrup, U. (2000) 'Fuzzy Borders and Adaptive Outsiders: Norway, Switzerland and the EU', *Journal of European Integration* 22(3): 237–270.

Lacey, J. (2014) 'Must Europe be Swiss? On the Idea of a Voting Space and the Possibility of a Multilingual Demos', *British Journal of Political Science* 44(1): 61–82.

Lenz, T. (2012) 'Spurred Emulation: The EU and Regional Integration in Mercosur and SADC', *West European Politics* 35(1): 155–173.

Leon, S. (2011) 'Who is Responsible for What? Clarity of Responsibilities in Multilevel States: The Case of Spain', *European Journal of Political Research* 20(1): 80–109.

Leon, S. (2012) 'How Do Citizens Attribute Responsibility in Multilevel States? Learning, Biases and Asymmetric Federalism: Evidence from Spain', *Electoral Studies* 31(1): 120–130.

Leuffen, D., Rittberger, B. and Schimmelfennig, F. (2012) *Differentiated Integration: Explaining Variation in the European Union*, Basingstoke: Palgrave Macmillan.

Lijphart, A. (1999) *Patterns of Democracy: Government Forms and Performance in Thirty-Six Countries*, New Haven: Yale University Press.

Linde, J. and Dahlberg, S. (2016) 'Democratic Discontent in Times of Crisis?'. In Y. Peters and M. Tatham (eds.), *Democratic Transformations in Europe: Challenges and Opportunities*, Abingdon: Routledge, pp. 72–95.

Linder, W. (2013) 'Switzerland and the EU: The Puzzling Effects of Europeanisation without Institutionalisation', *Contemporary Politics* 19(2): 190–202.

Liu, X. and Ornelas, E. (2014) 'Free Trade Agreements and the Consolidation of Democracy', *American Economic Journal: Macroeconomics* 6(2): 29–70.

Lloyd, P. J. and Maclaren, D. (2004) 'Gains and Losses from Regional Trading Agreements: A Survey*', *Economic Record* 80(251): 445–467.

Mahoney, C. (2007) 'Lobbying Success in the United States and the European Union', *Journal of Public Policy* 27(1): 35–56.

Mansfield, E. D. and Milner, H. V. (2008) 'Democracy, Veto Players and the Depth of Regional Integration', *The World Economy* 31(1): 67–96.

Marks, G., Hooghe, L. and Blank, K. (1996) 'European Integration from the 1980s: State-Centric v. Multi-Level Governance', *Journal of Common Market Studies* 34(3): 341–378.

Martin, P., Mayer, T. and Thoenig, M. (2012) 'The Geography of Conflicts and Regional Trade Agreements', *American Economic Journal: Macroeconomics* 4(4): 1–35.

Mitrany, D. (1966) *A Working Peace System*. Chicago: Quadrangle Books.

Mjelde, H. L. and Svåsand, L. (2016) 'Party Decline?'. In Y. Peters and M. Tatham (eds.), *Democratic Transformations in Europe: Challenges and Opportunities*, Abingdon: Routledge, pp. 51–71.

Oldervoll, J. A. and Kuhnle, S. (2016) 'The Sustainability of European Welfare States: The Significance of Changing Labour Markets'. In Y. Peters and M. Tatham (eds.), *Democratic Transformations in Europe: Challenges and Opportunities*, Abingdon: Routledge, pp. 120–142.

Ostrom, E., Burger, J., Field, C. B., Norgaard, R. B. and Policansky, D. (1999) 'Revisiting the Commons: Local Lessons, Global Challenges', *Science* 284(5412): 278–282.

Palermo, F. and Wilson, A. (2014) 'The Multi-Level Dynamics of State Decentralization in Italy', *Comparative European Politics* 12(4–5): 510–530.

Peters, Y. (2016) 'Displacing Politics: The State of Democracy in an Age of Diffused Responsibility'. In Y. Peters and M. Tatham (eds.), *Democratic Transformations in Europe: Challenges and Opportunities*, Abingdon: Routledge, pp. 163–186.

Peters, Y. (forthcoming) *Diffused Democracy. Displaced Governance, and Political Participation*, Abingdon: Routledge.

Pierson, P. (1996) 'The Path to European Integration: A Historial Institutionalist Analysis', *Comparative Political Studies* 29(2): 123–163.

Pius Kulipossa, F. (2004) 'Decentralisation and Democracy in Developing Countries: An Overview', *Development in Practice* 14(6): 768–779.

Pollack, M. A. (1997) 'Delegation, Agency, and Agenda Setting in the European Community', *International Organization* 51(1): 99–134.

Quittkat, C. and Kotzian, P. (2011) 'Lobbying via Consultation – Territorial and Functional Interests in the Commission's Consultation Regime', *Journal of European Interation* 33(4): 401–418.

Schakel, A. H. and Dandoy, R. (2014) 'Electoral Cycles and Turnout in Multilevel Electoral Systems', *West European Politics* 37(3): 605–623.

Schakel, A. H. and Jeffery, C. (2012) 'Are Regional Elections Really 'Second-Order' Elections?', *Regional Studies* 47(3): 323–341.

Scharpf, F. (1988) 'The Joint-Decision Trap: Lessons from German Federalism and European Integration', *Public Administration* 66: 239–278.

Scharpf, F. (1999) *Governing in Europe: Effective and Democratic?*, Oxford: Oxford University Press.

Scharpf, F. (2006) 'The Joint-Decision Trap Revisited', *Journal of Common Market Studies* 44(4): 845–864.

Schmitter, P. (2000) *How to Democratize the European Union . . . and Why Bother?*, Lanham, MD: Rowman & Littlefield.

Sinardet, D. and Bursens, P. (2014) 'Democratic Legitimacy in Multilevel Political Systems: The Role of Politicization at the Polity-Wide Level in the EU and Belgium', *Acta Politica* 49(3): 246–265.

Sorens, J. (2014) 'Does Fiscal Federalism Promote Regional Inequality? An Empirical Analysis of the OECD, 1980–2005', *Regional Studies* 48(2): 239–253.

Spina, N. (2014) 'Decentralisation and Political Participation: An Empirical Analysis in Western and Eastern Europe', *International Political Science Review* 35(4): 448–462.

Swenden, W. (2013) 'Conclusion: The Future of Belgian Federalism – Between Reform and Swansong?', *Regional & Federal Studies* 23(3): 369–382.

Swenden, W. and McEwen, N. (2014) 'UK Devolution in the Shadow of Hierarchy[Quest] Intergovernmental Relations and Party Politics', *Comparative European Politics* 12(4–5): 488–509.

Tatham, M. (2011) 'Devolution and EU Policy-Shaping: Bridging the Gap between Multi-Level Governance and Liberal Intergovernmentalism', *European Political Science Review* 3(1): 53–81.

Tatham, M. and Thau, M. (2014) 'The More the Merrier: Accounting for Sub-State Paradiplomats in Brussels', *European Union Politics* 15(2): 255–276.

Tiebout, C. (1956) 'A Pure Theory of Local Expenditures', *The Journal of Political Economy* 64(5): 416–424.

Toonen, T. A. J. (1990) 'The Unitary State as a System of Co-Governance: The Case of the Netherlands', *Public Administration* 68(3): 281–296.

Treib, O. (2014) 'The Voter Says No, But Nobody Listens: Causes and Consequences of the Eurosceptic Vote in the 2014 European Elections', *Journal of European Public Policy* 21(10): 1541–1554.

Tsebelis, G. (2002) *Veto Players: How Political Institutions Work*, Princeton: Princeton University Press.

Vibe, V. (2016) 'Minority Rights under Majority Rule: LGB-Rights in Europe'. In Y. Peters and M. Tatham (eds.), *Democratic Transformations in Europe: Challenges and Opportunities*, Abingdon: Routledge, pp. 231–251.

Vicard, V. (2012) 'Trade, Conflict, and Political Integration: Explaining the Heterogeneity of Regional Trade Agreements', *European Economic Review* 56(1): 54–71.

Weingast, B. R. (1995) 'The Economic Role of Political Institutions: Market-Preserving Federalism and Economic Development', *Journal of Law, Economics, & Organization* 11(1): 1–31.

PART 4

Conclusions

15

THE CONTEMPORARY STATE OF DEMOCRACY IN A TRANSFORMED EUROPE

Yvette Peters and Michaël Tatham

Two main themes run through the book as a whole. These are the impact of *inequalities*, on the one hand, and the re-definition and contestation of the concept of *community* as a basis for the running of political systems, on the other hand. These two concepts of inequality and community have direct consequences for democracy. They are also intertwined: community membership necessarily implies the definition of an in-group and an out-group[1] and therefore may function as a rationale for exclusion from certain rights or policies. These exclusionary processes can result in a rise in inequalities among individuals within the polity. Indeed, the idea of a homogenous community is a fiction. There will always be minorities, however defined. What differentiates political systems, then, is the extent to which minority rights can be safeguarded whilst at the same time guaranteeing that the preferences of a majority will translate into congruent policy outputs – in other words, how political systems balance responsiveness with responsibility, and decisiveness with inclusiveness.

In this sense, Dahl's understanding of democracy and its five necessary conditions all relate to the questions of equality and community. They all affect equality in terms of access to rights and in terms of participation in and influence over the policy-making process. They all rest on a broad understanding of community, and hence the *demos*- and citizenship-basis of the exercise of authority. We review as follows how the challenges that Europe 31 faces relate to Dahl's work, starting with his five necessary conditions and their implications in terms of political equality, citizenship rights, and preference-policy congruence. This leads us to discuss the observed trends in terms of two ideal-typical models of democracy: one following Madisonian logics and another following populistic logics. Our proposal is to inject existing Madisonian dynamics with doses of populistic empowerment through (1) multilevel direct elections, (2) the availability of direct democracy instruments, and (3) the "(re-)public-isation" of (a) non-majoritarian institutions and (b) services of interests to the general public.[2] These three measures are intended to revitalise Madisonian developments through indirect and direct citizen involvement and control.

Dahl's necessary conditions

As highlighted in the introductory chapter (Peters & Tatham, 2016, this volume), Dahl considered that a democratic process would achieve a certain level of congruence between popular preferences and policy outputs. Such congruence – or policy responsiveness – would stem from two core pillars of the political system: the fact that it should guarantee political equality and citizenship rights. Political equality and citizenship rights would be achieved through Dahl's 4+1 necessary conditions in order to achieve a democratic process (1989, 1998). These necessary conditions consist of the opportunity for the effective participation of the people in order to make their voices heard (1), the people's equal opportunity to cast a vote affecting with equal weight the system's policy output (2), the opportunity for people to obtain information on different policy options and their alternatives (3), the right to decide what issues should be placed on the political agenda (4), and finally that these four necessary conditions be fulfilled for most adults within the polity (+1). The thirteen challenges covered in this volume all impact Dahl's 4+1 necessary conditions and eventually what model of democracy Europe 31 is transforming towards – ranging from the ideal-typical Madisonian model to a more populistic one.

Effective participation

Dahl's necessary condition nr. 1 entails that people within the political system should have equal and effective opportunities to make their preferences, ideas, and considerations concerning a policy known. In essence it is an opportunity to voice their (political) preferences through (political) participation.

As illustrated by Bjånesøy and Ivarsflaten (2016: this volume), the rise of radical right populism in Europe represents a direct threat to Dahl's necessary condition nr. 1. Indeed, these parties and their supporters attribute weaker importance to living in a democratically governed country where free and fair elections take place and where the media has the opportunity of freely reporting on political affairs. That radical right populist parties also intend to curb the effective participation of people along ethnic, religious, or national lines is further illustrated by their attitudes towards the protection of minority groups' rights. For voters of these parties, minority rights are distinctively less important than for voters of other parties. Hence, these generally anti-Islam, anti-immigration parties represent a threat to the effective participation of all citizens in the political process. Far from being purely driven by variation in economic cycles (Mols & Jetten, 2016), their rise represents a clear threat to Dahl's first necessary condition in the exclusionary dynamics they promote (Sheets et al., 2015; Yılmaz, 2012).

There is only a small step from xenophobic, exclusive-nationalist, anti-immigration attitudes to the actual suspension or limitation of the political rights of ethnic, religious, linguistic, national, and non-national minorities. And this step has proved to be a feasible one to take under the justification of preserving the security of an imagined national community from the threat of terrorism, be it of a domestic or international form. As highlighted by Engene (2016: this volume), counter-terrorist measures have sometimes constituted a greater threat to Dahl's necessary conditions than terrorism itself. Indeed, the war on terror has represented an opportunity for the pre-emptive suspension of essential social and political rights of groups perceived as a threat to the existing political community.

Hence, counter-terrorism measures can negatively impact fundamental civil liberties such as the rights of free expression, association, and assembly, of free information and movement, of due process of law (e.g. searches without warrants or judicial order, detention without trial, use of torture, bypassing of judicial review), but also through the discriminatory targeting of individuals and the suspension of their (civic and individual) rights according to ethnicity, religion, language, or country of origin. Indeed, some counter-terrorist measures have been judged to breach human rights, as illustrated by the UK Anti-terrorism, Crime and Security Act of 2001, parts of which the Law Lords considered incompatible with the European Convention on Human Rights. Thus, the citizenship implications of counter-terrorism should not be belittled. These measures affect citizens unequally and may generate a further alienation of ethnic minorities from their political system. Various researchers have highlighted the extent to which anti-terrorist policies affect multiple dimensions of citizenship, including participation, identity, duties, and rights, thereby curtailing citizenship for some (mostly ethnic minorities), whilst leaving that of others (mostly white ethnic nationals) only remotely affected. Due to their unequal impact, anti-terrorism measures have the potential to generate "disconnected citizens" (Jarvis & Lister, 2013), only a small step away from another ominous concept – that of second-class citizens.

The consideration of counter-terrorism's negative effects on the health of democracy is all the more pressing as there are serious doubts as to whether extending executive power beyond its legal limits, hence bypassing institutionalized decision-taking processes and constitutional checks-and-balances (such as in a declared state of emergency) at all enhances security from terrorism. Dragu and Polborn (2014) in fact argue that an executive can achieve terrorism prevention more effectively when there are some legal limits on its counter-terrorism powers rather than when the executive has the legal flexibility to devise its own security policy. This implies that "some legal limits on executive counterterrorism powers can be beneficial *on security grounds alone*, and, therefore, strengthening institutions that uphold the rule of law in the fight against terrorism can be an effective way to achieve security from terrorism" (Dragu & Polborn, 2014: 512, emphasis original). In this way, Dragu and Polborn show that when confronted with "the paradox of suspending democracy in order to defend it" (Wilkinson, 2001: 23), democracies should not boundlessly maximize executive discretion, but instead should uphold legal limits and checks on executive power. This approach is consonant with a Madisonian perspective on the role of institutional checks and balances in the safeguarding of democracy when confronted by internal and external challenge.

All is not dark, however, in twenty-first-century Europe, and some developments give cause for optimism. The decline of political parties in terms of party membership, identification, volatility, trust, or turnout is well documented and points to a crisis of representation, which may well find its sources in some of the trends discussed previously. Parties as collective actors, articulating and aggregating policy preferences, acting as gatekeepers mediating the interface between the citizenry and state institutions, are contested and transforming. They are contested in the sense that parties have been criticised for their poor representation of everyday citizens (Ignazi, 2014). However, political parties are also evolving with their time, and one distinguishable development which may breathe new representational life into them is their growing internal democratisation. As discussed by Mjelde and Svåsand (2016: this volume), parties are increasingly opening up their selection procedure to decide on their leadership through (more or less inclusive) primaries, ranging from those which are open to all voters, to those open to supporters and party members only, all the way to "closed" primaries involving party members only, with different weighing and selection sequences possible (Kenig et al., 2015). Similarly, the nomination of parliamentary candidates has also opened up, whilst the drawing up of party manifestos, programmes, and policies has become less of a closed process despite the persistent stronghold of party leaders (Hertner, 2015).

Along with the democratisation of existing parties, the rise of new parties or the renewal of older ones through bottom-up processes of expanded membership are testimony to the capacity of some parties to still capture popular enthusiasm. Current illustrations include Podemos and Ciudadanos in Spain. These two parties are recent creations. Whilst Ciudadanos was formed in Catalonia in 2006, it only expanded as a state-wide party since 2013. By the December 2015 general election in Spain, it had gathered almost 14 per cent of the national vote share. The rise of Podemos is more striking still, as the party was only founded in March 2014 as a platform for ongoing discontent linked to inequalities and corruption. At the December 2015 general election, it became the third largest party in parliament with 21 per cent of the vote share, and the second largest party in terms of the number of party members (García, 2014). Similar trajectories have been observed outside of Spain. In Greece, for example, Syriza was only founded as a political alliance in 2004 and as a party in 2012, before becoming the largest party in the Hellenic parliament. Finally, as a result of the use of primaries, older mainstream parties have also had the opportunity to re-expand their membership and alter their ideological orientation. The British Labour party and the recent election of Jeremy Corbyn are a case in point (Garland, 2016). Though the interpretation of these developments is contested, we see some evidence of a democratic renewal. The offer of alternative political platforms, protagonists, and programmes appears to be attracting a large number of citizens back into politics, which can only serve to increase the effective participation of the citizenry.

The growing democratisation of parties can be viewed as a reaction to the desire of not only correcting for the professionalisation, bureaucratisation, and eventually cartelisation of parties (Katz & Mair, 1995, 2009) but also of greater direct citizen involvement. This desire has been expressed by different types of citizens, ranging from radical right populist voters and their stronger preference for referendums compared to other citizens (Bjånesøy & Ivarsflaten, 2016: this volume) all the way to dissatisfied democrats who feel that direct voting is more important but working less well than their satisfied peers do (Linde & Dahlberg, 2016: this volume). Hence, answering calls for the greater participation of citizens in the running of their political parties as well as the running of their polity through the use of direct democracy instruments goes some way towards the appeasement of both dissatisfied democrats and the less democratically inclined radical right populist voters. Whilst these two groups may be strange bedfellows, their converging aspiration for direct involvement and their resentment of the *status quo* are testimony to a malaise affecting very different strands of the citizenry. The consequences of the availability and use of direct democracy instruments, as well as their implications in terms of representation, responsiveness, and alternative forms of political participation are a continuing source of discussion. However, they respond to very concrete concerns that citizens express when assessing their political systems, and may well serve as a means of complementing or strengthening other sources of citizen participation in their polity (Peters, 2016b, 2016c).

Voting equality

Dahl's necessary condition nr. 2 is voting equality. Every individual should have the equal and effective opportunity to cast a vote in the decision-making process. Not only should every individual have one vote, but all votes should weigh equally.

This necessary condition is undermined by both radical right populist parties and by the re-emergence of nationalism (Bjånesøy & Ivarsflaten, 2016; and Knutsen, 2016, this volume). Both developments often aim at limiting voting rights to one group within the given polity: that of native nationals (Mudde & Rovira Kaltwasser, 2013: 163–4). This implies the non-enfranchisement of a number of minority groups and sometimes the disenfranchisement of nationals due to ethnic or religious criteria or due to perceived conflicts related to dual nationality. Hence, nationalist movements as well as radical right populist parties have sometimes proposed to strip some citizens from their nationality and hence from their voting rights. These disenfranchisement dynamics have been mostly studied in the U.S. context (Scher, 2015), but the rise of political movements advocating a nativist or narrowly republican vision of citizenship equally aim to exclude ethnically, religiously, or linguistically defined segments of the population. The result would further shrink the pool of residents endowed with voting rights, which already excludes the young (those under age 18, or in some countries under age 16), those deemed to be mentally unfit, those with criminal convictions, the homeless (or those leading a nomadic existence), and of course non-citizens.

The rise of multi-jurisdictional politics, however, has provided an opportunity to expand voting equality in Europe 31. It has done so in two ways. First, the EU, since the Maastricht Treaty (signed in 1992, in force in 1993) introduced a supranational form of citizenship applying equally to all EU citizens and complementing their national citizenship. This additive EU citizenship comes with a number of rights, including electoral rights. These rights imply that every EU citizen has the opportunity, in his or her state of residence, to vote and stand in two types of elections: European Parliament elections and local/municipal elections. In this sense, the EU has directly enfranchised non-citizen residents who are members of its ever-expanding Union. The implementation of this new right for non-nationals was not without resistance or difficulties (Lewis, 2003: 111–15), and some countries have added different residency requirements, ranging from thirty days before election day (e.g. Estonia), to six months (e.g. Bulgaria), to five years (e.g. Luxembourg or Czech Republic).[3] However, the end result is to directly increase voting equality among European citizens, irrespective of their nationality, and on residency grounds only. Hence, when studying immigrant rights, EU migrants – with their right to freely work and settle within the EU – clearly come across as a "privileged group of immigrants" compared to asylum seekers, third-country nationals, and of course undocumented migrants (Koopmans et al., 2012: 1209). As illustrated by the chapter on intra-EU migration and the welfare state (Cappelen, 2016: this volume), these rights are often reciprocally extended to the three non-EU states we also cover in the book: Norway, Switzerland, and Iceland. Norway and Iceland have gone a step further, having a purely residence-based local franchise, whilst other EU countries such as Belgium, Luxembourg, the Nordic countries, Ireland, the Netherlands, Hungary, Lithuania, Slovakia, Slovenia, or Estonia have extended local voting rights to third-country nationals, too (Bauböck, 2005: 685; Day & Shaw, 2002: 192; Koopmans et al., 2012: 1209).[4]

The positive effect of supranational integration in terms of voting equality does, however, have some very obvious limits. The enfranchisement of EU non-nationals falls short of granting voting or candidacy rights for national elections. Similarly, the treatment of third-country nationals remains at the discretion of the member states. Despite recommendations from EU institutions and pressures by the Council of Europe, the majority of Europe 31 countries tends to exclude rather than include them (Day & Shaw, 2002: 187–9). At any rate, multi-jurisdictional politics has nonetheless expanded voting rights in Europe 31, albeit selectively. Although calls abound for a more inclusive approach – for example, by promoting enfranchisement not only beyond the boundaries of citizenship but also beyond territorial boundaries (Song, 2009), or more creatively through the concept of "stakeholder citizenship", which combines insights from the republican and liberal perspectives of citizenship (Bauböck, 2005: 686) – multi-jurisdictional politics has, by partially supranationalising national citizenship, made significant inroads into greater voting equality in Europe 31.

Second, multi-jurisdictional politics also increases voting equality in two indirect ways. If EU citizens can vote in European Parliament and local elections, then the empowerment of these levels of government necessarily implies a greater weight of their voice in policy-making. As highlighted by Tatham (2016: this volume), central governments have both supranationalised and decentralised their powers. The strengthening of the European Parliament throughout the integration process – becoming a co-equal legislator to the EU Council in the "ordinary legislative procedure" introduced by the Lisbon Treaty – makes it an extraordinarily powerful legislature (Hix & Høyland, 2013). EU legislation has primacy and direct effect over national and subnational legislation. Hence, whilst non-nationals typically cannot vote in national elections, EU citizens can always vote (and stand for office) in European Parliament elections, and thus directly impact national policies "from above". Although debates are rife as to the precise amount of national legislation stemming directly from Brussels (Töller, 2012), the creation of a supranational legal order superseding the national legal order represents a clear opportunity for EU citizens to shape the policies of their host country despite their lack of voting rights at the national level.

In addition, the strengthening of the local and regional levels of government also means that votes in these areas have gained in significance, hence providing an opportunity for non-nationals to shape politics and policies "from below". Again, there are some caveats. EU citizens do not have the right to vote in regional elections in many of the most decentralized countries of Europe 31. For example, EU citizens cannot vote in regional elections in federal Austria, Belgium, or Germany, nor in regionalized Spain, Italy, France, the Netherlands, Greece, or the Czech Republic. They can, however, take part in these elections in Croatia and the UK (Scotland, Wales, Northern Ireland, and the Greater London Authority), and this right is even expanded to third-country nationals in Denmark, Sweden, Slovakia, and Hungary. Although these are countries where the regional level is modestly endowed (with the exception of the UK devolved governments), this nonetheless represents an additional avenue through which voting rights are extended to resident non-nationals of the EU and to third-country individuals. In sum, through (1) the introduction of a supplementary form of EU citizenship which includes voting rights at the local and European levels, and (2) through the strengthening of the powers of both the supranational and decentralised layers of government, the rise of multi-jurisdictional politics has gone hand in hand with the enfranchisement of individuals who were otherwise excluded from the electoral process. Obviously, multi-jurisdictional politics have only partially indented the exclusionary logics promoted by various strands of nationalist and radical right populist movements, but re-enfranchisement below and above the state is a step in the direction of greater voting equality.

In a more subtle way than through disenfranchisement, however, a significant restraint on voting equality is the differential weight given to distinct segments of society. As analysed by Alvarez (2016: this volume), liberal visions of democracy inherently adjudge a disproportionate weight to capital interests, to the detriment of both non-capital interests and the interests of the capital-less. This implies a dual inequality, in terms of which interests are promoted (capital vs. non-capital interests) and whose voices count most (the voices of those with capital vs. those without). This prioritisation of capital over people does not sit well with a conceptualisation of democracy relying on the ideal that all citizens' preferences should be weighed equally in the policy-making process (see also Talbot, 2016: this volume). As argued by Rodrik, the erection of economic growth as the prime objective of a political system inevitably clashes with the ideal of

> democracy for the simple reason that it seeks *not* to improve the functioning of democracy but to accommodate commercial and financial interests seeking market access at low costs. It requires us to buy into a narrative that gives predominance to the needs of multinational enterprises, big banks, and investment houses over other social and economic objectives.
>
> *(Rodrik 2011: 206, emphasis added)*

Empirical evidence has long suggested this is the case in the United States (Bartels, 2008; Gilens, 2012). More recent studies indicate that in Europe, too, the voices of the rich tend to weigh more heavily than those of the less wealthy (Peters & Ensink, 2015; Rosset et al., 2013).

An extension of (the logic underpinning) the prioritisation of capitalist interests can be found in the growing privatisation of the state and of its public services. As discussed by Peters (2016a: this volume), privatisation engenders two types of inequalities. First, there is an inequality in terms of the distribution of services. With their privatisation, non-profitable "services" may be discontinued – usually affecting remote, rural, or poorer areas in a variety of domains such as postal, transport, housing, educational, or healthcare services. Second, there is an inequality in terms of influence over outcomes. Private companies do not have an interest in weighing the preferences of their citizen-consumers equally, but instead seek to maximise profits, usually with a shorter rather than longer time horizon. This leads to lower *input legitimacy*, in terms of the possibility to voice one's preferences, but also to lower *process legitimacy*, in terms of a less transparent and accountable decision-making process and an unequal weighing of preferences. In this sense, as Peters (2016a: 179) argues, consumerism does not promote equality per se, or democratic values more widely for that matter. The cumulative effect of the prioritisation of capital interests on the one hand (Alvarez, 2016; Rodrik, 2011), and of privatisation on the other (Peters, 2016a), only further hinders the voting equality of citizens when seeking to shape policy outcomes.

Enlightened understanding

Dahl's necessary condition nr. 3 concerns the idea of members' enlightened understanding. This corresponds to the notion that all individuals should have equal and effective possibilities to learn about the relevant aspects of policies within a reasonable limit of time. This also implies that people should have the opportunity to obtain information relevant to the policy at stake, and to its alternatives.

The changing nature of parties in terms of their relation to the electorate, especially how trusted they are by the citizenry (Mjelde & Svåsand, 2016: this volume), certainly implies that their role as an information channel – at the interface between the state and the people – has diminished. However, if parties play a lesser role in terms of enhancing the understanding of the people with regards to existing policies and their alternatives, citizens have a number of alternative venues. These mostly consist in gaining policy insights through other platforms such as those provided by newer and older means of information, such as traditional media (television, newspapers, radio, magazines) and social media platforms relying on networks of virtual communities (e.g. Twitter, Facebook, LinkedIn, Pinterest, Google Plus+, Tumblr, Instagram, Vkontakte, Flickr, Qzone, or Myspace). It is hence of little surprise that views regarding the media differ significantly across categories of citizens. Whilst populist radical right voters consider that a free media capable of criticizing the government is much less important than other citizens do (Bjånesøy & Ivarsflaten, 2016: this volume), we also notice that dissatisfied democrats evaluate the performance of the media (as a watchdog and provider of information) far more critically than do their more satisfied peers (Linde & Dahlberg, 2016: this volume). In other words, whilst populist radical right movements put a lower emphasis on citizens' enlightened understanding of politics, dissatisfied democrats highlight that the media falls short of playing the crucial information role democratic politics entail.

Beyond the evolution of parties (in their relationship to the electorate) and the perception of the role the media should play (and to what extent it actually succeeds in playing such a role), one key development has generally constrained citizens' enlightened understanding: the rise of multi-jurisdictional politics. As discussed by Tatham (2016: this volume), the supranationalisation and decentralisation of Europe 31's political systems can be confusing to citizens. It renders a key assumption of electoral democracy – the attribution of responsibility – more difficult to sustain as the entanglement of policy competencies across levels (local, regional, national, supranational) and throughout the policy process (who is responsible for policy initiation, decision taking, policy implementation, and adjudication across these levels in different policy areas?) blurs the clarity of responsibility and hence the attribution of blame and credit for policy failures and successes. Simple questions of accountability become more challenging to citizens when they are called to cast their vote, and hamper the reward-punishment model of electoral accountability. At the supranational level, this has not been helped by (1) the fragmentation of the European public sphere, which still lacks institutionalised pan-European parties and media (Sicakkan, 2016: this volume) and (2) the technicality and lack of scientific consensus on different policy options available to solve (negative) externalities issues requiring international cooperation, as illustrated by the question of climate change mitigation (Talbot, 2016: this volume). Needless to say, further trends in privatisation, the horizontal dispersion of power to regulatory agencies, and the globalisation of our political systems similarly disempower the centre, fragment authority institutionally and territorially, and further contribute to the muddling of the policy process (Peters, 2016a: this volume). Taken together, these developments do not contribute to enlighten the citizens' understanding of (1) who is responsible for what and consequently (2) what the policy options available to them are, across levels of government and policy areas.

There are some causes for optimism, however. As illustrated by Leon (2012), citizens display a capacity to learn where power resides and hence can, over time, improve on their capacity to allocate responsibility across multiple levels of government and administration. In the meantime, as decentralisation has increased, the awareness of citizens towards this level of governance has similarly increased. This to the extent that traditionally "second-order" elections held at the sub-national level are gradually losing their second-order characteristics (Schakel, 2013a, 2013b; Schakel & Jeffery, 2012). Meanwhile, supranationalisation has shifted from a state of "permissive consensus" to one of "constraining dissensus" (Hooghe & Marks, 2009). This certainly implies a greater divisiveness of the issue of European integration, but also an increase in the saliency and politicisation of the question of integration. And with saliency and politicisation come greater exposure, greater discussion, greater information, and, *in fine*, a greater chance for citizens to enlighten their understanding (in the Dahlian sense) of the supranational policy-making process and of the different ideological and policy options available. As highlighted by Cappelen (2016: this volume), European citizens have become well aware of the practical implications of their European rights, as illustrated by their understanding of the right to free movement, settlement, and work anywhere within the EU-EEA area. Power dispersion through decentralisation, supranationalisation, privatisation, delegation, and globalisation has accelerated these past fifty years, but Europe 31 citizens are adjusting. And future generations of European citizens will have grown accustomed to life in multi-jurisdictional polities.

Control of the agenda

Dahl's necessary condition nr. 4 concerns the control of the agenda. This means that members of the political system must have the exclusive right to decide on what issues matter and should hence be placed on the political agenda. This control of the agenda also implies the possibility of reversing – or at least challenging – past decisions.

A number of trends described in this book suggest a loss of control of the agenda by Europe 31's people. Part of this phenomena is related to the shrinking role played by the state due to its diffusion of powers – vertically to the supranational and subnational levels, horizontally to non-majoritarian institutions, such as regulatory agencies or courts, and to non-state actors through privatisation processes (Peters, 2016a; Tatham, 2016; Vibe, 2016, all this volume). As has been described elsewhere (Levi-Faur, 2005), the state is doing less and less of the "rowing" (i.e. policy implementation, including service delivery) and is instead retreating to a "steering" role (i.e. leading and directing). However, one can wonder if the state is not gradually giving up significant portions of its steering activities, too. One can discuss the extent to which state steering is either constrained or abolished altogether in increasingly privatised and deregulated sectors (e.g. telecommunications, transport), or sectors falling under the remit of independent regulatory agencies, international organisations, and subnational governments (e.g. monetary policy, trade and investment/state-aid policies, education, or cultural policy).

A perhaps extreme illustration of the limitations states face in their steering activities comes from the spread of austerity policies in Europe 31 during the financial crisis. Just as the crisis has not hit all countries equally, all countries have not faced equal pressures to implement austerity measures. These measures were encouraged in a certain number of countries, but they were imposed in other countries in exchange for international support. Austerity "packages" taking the shape of a mix of measures aimed at the structural reform of the welfare state and of the labour market were either implicitly imposed through international financial market pressures or explicitly imposed (as part of conditionality clauses releasing "bailout" funding) by international actors such as the troika of the European Central Bank (ECB), the EU, and the International Monetary Fund (IMF). As highlighted by Armingeon and Baccaro, citizens were de facto excluded from the policy-making equation. It mattered little whether they individually protested, demonstrated, or voted out their governments, or whether they collectively resisted these measures through (older or newer) political parties, labour unions, or citizens groups. Externally imposed reform packages affecting key dimensions of welfare and labour policies had to be accepted. Hence, the sovereign debt crisis represents a "case in which domestic politics, either party- or interest group-based, does not matter: there is only one option and it is imposed from outside. All domestic actors can do is to find ways to blunt popular opposition to it" (2012: 162). In this sense, citizens and governments (of the national and sub-national types) have been imposed an agenda with very clear ideological underpinnings: its goals are to further roll back the welfare state and to liberalise as well as deregulate both the labour market and the existing systems of interest intermediation (e.g. Oldervoll & Kuhnle, 2016: this volume).

Such interference with the democratic process by markets and international organisations has logically resulted in a dramatic decline in support for national democracy, in terms of both trust and satisfaction with the way democracy works (Armingeon & Guthmann, 2014). The advent of what one could call "proxy-steering" has meant a loss of control of the agenda by individual citizens and the subjugation of the state's steering capacities by external actors. Although a return to the "laissez-faire capitalism" of the 1800s through 1930s, during which the state neither rowed nor steered, seems unlikely, the "regulatory capitalism" model, identified since the 1980s, where the state does not row but nonetheless steers (Levi-Faur, 2005: 15), appears to have been eroded by the power of financial markets and the growing influence of international organisations.

The advent of "remote steering" (i.e. steering at a distance) of domestic governments by international organisations not only curtails the effective participation of individuals, their enlightened understanding, and their control of the agenda, but it also generates a certain number of representation issues. First, not all countries are equally affected – and hence disenfranchised. Remote steering by supranational organisations has mostly affected Europe's southern states, such as Greece, Portugal, Spain, and Italy, its Baltic states, and to some extent Ireland. It has also set the agenda for reform in a number of other countries (e.g. the UK). Second, the top-down nature of agenda setting, away from citizen influence, is of concern because of the lack of congruence between citizen and élite preferences. This preference mismatch can sometimes take inclusive forms, such as when comparing general public and élite views on citizenship and identity (Sicakkan, 2016: this volume).[5] Other times, however, it takes less inclusive forms in terms of market (de)regulation and the social protection of the more precarious. As Hooghe (2003) discovered in a groundbreaking analysis of citizen and élite preferences on several dimensions of European integration, "élites desire a European Union capable of governing a large, competitive market and projecting political muscle; citizens are more in favour of a caring European Union, which protects them from the vagaries of capitalist markets" (2003: 296). This takes the form of desires for a more socially inclusive, health-caring, environmentally friendly, market-regulated, and redistributive Europe. Hence, the capture of the policy agenda by financial markets and international organisations not only robs citizens of their agenda-setting prerogative, but it also weakens the representative dimension of democracy, as citizen and supranational élite preferences fail to align. These élites tend to favour liberalising policies, whilst the general public tends to express a preference for "market flanking" policies (Hooghe, 2003: 296) aimed at containing, or at least mitigating, the labour market volatilities that were intensified by the expansion of the EU's single market within Europe 31.

State steering by proxy, or the advent of remote steering by international actors, has thankfully not had only negative consequences for Europe 31 citizens. As illustrated by Vibe (2016: this volume), the European Convention on Human Rights and the European Court of Human Rights have provided vehicles for the defence and promotion of people's rights, including those of minorities. In terms of greater equality and lesser discrimination, these have undeniably been positive developments. Similarly, although international organisations' agendas remain often both remote and inaccessible to citizens, there have been some developments towards their opening up to citizen influence, both directly and indirectly.

The EU's agenda setting has started to open up to *direct* citizen involvement. The steps are small, but they are illustrative of a shift towards citizens regaining control of their polity's agenda. The most notable of those small steps is the Citizen Initiative instrument introduced by the Lisbon Treaty of December 2009. The Citizen

Initiative allows for one million EU citizens coming from at least seven out of the EU's twenty-eight member states to call on the European Commission to make a legislative proposal. In essence, it provides a direct instrument for citizens to put items of interest on the European agenda. Successful initiatives have concerned the right to water and sanitation as a human right and their provision as public services, the phasing out of animal experiments, as well as issues related to the human embryo, with implications for abortion policies (and its public funding). The instrument has clear limitations, but also some potential (Monaghan, 2012), and represents a step towards further opening up the EU's agenda setting to the general public.

Citizens have also sometimes exerted pressures on their national government to pull out of the European integration project altogether, so as to regain part of their sovereignty. How much sovereignty can be recovered by formally leaving the EU is open to discussion. However, Greenland voted to leave the European Communities in a (consultative) referendum in 1982, leading to the Greenland Treaty of 1985 and the territory's formal withdrawal on February 1st of that year. The UK has had a tumultuous history regarding EU membership. It joined the European Economic Community at the third attempt in 1973 after two French vetoes (in 1963 and 1967). However, after joining under Conservative rule, the following Labour government upheld its manifesto promise to review its membership and hold an "in or out" referendum. The June 1975 referendum (67.2 per cent to stay, 64.5 per cent turnout) meant that the UK remained in the European Community. Following a similar campaign promise by the Conservative Party in 2013 that (if re-elected in 2015) it would review the terms of the UK's membership and then submit the "in or out" question to its people, a new EU referendum took place on June 23, 2016. The outcome of the consultation (51.9 per cent to leave, 72.2 per cent turnout) paves the way for the UK to be the first member to use the Lisbon Treaty's exit clause, formalizing the procedure for withdrawal from the Union.

In more *indirect* ways than via the Citizen Initiative or membership referendums, citizens have exerted growing influence on their polity's agenda through both supranational and subnational means. Supranationally, the notable empowerment of the European Parliament implies that European citizens directly choose their representatives in a key arena. This affects not only decision-taking (through Lisbon's ordinary legislative procedure) but also the EU's agenda setting. Indeed, the European Parliament has gained a right of legislative initiative through its capacity to ask the Commission to submit a proposal. Although the Commission can refuse to submit the proposal, this nonetheless represents an indirect instrument available to European citizens to influence the EU's agenda via the European Parliament. Similarly, in the context of the crisis, the European Parliament has also sought to increase its influence (and hence that of its citizens) with some successes (e.g. the Single Supervisory Mechanism) and some disappointments (the European Stability Mechanism) (see Rittberger, 2014). Nonetheless, the European Parliament's growing role in the EU political system shows no sign of decline, and even in cases where its Treaty-based powers are absent, it has been able to extract some concessions (such as information rights, see Rittberger, 2014: 1179).

At the subnational level too, citizens are clawing back some of their agenda-setting competences. The spread of the direct election of regional authorities has gone hand-in-hand with greater degrees of self-government at those levels. The rise of regional "self-rule" – understood as "the capacity of a regional government to exercise authority autonomously over those who live in its territory" (Hooghe et al., 2010: 6) – is a distinctive feature of the transformation of European states since the 1970s. Of course, regional self-government, though expanding, is limited in terms of the policy fields covered. These are often confined to a selection of economic, cultural-educational, or welfare policies. However, regions' policy scope has also been on the increase, especially in the case of regions with legislative powers. There are over seventy such regions in the EU, hence covering about 40 per cent of the EU's population.[6] Having the power of making laws applicable to one's own territory represents the climax of self-government and – coupled with representatives' direct election – contributes to bringing back agenda-setting and policy-making closer to the citizenry.

Two other subnational developments imply greater citizen control on the policy-making process, from agenda setting all the way to policy implementation. The first is the (more gradual) rise of "shared rule", defined as the co-determination by regional authorities of national decision-making (Hooghe et al., 2010: 6). This means that, through the empowerment of regional governments, citizens can now influence national policies directly through traditional channels of participation (i.e. national elections and referendums) but also indirectly through their regional governments. In the case of federalised and regionalised states, sub-national governments can now influence the national law-making process, their nation's executive powers, national taxation, and national constitutional reform (Hooghe et al., 2010: 22–9). Increasingly, these regions with high shared rule have also institutionalised their *domestic* power on EU issues, both at the pre- and post-legislative phases of the policy-shaping process (Tatham, 2011). Hence, if regional *formal influence at the EU level* – what one could call EU-level shared rule – remains somewhat limited (Tatham, 2014), formal influence on EU issues *at the national level* and *informal influence* in Brussels have both been growing (Jeffery, 2007; Tatham, 2015). In this way, through the spread of democracy at the regional level in an increasing number of policy areas (i.e. greater regional self-rule), and through the empowerment of regional authorities at the national level on both national questions (Hooghe et al., 2010: 22–9) and on EU ones (Tatham, 2011), citizens have gained new avenues to influence the policy-making process – from agenda-setting to implementation – at multiple levels of government. In this light, it is interesting to note that regional administrative élites (i.e. regional senior civil servants with policy responsibility) display both a clear preference for a greater degree of control over the European integration process (Tatham & Bauer, 2014) and a tendency to adjust their policy preferences to their specific regional context (Tatham & Bauer, 2016). These developments help to reduce the preference-policy gap at the subnational level and provide an indirect route for citizens to influence policy development nationally and supranationally through their regional governments.

Citizen rights

Dahl's necessary condition nr. 5 determines that all or most permanent adult residents should have full citizen rights, as described by the conditions 1 to 4. This entails political equality among the members of the political system.

As discussed above, the exclusionary logics advocated by radical right populist parties have benefited from the re-emergence of nationalism as a political force in Europe. In part resting on xenophobia and distinct attitudes towards immigrants (Knutsen, 2016: this volume), nationalism and radical right populism have tended to rely not only on authoritarian preferences (hence contradicting democratic principles) but also on "exclusive-nationalism" (Dunn, 2015). Coupled with desires to reduce immigration (Rydgren, 2008), the re-emergence of nationalism represents a direct threat to citizen rights by seeking to reduce the pool of individuals qualifying as full citizens of a given system. These exclusionary dynamics have fed right-wing populist movements throughout Europe 31, such as in Norway (*Fremskrittspartiet –* FrP), Sweden (*Sverigedemokraterna –* SD), Finland (*Perussuomalaiset –* PS), Denmark (*Dansk Folkeparti –* DF), the Netherlands (*Partij voor de Vrijheid –* PVV), Belgium (*Vlaams Belang –* VB), the United Kingdom (*UK Independence Party –* UKIP), Germany (*Alternative für Deutschland –* AfD), Austria (*Freiheitliche Partei Österreichs –* FPÖ), France (*Front National –* FN), Switzerland (*Schweizerische Volkspartei –* SVP), Italy (*Lega Nord –* LN), Greece (*Chrysí Avgí –* Golden Dawn; *Anexartitoi Ellines –* ANEL), Poland (*Prawo i Sprawiedliwość –* PiS; *Kongres Nowej Prawicy –* KNP), Slovakia (*Slovenská národná strana –* SNS), or Hungary (*Fidesz*; *Jobbik*) (see also Bjånesøy & Ivarsflaten, 2016: this volume).

At the heart of these movements are identity and community questions. As borders between states are eroded by European integration, and as territorial differentiation deepens within states through the rise of regional self-rule, the question of the delineation of a political community and the identity on which it relies becomes contested. Mounting criticism of the European integration project, perceived as a threat towards "national" identity, is symptomatic of the challenge of defining the legitimate territorial scale of government and the community dimension underlying it (Henderson et al., 2013; Hooghe & Marks, 2009). The successes of nationalist and populist parties at European elections, as well as the connection made between free intra-EU labour migration and welfare solidarity in the current "Brexit" discussions, are all further symptoms of these questions. How does one define identity, and hence community, and what should the link be to citizenship and individuals' rights within a given political system? As discussed above, the restrictive attribution of full citizenship rights to nationals implies that immigrants (i.e. resident non-nationals) fall short of achieving the status of full citizen, with complete rights in their host polity. This breaches Dahl's necessary condition nr. 5 of citizen rights and hence of political equality among the members of the polity. In this sense, resident non-nationals become "second-class citizens". There are degrees of exclusion and inequality. These range from illegal (i.e. undocumented) migrants who have next to no rights beyond some emergency healthcare or schooling for their children, to asylum seekers who have greater access to basic services but face clear limitations to fundamental rights nonetheless (e.g. restrictions on employment or free movement) (Koopmans et al., 2012: 1211). However, being granted nationality and hence full citizenship rights may not end *de facto* exclusionary processes, which take the form of discrimination on ethnic, cultural, linguistic, religious, or sexual grounds. These cleavages sometimes overlap with the national or nativist cleavage and form the basis for further exclusion from the political system. This discriminatory process can become institutionalised when the polity is perceived as under threat from within or from outside, as in the case of a perceived terrorist threat (Engene, 2016: this volume), hence leading to the targeting of minorities and in turn these becoming "disconnected citizens" (Jarvis & Lister, 2013). Again, these minorities are often identified on the basis of ethnic, cultural, linguistic, religious, or sexual markers. Hence, when counter-terrorist measures momentarily suspend democracy to defend it (Wilkinson, 2001: 23), it seems that democracy becomes more suspended for some (i.e. minorities) than for others (i.e. the nation's majority).

Other forms of exclusion are more subtle, however. While nationalist movements seek to exclude certain individuals from the political system and restrain their civil rights, access to welfare rights is also increasingly gate-kept via other means than membership to an imagined community (Anderson, 2006). In this sense, the evolution of the labour market in terms of access to employment, to what kind of employment, and with what sort of social protection, as described by Oldervoll and Kuhnle (2016: this volume), represents a clear though indirect threat to the principle of equal citizen rights and *in fine* political equality within the system. Indeed, labour market "dualisation" (with all the caveats that a dichotomous concept necessarily entails in terms of bluntness) is a clear source of inequality among individuals in how it affects social protection. Oldervoll and Kuhnle describe a process by which certain groups retain extensive forms of social protection, whereas others either lose such protection or fail to qualify for it. Such dualisation generates a system of privileged insiders and deprived outsiders – in other words, an asymmetrical coverage of the population in terms of individuals' rights and access to services. In this way, labour market inequalities, instead of being corrected by welfare policies, are actually magnified by them. Labour market dualisation hence leads to welfare dualisation, or a two-tier welfare state, helping and assisting some better than others. In this case, unfortunately, welfare dualisation leads to a "Matthew effect" of both entrenching and increasing inequalities. As the Gospel according to St Matthew (25:29) put it, those who have shall have more, while those who have least shall have less (Scientia Biblica, 1825: 247). The transmission belt from labour to welfare inequalities and the resulting Matthew effect widens the gap between the haves and have-nots. The reproduction and entrenchment of socio-economic inequalities via a dualised welfare state inevitably penetrates the political sphere. And the logical steps from labour, to welfare, to political inequalities become inevitable: as income inequalities spill over into health, educational, and social inequalities, the gap between citizens and their opportunity to equally affect policy outcomes widens, as already illustrated above (Bartels, 2008; Gilens, 2012; Peters & Ensink, 2015).

The link between socio-economic inequalities (and the reproduction of labour market inequalities in welfare policies) on the one hand, and a society's ethnic, cultural, linguistic, and religious cleavages on the other, is an obvious one to make. Although the latter cleavages do not always lead to socio-economic inequalities, the overlap is often consequential. And this link is particularly obvious to a certain class of citizens identified as dissatisfied democrats and who most likely perceive the threat that cleavage-driven inequalities entail for the polity as a whole. As Linde and Dahlberg (2016: this volume) highlight, dissatisfied democrats perceive minority protection and impartial courts as important as any other democrat; however, they evaluate minority rights' protection as insufficient in practice and observe that their country's court system is neither egalitarian nor impartial. Crucially, dissatisfied democrats relate political to economic inequalities: they consider their government's measures to reduce income differences as falling well short of expectations. This seems to be a key driver of their dissatisfaction towards how their preferred political system (i.e. democracy) is functioning in practice.

The convergence of the (1) minority, (2) political/rights inequality, and (3) economic inequality issues seems to be at the heart of the greatest tensions of early twenty-first-century Europe. These three dimensions appear to be structuring political developments and contestation. This is certainly the case regarding European integration, supranational judicial policy-making, and state decentralisation (Sicakkan, 2016; Tatham, 2016; Vibe, 2016, all this volume), regarding the exclusionary dimensions of nationalism and radical right populism (Bjånesøy & Ivarsflaten, 2016; Knutsen, 2016, all this volume), the evolution of the welfare state in times of labour migration and changing markets in the EU-EEA context (Cappelen, 2016; Oldervoll & Kuhnle, 2016, all this volume), the perceived threat of terrorism and the lack of climate change mitigation (Engene, 2016; Talbot, 2016, all this volume), the deepening disconnect between state institutions and the citizenry through the (partial) decline of parties, the primacy of capital interests, and the displacement of politics away from citizens' reach (Alvarez, 2016; Mjelde & Svåsand, 2016; Peters, 2016a, all this volume), culminating in the dissatisfaction of the proponents of democracy themselves (Linde & Dahlberg, 2016: this volume). The persistence of dissatisfied democrats on a continent harbouring the world's most advanced democracies only serves to illustrate that democracy is under threat in Europe 31. Following Dahl's insights, it seems that each and every necessary condition is threatened by core developments in this privileged group of countries. And each time a combination of questions related to the status and treatment of (1) minorities (ethnic, cultural, religious, linguistic, sexual), of (2) political and rights' inequalities, and finally of (3) economic inequalities seems to constitute a driving force focalising tensions and conflicts within our polities.

Conceptions of democracy: Madisonian vs. populistic

How a political system treats its minorities, how it distributes rights (political and civil) to its members, and to what extent it seeks to reduce economic inequalities all affect Dahl's five necessary conditions and hence determine the shape and nature of the political system. Contested concepts of identity and community are both mobilised and instrumentalised as legitimising tools to justify more inclusive or exclusive understandings of citizenship. Indeed, both identity and community are constructs, and their meaning, definition, and delineation in turn affects the placement of the polity on the inclusive-exclusive continuum, thereby also affecting the access to and (re)distribution of economic, social, and civil rights, hence generating winners and losers, majorities and minorities within the political system.

The extent to which a political system not only defines clear majorities and minorities but also empowers or disempowers them can be described in terms of two ideal-types: a Madisonian system as opposed to a populistic system. The Madisonian system rests on the idea of preventing the tyranny of any majority – and even of any minority – through (1) the division of powers and (2) systems of checks and balances on each branch of power (typically the executive, the legislature, and the judiciary). It is similar to concepts such as consensus democracy or consociational democracy (Lijphart, 1999) in the sense that it implies compromise and agreement among the different institutions of government in order for it to function. At its core, one can find the division of power (among branches of government, but – by extension – also among layers of government or across functional areas), its constitutional enshrinement, the respect of the rule of law, and hence the respect of minority rights. As described by Dahl, the Madisonian theory of democracy "is an effort to bring off a compromise between the power of majorities and the power of minorities, between the political equality of all adult citizens on the one side, and the desire to limit their sovereignty on the other" (Dahl, 2006: 4). The essence of this Madisonian model is to avoid the tyranny of groups of individuals by other groups of individuals through checks which are "external" to those groups, which rely on the fragmentation (as opposed to the concentration) of power, and hence avoid tyranny understood as the "severe deprivation of a natural right" (2006: 6). In the absence of external checks, the tyranny can equally be of the majority over the minority, or of the minority over the majority as, following Hamilton, "give all power to the many, they will oppress the few. Give all power to the few, they will oppress the many" (cited in Dahl, 2006: 7). Hence, in the trade-off between system responsiveness and responsibility, Madisonian democracy puts a greater emphasis on responsible government.

This contrasts with a populistic conception of democracy. This understanding of democracy puts a greater emphasis on liberating the will of the people from external checks and balances, and hence equating democracy with unconstrained popular sovereignty. This implies that the majority view within the political system is free from past expressions of the popular will and does not constrain future expressions of the popular will. Government by the people should be as unchecked as possible. Similarly, it tends to favour direct forms of political participation so as to bypass existing institutional setups, as systems of interest intermediation are viewed as diluting, filtering, and to some extent corrupting the popular will. The populistic conception seeks to shrink the interface between the state and the people, with the state minimally considered as the political arm of the people, a mere executant of its will. This conception of democracy is obviously at odds with a Madisonian view. It is also silent on how "the people" is identified.[7] Interpretations range from a nativist conceptualisation of the people (relying on *Blut* or *Bodenrecht*, for example) to an inclusive but majoritarian conceptualisation (the will of the people is the majority of individuals). At any rate, it is inimical to minorities, however defined. This conception of democracy is also ambiguous as to the (extent of) constraints placed on the will of the majority. This leads to the contradictory conciliation of two opposites. On the one hand that of the *absolute* sovereignty of the majority, and on the other that such a conception somehow does *not* advocate "that a majority would or should do anything it felt an impulse to do" (Dahl, 2006: 36). As Dahl summarises, "in practice, however, the attempt to identify democracy with the *unlimited* power of majorities has usually gone hand in hand with an attempt to include in the definition *some concept of restraints on majorities*" (2006: 35, emphasis added). Notwithstanding these internal tensions and others still,[8] in the trade-off between system responsiveness and responsibility, populistic democracy puts a greater emphasis on responsive government.

How does the evolution of democracy in Europe 31 relate to the two ideal-types of Madisonian and populistic democracy, and where can one place it on the responsible-responsive continuum? We find that there are demands for both more Madisonian and more populistic democracy, resulting inevitably in tensions regarding the desired direction of change (1). Conversely, it also appears that whilst the populist model can drift towards non-democratic forms, the Madisonian trend has the potential to generate an anti-system backlash among citizens. Yet, despite the potential for a negative backlash, this more responsible and fragmented model displays some clear advantages which – if combined with the strengthening of public authority in sectors of general interests as well as with populistic elements of direct election and direct democracy – may provide the foundations for the *least inacceptable* balance between responsiveness and responsibility, between inclusiveness and decisiveness (2).

Madisonian, populistic, or both? Paradoxes and countervailing citizen demands

Critics of the status quo are often advocates of either a more populistic or a more Madisonian vision of democracy. However, they sometimes overlap in their preferences, forming unlikely coalitions. Populist radical right voters and dissatisfied democrats have little in common (Bjånesøy & Ivarsflaten, 2016; Linde & Dahlberg, 2016, both this volume). They weigh differently the importance of living in a democracy, of minority rights protection, of free and fair elections, and of the media's role. However, they do not diverge on one issue and actually converge on another. Populist radical right voters do not diverge from other citizens in their view of the role of courts. They actually find that courts have an important role to play in their polity through their capacity to stop governments from acting beyond their authority. Meanwhile, dissatisfied democrats also value courts highly, especially in terms of their impartiality, but they complement the perceived importance of courts by highlighting how they consider courts should, in practice, be even more impartial than they currently are. In this sense, when seeking to strengthen the role of courts, dissatisfied democrats will encounter little opposition from radical right populist voters. This lack of divergence on the importance of courts in curbing over-stepping executives and providing impartial protection is somewhat surprising. Strong and independent courts with powers of judicial review contribute to making a political system more Madisonian than populistic, as they represent an "external check" (Dahl, 2006: 6) and have been mobilised to promote and upheld minority rights against discriminations of different kinds (e.g. Vibe, 2016: this volume).

More surprising still, dissatisfied democrats and populist radical right voters actually converge on one issue: that of direct democracy. When populist radical right voters are asked how important they think it is for democracy that citizens have the final say on political issues by voting directly in referendums, the gap with the other citizens is a highly significant one. That these types of voters are in favour of a populistic vision of democracy which bypasses institutional structures to allow direct input (and in this case decision-making) by the citizenry is hardly counter-intuitive. What is striking is that dissatisfied democrats unambiguously converge with their populist peers on the question of direct voting. Indeed, whilst dissatisfied and satisfied democrats tend to ascribe similar levels of importance to the various elements of democracy and only diverge on the evaluation of their implementation, they significantly diverge on direct voting. Dissatisfied democrats are not only much more critical of the implementation of direct voting (i.e. they want more), but they also find direct voting much more important than other democrats do. Whilst dissatisfied democrats seem mostly characterised by desires for greater accountability and stronger checks and balances on government action via enhanced party competition, freer opposition parties, a freer and more reliable media, more impartial courts, or through better protection of minority rights, they depart from these Madisonian characteristics to embrace a more populistic vision, finding direct democracy both more important and more lacking than their satisfied peers do. Hence, in the critical and discontented eyes of dissatisfied democrats, Madisonian preferences are not wholly incompatible with some populistic instruments, such as the exercise of direct democracy. Indeed, they seem to advocate that Madisonian logics be balanced by injecting some populistic elements into the political system.

One last item seems noteworthy in the list of paradoxes linking populistic and Madisonian visions of democracy. Whilst the populistic vision seeks to empower the will of the majority, concentrating power in the hands of the people with minimal external checks, the Madisonian ideal to a great extent seeks to entrench power dispersion and fragmentation, cooperation and compromise. It is hence not surprising that populist radical right voters differentiate themselves from other voters in how important they think it is for democracy that politicians take into account the views of other European governments (i.e. a quintessentially "external check") before making decisions. This ties in well with the literature describing these voters and ensuing parties as state-centric and generally suspicious of any supranational or sub-national developments which may limit the capacity and independence of the centre to act unilaterally in its unmediated execution of the people's will. It is then somewhat ironic that many populistic parties have been especially successful at so-called second-order elections (i.e. elections at the sub-national or supranational level). Whilst decentralisation and supranationalisation both lead to more power sharing and greater constraints on central executives in day-to-day policy-making, the democratisation of both political arenas through the direct election of regional bodies and of the European Parliament has provided new electoral platforms for populist parties where they have often outperformed their national electoral scores. It is one of the paradoxes of Europe 31 that populist parties of the radical right type have built much of their electoral success in arenas that are inconsistent with their ideology. Indeed, institutionalising interdependence with other states and the subjugation of the nation's will to a pan-European Parliament goes against their nation-centric ideology, whilst their nationalist framework sits oddly with the institutional empowerment of territorial minorities in the state's regions. Their agenda for change by strengthening the centre and loosening supranational ties may well be self-defeating. Withdrawal from the EU and re-centralisation of powers may well deprive them of not only essential electoral resources but also of their appeal among voters. Clearly, there are other determinants to their successes, such as mobilisation on identity and community dimensions of contestation (Hooghe & Marks, 2009), the tabloidisation of politics, the persistence of the economic crisis, and these parties' capacity to learn, adapt, and build on their own success (Mudde, 2013). However, the electoral success of these populistic parties in arenas they contest – due to their Madisonian characteristic of further constraining and disempowering central government – is a further paradox linking the Madisonian and populistic visions of democracy.

The least inacceptable system? a Madisonian– populistic compromise

The drift towards a bound or constrained form of government, inimical to the populist vision, and moving towards the Madisonian ideal through the dispersion of central government powers downwards (regional and local levels), upwards (European integration, international organisations), sideways (judicial review, regulatory agencies), and the associated "checks" on governmental activities this implies, may contain the seeds for a popular backlash against what one could call "encumbered democracy".

As discussed in the various chapters and above, the diffusion and dispersion of power negatively affects a number of conditions necessary for democracy, such as citizens' enlightened understanding or their control of the agenda. The lack of clarity of responsibility (Hobolt & Tilley, 2014; Leon, 2011), the deadlock-inducing properties of power sharing at multiple levels (Falkner, 2011; Scharpf,

2006), the capture of reform agendas by international institutions and international markets (e.g. credit rating agencies such as Standard & Poor's, Moody's, or Fitch) to the detriment of electoral democracy (Armingeon & Baccaro, 2012; Armingeon & Guthmann, 2014; Rodrik, 2011), the outsourcing of government rowing and steering (Levi-Faur, 2005), and many other developments threaten democracy beyond concerns regarding the optimal trade-off between responsiveness and responsibility, or between inclusiveness and decisiveness. It is hence of little surprise that the most Madisonian projects of all, that of bringing European states in an "ever closer union . . . united in diversity" is increasingly contested, shifting from permissive consensus to constraining dissensus as it deepens over time (Hooghe & Marks, 2009).

However, whilst these Madisonian developments can have adverse consequences, they also come with more positive effects regarding other necessary conditions for democracy, such as enhanced effective participation, greater opportunities for voting equality, or the spread of (citizenship) rights (see above). The parallel with Lijphart's (1999) model of consensus democracy, also relying on power sharing, checks and balances, and more inclusive policy processes, is encouraging as Europe 31 moves towards such a model. As outlined throughout the book, these predominantly Madisonian elements are often complemented by populistic instruments such as direct elections (at the local, regional, national, and supranational levels) and direct participatory measures (such as recalls, constitutional referendums, legislative referendums, popular initiatives, or agenda initiatives – variously available at each level of government). How these different developments affect political participation (Peters, forthcoming), policy-making inclusiveness and decisiveness (Scharpf, 1999), and in turn affect input and output legitimacy as well as procedural and substantive dimensions of democracy is open for discussion. However, the evidence available does highlight that the greater openness and the more consensual approach associated with power-sharing arrangements resting on compromise and the protection of minority rights seem to lead to "kinder, gentler" forms of government (Lijphart, 1999: 275).

Findings by Engene (2016: this volume) and Sicakkan (2016: this volume) provide some cause for optimism. As reported by Engene (2016), if one considers domestic terrorism as an extreme expression of political dissatisfaction, then it is least likely as the political system adopts traits associated with the consensus model. In the words of Qvortrup and Lijphart,

> the risk of fatal terrorist attacks is almost six times higher in majoritarian democracies than in their consensus counterparts, and . . . this indicator is stronger than factors such as economic development and a large youth population and levels of urbanisation.
>
> *(2013: 471)*

Similarly, whilst supranational integration has historically been a top-down, élite-driven project, the incongruence between élite and citizen preferences may not always be detrimental to the spread of a more inclusionary type of democracy. Although élites have failed to reflect their citizens' preferences for "market flanking" policies (Hooghe, 2003), they do tend to exhibit more inclusive and pro-diversity conceptions of citizenship (Sicakkan, 2016: this volume). Hence, while the European Madisonian project can impair responsiveness and electoral democracy, it may also reinforce the inclusiveness of citizenship, hence strengthening a core dimension of Dahl's democratic model.

In sum, in the quest for an elusive balance between responsible and responsive government, and between system inclusiveness and decisiveness, the ills of the populistic vision of democracy appear to us as greater than the evils of the Madisonian model *if and only if* the latter is complemented with doses of the former. Clearly, Europe 31 is not in an either/or scenario, but searching for the optimal equilibrium on the democratic continuum delineated by those two ideal-types implies movement towards one and away from the other. We therefore observe the messy emergence of a system which is more Madisonian than populistic, more consensus than majoritarian. But this evolving system is also one where with every institutional check-and-balance mechanism, with each new instance of power sharing, with any creation of new policy players, a dose of popular involvement is also injected in the shape of a multiplication of direct elections across levels of governments and new institutionalised opportunities for direct citizen involvement, ranging from different types of referendums (constitutional, legislative, consultative) to various citizen-based initiatives (recalls, popular or agenda initiatives). As persistent dissatisfaction and feelings of anti-system and even anti-establishment illustrate, our evolving political systems have yet to reach their zenith. The disempowerment of the people, as well as that of their governments, is very real. In this vein, the primacy of capital and financial interests over that of the citizenry as a whole is particularly worrying (Alvarez, 2016: this volume) and leads to the disproportionate influence of the more affluent (Bartels, 2008; Gilens, 2012; Peters & Ensink, 2015). In turn, these inequalities of input (i.e. who has influence) and output (i.e. who gets what) only further feed the discontent of citizens, expressed through more or less extreme forms, from mere dissatisfaction with the way democracy works, to the support of anti-establishment movements, all the way to acts of domestic terrorism. In this light, both the substantive and procedural dimensions of democracy need strengthening.

We believe this can be achieved through the further *democratisation* of subnational and supranational decision-taking arenas, ranging all the way from local government to the governance of international organisations. Whilst the local, regional, and European levels have been democratising, this process needs to go further. Only through democratisation will the politicisation of decision-taking bring the system's inputs and outputs closer to its citizens. Similarly, while we advocate that power dispersion should go hand-in-hand with the democratisation of these dispersed powers, we are also in favour of a "(re-)public-isation" of services of general interest. By this we mean that services of general interest to the people either should be owned by public authorities or that, at the very least, the delivery of these services should be controlled by public authorities – public authorities being by definition subject to democratic scrutiny. Unlike "nationalisation" policies, the control over these services need not be recaptured by "national" authorities, but by public authorities broadly defined, be they local, regional, national, or supranational. But these authorities need to be "public" in terms of their direct or indirect accountability to the general public. We advocate "(re-)public-isation" both for services of general interest and the bodies/institutions involved in the public policy cycle, such as regulatory agencies or international institutions.

An illustration of this is the European Commission. This is a non-elected supranational bureaucracy, but it has come under increasing popular scrutiny through a variety of procedures and instruments affecting its composition, tenure, and day-to-day work. Its leadership (the President and the college of Commissioners) is nominated (President) and voted in (college) by national governments taking into account the results of the last supranational election. It is invested by a directly elected parliament (election of the President and approval/rejection of the college as a whole). It is regularly scrutinised by this same democratic parliament (in terms of requesting policy proposals, reviewing its work programme, questioning its activities, but also voting a motion of censure obliging it to resign) and by a supranational court of justice which reviews the legality of its acts and non-acts (i.e. "actions for annulment" when it oversteps its role, "actions for failure to act" when it falls short of its duty to act) against treaties drawn by heads of states/governments and ratified by the people of Europe or their legislatures. Finally, it can be called upon directly by citizens to make a legislative proposal (i.e. Citizen Initiative, see above). The evolution of the European Commission illustrates how tasks can be delegated to non-majoritarian and supranational institutions whilst still achieving a certain degree of public oversight and hence control. This model can certainly be improved, but it could also be extended to other supranational institutions or non-majoritarian institutions.[9]

Absent of such "(re-)public-isation" of key policy institutions and of general services such as education, healthcare, security, banking, and in some cases essential transport or telecommunication facilities (e.g. in remote/rural/poorer areas), policies and services will be delivered unevenly and asymmetrically, reinforcing rather than correcting for existing inequalities and further entrenching specific interests as opposed to citizen interests, thereby undermining Dahl's five necessary conditions. In this sense, "(re-)public-isation" implies that (1) policy institutions such as regulatory agencies or international organisations should be brought back within the reach of democratic control so as to prevent their capture by specific interests and that (2) services of interest to the general public (e.g. education, healthcare, security, banking) should also be brought back within the reach of citizens, either through public ownership (but not necessarily delivery) or through public oversight of the institutions responsible for the delivery of these public goods. We do not argue that these measures will lead to an optimal political system, striking the right balance on key dimensions of responsiveness and responsibility or inclusiveness and decisiveness. However, we do believe that injecting a Madisonian setup with doses of populistic measures such as direct election, direct democracy, and the (re-)public-isation of institutions and services of general interests has the potential to lead to the *least inacceptable system*. In the words of Winston Churchill (House of Commons, 11 November 1947),

> many forms of Government have been tried, and will be tried in this world of sin and woe. No one pretends that democracy is perfect or all-wise. Indeed it has been said that *democracy is the worst form of Government except for all those other forms that have been tried from time to time.*
>
> *(Langworth, 2008: 574, emphasis added)*

We hope that the above can contribute to taking further steps towards a democratic system which would represent the least inacceptable compromise to the individuals it governs.

Further reading

Dahl, R. A. (1998) *On Democracy*, New Haven: Yale University Press, chapters 1–3.
Lijphart, A. (1999) *Patterns of Democracy. Government Forms and Performance in Thirty-Six Countries*: Yale University, pp. 274–310.
Peters, Y. and Ensink, S. J. (2015) 'Differential Responsiveness in Europe: The Effects of Preference Difference and Electoral Participation', *West European Politics* 38(3): 577–600.

Key questions for discussion

1 How do you see the evolution of Europe 31 in terms of the Madisonian vs. populistic ideal-types defined by Dahl?
2 In which other ways have Dahl's five necessary conditions been affected by the trends described in the book?
3 What reforms would you suggest to improve democracy in Europe 31?

Notes

1 That is, members who are perceived to belong to – or to legitimately be part of – a constructed community.
2 The election principle should be applied to the designation of representative bodies (e.g. councils, assemblies, parliaments) at the local, regional, national, and international levels. It should *not* be extended beyond these bodies. Non-elected institutions and their policies, however, should be held accountable to these directly elected bodies (what we call a (re-)public-isation of institutions and policies, i.e. that they fall under the reach, or at least the scrutiny of public authorities). Election campaign expenses should be capped and publicly subsidized to avoid their capture by specific (and affluent) interests.
3 See the European Union Democracy Observatory on Citizenship: http://eudo-citizenship. eu/ [last accessed 4 January 2016].
4 See also the European Union Democracy Observatory on Citizenship: http://eudo-citizenship.eu/ [last accessed 4 January 2016].

5 As a side note, the more inclusive nature of élites in the European public sphere on questions of citizenship and identity, as mapped out by Sicakkan (2016: this volume), may well provide an explanation for the electoral success of radical right populist parties (Bjånesøy & Ivarsflaten, 2016: this volume), and more particularly their success at European elections. This success can be interpreted as a nationalist, exclusionary, and to some extent nativist backlash aimed at counter-balancing European élite preferences on these identity, citizenship, and community questions. It is maybe not so surprising that if European élites have more inclusive conceptions of identity and citizenship than the general public has, that this public in turn counteracts by sending radical right populists to sit in the European Parliament.

6 See http://regleg.eu/index.php?option=com_content&view=category&layout=blog&id= 4&Itemid=5 [last accessed 15 January 2016].

7 Be it in terms of which individuals legitimately qualify as belonging to the system, but also in terms of the geographic boundaries of the said system (Dahl, 2006: 52–4).

8 Dahl specifies that the populistic conception whereby majorities should have unlimited sovereignty requires the necessary "condition of political equality" (see Dahl, 2006: 37, especially Definition 1 and Definition 3). Political equality hence seems to be a *consequence* of a Madisonian system (the protection from "severe deprivation of a natural right", 2006: 6, 12) and, by extension, a consequence of a non-populistic system, but at the same time a necessary *precondition* for the exercise of populistic democracy.

9 Courts are excluded from this argument. They should remain independent, non-majoritarian institutions.

References

Alvarez M E (2016) The Struggle between Liberalism and Social Democracy. In Peters Y and Tatham M (eds.), *Democratic Transformations in Europe: Challenges and Opportunities*. Abingdon: Routledge, pp. 99–119.

Anderson B (2006) *Imagined Communities: Reflections on the Origin and Spread of Nationalism*. London: Verso.

Armingeon K and Baccaro L (2012) The Sorrows of Young Euro: Policy Responses to the Sovereign Debt Crisis. In Bermeo N and Pontusson J (eds.), *Coping with Crisis: Government Reactions to the Great Recession*. New York: Russell Sage, pp. 162–198.

Armingeon K and Guthmann K (2014) Democracy in Crisis? The Declining Support for National Democracy in European Countries, 2007–2011. *European Journal of Political Research 53*(3): 423–442.

Bartels L M (2008) *Unequal Democracy: The Political Economy of the New Gilded Age*. Princeton: Princeton University Press.

Baubóck R (2005) Expansive Citizenship – Voting beyond Territory and Membership. *Political Science and Politics 38*(4): 683–687.

Bjånesøy L L and Ivarsflaten E (2016) What Kind of Challenge? Right-Wing Populism in Contemporary Western Europe. In Peters Y and Tatham M (eds.), *Democratic Transformations in Europe: Challenges and Opportunities*. Abingdon: Routledge, pp. 33–50.

Cappelen C (2016) Intra-EU Migration and the Moral Sustainability of the Welfare State. In Peters Y and Tatham M (eds.), *Democratic Transformations in Europe: Challenges and Opportunities*. Abingdon: Routledge, pp. 143–162.

Dahl R A (1989) *Democracy and Its Critics*. New Haven: Yale University Press.

Dahl R A (1998) *On Democracy*. New Haven: Yale University Press.

Dahl R A (2006) *A Preface to Democratic Theory*, Expanded Edition. Chicago: University of Chicago Press.

Day S and Shaw J (2002) European Union Electoral Rights and the Political Participation of Migrants in Host Polities. *International Journal of Population Geography* 8(2): 183–199.

Dragu T and Polborn M (2014) The Rule of Law in the Fight against Terrorism. *American Journal of Political Science* 58(2): 511–525.

Dunn K (2015) Preference for Radical Right-Wing Populist Parties among Exclusive-Nationalists and Authoritarians. *Party Politics* 21(3): 367–380.

Engene J O (2016) Terrorism, Counterterrorism and Democracy. In Peters Y and Tatham M (eds.), *Democratic Transformations in Europe: Challenges and Opportunities*. Abingdon: Routledge, pp. 189–208.

Falkner G (Ed.). (2011) *The EU's Decision Traps: Comparing Policies*. Oxford: Oxford University Press.

García G (2014) Podemos ya tiene más 'militantes' que el PSOE. *El Boletín*. http://www.elboletin.com/nacional/106784/podemos-psoe-segunda-fuerza-militantes.html

Garland J (2016) A Wider Range of Friends: Multi-Speed Organising during the 2015 Labour Leadership Contest. *The Political Quarterly* 87(1): 23–30.

Gilens M (2012) *Affluence and Influence: Economic Inequality and Democratic Responsiveness*. Princeton: Princeton University Press.

Henderson A, Jeffery C and Wincott D (eds.). (2013) *Citizenship after the Nation State: Regionalism, Nationalism and Public Attitudes in Europe*. Basingstoke: Palgrave Macmillan.

Hertner I (2015) Is It Always Up to the Leadership? European Policy-Making in the Labour Party, Parti Socialiste (PS) and Sozialdemokratische Partei Deutschlands (SPD). *Party Politics* 21(3): 470–480.

Hix S and Høyland B (2013) Empowerment of the European Parliament. *Annual Review of Political Science* 16(1): 171–189.

Hobolt S B and Tilley J (2014) Who's in Charge? How Voters Attribute Responsibility in the European Union. *Comparative Political Studies* 47(6): 795–819.

Hooghe L (2003) Europe Divided? Elites vs. Public Opinion on European Integration. *European Union Politics* 4(3): 281–304.

Hooghe L and Marks G (2009) A Postfunctionalist Theory of European Integration: From Permissive Consensus to Constraining Dissensus. *British Journal of Political Science* 39(1): 1–23.

Hooghe L, Marks G and Schakel A H (2010) *The Rise of Regional Authority: A Comparative Study of 42 democracies*. Abingdon: Routledge.

Ignazi P (2014) Power and the (Il)legitimacy of Political Parties: An Unavoidable Paradox of Contemporary Democracy? *Party Politics* 20(2): 160–169.

Jarvis L and Lister M (2013) Disconnected Citizenship? The Impacts of Anti-Terrorism Policy on Citizenship in the UK. *Political Studies* 61(3): 656–675.

Jeffery C (2007) A Regional Rescue of the Nation-State: Changing Regional Perspectives on Europe. *Europa Institute Mitchell Working Paper Series* 5: 1–16.

Katz R S and Mair P (1995) Changing Models of Party Organization and Party Democracy: The Emergence of the Cartel Party. *Party Politics* 1(1): 5–28.

Katz R S and Mair P (2009) The Cartel Party Thesis: A Restatement. *Perspectives on Politics* 7(4): 753–766.

Kenig O, Cross W, Pruysers S and Rahat G (2015) Party Primaries: Towards a Definition and Typology. *Representation* 51(2): 147–160.

Knutsen T (2016) A Re-Emergence of Nationalism as a Political Force in Europe? In Peters Y and Tatham M (eds.), *Democratic Transformations in Europe: Challenges and Opportunities*. Abingdon: Routledge, pp. 13–32.

Koopmans R, Michalowski I and Waibel S (2012) Citizenship Rights for Immigrants: National Political Processes and Cross-National Convergence in Western Europe, 1980–2008. *American Journal of Sociology 117*(4): 1202–1245.

Langworth R (Ed.). (2008) *Churchill by Himself: The Definitive Collection of Quotations*. New York: Public Affairs.

Leon S (2011) Who Is Responsible for What? Clarity of Responsibilities in Multilevel States: The Case of Spain. *European Journal of Political Research 20*(1): 80–109.

Leon S (2012) How Do Citizens Attribute Responsibility in Multilevel States? Learning, Biases and Asymmetric Federalism: Evidence from Spain. *Electoral Studies 31*(1): 120–130.

Levi-Faur D (2005) The Global Diffusion of Regulatory Capitalism. *The ANNALS of the American Academy of Political and Social Science 598*(1): 12–32.

Lewis J (2003) Institutional Environments and Everyday EU Decision Making: Rationalist or Constructivist? *Comparative Political Studies 36*(1–2): 97–124.

Lijphart A (1999) *Patterns of Democracy: Government Forms and Performance in Thirty-Six Countries*. New Haven: Yale University Press.

Linde J and Dahlberg S (2016) Democratic Discontent in Times of Crisis? In Peters Y and Tatham M (eds.), *Democratic Transformations in Europe: Challenges and Opportunities*. Abingdon: Routledge, pp. 72–95.

Mjelde H L and Svåsand L (2016) Party Decline? In Peters Y and Tatham M (eds.), *Democratic Transformations in Europe: Challenges and Opportunities*. Abingdon: Routledge, pp. 51–71.

Mols F and Jetten J (2016) Explaining the Appeal of Populist Right-Wing Parties in Times of Economic Prosperity. *Political Psychology 37*(2): 275–292.

Monaghan E (2012) Assessing Participation and Democracy in the EU: The Case of the European Citizens' Initiative. *Perspectives on European Politics and Society 13*(3): 285–298.

Mudde C (2013) Three Decades of Populist Radical Right Parties in Western Europe: So What? *European Journal of Political Research 52*(1): 1–19.

Mudde C and Rovira Kaltwasser C (2013) Exclusionary vs. Inclusionary Populism: Comparing Contemporary Europe and Latin America. *Government and Opposition 48*(2): 147–174.

Oldervoll J A and Kuhnle S (2016) The Sustainability of European Welfare States: The Significance of Changing Labour Markets. In Peters Y and Tatham M (eds.), *Democratic Transformations in Europe: Challenges and Opportunities*. Abingdon: Routledge, pp. 120–142.

Peters Y (2016a) Displacing Politics: The State of Democracy in an Age of Diffused Responsibility. In Peters Y and Tatham M (eds.), *Democratic Transformations in Europe: Challenges and Opportunities*. Abingdon: Routledge, pp. 163–186.

Peters Y (2016b) (Re-)join the Party! The Effects of Direct Democracy on Party Membership in Europe. *European Journal of Political Research 55*(1): 138–159.

Peters Y (2016c) Zero-Sum Democracy? The Effects of Direct Democracy on Representative Participation. *Political Studies 64*(3), forthcoming.

Peters Y (forthcoming) *Diffused Democracy. Displaced Governance, and Political Participation*. Abingdon: Routledge.

Peters Y and Ensink S J (2015) Differential Responsiveness in Europe: The Effects of Preference Difference and Electoral Participation. *West European Politics 38*(3): 577–600.

Peters Y and Tatham M (2016) The Transformation of Democracy. In Peters Y and Tatham M (eds.), *Democratic Transformations in Europe: Challenges and Opportunities*. Abingdon: Routledge, pp. 1–9.

Qvortrup M and Lijphart A (2013) Domestic Terrorism and Democratic Regime Types. *Civil Wars 15*(4): 471–485.

Rittberger B (2014) Integration without Representation? The European Parliament and the Reform of Economic Governance in the EU. *JCMS: Journal of Common Market Studies* 52(6): 1174–1183.

Rodrik D (2011) *The Globalization Paradox: Democracy and the Future of the World Economy.* New York: Norton.

Rosset J, Giger N and Bernauer J (2013) More Money, Fewer Problems? Cross-Level Effects of Economic Deprivation on Political Representation. *West European Politics 36*(4): 817–835.

Rydgren J (2008) Immigration Sceptics, Xenophobes or Racists? Radical Right-Wing Voting in Six West European Countries. *European Journal of Political Research 47*(6): 737–765.

Schakel A H (2013a) Congruence between Regional and National Elections. *Comparative Political Studies 46*(5): 631–662.

Schakel A H (2013b) Nationalisation of Multilevel Party Systems: A Conceptual and Empirical Analysis. *European Journal of Political Research 52*(2): 212–236.

Schakel A H and Jeffery C (2012) Are Regional Elections Really 'Second-Order' Elections? *Regional Studies 47*(3): 323–341.

Scharpf F (1999) *Governing in Europe: Effective and Democratic?* Oxford: Oxford University Press.

Scharpf F (2006) The Joint-Decision Trap Revisited. *Journal of Common Market Studies 44*(4): 845–864.

Scher R K (2015) *The Politics of Disenfranchisement: Why Is It So Hard to Vote in America?* Abingdon: Routledge.

Scientia Biblica (1825) *Scientia Biblica: Containing the New Testament in the Original Tongue.* Grand Rapids, MI: Booth.

Sheets P, Bos L and Boomgaarden H G (2015) Media Cues and Citizen Support for Right-Wing Populist Parties. *International Journal of Public Opinion Research.*

Sicakkan H G (2016) Is the European Public Sphere Good for Democracy? In Peters Y and Tatham M (eds.), *Democratic Transformations in Europe: Challenges and Opportunities.* Abingdon: Routledge. pp. 252–268

Song S (2009) Democracy and Noncitizen Voting Rights. *Citizenship Studies 13*(6): 607–620.

Talbot F (2016) Climate Change Mitigation. In Peters Y and Tatham M (eds.), *Democratic Transformations in Europe: Challenges and Opportunities.* Abingdon: Routledge, pp. 209–230.

Tatham M (2011) Devolution and EU Policy-Shaping: Bridging the Gap between Multi-Level Governance and Liberal Intergovernmentalism. *European Political Science Review 3*(1): 53–81.

Tatham M (2014) Limited Institutional Change in an International Organisation: Accounting for the EU's Shift Away from "Federal Blindness". *European Political Science Review* 6(1): 21–45.

Tatham M (2015) Regional Voices in the European Union: Subnational Influence in Multi-level Politics. *International Studies Quarterly 59*(2): 387–400.

Tatham M (2016) Multi-Jurisdictional Politics: State Adaptation and Mixed Visions of Democracy. In Peters Y and Tatham M (eds.), *Democratic Transformations in Europe: Challenges and Opportunities.* Abingdon: Routledge, pp. 269–293.

Tatham M and Bauer M W (2014) Competence Ring-Fencing from Below? The Drivers of Regional Demands for Control Over Upwards Dispersion. *Journal of European Public Policy 21*(9): 1367–1385.

Tatham M and Bauer M W (2016) The State, the Economy, and the Regions: Theories of Preference Formation in Times of Crisis. *Journal of Public Administration Research and Theory 26*(4): 631–646.

Töller A E (2012) Causality in Quantitative Approaches. In T. Exadaktylos and C. M. Radaelli (eds.), *Research Design in European Studies: Establishing Causality in Europeanization.* London: Palgrave Macmillan, pp. 44–63.

Vibe V (2016) Minority Rights under Majority Rule: LGB-Rights in Europe. In Peters Y and Tatham M (eds.), *Democratic Transformations in Europe: Challenges and Opportunities.* Abingdon: Routledge, pp. 231–251.

Wilkinson P (2001) *Terrorism Versus Democracy: The Liberal State Response.* Abingdon: Routledge.

Yılmaz F (2012) Right-Wing Hegemony and Immigration: How the Populist Far-Right Achieved Hegemony through the Immigration Debate in Europe. *Current Sociology* 60(3): 368–381.

INDEX

Note: figures and tables are denoted with italicized page numbers; end note information is denoted with an n and note number following the page number.